THE BEST OF
Inc.
GUIDE TO

FINDING
CAPITAL

THE BEST OF

Inc.
GUIDE TO

FINDING
CAPITAL

BY
THE EDITORS OF
Inc. MAGAZINE

PRENTICE HALL PRESS
NEW YORK · LONDON · TORONTO · SYDNEY · TOKYO

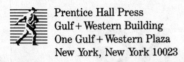 Prentice Hall Press
Gulf+Western Building
One Gulf+Western Plaza
New York, New York 10023

Published by the Prentice Hall Trade Division

PRENTICE HALL PRESS and colophon are registered
trademarks of Simon & Schuster, Inc.

Library of Congress Cataloging-in-Publication Data

    Inc. guide to finding capital.

    (The Best of Inc.)
    Includes index.
    ISBN 0-13-453986-9
        1. Business enterprises—Finance. 2. Bank loans.
    3. Venture capital. 4. Going public (Securities)
    5. Business enterprises, Sale of. I. Inc. II. Series.
    HG4026.5.I53   1988   658.1'5224   87-43160

Designed by Stanley S. Drate / Folio Graphics Company, Inc.

Produced by Rapid Transcript, a division of March Tenth, Inc.

Manufactured in the United States of America

CONTENTS

PART
V

VALUING, BUYING, AND SELLING A BUSINESS *213*

BANKS

The first stop for financing is traditionally the bank. But banks don't always say yes, and even when they do their decision can be based on broad criteria ranging from healthy financial statements to community involvement.

"Banks," Part I of our guide to finding capital, shows you how to elicit approval from banks and describes how to prepare a loan proposal, what to expect at the interview, and which types of loans to consider. The second half provides an overview of some alternatives to traditional bank financing: establishing a credit line with a supplier, securing an asset-based loan, or building a limited partnership.

In "Tough Talk About Bank Financing," Asbury Industries Inc. CEO Edward Asbury and Commonwealth Bank president and CEO Arthur F. F. Snyder face off over the topic of borrowing for growth. Asbury speaks frankly about his bitterness toward the several banks unwilling to lend him capital at an important growth period in his company's history. Currently the owner of an 18 percent interest loan from a commercial credit company, Asbury blames his company's slow growth and narrow profit margin on short-sighted and overly cautious bankers who refused him a fair hearing when he needed capital. Equally blunt, Snyder points out that some of the characteristics Asbury values most in his company are interpreted as weaknesses by wary bankers.

"Don't Leave Banking Up to Chance" counsels the importance of fostering a solid relationship with your banker. Warne and Doreen Boyce depended completely on the loans they acquired to build Microbac Laboratories Inc. During their search for the $355,000 they've borrowed over the past ten years, the Boyces learned the value of keeping their banker informed about new ideas, the status and development of existing enterprises, problems the business encounters,

1

and other finance-related topics. In seventeen trips to the bank, the Boyces have only been rejected twice. By recognizing the banker as an adviser and ally, not an opponent, the Boyces have borrowed enough to develop Microlab from a single laboratory to a successful $2 million chain of seven labs.

The next article, "A Dozen Ways to Borrow Money," is a guide to acquiring loans. It defines several types of short-, medium-, and long-term loans, suggests which is the most appropriate in specific circumstances, and provides inside tips you'll need to be prepared at the bank. The article also includes a step-by-step guide to writing an effective loan proposal, and seven "Tips from a Banker" aimed at improving a loan applicant's batting average at the bank.

In "How to Choose a Bank," "What Do Bankers Want?" and "Of Growing Interest," a banker speaks out and explains what you should look for in a loan officer, what bankers will look for in you, and the options you should consider when negotiating a loan.

The results of an *Inc.* survey of 150 banks on the problems of lending to small businesses appear in "How Banks View Small Businesses."

In "Hidden Perils in a Volatile Economy," another banker discusses with *Inc.* how smaller companies should approach their capital needs in an uncertain economy. And finally, "Smart Money" is a portrait of an innovative bank at work.

BANKING GURU ALEX SHESHUNOFF

In the banking industry, they are known simply as Sheshunoff ratings—quarterly surveys of the performance of every federally insured bank in the United States. And now, with nearly every bank either plotting an acquisition or expecting to be the target of one, these dry statistical reports have become nothing less than required reading among bankers, regulators, and a growing audience of corporate-finance officers.

Alex Sheshunoff's first book, *The Banks of Texas: 1974,* was an instant best-seller when it came out during the go-go years of Texas banking, something of a Sears, Roebuck catalog of Texas banks available for acquisition. Since then, his Austin firm has gone national, cornering the market on packaging and analyzing the mounds of information the government has available about individual banks. So thoroughly, in fact, does Sheshunoff & Company dominate the flow of bank information that it counts the Federal Deposit Insurance Corporation itself among its most loyal customers.

During the past three years, more than 600 bankers have sought Sheshunoff's advice as they contemplated various proposals for mergers and acquisitions. *Inc.* senior writers Bruce G. Posner and Tom Richman traveled to Austin with a slightly different question in mind: How does all this reshuffling of the banking industry affect the prospects of the small-business borrower? The answer, it turns out, is that prospects have been greatly improved.

INC.: From the outside, it looks as if the banking industry is going through a rather dramatic restructuring. What does it look like from the inside?

SHESHUNOFF: We're seeing banks being forced to abandon their old, somewhat passive ways of doing business. What has happened is that the bank spread is being squeezed rather hard—the spread, that is, between what banks pay for money and what they sell it for. Not too long ago, banks could rely on low-cost deposits. But with the phaseout of Regulation Q by 1986, the banks' cost of money—either on the open market or from depositors—has risen toward the money-market rate. That means that banks can no longer survive taking their money and putting it into T-bills—the profits from that kind of investment have disappeared. So the real challenge for banks today is to find something better to do with that money, and for most banks that means generating good loan demand.

INC.: And that includes small-business loans?

SHESHUNOFF: In the case of most commercial banks, I'd say the small-business borrower is a key, if not the key, factor.

INC.: That would come as something of a surprise to most businesspeople, to know that bankers are anxious to make them loans.

SHESHUNOFF: Obviously, it will depend on the market. But think of it from the point of view of the bank that wants to grow and become more profitable. In today's environment, a business is much more valuable as a borrower than as a depositor. If you, as a company treasurer, have a couple of hundred thousand to invest in certificates of deposit, for instance, you are going to want something that approaches a T-bill rate on your money. You may think you're a good customer, but it won't be a very profitable piece of business for the bank. If you borrow money, on the other hand, you enable the bank to realize a gross margin of 3 percent to 3.5 percent over its cost of funds.

INC.: But why small businesses? It's a lot easier for a bank to make very big loans isn't it?

SHESHUNOFF: It is. But look at what has been happening in the marketplace for big-business loans.

First of all, the overall market for loans has been shrinking. Companies, especially big companies, are doing a better job at managing their cash flows, so they have less borrowing short-term. And long-term, some have found other sources of capital, most notably commercial paper. And then there is the competition from the "nonbank" competitors—General Motors, Sears, and so forth—that have been able to borrow money from the public using their own commercial paper and lend it out at bank rates or even a little bit lower. Add to that some very aggressive marketing by a few of the more active and forward-looking banks, and what it means is that the other banks are looking at a loan market that has shrunk by 15 or 20 percent over the past five years.

The other thing to remember is that you have a very thin spread when you lend to *Fortune* 500 companies. You're selling a commodity—all the borrower really cares about is price. Maybe there is a little cash management in there, a little technology, but mostly the profits come from volume, not margin. Now volume is shrinking. At first, these banks responded by going abroad, which hasn't always worked out. So now even the really big money-center banks have discovered the middle market—small and midsize companies—and they have begun to work it aggressively.

INC.: Give us a quick primer on where banks are earning their money these days. What are the profit centers?

SHESHUNOFF: Well, one thing I can tell you is that corporate checking accounts, generally speaking, are a lot less profitable to banks than they used to be. Even though banks usually require balances or fees to maintain these checking accounts, the data show that a quarter of all corporate checking accounts end up costing banks money, and another half are barely profitable. Personal checking accounts aren't as profitable as they once were either, for the same reason.

The best way for banks to make money today is by making loans. Home mortgage is one area that's been attractive—especially variable-rate mortgages, where there's no interest-rate risk. The operating costs on mortgages are very low, and often the loans are repackaged and sold into the secondary markets. Credit cards are also extremely profitable for many banks, although it's an expensive business to get into and to administer, and credit quality can be a problem. Another lucrative area for a lot of banks lately has been loans for the more expensive foreign cars—lending money on a Mercedes looks a lot like a small commercial loan used to look. But having said all that, the best source of loan volume and quality is still for banks to expand their commercial portfolios—and that means lending to small companies.

INC.: Which for many will be something of a new frontier.

SHESHUNOFF: You know, I've always been amazed by the fact that we've been here in Austin for fifteen years, and I don't think I've had more than one or two banks call on us for our banking business. And most of them are our clients! I mean, it's ridiculous. If somebody had just come by, told us what they were doing, and asked for the business, there would have been a good chance of their walking out with some kind of an account. Come to think of it, we've been in this building for two years, and it was a year before the bank located on the bottom floor of this building came up.

But that is going to change—and change very quickly now—if only as a matter of survival. The good banks, the ones that will come out on top at the end of all this, are becoming much more proactive in their selling—picking up the phone, calling on customers in person. There is a bank in Fort Lauderdale, Florida, for example, that used retired bank chief executive officers to go out and make calls on small and midsize businesses, with good results. And there's a bank in southern California that provides commercial customers with free courier service, so they never have to go to the bank. So there are some successes out there, although you don't hear much about them. The people who do them don't write them up—they go out and buy another bank and do it all over again.

INC.: In the context of the banking industry, you're describing something of a cultural revolution.

SHESHUNOFF: Very much so. In the old days, the objective was to man your desk and wait for people to come to you. It was a processing-oriented culture—good risk-free, indoor work. If you wanted to sell, you went to work for IBM. Now a lot of banks are trying to change their cultures, but it's hard. In the end, I think you're going to end up with something on the model of an insurance company, where you have the salespeople out looking for customers and somebody back in the office who has the underwriting or credit-granting authority—a separation of the two functions.

INC.: Was it merely the culture that defined the dynamic, or are there sound business reasons for it?

SHESHUNOFF: Well, let's say that there was no reason to get very aggressive. Banks consistently had been making 11 to 12 percent return on equity year after year, with the better ones making 15 percent or higher through good times and bad. Now, to many businesspeople, that doesn't sound like a very interesting return. But for the risk involved, which was minimal, it was a good deal.

INC.: But was it—is it—a good deal gained at the expense of the borrower?

SHESHUNOFF: I don't think so. The fact that the banker takes collateral and charges interest instead of taking equity and becoming your lifelong partner—there ought to be some advantage to that, something worth one or two extra percentage points of guaranteed return. In the long run, what you need to offer a banker in terms of repayment is, in most cases, still a lot less than what you have to give an equity investor—a limited partner or a venture capitalist. Think of it as the bank does. When it wins, it wins 4 percent over the cost of its funds—if it's lucky. But if it loses, it can lose 100 percent plus attorneys' fees.

INC.: Other than perhaps separating the selling function from the credit-approval function, is there anything else that banks will have to do to change the culture of their business-lending operations?

SHESHUNOFF: Certainly one of the changes will come in the way loan officers are rewarded. We are always telling bankers that the value of money as a motivator has been grossly underestimated. Bank salaries are very low. A senior loan officer who might control a portfolio of $10 million, say, may make between $50,000 and $60,000.

INC.: And you're saying that's low?

SHESHUNOFF: Low relative to the amount of responsibility and the income produced. A $10-million loan portfolio with a 3 to 4 percent net interest spread is generating at least $300,000 for the bank.

INC.: So how would you structure a loan officer's compensation?

SHESHUNOFF: You have to define it in terms of both the loan portfolio's growth and the quality. I mean, if you put every loan officer on a sales commission and give each of them all the lending limit of the bank, you could probably break any bank in America in twelve to eighteen months, because of all the bad loans you would have on the books. We've not really seen any commission-driven schemes that we've been particularly impressed with.

But there may be ways to refine it. Perhaps you could say, "Okay, Charlie, you did a great job of bringing in the loans this year, so we've decided to give you a bonus: a new Mercedes. It's over there in the parking lot and you can walk by it every day on your way past your old car, and as soon as all those loans are paid back, you can drive the Mercedes right off the lot." And with some scheme like that, you can reward people based not only on the quality of business they're bringing in, but also on the quality of the credit they give.

At the same time, I think you have to change the career paths that have also defined the bank culture, in terms of status. Banking is still a very hierarchical activity, where titles are jealously guarded and a lot of prestige is attached to the number of people or departments reporting to you. A loan officer who is an excellent lender with a large portfolio and a decent spread with few losses doesn't receive the same status. That's got to change. There has got to be more emphasis on the producers rather than on the managers.

INC.: You've sketched the brave new world of aggressive banking from the point of view of the banker. What about the business borrower? Is an aggressive bank preferable?

SHESHUNOFF: Doing business with an aggressive bank may be a very good short-term strategy. If it is known to be aggressively making loans to companies like your own, it is much more likely to be a good source of capital than a bank that has a more conservative reputation. But the problem that we have found, and one that is key to a bank's long-term success, is knowing when to leave the party. A good bank starts backing off before it's finally over, so as to be sure it doesn't give back the money made during the boom times when things begin to tighten up. You see that in all of the high-growth markets. They go three, four, five years making very good money and then give it back over a one- or two-year span, and when that happens, it is not so pleasant to be one of their customers.

INC.: What's a good bank, then?

SHESHUNOFF: First of all, you need a healthy bank, one that is not beset by a siege mentality, one that hasn't gone through a lot of trauma in terms of loan losses. For an individual loan officer, that's a tough environment in which to champion the case of a particular customer, no matter how good a customer. You also want a bank that is growing, from the standpoint of profitability, capital, assets—growing at least as fast as the regional economy. And, given a chance, lean toward a bank that's earning 1 percent or more on assets—that's in the upper half among all banks, although there are lots of good banks earning less than that.

You might be interested, by the way, in knowing how bankers themselves evaluate banks. We did a big survey of more than 2,000 bankers recently, and the factor they mentioned most often as the indicator they cared about the most wasn't profitability or capital or liquidity. It was quality of assets: the percentage of the portfolio tied up in nonperforming assets. As far as bankers are concerned—and it doesn't really matter what size bank you're talking about—asset quality tells you more about the overall health of the bank than any other single factor.

All of those factors are ones you can measure pretty easily. Less easy to measure, but just as important, is the degree to which a bank invests in the quality of its loan officers—in compensation that allows it to attract and retain good people.

INC.: How do you determine the quality of a loan officer?

SHESHUNOFF: I think some of it is simply sitting down and interviewing the banker the same way you interview anybody else who is going to provide you services. You try to get a feel for it. Tell him or her that you've got some credit needs, some short-term, some long-term. And then ask, "What can you provide me in the way of expertise, professionalism, and so on?" Ask about the turnover on the bank's staff. Find out if there are other people from your industry—suppliers, customers, competitors—who use the bank's services. To some loan officers, your loan may be a terribly complex piece of business—and one that they don't want to bother understanding. You don't want to waste your time with them.

INC.: Do you really think most businesspeople feel comfortable going in and conducting an aggressive interview like that with a banker, somebody who may very well hold the future of their business in his or her hands?

SHESHUNOFF: Well, a lot of people have that fear, but if theirs are well-managed, growing companies with significant credit needs, and if they have actually accomplished what they said they were going to do—paid off loans when they said they would and so on—there is no reason to go hat in hand to a bank. What they are really doing is going cash in hand—they are the major source of earning growth for the bank, remember. And if the bank is going to get those earnings by charging 3 to 4 percent over its cost of funds, then the person who is going to borrow $100,000 over the next year has to ask himself, "Okay, who is going to give me the most service for the four thousand dollars I'm going to spend?" And the banker is going to say to himself, "What service can I afford to give him? Do I give him two hours of my time this year? Obviously, yes. Can I give him two hundred hours of my time? Probably not." But somewhere in between there is a level of service that customers can expect for the money that they're spending. And customers are perfectly within their rights to ask about that.

INC.: Realistically, though, how demanding can you be about what loan officers can do for you other than help you get the money?

SHESHUNOFF: In this environment, you can be quite demanding. How well does this guy understand my industry? How does he understand the regional and national and international economic trends and how they might affect the business that I'm in? Does he understand the alternative financing sources that might be important to me? How plugged in is he to venture capital? Can he help secure an IRB [industrial revenue bond]? Is he able to do a good cash-flow analysis on his personal computer? Does this loan officer appear to have influence upstairs?

INC.: You mean a banker might say, "Well, you probably ought to see about increasing your trade credit over here, and I can set you up with a couple of venture capitalists on your R and D, and we can finance the receivables." There are bankers who actually talk that way?

SHESHUNOFF: There are—or we understand that there are. We've met a few of them, although there are not many. One reason is that when they get that good, they go into business for themselves. After all, once they understand a business that well, they get frustrated. Real estate has been the prime example. They say, "Hell, I don't want to *lend* to a developer. I want to *be* one."

INC.: And begin to make some real money . . .

SHESHUNOFF: The compensation is part of it. But another part of it is wanting to be a player, not a provider of services to players. There's an ego thing there.

INC.: You have talked about shopping around for quality of service from a bank. What about price?

SHESHUNOFF: I don't think that compensation will take the form of price competition. From the standpoint of the business borrowers, most probably would rather pay 1 percent extra to know that a well-qualified lender is going to be there in good times and bad, and is someone who understands the business. That's a small price to pay for something that important. On a $100,000 loan, 1 percent translates into only $83 more a month.

INC.: But is it true that some banks consistently charge more than other banks?

SHESHUNOFF: Sometimes that is because they offer a better-quality service. Other times I think the reason they get the higher loan rates is that they just ask for them—and because what's most important for so many customers is that they get the loan, they often pay it. Of course, the customer can avoid that by shopping around before he actually needs the loan.

INC.: Do you recommend doing business with more than one bank at a time to help keep things competitive?

SHESHUNOFF: The history of Western civilization has been a search for second sources. It has been true in salvation and sex, and it is true in banking. You can't put all your eggs in one basket or pin all your hopes on one bank or one loan officer. You might have a primary bank with 80 percent of your business and a secondary one that you use for some other purpose. But the secondary one can still be kept up to date on your business in case the primary bank is taken over or is going through a bad period.

INC.: Hardly a day goes by now that there isn't a new bank takeover or merger announced in the papers. What is the shape of things to come? How can the climate continue to be competitive with fewer and fewer banks?

SHESHUNOFF: You know, ten years ago there were something like 14,000 commercial banks in the United States. Today, we still have about that number. Oh yes, banks get very big. But in more than a few cases, some of the good people who work in those big banks decide that they've lost touch with their work, with their customers, and—voilá—they go out and start their own bank, taking their customers with them. And then eighteen months or two years later, they sell out at two and a half times book value and go out and start it all over again. It has been happening in California for years, and you see it happening now in Florida and New England.

INC.: So, in spite of the frenzy of consolidation going on at one level, you see banking as continuing to be quite competitive, even entrepreneurial, with smaller banks and regional banks holding their own against the interstate giants?

SHESHUNOFF: I don't think size will be as important as how aggressive a bank is. Those banks that are actively selling are going to take business away from those that are depending on old, passive marketing techniques, and they are going to move market share very fast.

INC.: And the others?

SHESHUNOFF: The others are either going to respond, or they are going to have to worry about survival.

INC.: And aggressive banks will come in every size—is that what you are saying?

SHESHUNOFF: Yes, Some will be the money-center banks in New York and Chicago. You'll also be hearing more about the North Carolina banks like First Union, Wachovia, and NCNB. They have all acquired banks in Georgia and other southern states, and I anticipate their business will extend throughout the South. But a bank can be small—much less than $1 billion in assets—and still be profitable and aggressive. The fact is that banking is one of those endeavors where there aren't many economies of scale. And often, the larger the entity, the more difficult it is to run efficiently.

INC.: So if economies of scale are not driving the consolidation, what is?

SHESHUNOFF: Mostly it is the need to find new earning assets: If you can't make any more new loans, then buy them. And that, in effect, is one of the things you have to do when you buy a bank.

The other thing you buy is the good loan officers with their contacts and their established customers. Of course, what some banks have found is that it is much cheaper to buy the banker than to buy the bank. In other words, if the banker has $5 million in good loans with a 4 percent spread on them, that's $200,000 a year of income that he brings with him. And what we see is that some of these acquiring banks are stealing away these aggressive loan officers and putting them in very small two- and three-person storefronts with the idea of hustling business from their old customers. And it is a very cost-effective way for a bank to develop new markets—even out of state.

INC.: Where would you open such a storefront?

SHESHUNOFF: Right next door to a bank that has lots of unhappy customers.

INC.: Looking to the future a bit, do you see a movement toward merchant banking where banks might offer some combination of equity and debt financing?

SHESHUNOFF: There has been some of that in the real estate area, where a bank might get its principal and interest back and then share in the equity after payout—and if the project is sold, maybe get a percentage of the profit. Recently, I heard a story about a major bank in New York City that loaned money for some coal-mining equipment: In addition to the monthly payments, the bank participates in the success of the business by getting a royalty on the production. But, in general, I think banks have been reluctant to get into this kind of lending. And, frankly, I think a lot of people would feel that the bank would be too conservative to have as an equity partner. Even as it gets more aggressive in its marketing, banking should remain a fairly simple business. As someone else once said, When it gets complex, it's wrong.

TOUGH TALK ABOUT BANK FINANCING

Neither a borrower, nor a lender be:
For loan oft loses both itself and a friend,
And borrowing dulls the edge of husbandry.
—*Hamlet*, Act I, Scene 3

W ere Shakespeare's Polonius to meet Edward Asbury, the forty-seven-year-old president of Asbury Industries, their discussion would be heated. When *Inc.* asked Asbury and several other smaller company managers to tell how they have—or haven't—financed their companies, Asbury didn't mince words. He said he'd gone to bankers six times since 1957, when he took over his father's repair and welding shop in Pittsburgh. He went because he needed money to expand as he took the business out of repairs and into the manufacture of underground mining tools and attachments for construction machinery. He never got it; as a result, he now pays as much as 18 percent interest to a commercial credit company, the last source that would loan him money. Asbury Industries has grown slowly from twenty to sixty-five employees and from $250,000 to $3 million in sales. With expansion money from a bank, it could have gone farther, faster, says Asbury.

"My problems are the same as those a lot of small businesses face—coming up short of capital and short of borrowing power. As a result, many small companies are forced to sell. At least I've held on to my company. We all need help. We want to know how to get the money we need—and we don't want to hear a lot of the stuff we read but don't believe.

"People have told me, 'Come up with pro formas, cash flow charts. Go into the bank with a good dog-and-pony show and you'll get your loan.' Nonsense. I've done that and I didn't get my money. Maybe it works somewhere, but it doesn't work in Pittsburgh."

We decided the best way to get some answers for Asbury and other *Inc.* readers was to go to the source. We called Arthur F. F. Snyder, sixty-year-old president and chief executive officer of Boston's Commonwealth Bank. Over his twenty-five-year career in the financing of smaller companies, Snyder claims to have created seventy mil-

12

lionaires. His biggest successes have been in the finance of high-technology companies, mainly electronics, and his average customer today has $5 million in sales.

We arranged for Asbury and Snyder to face off across *Inc.'s* conference table, rather than a banker's desk, for a frank discussion.

ASBURY: My current money problems were created because I wasn't able to borrow money five years ago when I really needed it. We were a small business that was growing at the rate of about 25 percent a year, dollarwise, before double-digit inflation.

SNYDER: You were growing nicely.

ASBURY: Yes, and it wasn't just that I wanted to expand. The fact is, I *needed* to expand to hold my customers. They were asking me to expand. They were concerned about my being able to handle their business volume. In fact, when I started to put together a plan for an expansion program, my major customers wrote testimonial letters, which I needed in order to approach the Pennsylvania Industrial Development Authority, our state lending authority. The state was willing to kick in 40 percent of the total if I could get 50 percent from a bank and the other 10 percent either from a local industrial development source or out of my own pocket. But I couldn't get the bank participation. I was led to believe by the president of the bank that they were going to go along with the plan. Then the loan officer changed his mind and rejected the loan application, and I was out in the cold.

SNYDER: Let me go into something that might throw some light on the incident. There is something in a company called "P&T disease," and it occurs when the president and treasurer are the same guy. That can't work; it's corporate cancer. The president should be responsible for the left-hand side of the balance sheet—the assets, the people. His job is to run them as hard and as effectively as possible.

The right-hand side of the balance sheet should be run by the treasurer. His job is to say, "Yes, but . . . if you expand the sales, who's going to find the receivables? Who's going to find the inventory? How are you going to expand the balance sheet that fast?"

Now, if the treasurer is stronger than the president, he will control growth too tightly. If the president is stronger, he might expand the business too fast and get in the bind where he has to go to the banks in a crisis, begging.

But if he plans correctly, the president first goes to the bank when he has opened an account but doesn't need to borrow. He goes to the banker and says, "Hey, you crummy little kid, I want to have lunch with you. I want to tell you about my business because a year from now I'm hoping to expand." Did you do anything like that, Ed? Did you massage the banker before you came in, play up to him a little?

ASBURY: Yes, for years. Every month I walked in there and I sat down with the president. We would go over the previous month's statement. I'd explain our products, our markets, our new plans, and he seemed to be on our side. But his loan officer still turned me down.

Another time when I needed money, I went to a major Pittsburgh bank with a big presentation—just like everyone says you should do. I have my auditor with me, and we've put together three-year cash-flow projections, a customer base analysis, the whole bit. I want to borrow $300,000 for a $600,000 building project. We go through our entire presentation and after we're all done, the banker shakes his head. "No," he says. "Ed, you need more equity in the business."

We talk about that a little bit, and finally my auditor asks, "Mr. Banker, just how much do you think Ed needs in additional equity before you would consider this loan?" The vice-president looks up at the ceiling for a minute, and then he looks back down at me. "Well, we think you need another three hundred thousand dollars of equity," he says. And I'm in there to *borrow* $300,000.

Well, I went right through the roof. I said, "If I had another three hundred thousand dollars to invest in equity, I wouldn't be in here trying to borrow." Now, that's their level of thinking.

SNYDER: Of course I don't know the specifics of that conversation, but I have to admit that many bankers are chicken. They are afraid of being candid. They don't come out and say, "Fella, I don't like this." They say, "What you need is more capital," when really they don't like something else that you will never know about. Nobody can ever sue a banker for saying you need more capital in your business. You can say it to General Motors if you want to. It's the easiest cop-out ever created.

I try never to say that. If you need more capital, I try to say, "Look, you need three hundred thousand dollars in the business. If you can get fifty thousand or one hundred thousand dollars more capital, I would lend you the two hundred thousand or the two hundred fifty thousand dollars." You see, there's a balance there. You can borrow $200,000 if you have $100,000. Most bankers feel comfortable with a two-to-one debt-to-equity ratio like that.

Besides, for me, money isn't even the main issue. The main issue is the CEO. Who is he? What does he know about his business? Does he understand the people he has working for him, their capabilities? Were they hired because they did the job somewhere else, or because they are brothers-in-law? The statistical chances of your brother-in-law being competent enough to be your controller or your salesman are almost zero.

The person who runs a business has to have judgment above all things. When he hires, he has to hire the right people. When he fires, he has to fire the right people and do it humanely.

ASBURY: I just fired my son. What does that tell you?

SNYDER Hallelujah, baby. That would tell me to make a credit judgment to lend you money. I never make a loan without putting my finger in the salad oil. Does that make any sense?

ASBURY: No. Explain it.

SNYDER: Well, there was a guy named Tino DeAngelis down in New Jersey who was dealing in salad oil futures. He had an accounting firm, but the accounting guy never climbed up the ladder of the big tanks to put his finger in the salad oil. It was all water, or at least it was water up to the top six inches. A big scandal about twenty years ago.

So some banker has got to put his finger in the salad oil. Somebody has got to go out and look at the plant, the people, the organization. Very important.

ASBURY: I've talked to every major bank in Pittsburgh, and some smaller banks. I have never yet had a banker delve into my personal character or the way I run my business. You're an exception. In fact, I have never been able to get one of the principal officers of a bank to walk into my building to look and see what the hell we do—to know we really exist.

SNYDER: Does that indict them or you?

ASBURY: I think it indicts them.

SNYDER: Ed, I'm not so sure. It would be presumptuous of me as a banker to say I know all your business. I have no way of really knowing because I've never seen your balance sheet and your P&L statement, much less walked into your building. But, in looking at your company, let's be sure we understand what a business is all about. A business has to serve somebody a profit. Each bank customer is a business. I look to see what the service is—what the business is really doing for the customer—before I ever look at any income statement. The first thing I learned about your business was that you sell stuff to a very significant industry, the front-end loader business. You make stuff those guys really need. They use it all the time, and I suppose it breaks.

ASBURY: Sure, it wears out.

SNYDER: You're in a real business. That's my personal decision. With that decision, I start asking a borrower like you questions about the financial aspects of the business. I want to know what *you* know about it. I don't want to know what your accountant knows about it, or your controller. I want to know what you know.

You knew your figures. I was thrilled. Every question I asked you, you answered me right off, with a figure.

So far, so good. I like you, I like your company, and I would like to have you as a customer. But, I look at your earnings and you haven't ever really made money. You've earned marginally over all these years. Marginally. And then you had two years of losses. I can't quite understand this because you seem to have financial control of your business.

So, I asked some more questions, and I found out some things that disturb me. I found out that you own and operate an airport. Not only that, but you tell me you're flying tomorrow to a meeting of the Boy Scouts because you're a regional director. Then you mentioned that you've done some guest lecturing at some university, you've taken all kinds of management courses, and you're active in Pittsburgh's Smaller Manufacturers' Council, too. Quite simply, you spend too much of your time on other things besides running your business.

ASBURY: Let me tell you why I do some of these things. I do them because of what's happening to the business climate in this country. We're going to be regulated out of business, taxed out of business, and we'd better start doing something about it. I feel strongly about people getting involved in government. I also think we've got to train the youth of today, who are going to be running the country when you and I are thinking of retiring.

Who should be involved if it's not the small businessman? I go to bed at night and I can sleep. I know that I've done something—maybe through my Boy Scout activities or government relations or whatever—something to maybe better the world a little bit. And, I know that sixty-five people are making a living because of Asbury Industries. All that means a lot to me.

So, frankly, money isn't the whole thing. Sure, I'm concerned that I'll have enough to live on when I retire, concerned that the business will succeed. But your philosophy that the business should take 100 percent of my time is representative of other bankers. You know, sometimes I think you're all a little jealous. Here are these excited young people looking for money—people who have an opportunity to go somewhere. And bankers lecture on how they should do it, rather than help them. A banker sees these young people who have a shot at making more money than he ever will—and even more if they can get the right kind of backing. And I think it grates on him, gets to him.

So the banker sits up there and says, "Now listen, son, don't tell me what business is all about. I've been around here sixty years and you're only thirty." And the young guys say, "But, I've got a new gadget, or a new way to sell something." "Oh, I've heard that story before," the banker says.

Yes, bankers like to think they're experts in all fields, but, actually, they don't understand a lot of things about small companies. For example, the biggest asset in any business is not the building, the furniture, the machinery and equipment. It's the people. You spend a lot of money on people.

For four months last year, a coal strike reduced our business by about 50 percent. Now, what do I do during those four months? Do I lay off all my people? This is a tough thing for small companies to handle and bankers don't understand that.

SNYDER: Wait a minute, Ed. I think you've got a lot of character, a lot of integrity. You've got an understanding of what a business is, but you're off on a tangent here. Let's get this in focus. You have all this peripheral activity, plus you've got a $3-million family business, which fundamentally requires 100 percent of your time or it won't go.

ASBURY: You're wrong there. I run an unusual business. I probably have one of the most sophisticated business management systems of any business our size. And, because of that, I don't have to run my business on a daily basis. I oversee the people that run the business.

SNYDER: What do you think this is costing? Has it cost you your business?

ASBURY: No, it hasn't cost me the business. I still have the business. But I probably know more about my business financially, and what we're doing, than most people do.

SNYDER: But all of this took your time.

ASBURY: Sure, it took time. I had to get involved. But the real reason I did it was so that I could become uninvolved. I wanted to work my way out of the day-to-day decision making. Now I spend my time on long-range planning. But no banker has ever taken all of that into consideration.

I've banged my head against a wall for so many years trying to get this thing to grow. A lot of people besides me don't understand why we can't move. Why this company won't go.

Okay, so I decided there must be something I'm doing wrong. Maybe I need some young blood. So I bring in new people, train people to run the business, to grow within, to plan their futures around it, and all of a sudden they start to see the bottlenecks. It wasn't going according to plan, and it was because of the bank arrangement.

SNYDER: Somewhere along the line you got involved with too much theoretical management and maybe not enough day-to-day hands-on work. And then you got involved in all these other activities that take your time away from your business. Can we really blame it on the banks?

ASBURY: Well, I did what you're saying a small business guy should do. Confide in your banker, tell him what you're going to do, tell him your plans, take his advice. Bankers had been after me for years to put in more managers. "Who's going to run the thing if you get laid up, sick, or you're in an accident, or something like that?" This is one of the excuses they gave me for being afraid to loan me money. So, that was one reason I started to think about professional management.

Let me tell you the other reason.

One day as my secretary was going out to lunch, I had a chest pain and tumbled over. She had me rushed off to the hospital, even though I didn't want to go and went fighting all the way. When we got to the hospital, the doctors said, "Thirty-seven-year-old man with chest pains," and I ended up in the cardiac ward, the whole bit.

As it turned out, it wasn't a heart attack; it was nerves. But they kept me for a week. The psychiatrist probably did more for me than anyone else. He asked, "Ed, did you ever think about getting rid of that business?" And I said, "No, why? That's all I know, this has been my life. I've worked there since I was a kid."

And he said, "Well, you'd better think about doing something, because it's going to kill you if you don't change your ways."

That's when I got hooked on professional management. I said, "There's a message there." I took a management course for presidents, which is basically the Harvard Business School professional course, all crammed into seven days of twelve hours each. We really hammered at it. I got hooked on that, and I took several other courses to help me implement professional management. This was my way of changing my business. I wanted to get out of the day-to-day thing of putting out fires.

SNYDER: For fifteen years, you've earned a marginal sum each year after taxes—not enough to expand a $3-million business. You aren't earning enough money to cover the cost of money inflation-wise. Now you say you have all these excellent programs. Those belong in a

$50-million business, not a $3-million business. You can't afford it. A business with a 25 percent gross margin can't support all that. You've got to tighten down to get out from under. You're not going to solve your money problems by borrowing money.

ASBURY: I know that. My money problems now are created because I wasn't able to borrow money when I needed it. That's the tough part . . . I can't back up four or five years. I have to solve the problems that I have today from within.

I'll admit that we spent a lot of money on things like training people, and that has reduced the bottom-line profit. But, then again, it isn't the smartest thing in the world for a small, private business to show big profits before taxes when it's in a growth situation.

SNYDER: Ed, I still think the solution is to tighten the business down, not to worry about extras. Right now you're borrowing at 18 percent. You can't earn anything paying 18 percent on money. You make money for the bank's commercial finance arm, and when they get tired of making money on it—and scared—they're going to sell your assets off.

So, just make the company as tight and neat as you can, to get away from the moneylenders and into regular banking, and then from regular banking into unsecured borrowing. You don't need a scalpel—you need a meat cleaver. Otherwise, your company's going to roll over and put four feet in the air.

ASBURY: I doubt that, and it's obvious, Art, that you and I don't agree on how to run a small business. I *have* been successful over the years by my standards, so I'll probably continue to run my company just the way I have in the past. And I'll probably continue to fight with bankers just as long as I'm in business.

DON'T LEAVE BANKING UP TO CHANCE

On a hot summer day in 1975, Warne Boyce stood quite still outside Mellon Bank in downtown Pittsburgh. He'd just been refused a loan and he felt humiliated. Humiliation turned to anger as he realized that being turned down was all his fault.

Boyce had built his company on the strength of his relationship with his bank. In the years since he started Microbac Laboratories Inc. in 1969, Boyce had expanded through acquisitions financed by bank loans. Microbac had averaged an acquisition a year by the time Mellon turned down Boyce's application that summer.

And Boyce had known almost as soon as he sat down in Bob Off's office at Mellon Bank that he was going to be rejected. He knew it because he was breaking all the rules he'd followed for six years in his dealing with the bank—rules he had only intuitively understood until he broke them.

Boyce's cardinal rule is this: Let your banker know what you're up to, even before you're up to it. All the other "rules according to Boyce" are variations on that theme.

Boyce broke his rules in a couple of ways on that visit to Mellon Bank. First, Bob Off had heard nothing of Boyce's plans to acquire still another testing laboratory until the morning Boyce called for a loan interview. Second, Boyce compounded the error by walking in with only some doodlings on a legal pad to back up his application.

"I was so caught up in day-to-day operations of the company," recalls Boyce, "that I failed to see how much we had grown. I needed a much more sophisticated balance sheet. We'd been so successful in the past, I became a little too casual."

Boyce was scheduled to leave for Montreal on business immediately after his stop at the bank. But before he left, he called on his accountant. Then, his briefcase stuffed with financial papers and legal pads, he set off for the airport.

"I'd been so looking forward to that trip," Boyce recalls. "Montreal is lovely and there are some wonderful restaurants. But both nights there I ended up working until early in the morning transferring our figures onto the cash flow projections we'd worked up."

Back in Pittsburgh, Boyce returned immediately to Mellon Bank.

19

This time, he got the loan. His effort to repair damage he'd done himself reflects the importance he places on credibility. Rejections tarnish credibility. And credibility with banks is like honor in battle—you lose it just once.

Looking back on that loan refusal, Boyce finds it was an invaluable experience. "It was a bad jolt psychologically," he says, one he was determined not to repeat. And he hasn't. Today, Microbac Labs is a $2-million chain of seven laboratories (several were merged after they were acquired) that stretches across western Pennsylvania into Kentucky. Microbac tests and analyzes for industry everything from food, water, and waste water to heavy metals, oil and hydraulic fluids, and coal.

In the past decade, Boyce has looked to the bank for loans that have forged each new link in his chain of testing labs. In those ten years, he has borrowed $355,000 in seventeen trips to the bank. He's been turned down only twice. That 15-2 won-lost record makes him something of an expert on the relations between small business and banks.

Boyce knows how important it is to get on the right side of a bank—and to stay there. "You can't treat your banker as an adversary," he says. "He has to be an ally. If you're a success, your banker is also. You're a hero to your banker."

Mellon Bank was the first place Warne and his wife, Doreen, had turned to when all they had was a dream. They chose Mellon because they'd been doing their personal and business banking there.

"We had only an idea," says Warne. "We didn't know how to bring it about. But we wanted to let the bank know what we were thinking about. We asked them if there was anyone we should be talking to. Banks know a lot of people in the community."

Warne and Doreen had come to the United States from England in 1962 when Warne was offered a position as executive vice-president of Megator Corporation's American subsidiary. Megator built pumps of all sizes and types, each for a specific use. But, the Boyces realized, Megator's customers bought pumps without knowing what they pumped.

"They had no idea of the acidity or viscosity of the fluids they were pumping," says Doreen Boyce. Their customers' ignorance set the Boyces to pondering the need for testing and analysis in industry.

When the Boyces went in to talk to Jim Karras, a loan officer at Mellon Bank, they were practical above all. "We didn't pretend to be thinking of anything on a tremendous scale," says Doreen. "We recognized our limitations. On the other hand, we recognized our strengths."

Both strengths and limitations were considerable. Warne was a metallurgist with a background in engineering, and he had experience running a company. Doreen was an economist, then teaching at Chatham College in Pittsburgh.

On the other hand, the Boyces' assets were meager. They couldn't muster $15,000 even if Doreen cleaned out her personal bank account.

And it couldn't have impressed the bank that neither of the Boyces had ever lived anywhere for more than six years. (Warne was born and raised in South Africa, Doreen in Chile; both are now American citizens.)

But the Boyces have a way of turning negatives into positives. Although she wasn't aware at the time that she was blunting a potential liability, Doreen found herself stressing their commitment to Pittsburgh. She was already serving on a local school board. And Jim Karras could see that they were willing to throw all their assets behind their idea.

Perhaps the most impressive thing about the Boyces was their compelling and articulate presentation. It was clear that even at this exploratory stage they had carefully thought through their idea for a company. They pointed out that Pittsburgh, dominated as it is by industry, had a need for testing and analysis that was bound to grow. Stricter air and water pollution standards were on the way. Concern over safety in the workplace would create a demand for materials testing. Consumer concern about diet, nutrition, and health meant a greater need for food testing.

Jim Karras told the Boyces their lack of assets was the greatest obstacle to their starting a company, but he suggested an alternative. "It may seem queer that when you're short on capital it could be reasonable to acquire a company," Warne says. But that's what Karras suggested. "It made sense. With an existing company, there is equipment, a building, and cash flow."

Karras told them the bank would tune in its communication network and see what it could find. By involving the bank from the start, the Boyces had given it a stake in their dream. Six months later, Karras called the Boyces. Mellon Bank had located a company they might be interested in acquiring.

Although they didn't realize it at the time, the Boyces now know how closely Mellon Bank was watching when they went out to talk with the owners of Dairy Products Lab, John and Ann Davis.

"The Davises were more comfortable with Doreen," Warne says. "I have a tendency to come on too strong sometimes." The trust and reassurance that Doreen conveyed to the Davises led to an honest discussion of needs and goals.

The Boyces recognized the need the Davises felt for long-term security. And they saw how traumatic this sale could be for a couple who had worked long and hard to build their company. So they proposed an installment loan, with a one-third down payment and annual installment payments plus interest on the balance over ten years. And Warne asked the Davises to stay on at the lab on a three-year noncompetitive contract.

The installment loan buyout solved the Boyces' capital problems. It also eased the Davises' tax burden, which would have been much greater with a lump-sum payment, and it gave them long-term security. Moreover, the agreement would permit the Boyces to finance their acquisition essentially on the cash flow the lab itself would generate. Keeping the Davises on board meant the Boyces had two experienced, dedicated employees who had a stake in the lab's continued success. The installment buyout would ease any jolt Dairy Products' customers might feel during the transition and minimize the trauma of separation for the Davises.

"It's important to establish trust when negotiations get complex," Warne says. "Egos and personalities get involved, and the bank listens very carefully when you talk about these things."

The Boyces were gradually molding a very good image at Mellon Bank. And Warne was aware how much that image is affected by the quality of people with whom a businessman surrounds himself. So it was not without foresight that Warne Boyce approached Brent Wilson to invest in his yet-to-be-launched company. Boyce had been introduced to Wilson, president of Harbison Walker, the world's largest refractory company, back in 1962. When Boyce described his idea for a business, Wilson accepted an offer to become 30 percent stockholder and serve on Microbac's board.

"Many small companies don't give their boards enough attention," says Boyce. "If you can get someone like Brent Wilson to invest and give good advice at the same time, it's a tremendous plus."

For accounting and legal expertise, the Boyces turned to firms that matched Mellon Bank in size and prestige. "There's a great temptation to look to a small accounting firm or a lesser-known legal firm when you're a small business," Doreen Boyce says. "It's natural to think that a small firm might give a small business more attention. But you want someone who moves in the same circles with your banker. They meet at banquets or the Duquesne Club, and it's nice to know that on an informal basis they're communicating with each other."

The Boyces are a handsome couple. Their British accents suggest culture and urbanity. That they are not typical of small-business owners in Pittsburgh prompts skeptics to argue that they are among an elite few who can deal successfully with banks in a city dominated by big business.

Yet that argument underscores the importance of image. It may not pay to affect a British accent, but the Boyces are proof that it is important to cultivate an image that will open doors at the bank.

Before Warne Boyce opened the door to Mellon Bank, he and Doreen practiced their presentation. Doreen played devil's advocate to Warne as they ran down all the "what if" scenarios. "It's important to have someone to talk to," she says, "someone to critique your performance."

Tutored by Doreen, schooled inch by inch on the intricacies of the installment loan by his attorney, and armed by his accountant with projections of income and cash flow over five years, Warne Boyce set off for the bank.

"The last thing you want your banker to think is that you're naive," says Boyce of a loan interview. "Even if you don't have the answers, he should at least realize you know the questions."

Boyce knew the questions and he had the numbers. As he walked through the door, he straightened his tie. When he came out, he carried a check for $26,000. Microbac Labs was born.

Even with his company off and running, Warne Boyce did not consider his work with Mellon Bank complete. Intuitively following what would become Boyce's first law of banking, he would drop by occasionally to talk with his loan officer. "If you see your banker only once every nine months," he says, "you shouldn't be running a business." He makes a habit of inviting his banker along for tours of new acquisitions, and he always invites new loan officers out to Microbac. The Boyces discuss any potential acquisition with their banker, because "banks know a lot more about the community," says Doreen. "They can raise little red flags about things you'd never think of."

Warne and Doreen Boyce don't dwell on the subject, but they are realistic about the possibility of sickness or accident. Doreen makes a point of letting Microbac's bankers know that she is fully prepared and qualified to step in and run the company should anything ever happen to Warne. That possibility was difficult for the Boyces to confront initially. But it was an important issue to come to terms with, they both now agree, because bankers are quite concerned about the continuation of a business in the event of death.

Doreen Boyce does not hesitate these days to point out how knowledgeable and qualified she is to run Microbac Labs if she had to. And that is just one more way the Boyces have learned to reassure their banker and cement their banking relationship.

Microbac provides Mellon with more than it has to. "It's crazy not to," says Boyce, who as a matter of course sends along an income statement. "Once a quarter," he says, "although we might send it once a month prior to an acquisition. And we send the bank a cash flow statement every six months."

Keeping their banker informed of everything they're doing is the Boyces' approach to preventive banking. An informed banker can act in a crisis because he understands the inner workings of a company and its manager. And crisis, according to Boyce, greets just about every four-year-old company.

Three or four years down the road, the reservoir of good feeling extended any start-up by the public, its customers, and the bank will have evaporated. "By this time, you're expected to stand on your own two feet," says Boyce. The marginal economics of a small business are critical at this point. You're strapped financially, cash flow is tight, and you're paying high interest rates on your debt.

The natural reaction, Boyce says, is to conceal your problems from the bank, for fear it will think you don't measure up. But it's the wrong reaction. "This is not the time to withhold information from that ogre of a banker you have to face to get money to survive," says Boyce. "Your loan officer is just as anxious about your business as you are. He has to go before a committee that doesn't know you from a cake of soap. He needs as much ammunition as you can provide him to sell your case to the loan committee."

As a rule, the Boyces provide forecasts of sales for the year, broken down by month and service category. Monthly breakdowns of costs and expenses and net profit before and after taxes are included. A pro forma cash budget is delineated, with accounts receivable on 30/60/90 term bases, total cash available, income tax deductions, cash surplus, and anticipated loans and repayment schedules with an analysis of their impact on cash flow. A cash balance completes the package. The same information is provided on any acquisition.

According to Boyce, the next growth crisis is likely to come when the company is about seven years old. At that point, "a banker says to himself, 'These people have grown pretty well, but their long-term indebtedness is still pretty stretched. Maybe they ought to cool down a bit and establish themselves as a reputable little business by all the commonly accepted balance sheet standards.'"

This might be good advice if the company has any sign of internal management problems. But in Boyce's case, it would have been the wrong strategy. "Had we thrown our game plan out the window just to make our long-term debt look better," he says, "the company would have closed right in on itself." There's a difference, Boyce stresses, between being sensitive to a banker's position and being intimidated by him.

In 1978, the Boyces were homing in on their ninth acquisition. With the coal industry depressed, coal labs were on their knees, ripe for Microbac's acquisition tactics.

In this case, the Boyces were dealing with a small bank in Johnstown. Whenever possible, they place part of a loan with a local bank, partly because the Regional Industrial Development Corporation encourages them to do so, partly because it's good public relations for a big-city company that's taking over a business in a small town. Mellon Bank understands this and supports them.

But the Johnstown bank turned down the Boyces' application. "They badly misread our capabilities," Warne says. "They felt our long-term debt was rather too substantial for our assets, so they would grant us only a portion of the one hundred thousand dollars we were after. In the long run it worked out better for us because it led to a private deal. But the bank lost out on a very secure loan."

Even so, Boyce didn't give up on the Johnstown bank. He continued to send it Microbac's statements and to keep it informed about the company's plans. So last year, when he called about a $10,000 loan for new equipment, the bank granted it immediately.

Diligent care and feeding of bankers pays off when unexpected opportunities arise. Late in 1978, Boyce got wind of a real steal on some lab equipment. A coal testing lab had gone out of business before it even opened. There was a fully equipped lab—grinding and sorting machines, calorimeters, sink and flotation gear, muffle furnaces, even a computer—worth between $70,000 and $100,000. It was his for only $35,000 if he could come up with cash on the barrel.

"I explained to Mellon Bank what the situation was," Boyce says. "My loan officer said the money would be ready. And when we discussed the terms of the loan the next morning, I got it at the lower two-tier rate for small businesses—one and a quarter percent below prime."

More recently, in March 1979, Microbac was bidding on a testing contract. Boyce was certain that Microbac's $55,000 bid was too high, but to lower it he needed more sophisticated equipment that would increase productivity. Boyce turned to Mellon Bank. He explained that a new Perking-Elmer 703 Atomic Absorption unit and a P-E Gas Chromatograph would enable him to lower his bid to $52,000. And if he won the contract, Microbac could begin writing off that equipment immediately.

Mellon gave him the go-ahead. Later Boyce learned that he'd just beaten out a competitor's bid of $53,000.

Boyce was able to react swiftly because he'd enabled his loan officer to react swiftly. Warne Boyce makes his banker an expert on Microbac, one of his inner-circle advisers. As a result, the banker feels confident about making a quick decision when he must.

"We give them the bad news as well as the good," says Doreen. "We try to keep them fully informed. A manager doesn't like surprises; why would a banker?"

"We don't get the most senior people," adds Warne. "But one of the advantages of being with a bank for a while is that as your loan officers move up in the organization, more and more senior people know who you are."

In return for his hospitality, Boyce has found that he and Doreen are often invited to functions associated with the bank. Recently, his loan officer made a point of introducing the Boyces to an officer of a fish importing company he thought would be interested in doing business with Microbac. The company has since become a valuable account.

"Bankers are very similar the whole bloody world over," says Boyce. "You expect the Pope to be Roman Catholic; you expect a banker to be a banker."

Yet in Pittsburgh, small businesses take an almost perverse pride in the belief that their city has the most hostile small-business banking climate in the country. To Warne Boyce, the perception of bankers is the crux of the problem: Expecting your banker to be an ogre becomes a self-fulfilling prophecy. Boyce should know. He has succeeded in a city of banks small businessmen love to hate.

—JOHN R. HALBROOKS

A DOZEN WAYS TO BORROW MONEY

Bankers, even those who are hot on the trail of new clients, play by some pretty conservative rules. They may take you to lunch, tour your offices, peruse your financials enthusiastically, and then turn down a loan request for reasons that seem absurdly technical.

In fact, banks want to lend money. It's the main product they have to sell, and small business is rapidly becoming one of banking's most attractive customers. But lending officers aren't standing at the door counting out bills. They still have to cope with both federal and state banking regulations, traditional lending standards, and a persistent desire to keep the funds they lend from straying beyond their control

The starting point to overcoming these obstacles, most lending officers agree, is to put together a proposal that fits into the conventional categories the banking world uses to describe most loans. There will still be countless variations on these categories, as well as individual terms and conditions to deal with for each borrower. But at least you'll be speaking a language your banker respects—and that can't hurt.

Here then are the twelve basic loan categories that bankers generally use to classify loans, grouped according to the expected duration of the loan.

Short-Term Loans

Business runs on short-term loans. Technically "short term" means less than a year, but in practice often expands to two or three years. Small companies usually seek short-term loans to finance receivables or inventory, especially in seasonal or perishable lines. But short-term loans can also be turned to many other purposes, from taking advantage of an inventory bargain to taking care of an emergency.

Most short-term loans fall into one of five classes:

• *Line of credit.* A widely used mode of short-term lending, a line of credit consists of a specific sum marked off for a company to draw on, as needed, over a prescribed period. The period may run only thirty days, or may stretch to two years, since repayment is tied to anticipated receipts. Interest is computed only on the amount actually drawn, but a commitment fee of ½ to 1 percent of the total credit line is usually imposed, to pay the bank for reserving funds that may not be tapped. Some banks waive the fee in favor of a compensating balance, a sum that must be kept on deposit throughout the loan period; others work out a combination of compensating balances and commitment fees.

Lines of credit are popular because of their simplicity, but banks have developed several credit line arrangements that fit different borrowing needs. The cheapest, the nonbinding line of credit, may be your best buy if you're willing to risk the line's drying up. With no guarantees, your credit may be curtailed if your company's financial position deteriorates, or even if your industry seems headed for hard times. Moreover, when the economy is tight—and your need is greatest—the bank may develop liquidity problems that force a cutoff, although the larger money-center institutions can usually ride out such crises.

The risks of losing the line can be avoided by paying a premium to insert the word *committed* in the loan agreement. The commitment fee will probably double, going as high as 2 percent, but you're assured that the funds will be there when you need them.

Nonbinding or committed, a short-term line of credit must be "cleaned up" periodically, under most banks' rules. You must be "out of the bank," or fully paid up, for thirty days a year, in the typical agreement.

If cleaning up a line of credit will constrict your cash flow, there's a third form that may be useful—the revolving line of credit, which requires an annual review and renewal but no cleanup. This is similar to a revolving charge account: As you withdraw funds, your available credit diminishes, and as you repay, it expands by a like amount. Interest is computed only on the funds actually borrowed, and there's usually no additional cost.

Ordinarily, revolving lines are repaid in monthly installments of interest plus principal, but some banks offer other options. At Citibank in New York, for example, you can arrange to restrict some installments to interest, holding off on payments of principal until your cash flow improves.

• *Inventory loan.* When a small company with seasonal borrowing needs comes in for a loan of $25,000 to $200,000, some big banks shy away from the formal line of credit, preferring to write what they may call "short-term loans to carry inventory." The bank's collateral is the inventory itself—sometimes, under an arrangement called "floor planning" that big-ticket retailers use, loans are collateralized by specific inventory items—so your banker is likely to feel in control of the situation. From the customer's point of view, however, an inventory loan might just as well be a line of credit. Funds are made available to be "taken down," or borrowed, as needed; repayment is made in installments as inventory is sold and receivables satisfied.

The usual inventory loan runs six to nine months, and requires the same thirty-day annual cleanup as a line of credit, if you want an extension.

• *Commercial loan.* Some big banks funnel much of their short-term lending into commercial, or "time," loans which minimize book-keeping for both lender and borrower. Requiring no installments, a commercial loan is simply repaid in a lump sum at the end of the term, typically three to six months. In practice, commercial loans are often used to finance inventory, but they may be applied to any other purpose that wins bank approval. In making a commercial loan the bank's chief concern, in addition to the company's credit rating, is the source of repayment. How will the company amass the lump sum to meet its obligation?

• *Accounts receivable financing.* Small companies in almost every industry today find receivables are tying up inordinate amounts of working capital, so they're turning to their banks for loans that will convert unpaid accounts into fast cash.

Which accounts, and how much? Generally, accounts must be less than sixty days past due, and the customers themselves must qualify as creditworthy. For receivables meeting these criteria, banks will advance 65 to 80 percent of face value, repayable as customers' checks come in. The usual arrangement calls for you to pass the checks on to the bank, which takes its portion and deposits the rest in your account, charging interest only on the amount outstanding.

Although the contract is ordinarily written for one year, many banks are prepared to work out a revolving format. Under such an agreement, which is subject to annual review and renewal, they will continue to advance funds against your incoming receivables. One limitation on receivables financing that doesn't apply to other short-term loans is that most banks set minimums based on the cost of monitoring such loans. At the Southeast First National Bank of Miami, for example, qualified receivables must amount to at least $250,000, which translates into annual sales of at least $2.5 million.

• *Factoring.* Perhaps the oldest method of commercial lending, factoring is a variation of accounts receivable financing in which the bank (or a factoring company) buys receivables outright. A couple of decades ago, factoring was largely restricted to the apparel and textiles industries and was disdained in other quarters. Today, many more industries draw on factoring services. In addition to textiles, major users include the electronics, importing, wood and wood products, plastics, home furnishings, and appliance industries.

Since receivables are purchased without recourse, ordinarily you're no longer involved once the transaction is completed. The bank assumes credit risks and takes on collection responsibilities, receiving payments directly from your customers. But if you don't want your customers to know you're involved in a factoring arrangement, you have other options. Some banks offer "non-notification" factoring, in which you continue to collect payments on the purchased receivables and forward them to the new owner.

There are some limits to factoring. The bank subjects receivables to rigid scrutiny before making any purchases, to screen out the poorest risks. Further, your costs, in the form of discounts from face value, may be quite high; often, in fact, they are higher than in most other forms of short-term financing.

Medium-Term Loans

Short-term loans tend to be granted by banks without too much concern for collateral since these loans are usually self-liquidating from sales made in the ordinary course of business operations. More likely to require collateral are medium-term loans, of one to five years, which are the usual way to finance machinery and equipment, including furniture and fixtures, plant alteration, and expansion. While you may view the asset you're purchasing as security, don't be surprised if the bank doesn't see it that way and asks for additional collateral, particularly if you're starting a new company. The bank will, however, expect the asset to serve as the source of repayment, in terms of generating increased revenues.

There are two kinds of medium-term loans:

• *Term loan.* Most term loans providing 80 to 90 percent of total costs are written either for five years, with a refinancing clause, or for the useful life of the asset. The typical repayment schedule calls for quarterly installments of principal plus interest. Principal payments remain constant, but interest, computed on the amount outstanding, declines over the term of the loan. In consequence, installments are highest at the start, although you can often arrange to tailor the repayment schedule to meet your anticipated cash flow.

• *Monthly payment business loan.* Even with this deferral, the quarterly installments may prove initially burdensome. Accordingly, some banks offer a variation permitting you to make approximately equal monthly payments over the entire period. At Union Trust in New Haven, Connecticut, for example, you can work out a schedule, tailored to your company's needs, that will allow you to repay a much smaller amount in the first year or two than would be demanded by term-loan conditions. Toward the end of the loan period, though, you'll be paying more, under the monthly payment plan. While these payments remain the same, the quarterly term-loan installments decrease, as interest drops along with principal owed.

Many companies find the reduced early payments advantageous, but whichever method of repayment suits you better, you should be aware that medium-term loans, in contrast to short-term loans, may impose operating restrictions on your company. The bank may insist on your maintaining a certain level of working capital or current ratio (current assets/current liabilities); or limits may be enforced on the distribution of dividends or on other debt. If you don't like the conditions laid down by one bank, however, try another; you're sure to find differences.

Long-Term Loans

Loans of five or more years, least often sought and probably the hardest to get, will be linked to specific business purposes. The most common include purchase of real property, major expansion, acquisitions, and start-ups.

• *Commercial and industrial mortgages.* Banks ask sharp questions about potential real estate purchases because, as a Bank of America lending officer cautions, "Pride of ownership can mean business failure." Nevertheless, if you get the chance to buy the building you're now renting, most banks will consider a mortgage loan of up to 75 percent of appraised value. Commercial and industrial mortgages may be written in a variety of ways, depending on the value of the building, your company's long-range profit projections, and the bank's lending policies. Under the best circumstances, you might get a twenty-five-year mortgage, to be paid off in regular monthly installments. More likely, though, you'll have to settle for a mortgage of five to ten years, but your monthly payments probably won't reflect this short period. Rather, they'll be geared to a fifteen- or twenty-year amortization period. When the mortgage comes due, you'll be faced with a "balloon" payment of the entire amount still owed. Many companies manage to refinance at this point, but a new loan won't be guaranteed.

• *Real estate loan.* Many companies face just the opposite problem: They already own real estate and want to borrow against its value to finance an acquisition or other form of expansion. You can tap this equity, without giving up a low-interest first mortgage, by adding a second mortgage—if you have sufficient equity and good financial standing. If you're in a less solid position, a "wrap-around" mortgage could be an alternative. This differs from a second mortgage in one detail: The bank tightens its control by receiving all your mortgage payments, and then passing on the amount due to the holder of the first mortgage.

If your mortgaged property has appreciated substantially, you might consider refinancing. You can probably get a new mortgage based on current value, but you'll have to give up your old interest rate and take on today's higher rate. Your banker may try to discourage you from refinancing—unless you're certain you can turn the cash you get into long-term profits.

• *Personal loan.* Most bankers believe an owner's personal assets should provide much of the financing for major expansion and acquisition, so you may have to think about including a secured personal loan in your long-term financing plans. Any property in your own name can be used as collateral, along with marketable securities, savings passbooks, and certificates of deposit. Such collateral is readily acceptable, and a personal loan may be easier to negotiate than a business loan.

To help you put the proceeds to most productive use, the bank may recommend a sophisticated leveraging technique. For example, you may be advised to turn the funds over to your company as a "subordinated loan," repayable to you only after other company debt is discharged. While this kind of loan doesn't create real equity, it will appear on your balance sheet as "surplus capital," a source of leveraging further loans up to three times the amount of the surplus.

• *Asset-based loan.* Long used by big corporations, but relatively new to the repertory of small companies, is the leveraged buyout, in which the target company's own assets are used to finance the takeover. Virtually every asset can be used—receivables, raw materials, inventory, machinery, and equipment. Under the most favorable conditions, a combination of these assets may generate as much as 70 percent of the acquisition cost. But you'll be charged the prime, or "base rate," as some banks are starting to call this benchmark figure, plus 2 percent or 3 percent. Moreover, the bank is likely to insist on various operating restrictions as well as keep close tabs on the assets. But once again, not all banks make the same demands, so you can shop around for the best deal.

• *Start-up loan.* Starting up parallels expansion and acquisition, in the banks' view, which means that you'll have to pour much of your own money into the project. In addition to funds raised by personal loans and partners' investments, you may be able to get a term loan from the bank's venture capital specialists, though a Small Business Administration guarantee, which protects 90 percent of the total, is frequently a condition. This procedure can involve a fair amount of paperwork and delay, unless your bank participates in the SBA's Certified Lender Program.

How to Write a Loan Proposal

The heart of most lending decisions is company value. Every banker wants to hear how his loan will improve the worth of your company. Address your presentation to this question and you'll improve your chances of coming away with the money. Here are some guidelines, along with specific tips.

A loan proposal consists of eight parts. It's virtually written already, though, if you have an up-to-date business plan on hand. A simple shift of emphasis toward your new audience will convert a business plan into a loan proposal.

• *Summary.* On the first page, give your name and title, company name and address, nature of business, amount sought, purpose, and source of repayment.

• *Top-management profiles.* To sell yourself and your partners or top executives to the bank, develop a paragraph or two on each of you, touching on background, education, experience, skills, areas of expertise, accomplishments. *Bankers seek their ultimate security in experienced management.*

• *Business description.* Give details of your company's legal structure and age, number of employees and union status, and current business assets. Define your products and your markets, identifying customers and competitors. Describe your inventory in terms of size, rate of turnover, and marketability. *Bankers favor established and conventional merchandise, as opposed to trendy or perishable items.* Report the status of your accounts receivable and accounts payable. *Bankers look for accounts to be less than sixty days old and for receivables to be spread among many customers, not concentrated in a few big ones.* If you have any "contingent liabilities," or potential expenses, acknowledge them here.

• ***Projections.*** Basing your figures on your current share of market, explain your growth opportunities and describe how you plan to exploit these opportunities for the next year and the next five years. List your alternative and fallback plans. Work out a realistic timetable for achieving your goals. *Bankers judge your plans and goals in terms of your industry's practices and trends.*

• ***Financial statements.*** Get together balance sheets and income statements for the past three years, including current figures, and make projections for the next three years. Past and current statistics must be exact. *Bankers are more comfortable with audited statements.* If you can't afford a full audit, ask your accountant for a financial "review." While less convincing than an audit, this new intermediate procedure gives your banker more assurance than an unaudited statement. Prepare two sets of projected balance sheets and income and cash flow statements, one predicated on receiving the loan and the other on going forward without it. Although critical to proving your claim that the loan will increase company worth, your projections must be realistic. *Bankers match projections against published industry standards,* searching for padded earnings and meager cost estimates. Personal financial statements, including tax returns for the past three years, must also be submitted, since your own net worth is a factor. *Bankers check your personal credit rating, as well as your company's.*

• ***Purpose.*** Pinpoint your proposed use of the loan. A request for "working capital" will elicit questions, not money. Instead, explain what the working capital is for, e.g., "To build up Christmas inventory by increasing production, starting in late summer."

• ***Amount.*** Ask for the precise amount needed to achieve your purpose, and support your figures with estimates from suppliers, for example, and previous years' cost figures. Don't ask for too much, expecting your request to be trimmed, or for too little, hoping that the smaller the request, the more likely an approval. *Bankers know costs.* They'll suspect you don't, if you seek an inappropriate amount.

• ***Repayment plans.*** The pivotal aspect of your proposal, repayment plans, should be formulated in the light of several banking axioms. First, asset must match loan: *Any asset you want to finance must last at least as long as the loan period.* Second, *the asset should generate the repayment funds,* by increasing sales, slashing costs, or heightening efficiency. Third, *your projected balance sheet should clarify your company's capacity to meet interest as an expense, and to repay* *principal from net profits.* Finally, *you must provide "two ways out,"* or two different sources of repayment. The bank wants assurance that if the first way—the asset and your company—is blocked, there's a second, ordinarily comprising your own and perhaps others' guarantees, validated by an accountant.

Weaving these axioms into a repayment schedule is a complex task, but you won't be required to do it all yourself. Lending officers anticipate calls for advice on this and all other elements of your loan proposal. They look for you to be an expert only on your business; however, *you will be expected to come in with all the requisite financial data.* "I'll have to look that up" or "Let me check that out and get back to you" will put you in the amateur league, as far as bankers are concerned.

Bad as it is to lack financial information, it's worse to try to hide anything you fear may damage your chances. *Be candid,* bankers urge, pointing out that a good relationship is rooted in trust. Further, if you've made some misstep that's eating into your profits, the banker probably has the tools to effect a rescue.

Is there any other action you can take to swing the odds in your favor? Most bankers admit there is: *Don't confine your patronage to the loan department.* Buy additional services and refer other depositors. A bank, even a big money-center bank, is a business like any other, and will go to some lengths to satisfy customers—especially now, as competition for the small-business market heats up.

—JOAN FORD

HOW TO CHOOSE A BANK

A friend recently observed that bankers are people whom everyone loves to hate. He then proceeded to tell me about the banker with one glass eye . . . you could tell which eye it was—the one with compassion. Having been a banker for thirteen years and a bank regulator for one, I can't say I was surprised at his story. Still, if you could put aside your urge to hate for a while, I'd like to tell you about the view from the other side of the desk.

To begin with, we bankers are not all alike. Some of us will do better for your business than others, which is why you should shop around. Most loan officers are doing what their bosses want done so they can get a raise and a promotion. (Banks are notorious for giving the latter in place of the former.) They enjoy saying yes to loan proposals, but they also fear making bad loans. At the very least, bad loans will affect chances of promotion; at the worst, they can get a loan officer fired. It's no accident that bankers are risk averse.

Frequently, your proposals will be viewed in light of where a loan officer is sitting on a particular day—along the spectrum between the ecstasy of saying yes and the agony of a recent loan loss. One of the best bankers I know, for example, is absolutely the person you would want to approach about most loan propositions. He is honest, consistent, trustworthy, smart, and willing to meet with you anytime. If you want a restaurant loan, however, he is the wrong person to see. He was burned early in his career by a large loss on a restaurant. When Joe Businessman comes in to him and says, "I want to talk to you about a restaurant loan," he might as well say he'd like to talk about rape, incest, spiders, and taxes.

So, in your scouting around, it is important for you to get to know what businesses prospective loan officers like and what they dislike. This is not difficult to do—just ask about their best and worst lending experiences. They won't give you names, but they'll probably tell you all you need to know. You'll also want to know what they have done successfully in the past, not only because they are likely to look favorably on a similar proposal today, but also because the expertise gained from a successful venture in your industry can be invaluable to you.

Other key qualifications for you to consider include the following:

34

• *Is your loan officer someone you can consistently count on?*

As Mark Twain said, there are bankers who will loan you an umbrella when the sun is shining and then want it back when the rains come. There are solid, consistent, trustworthy bankers, and there are bankers who don't even have a compassionate glass eye. Ask around to see how different bankers treat people who have run into trouble.

In terms of reliability, you'll also want to know your banker's job history. Even if you think a loan officer would be wonderful to work with, one who is merely touching down at this job en route to greener pastures will probably not be there when you need help. It's better to have a reliable workhorse than a racehorse who is here today and gone tomorrow.

• *Does your loan officer have the authority to approve your loan or the influence to get it approved?*

All loan officers have specific lending authority or loan limits, and within those limits, they can approve a loan right away. If a request exceeds that authority, the loan officer will have to go to a more senior officer or to the loan committee. It's important that your loan officer either has the authority to decide or the influence to get affirmative decisions from higher up.

Of course, it would be nice if everybody could deal with a senior officer, but that's not always possible. You can, however, be equally well served by a respected rising star. In any bank, the key to a young loan officer's success is the ability to develop a high volume of low-risk loans. I've seen several bright young loan officers who work hard for their customers and are able to sell their proposals to the senior management or loan committee.

• *Is your loan officer competent enough to explain your loan to others?*

Your loan officer is your in-house advocate. Even if your loan is approved on the spot, it still will have to be reviewed by the credit department and, if it's a large loan, by the loan committee. Their ratios and formulas may seem like another language compared with your loan proposal, and it's up to your loan officer to serve as an interpreter, providing what they need to analyze your request.

Loan officers need to be able to explain who you are, how you are organized corporately, how you fit into your market, what you are using the money for, why the terms and conditions are a good deal for the bank, how you are going to pay the loan back, what your financial condition is, and when they can expect to receive progress reports on your operations.

I've seen presentations that left senior management with the impression that the loan was a low risk and a highly profitable bank asset. I've also seen loan officers appear before the loan committee like a hog on ice: They didn't know much about the borrower's financial condition; they described the purpose of the loan as working capital, which means absolutely nothing; and they weren't sure how the loan would be repaid. Needless to say, such a presentation leaves senior management cold.

- **Is your loan officer willing to be creative and take a reasonable risk?**

By that, I don't mean does the banker make unsecured, five-year loans to pay this year's taxes. That's not creative, that's stupid. But loan officers are under a lot of pressure to make a high volume of loans with a low level of risk. Individual loan officers react to these pressures in one of four ways. Some will make a high volume of high-risk loans. You don't want one of them as your banker, because he won't be around long, and when he's fired, your loan will look bad by association. Some will make a low volume of low-risk loans. You don't want that kind of loan officer either, because he will probably be promoted off the loan floor and into the credit department. Some will make no loans at all. If you run across someone like that, he or she is an FDIC employee and your bank has failed. Finally, some may succeed at making a high volume of low-risk loans. You want one of them. That officer will get your loan approved with creative structuring and will make sure the bank feels well secured.

Once you've settled on a good banker to work with, you then have to manage the relationship. The best way to do that is to follow four simple rules of banking etiquette. The idea is to build a solid partnership when times are good, so that you can work together should hard times fall on your company.

The first rule is that when it comes to sharing financial information, treat your banker as a full partner, not as a difficult minority shareholder. The thing a banker fears most is a bad loan. If your loan officer thinks you are not telling the truth, or if you are telling only partial truths, or if you are not talking at all, that will bring out the worst side of his personality—fear of an impending loss takes over. And there goes your advocate.

The second rule is to invite your banker to your place of business. Let him meet your key employees and see how the business works. Show him your accounts receivable billing-and-collections process and your inventory ordering and control. Then when he goes to the loan committee with your current or future proposal, he can enthusiastically explain why your company is successful: "I've been there and I've seen it myself." There is nothing as persuasive to a loan committee as that sort of personal endorsement.

The third rule is never become overdrawn; never become past due on a payment; and never fail to deliver your regularly scheduled financial statement. Repeat these words again and again until they become a mantra. Your loan officer has been taught from his first day as a trainee that the first signs of a bad credit risk are overdrafts, past dues, and late financial statements. For you to violate any one of these rules is like pouring gasoline onto a stack of wood. At the first sign of trouble, your banker will have visions of your loan going up in a blaze, exactly what he fears most.

The fourth rule of banking etiquette is to answer your banker's questions openly and honestly. If he makes recommendations, give them serious consideration. Accept his advice as well-intentioned observations that are meant to help you do better. The good banker views part of his role in life as helping businesspeople succeed. As one of my bank's customers put it, "Having to report to the bank and answer questions took a lot of time and cost a lot of money, but it helped me keep focused on how the business was doing financially. It helped us to become very successful."

Businesses tend to fail for one of two reasons: poor management or inadequate financing. It's up to you to provide the good management. To provide the adequate financing, you need to find a good banker. Selecting a banker, and then learning how to work with him, is the same as developing any kind of good partnership. Both partners have to be sensitive to the other's needs.

Banktalk

When bankers describe a good loan prospect, they are talking about four key areas:

1. The borrower has good character. This is not to be confused with being a "real character," which could work against a borrower. Bankers are talking about financial character. When I'm evaluating the character of a prospective borrower, I look at such things as credit reports (as evidence of his past record of repaying other people); experience in his line of business (degree of responsibility and how effectively he performed); education or training in business management (such areas as financial records, credit underwriting, accounts receivable collection, and inventory control); and understanding of the market for the proposed product or service.

2. The borrower has good capacity to repay. In evaluating capacity to repay a loan, I'll be looking at the flow of cash through the business to see if there is enough "excess cash." It is very important to understand that loans are not repaid merely out of profits. (It is also true, of course, that they are not repaid out of losses.) Profits frequently are tied up either in accounts receivable or in the purchase of new inventory for future sales, or both. It is the excess cash remaining after the entire business-transaction cycle that repays loans.

3. The borrower has good collateral *to support the loan.* Bankers don't make loans solely based on collateral value, or at least they shouldn't. Character and capacity to repay are considered much more important. However, while we usually anticipate being repaid from the excess cash flow from the normal operations of the business, sometimes things don't work out as planned. If we fail to take collateral at the outset of a loan and things do turn bad, it is unlikely that we can get collateral later. So, we think of collateral as a prearranged "Plan B."

4. The borrower has an appropriate purpose for the money. Many of my customers have responded to the question "Why do you need the money?" with the response "To pay my bills." That does not answer my need to know about the original purpose of the loan. I expect a good business operator to plan his cash flow sufficiently far in advance that he will be coming to me with loan requests to finance seasonal inventory buildups, to get through an unusually large contract, to purchase new equipment, or to purchase real estate for growth. The idea that he is surprised that the bills have come in and has no cash to pay them suggests lack of forward planning, slow accounts receivable collection, slow inventory turnover, operating losses, or all of the above. If, in fact, one or all of these is the purpose of the loan, I would like him to be able to tell me which one it is and what he is going to do to correct the situation.

—THOMAS E. BENNETT, JR.

WHAT DO BANKERS WANT?

If you've ever been turned down for a loan, or suffered through endless meetings before your loan proposal was approved, your kindest thoughts were probably that the banker didn't like you, didn't trust you, had poor judgment, or was an extreme pessimist. It's possible that you were right. It's also possible that you and your banker weren't speaking the same language.

One of the adages I learned as a young banker was "You can loan a good man enough money to break him." If you keep in mind that all bankers have been taught some version of this principle—keep a borrower's debt proportional to his ability to repay—you will better understand our language and our questions. Responsible bankers don't see it in either your interest or the bank's to loan you money that they don't believe you can repay. But there are a number of steps you can take that will increase our confidence in your ability to do so.

Let me tell you how the loan process looks from our side of the desk. When you explain your business to a banker, think of describing a tree. Most people are apt to wax eloquent about the beautiful leaves, majestic branches, and solid trunk. But bankers are the kind of people who want to know about the root system that supports the tree. And they feel the same way about a business. They want to hear about stability, integrity, and a good reputation. Since they're primarily interested in how you're going to repay the loan, they want to know where the essential nutrient—cash—is going to come from, however successful your company may look on the surface.

The way we view your management is a good example. Let's say that you walk into my office and explain that since you are a great manager, your skills and enthusiasm will more than make up for any inadequacies in your company. For argument's sake, let's say that I agree that you are, in fact, a super manager. But if you are the only good manager in your company, one of the questions on my mind is "What's going to happen to my loan if you should walk out of my bank and in front of a Mack truck?"

Or say that you are sixty-seven years old and there is no one in line to take over when you retire. In that case I'll wonder whether I should make your company a loan that will take it five to ten years to repay. I'll be much more positive if I see several good managers with balanced talents, mixed ages, and a fairly clear management-succession plan. A second adage that I learned early was "Bankers lend money to people, not to corporate structures." This attitude could be a real advantage to you, because as I become acquainted with your talented managers, you'll have a good chance of convincing me that your team can in fact make up for any other weaknesses I may find.

After you've made your presentation, one of the first things I'll do is order a credit report on your company from Dun & Bradstreet Credit Services and/or other credit agencies. I'll also call the other bankers you have worked with and ask about the size and repayment program of your loans and how well you met your payments. I may call your major suppliers to find out how much credit is available to you, how much of it you have used, and how well you have performed on your credit line.

If I find that you've had some financial trouble in the past, it doesn't necessarily mean that I'll turn you down. I will, however, be curious about how you responded to the trouble. I have had creditors describe to me at length problems suffered by prospective borrowers. The company may have gone through a period of slow sales, for example, or have had difficulty collecting on a large contract. If creditors follow up by explaining that the chief executive officer lost no time in letting them know about the problems and quickly arranged extended terms, I begin to see a person of integrity responding appropriately to trouble. If the creditors go on to rate the company's credit good or excellent under the altered terms, I consider that a real credit strength. What I'm interested in is solid character and appropriate credit management, in good times and bad. On the other hand, if I find a person who folded under pressure, I will probably turn down the proposal.

Once I'm satisfied that you are creditworthy, I'll evaluate your financial statement, and I'll take a particularly hard look at how closely the value you place on your assets reflects their true quality. Sometimes I find that the assets are actually worth more than a loan applicant claims. This has happened, for instance, in inflated real estate markets when a company has purchased a building years earlier and has depreciated its value on the balance sheet. I've also seen it happen when the borrower has depreciated equipment down to salvage value, but has maintained it in excellent marketable condition. This gives me a lot of confidence in the strength of the financial statement.

The more common discrepancies, however, turn up when people list assets that are about as realistic as claims of owning a flock of wild geese. For example, inventory may be carried at its original purchase price even though it hasn't sold in more than a year. I'm interested in financing inventory that moves quickly and turns into cash to repay my loan. I assign little value to antiques. I don't put much stock in accounts receivable listings over ninety days past due, either. I know that my loans over ninety days past due have questionable collectibility, and I would have to be convinced that you are a better lender than I am to believe that yours are much more sound. These sorts of findings can't help but raise questions in a banker's mind. When a borrower overstates his or her assets, I find it hard to believe any of the rest of the presentation.

Another point on the quality of assets: I'll pay close attention to how diverse your accounts receivable are. If 50 percent or more are due from one or two companies, I will be very concerned about *their* credit-worthiness. I'll also have to wonder what would become of you—and my loan payments—if they shifted their business to somebody else. As a result, I will probably expect you to maintain more equity in the business than might otherwise be necessary.

In my experience, you and your banker are most likely to talk past each other in the area of profits and cash flow. Borrowers often think that all of their profits are available to repay debt. Unfortunately, that is seldom true.

A company's cash flow is its profits plus depreciation *minus* increases in assets, and it's the subtraction of increases in assets that is usually forgotten. Say a company earns $100,000 and increases its assets by $75,000. That leaves only $25,000 available to repay debt. If this company has current debt-service requirements of $25,000 a year, it will have to manage growth in inventory and accounts receivable with care in order to have the cash to service its debt properly. If the CEO came to me wanting a loan that would require an additional $20,000 a year in payments, I would be very worried about the company's ability to pay. The fact is, I don't want you to repay my loan by giving me $20,000 worth of inventory or accounts receivable. Like most bankers, I want cold, hard cash.

When you go to your banker well armed with your financials, satisfied with your creditworthiness, and proud of your management team and succession plan, you're still not home free. That's because we won't look at your company in isolation. To some extent, at least, how we judge your riskiness will be influenced by the performance of your peers. We subscribe to several services that evaluate the riskiness of various industries, and we also have firsthand experience in our own marketplace. If you are one of ten area firms in a given line of business, and three others have recently failed, I'll look at your application with a jaundiced eye. If you are part of an industry from which bankers across the country have been reporting substantial losses, I'll have to question whether or not your company will fall prey to the same problems. Of course, the opposite is also true. If you had been in the oil business in the late 1970s, you would have found bankers tripping over each other to lend you money.

In any case, I'll expect you to know the trends—both problems and opportunities—in your industry. You may even have to educate me about the nature of industrywide problems and how they affect your business. One bit of advice, though. It doesn't help to tell me how terribly your competition is doing in an effort to make yourself look good. The truth is, as I said earlier, bankers are preoccupied with risk.

If your competition is doing well and you stumble, at least you could sell off your assets to them. If they're doing poorly and you stumble, there aren't many options but to shut down your business.

Your position within your industry will also interest me. I'll want to know whether you are a leader, or ninety-ninth out of a hundred. I'll compare your operating results or balance-sheet position to your peers'. If your industry has an average inventory turn of four times a year and you have only two, you look bad. If your industry is earning an average 44 percent gross profit on sales and you have a 57 percent gross profit, you look good.

Another measure of your industry standing is how up-to-date you are. One of the realities of business—every business—is change, and I'll want to be sure that you are keeping up with your competition. I'll look to see if you are an innovator with the latest equipment or a follower with equipment that will soon have to be replaced. I'll also want to know how strong the market is, and will be, for your product or service. If your prospects are good, that'll certainly raise my spirits.

As your banker, I would be very impressed by a business that has a vibrant and diverse root system. This would mean to me that you are the kind of customer whose growth I can finance today, and that we can grow old together with you as the lender, via deposits, and our bank the borrower. If, on the other hand, you have a fancy presentation about your trunk, branch, and leaves, but a weak root system, I'd be afraid that my money would dry up with your money, and that we'd both topple.

—THOMAS E. BENNETT, JR.

OF GROWING INTEREST

You can be certain of one thing when it comes to interest rates: They will change. And many forecasters are predicting that the next change we see will be an increase. Whether that will happen this year, next year, or the year after is open to debate. But a rise sometime soon seems inevitable, which means that this is a good time for you to understand how your bank arrives at its rate—and how you can negotiate to keep the cost of your loan within your ability to repay.

In a way, you and your banker are in the same position. You each want to come up with the best interest rate based on your estimates of whether the rates will go up, down, or stay the same over the term of your loan. Your banker, of course, can make a profit only if what he charges over time exceeds the cost of the funds he lends out. And you want to keep your monthly payments as low as possible while getting the services you need. That leaves you with a few points of negotiation. One is over the rate itself, often based on the bank's prime rate. (Prime rate is called "best" or "base" rate by some banks.) Another is how variable that rate will be over the life of your loan. Still another is how you might tie the terms of your loan to other business you do with the bank.

While changes in a large New York City bank's prime rate suggest the direction in which the financial markets are headed, there are many prime rates in today's market. The prime is usually described as "the rate that bankers charge their most creditworthy customers," but the truth is, the prime is merely an index from which each bank prices its loans, hoping to earn an appropriate yield on its investment. Ordinarily, banks have a lot of leeway: They can price loans off their prime, another bank's prime, the rate on their certificates of deposit, the average cost of various pools of funds, or other exotic indexes. Whatever your bank uses, you can try to negotiate a lower rate based on other factors.

You might be able to arrange to pay an up-front loan commitment fee, for example, in order to get either a lower interest rate or better terms. Before you go this route, though, check out your bank's financial statement. If its earnings are down, it may be especially willing to negotiate a very favorable long-term rate in order to get a higher up-front fee. You should also ask whether the bank is planning to keep your loan or to sell it. In the latter case, the up-front fee is the bank's primary source of income, and it may be willing to search more diligently for the long-term rate you desire if you are willing to pay a higher fee.

Another tack when you're negotiating interest rates is to be aggressive in reminding your banker about all the deposits you have in that bank, and to point out the income you generate for it by the other services you use, such as trust services or discount brokerage services. Many companies, especially those that keep large cash deposits anyway—retail establishments, for example, or construction companies or restaurants—maintain "compensating balances" in the banks where they have loans. These are funds deposited in noninterest-bearing checking accounts, which the bank can invest in exchange for giving a lower interest rate. For these companies, it often makes more sense to use the cash to reduce their interest rates than to shift it to savings accounts.

You can also tie your loan rate to the provision of a variety of banking services. Say, for instance, you have excellent credit and borrow money only on a short-term basis, which would qualify you as a prime borrower. You might not benefit as much by negotiating for a low interest rate as you would by paying a slightly higher rate and pushing for no service charges on your depository account.

When it comes to the terms of your loan, your banker usually will quote you a rate that best matches the rate he's paying on the deposits he has purchased. There are, however, at least three options you should think about. One is a floating-rate loan (tied to something like a prime); another, a floating-rate loan with a ceiling or cap; and the third, a fixed-rate loan. The one you choose to bargain for will depend on where you think interest rates are headed. Let's assume you want to borrow $100,000, to be repaid in monthly payments over five years, and that your bank's prime rate is 9 percent. The three options would look something like this:

1. Prime plus 1 (10 percent), adjusted quarterly with no ceiling. Beginning monthly payments: $2,125. If you expect the prime rate to hold steady or to drop (not likely in today's economy), this is probably your best option—a floating-rate loan with no ceiling. On the other hand, if the prime rate rose to 21 percent (as it did in 1981), you could wind up paying $2,762 per month—a whopping $637 per month increase.
2. Prime plus 2 (11 percent), adjusted quarterly with a ceiling of 14 percent. Beginning monthly payments: $2,175. If you expect rates to rise over the next five years, which seems likely, then having a ceiling would give you a maximum payment of $2,327, which you can budget into your operations.
3. Prime plus 3 (12 percent) with a fixed rate for the life of the loan. Fixed monthly payments: $2,225. If you expect rates to rise to the 14 percent ceiling soon and stay there for the life of the loan, then the

fixed rate at prime plus 3 is the best deal. (Often, to get a fixed-rate loan, you'll be required to pay an up-front commitment fee as well.)

I usually advise clients to take the lowest rate—usually the most variable—on short-term loans or loans that are small in the context of their total operations. On longer-term loans or loans that will require a large portion of your cash flow to repay, you'll probably want a loan with a ceiling. The reasoning is that it's worth paying a higher current rate to have the assurance that payments won't go above what your company can afford.

You should also consider how long you want to take to repay the loan. Normally, you will pay a higher rate for a longer-term loan, but it may be worth it. A two-year loan of $100,000 at 10 percent will mean monthly payments of $4,614. If you borrow the same amount for four years at 12 percent, your payments would drop to $2,633. That's a difference of almost $2,000 in monthly cash flow, which may be more valuable to your company than the lower rate.

Throughout history, the primary issues for lenders have been perceived risk and local cost of funds. The same is true today, so when you set out to negotiate with your banker over loan terms, your best strategy is to do what you can to lower his perception of your risk as a borrower and show how you can reduce his cost of funds by, for instance, keeping compensatory balances in the bank. You'll need to be knowledgeable about what you want and what the bank can offer.

—THOMAS E. BENNETT, JR.

ARE BIGGER BANKS BAD
FOR SMALL BUSINESS?

The old signs have just come down from the twenty-three branch offices of the Syracuse Savings Bank, the oldest and most venerable financial institution in this upstate New York city. Since 1849, the bank has been a pillar of the Syracuse business establishment. But from now on, Syracuse Savings will be part of Norstar Bancorp Inc., the "Beast of the East," as it is known in the banking community—an $11-billion regional powerhouse based in Albany that itself is slated to lose its independence when it joins forces with Providence-based Fleet Financial Group to form a superregional bank with $25 billion in assets.

Welcome to the brave new world of big-bank banking. Thanks to computer technology, government deregulation, bank failures, and competition from other financial institutions, consolidation is the name of the game in banking these days. By one estimate, the number of U.S. banks could drop from about 15,000 to 5,000 by the end of this century. And the prospect raises some profound and disturbing questions for American business owners and Washington policymakers.

The common fear is that big banks and small business just don't mix very well. Loan authority becomes centralized in faraway headquarters where decisions are made by number-crunching young MBAs who know nothing about you, your business, or your community. And as part of the culture of large institutions, loan officers rotate from place to place and job to job, so that just when you think you've got one trained, another takes his place.

"Lending to small business is very tough," explains Oklahoma banker Bob McCormick, "because the most important part of the underwriting process is the evaluation of management. It is subjective, it is personal, and it takes time and effort by an experienced person. But with consolidation, I think you'll see that kind of personal touch go by the boards."

McCormick is president of Stillwater National Bank & Trust Company and a past president of the Independent Bankers Association of America. Over the years, he has made something of a crusade against

46

what he calls, ominously, the "evils of bank consolidation." And he thinks the federal government should stop it before it threatens the very sector of the U.S. economy that lately has been producing all the new jobs and most of the new products.

"One reason small companies do so well in the United States is that we have thousands of small banks for them to work with," McCormick says. "And if those small banks disappear and you have to go into Bank of America, say, to find your loan, you are hurting."

Only time will tell if his gloomy predictions prove valid. In many areas, the first round of bank consolidation has only just begun. But it may be possible to take a glimpse farther into the future in a place like Syracuse, where the proximity of New York City's megabanks has already made bank consolidation a small-business reality.

It has been more than a decade since New York State ushered in the era of bank deregulation. In 1976, the state legislature, over the objections of independent bankers and business owners, abolished the banking districts that had made it difficult for the Manhattan megabanks to move upstate. Cities such as Syracuse seemed easy pickings for the likes of Citibank, Chase Manhattan, Chemical Bank, and Manufacturers Hanover. Local bankers braced themselves for the invasion.

"Those big banks came up thinking they were going to blow away the locals," says a Syracuse banker who lived through it. "They thought everyone would want to do business with them because of their size. And it was almost the reverse reaction. The people here were comfortable with their banks, they felt loyalty to them, and they didn't switch."

Manhattan bankers may be callous, but they aren't stupid, and before long most found themselves paring back their Syracuse plans. Chase, however, came up with a different strategy: If you can't beat 'em, buy 'em. Faced with lackluster performance in Syracuse under its own name, in 1984 Chase Manhattan Corporation purchased the Rochester-based Lincoln First Banks Inc., with its twenty-five or so branches in the Syracuse area alone. In deference to local sensibilities, the new operation was called Chase Lincoln First Bank, and bank officers were told to continue to answer to a regional headquarters in Rochester.

Even before the change in state law, however, the colonization of Syracuse had already begun. Irving Trust Company used its holding company to buy up the seventeen-branch Merchants National Bank & Trust Company of Syracuse, and the Bank of New York had taken over Metropolitan National Bank of Syracuse. From Albany, the old National Commercial Bank & Trust Company snatched up the thirty-branch First Trust & Deposit Company in Syracuse in 1971, later renaming the combined organization KeyCorp. And Buffalo's giant Marine Midland Banks, which was most recently a subsidiary of Hongkong & Shanghai Banking, had been operating more than a dozen branches in Syracuse since the 1950s.

As a result of these buys, and Norstar's purchase of Syracuse Savings, the big-bank sweep is now virtually complete in Syracuse.

Within a fifty-mile radius of the city, only two small banks and a few savings institutions remain independent. "Things are pretty well picked over," says an attorney who handles KeyCorp's acquisitions.

But if small banking is dead in Syracuse, small business definitely is not. Although the city's start-ups are relatively few, the annual *Inc.* survey of metropolitan areas shows a healthy percentage of fast-growth companies among them. And although many of the business owners I spoke with have had their troubles with the big banking outfits, they've found that, so far, there has been enough competition among the banks to provide for their needs eventually.

When Jake Berdan bought EDRO Business Forms Inc. fifteen years ago, for example, his bank was First Trust & Deposit. After First Trust was bought by KeyCorp and renamed Key Bank, "we just stuck with them," he says. "The personnel was the same, and I could see no change in their operations for the first eight or ten years. I had a good loan officer, and he took a real personal interest in us."

Since then, EDRO, a printer of customized business forms, has grown to twenty-nine employees and annual sales of $1.7 million. Now, with three sons in the business, Berdan sees this as a perfect time to expand into the printing of continuous computer-printout forms, which he now brokers out of state. His problem: After eight months of consideration, Key Bank still won't lend him $200,000 for the new press.

"I just feel that he doesn't understand what I'm talking about," says Berdan. "He has no enthusiasm for this piece of equipment. So I may have to go elsewhere to arrange my financing."

Berdan looks back somewhat longingly to the good old days of First Trust & Deposit, when he thinks this loan request would have been a *pro forma* matter. And he can't help but think that the reason for the bank's indifference has to do with the fact that his company is small.

Martin Yenawine's Eastern Ambulance Service Inc. is also small—$2.7 million in sales last year. And because ambulances wear out every four years, banking is almost always on his mind. His bank is Norstar, and although he has been through three loan officers in seven years, he has few complaints.

"The thing is, we work at it," explains Yenawine. "As soon as we know we are getting a new banker, we ask the old banker to bring the new guy down to see us. A small firm that wants a successful relationship with a big bank has to constantly work at it—just as hard as the bankers do."

And, indeed, Syracuse's big banks have been working at it. For the most part, they quickly learned to adapt their procedures to the sensibilities of local business owners. Bank officials in each region are allowed to set their own policies, develop their own products, and make their own loans—as long as overall performance is in line.

"When Irving bought Merchants National, it promised that it would let Merchants run with relative autonomy," says Roger W. Eck. "A lot of bankers, myself included, were skeptical of that. But it turned out to be the case. We make our own loans up to about four million dollars per customer. That's going to handle most small and midsize firms, and we compete for that market very aggressively—frankly, it's quite profitable."

As Eck speaks, he is sitting in the office of Mike Busse, president of Microwave Systems Inc., in East Syracuse. Busse listens and nods in agreement. Two years ago, when he bought Microwave in a leveraged buyout from a Virginia company, it was Merchants that saw him through.

"When I walked into the bank and sat down with a loan officer, I told him what I wanted to do with the company," Busse remembers. "I had no money. I said I needed at least one hundred thousand dollars and I really needed four hundred thousand dollars on top of that. And the bank didn't throw me out."

At the time, Microwave was in sorry shape—"essentially bankrupt," Busse admits. "Other than myself, there were three employees— the former president and his daughter, who were on their way out, and a foreign-born engineer who couldn't be cleared for defense work. How many banks would take a flyer on something like that?"

Merchants stood him $100,000 at a time when even the Small Business Administration thought him too risky. And the rest of the buyout was financed by the seller. "We didn't do it stupidly," explains Dave DiRoma, the banker who handled the deal. "We felt there were sufficient personal assets to cover our tails." Nonetheless, Busse so liked the way DiRoma finessed the package that he hired him away from the bank to be his chief financial officer.

The bank's gamble has paid off handsomely. Busse now has thirty employees making customized electronics components for everything from TV sets to navy antisubmarine aircraft. He expects to do $2 million this year and projects $9 million by 1989. Merchants has upped his line of bank credit from $100,000 to $200,000.

More money, more sophistication, more competition—these have always been the promises held out for a deregulated, big-bank environment. And yet for every Mike Busse you meet in Syracuse who's pleased with how things have turned out, you also meet someone like Tom Holmes.

T. A. Holmes Inc. fabricates the clear plastic bulk-food bins that you see in supermarkets. The company operates from a low, nondescript building on the east side of the city, and while its growth has not exactly set the world on fire—sales last year were $600,000—it has done well enough to provide its owner with a comfortable living.

Holmes used to bank with Key Bank but grew restless after it rejected his application for $50,000 in working capital. As it happened, Citibank was just opening up in Syracuse and was hungry for new business, and Holmes got his line of credit there. But several years later, he noticed a shift in Citibank's attitude.

"I think they decided that, hey, this small-business stuff isn't too attractive," he says. "So they handed their small-business customers to the same guy who handled used-car loans. I'd be in there to discuss what was to me a terribly important matter, and the phone would ring. He'd pick it up, and I'd hear him say, ' . . . a seventy-seven Chrysler—wait a minute. . . .' After that, I got out of Citibank fast."

Holmes ended up at the Bank of New York. He borrowed $70,000 to help finance his move to larger quarters and his switch from distribution to fabrication. When Syracuse's six Bank of New York outlets were bought by Norstar recently, Holmes saw few changes. Even his loan officer remained the same—"they just gave him a different sweatshirt to wear to the softball games."

But 1986 proved to be a dismal year for Holmes's firm. His best salesman suffered serious health problems; his son, his right-hand man, up and quit; and Holmes had to fire his bookkeeper. The company lost nearly $50,000 that year, and Holmes had to put in $40,000 of his own funds to tide things over. And although in five years he never missed a payment to the bank (a few were late, he concedes), Norstar apparently wasn't satisfied.

"They came in not long ago and wanted additional collateral—a mortgage on my house and my summer place," Holmes says. "And worse, they wanted me to pay the thousand dollars to have the papers drawn up. That's what really galled me." But Holmes, for all his anger, is now complying with the bank's demands.

"My hunch is that Norstar laid out all this dough for acquisitions, then made the decision to really tighten up and get their risks as close to zero as possible," concludes Holmes. "I think that's the trouble when banks get out-of-sight bigger. Their disregard for individual situations becomes accentuated. They lose the feel for the man, the owner. You become just a number."

Holly Barlow Burns and Carroll Murray Palmer know the feeling. When their six-person advertising agency, Barlow Murray Advertising Inc., outgrew its offices, they shopped for a $200,000 loan to refurbish a large Victorian house, hard by the sprawling campus of Syracuse University. Key Bank was swift to offer the funds.

"Key was quick with a decision, but then they proceeded to give us a hard time as we progressed with the renovation—they just hassled us right down the line," says Burns. "We drew money as we went along, until we got down to the twenty thousand dollars to finish the top floor. And they refused to give it to us until we had a tenant for it. We told them we couldn't get a tenant until it was finished. And they said, 'Too bad.' It was absurd."

Instead of fighting, the two marched out to Skaneateles Savings Bank, one of the area's few remaining small independents, less than half an hour's drive from Syracuse. In less than a week, the bank agreed to lend them $210,000—enough to pay off the loan to Key Bank, complete the renovation, and help recoup some of the personal funds they had invested in the project. Things have been copacetic ever since.

Even today, Burns complains about the annual turnover in loan officers she experienced at Key Bank—a situation that had led to problems even before the renovation. "We had a ten-thousand-dollar line of credit with Key, and our last lending officer—he was really a disaster—just let it slip through the cracks," she remembers. "We called to see if we could increase our line of credit to fifty thousand dollars, so we could buy some equipment, and he said, 'Well, your line of credit is no longer in existence.' He said we hadn't updated our financial information. We suggested that he might have called to remind us. So we took a new line of credit from the bank in Skaneateles, and Key has never even bothered to call to see why we aren't doing business with them anymore."

Burns and Palmer are not the only Syracuse business owners I found to have opted for a nearby independent country bank. Out in Cazenovia, a picturesque lakeside village half an hour southeast of the city, Nicholas Christakos's Continental Cordage Corporation sells cords and braided-wire products for everything from venetian blinds to windshield-defogging systems. His customers include IBM, General Electric, 3M, General Dynamics, and Boeing. And his bank is the tiny State Bank of Chittenango.

Back in the early days, when Continental Cordage was based in a Quonset hut and funded by $85,000 of his own money, Christakos went to Key Bank for a modest loan. The local branch manager in Cazenovia said that all he could do was give him a $5,000 line of credit on his MasterCard. "That was my very first business loan, and I will never forgive them for the way they handled it," Christakos says.

Two years later, a stranger walked into the Quonset hut on Good Friday afternoon. His name was Bob MacDonald, and he was president of the State Bank of Chittenango. He wanted to do business with Continental Cordage. Christakos remembers being flattered by the call.

"We were very small then, and we needed twenty-five thousand dollars in a hurry to buy some machinery, and he loaned it to us virtually that same day," he recalls. "Then he said, 'Why don't I give you a line of credit?' So he gave us one for seventy-five thousand dollars. The funny thing was, right after that, we learned of another machinery deal, for ninety-five thousand dollars, down in Albany. We had to move on it or we'd lose it. I called him and he said, 'I'll have to run it by the board, but you guys go ahead with the deal; you'll end up with it.' So we went ahead with the negotiations, and we got the loan."

These days, now that he has annual sales of $7 million, all the big banks are knocking on Christakos's door wanting to loan him money. They point out that an independent such as State Bank of Chittenango, with only $35 million in assets, has limits on how much it can lend him, and possesses little sophistication when it comes to things like international letters of credit. The big banks also remind him that their loan rates can be as much as two percentage points below what State Bank of Chittenango is charging him. But Christakos isn't impressed. It would take a team of wild horses to drag him away.

Wild horses, that is, or an acquisition. For what worries Christakos most about his bank is that, sooner or later, some megabank will zero in on the profitable little Chittenango bank. President Bob MacDonald says so far there have been no formal offers. But some of the big boys have been around, he adds, "kind of kicking the tires."

Does big banking spell the end for small business? Probably not, if this unscientific sampling is any indication. In Syracuse today there are big banks that take risks, show loyalty to customers, and keep an eye on service, and there are big banks that don't.

Whether it is desirable or not, the trend toward ever bigger banks seems as inevitable as the changing seasons. The Reagan Administration is content to let the consolidation continue, while Congress has been reluctant to intervene. At the Federal Reserve Board, the idea of prohibiting mergers among the country's ten, twenty-five, or fifty largest banks has been tossed around, but as yet there is no consensus on how much consolidation is too much.

Stillwater National Bank's Bob McCormick probably overstates the case when he warns that big banking threatens the viability of America's small-business economy. But in raising the issue, he expresses a common fear—a fear about excessive concentration of economic power—that has kept national banking at bay since the days of Andrew Jackson. There may now be some good reasons for setting aside some of those fears and proceeding with bank deregulation. But as we learned with telephones and airlines, deregulating an industry shouldn't be the same as ignoring it. Banking is too important to be left simply to the bankers.

—Jay Finegan

HOW BANKERS VIEW SMALL BUSINESS
(Source: *Inc.* survey of 150 large and regional U.S. banks)

These responses come from bank officers responsible for small-business accounts. The questions were "open-ended"—that is, not multiple choice: Respondents gave these answers unaided by suggestions from the interviewer. An independent research firm conducted the interviews by telephone. In order to avoid possible pro–small-business bias, the interviewees weren't told that *Inc.* had commissioned the study. Totals exceed 100 percent because the bankers were invited to give more than one response to each question. Omitted are "don't know," "no answer," and items mentioned by fewer than 1 percent of the respondents.

Question: What were the major reasons for rejecting small-business loan applications over the past year?

	Percent of respondents who mentioned factor
Undercapitalization or too much debt	32
Lack of collateral	20
Inability to demonstrate source of repayment	15

	Percent of respondents who mentioned factor
Poor credit history	15
Inadequate financial information	12
Weak management	8
Applicant lacks experience in his field of business	7
Poor track record or poor profitability	7
Insufficient cash flow	5
Unprofessional financial statements	2

Question: How would you characterize the ideal small-business borrower?

Good capitalization, decreasing debt-to-equity ratio, or retains earnings in business	31
"Good management"	22
Good profit history	21
Good accounting or financial statements	13
Knowledge or experience in this business or product area	11
"Good character"	11
Good credit history	9
Steady growth or growth potential	9
Good cash flow	7
Strong or increasing sales revenue or market share	5
In business a reasonable length of time	5
Good collateral	5
Keeps bank informed	4
Good planning	3
Good product, market, or industry	3
Liquidity	3
Personal equity invested in company	1

Question: What are the major problems in dealing with small business?

Undercapitalization	19
Inadequate or unreliable records	15
Lack of capable management	15
Inexperience or lack of financial knowledge	11
Inadequate credit rating	5

	Percent of respondents who mentioned factor
High interest rates	4
Don't use bank services to full advantage	4
Poor planning or overextension	3
Insufficient profit margins	3
Poor cash flow	3
Unaudited financial statements	2

HIDDEN PERILS IN A VOLATILE ECONOMY

E ver since Dean Treptow abandoned a promising career as a chemicals salesman in order to try his hand at banking, he has been quietly building a national reputation as one of the shrewdest small-business bankers around. He has done it, moreover, from the unlikely vantage of Brown Deer, Wisconsin, a small suburb of Milwaukee. There, as president of Brown Deer Bank, he has combined skillful marketing with imaginative lending practices to transform a sleepy little consumer-based institution into a exemplar of innovative banking, catering principally to closely held smaller companies. The bank's assets, meanwhile, have grown from $14 million in 1973 to more than $80 million in 1986.

Along the way, Treptow has emerged as an authority on the capital needs of smaller companies. He is frequently called on to testify in Congress on small-business matters and to serve on special commissions. And two years ago, when *Inc.* set out to identify some of the country's leading small-business bankers, he was at the top of everyone's list.

So it is hardly surprising that his name came to mind recently as we were puzzling over the latest rash of confusing, and often contradictory, economic prognostications. We invited Treptow to share his views on the state and direction of the economy and on how smaller companies should be approaching their capital needs.

INC.: What kind of advice are you offering business borrowers these days, given the possibility of a major slump, at least in some sectors of the economy?

TREPTOW: In these times, businesses need to place a real emphasis on their earnings coverage and cash flow related to capital investments. Forget the tax rules. The question people should be asking is, Can you recover the investment in fixed assets within the likely product or equipment life? I believe that recovery periods on fixed assets need to be shortened in view of shorter cycles. You used to buy a machine that had a useful life of fifteen years and depreciate it over seven years. Now we're talking about useful lives on machinery or major components of more like three to seven years—in some cases, their useful lives are substantially less than their tax depreciation lives.

This means companies are going to have to maximize their flexibility on fixed costs and scrutinize their investments, particularly on items that aren't directly related to increasing productivity or turning out a product. Now isn't the time to be buying office buildings and other trappings. When you're dealing with shorter economic cycles, you need to be careful about adding fixed assets that don't increase your productivity but still have to be fed, whether business is growing or not.

INC.: Are there other things companies should be watching?

TREPTOW: I think companies need to be tightening their internal controls as much as possible, particularly in the areas of inventory management and trade credit. There's been a lot of discussion of inventory management programs, such as Just in Time. But I think trade credit has the potential to become a far more dangerous problem for businesses. There's greater pressure on banks these days, and so more and more credit risks are being shifted from banks to individual businesses, which typically offer customers credit of at least thirty days. Increasingly, you'll see banks holding the secured portion of the credit, protected by collateral, and vendors will be the unsecured lenders.

INC.: Why is it any more risky for a company to extend trade credit today than it was, say, a year ago?

TREPTOW: The speed of change is causing many companies to be more fragile and less creditworthy. Combine that with the fact that banks are scrutinizing their customers more closely than before, forcing businesses to find other sources of working capital.

INC.: Why is that?

TREPTOW: Because of the number of bank failures we've seen in the past couple years. The federal bank regulators are more concerned now about the safety and soundness of the banking system, so they're asking banks to improve their credit quality. In fact, there's a lot of pressure on banks to increase their capital-to-asset ratios from a minimum of 6 percent of assets to 9 percent. It isn't mandated yet, but in all likelihood banks will have to do that over the next few years. The upshot is that bankers will be more careful about the assets they will be putting on their books and will be inclined to make loans at a slower rate.

INC.: So it sounds as though many companies may be heading for trouble with their bankers.

TREPTOW: Banks are going to be asked to function with less leverage on the balance sheets than before. You can improve capital ratios in only one of two ways. You sell stock or slow your asset growth. I predict bankers will be more cautious in their growth rates so as to minimize the need for additional capital. There will be less appetite to grow with risky investments, and they'll be weeding out some of the customers they have.

INC.: We're hearing some talk about a slowdown in the economy. Do you think that a major recession is inevitable in the next couple of years?

TREPTOW: I don't believe we're going to see a general recession in the next two years. But I do think that we're going to see a series of selective recessions in different industry and product groups.

INC.: If you believed that a customer's business might be hit by the ripples of a recession a year or so out, what would you be advising him now? Would you tell him, for instance, to scrap his capital spending plans?

TREPTOW: If I saw some softness in the market, then I'd certainly tell him to pull in his horns. I'd tell him to concentrate on the areas that are most profitable in the short term. But I'd also advise him to stay in markets where he had long-term confidence, even if it meant losing money.

Of course, those two may be in conflict, in which case you'll have to choose between them. It's easier to make such choices when you have a good understanding of what you do best and where it fits into your overall strategic plan.

INC.: Let's say I was outgrowing my production facility and asked you to finance a plant expansion. What kinds of concerns might you have?

TREPTOW: If your business was fairly labor intensive, I'd want to see some analysis showing why the plant expansion, with the continued labor intensity, was the right way to go. I'd want to know why you weren't spending some money on automation equipment to increase productivity. Over the long term, that might serve you better. In the end, the question is how you're going to get the product out the door for the lowest cost. Obviously, you can't focus on cost and ignore concerns about quality. More and more manufacturers today are requiring strict quality control because the market demands that they do it.

INC.: If you were to advise chief executive officers on how to read the economy, what kinds of signals would you say they should be watching?

TREPTOW: People should keep an eye on some of the economic data that's published on a regular basis. I get a publication called *Economic Indicators,* which is put out monthly by the Council of Economic Advisers. And while I don't bother following money supply, I do keep track of things like the consumer price index, personal income growth, consumer spending, and capital investment.

These kinds of numbers can help you keep track of what's happening, but it's more important to have detailed discussions with each of your significant customers about their own projections for their business. I'd want to know everything they could tell me about their demand for the kinds of products or services that I provide. I'd also watch for signs of what the competition is doing. But your own customers are probably the best intelligence sources you have.

INC.: You've seen a few recessions in your time. What are the most important lessons that managers should keep in mind for the future?

TREPTOW: The biggest single mistake that many businesses made in 1982 was to construe the recession as an ordinary downturn, with the expectation that eventually we'd be back to business as usual. It didn't happen, because, in large part, the last recession reflected our entrance into an increasingly global economy. It's hard to insulate yourself anymore. The materials you buy, the products or services you compete against—they're all affected by international forces.

INC.: Contrary to many expectations, interest rates have been falling in recent months. Should companies try to take advantage of the decline now?

TREPTOW: This is probably a very good time to stretch out long-term financing commitments if you can lock in favorable interest rates. I don't think rates can go much lower than they are now. But a word of caution: I happen to believe we're in a noninflationary or deflationary economy that may last for some time. Interest rates may be down, but borrowing could possibly be more expensive now than it was previously, when rates were higher. With today's lower inflation, borrowers pay something closer to a real rate of interest—you can't count on paying the loan back tomorrow with cheaper dollars. Managers need to be aware of that.

And I also want to reiterate the point I made earlier about paying close attention to earnings and cash flow. If you're making a good, productive investment and you're planning to borrow for it, rates are better than they've been in many, many years. But because of volatility in the economy overall, as well as in specific markets, I think you have to be especially careful about the earnings coverage—the return on assets, for instance—and the cash flow associated with an investment. Volatility means that a lot of individual companies will have upward spikes in profitability, and they will also have down periods. Those companies will have to make enough money in the upturns to get through the downturns. If you go by the old guideline that you should be averaging a 10 to 15 percent return on your equity, you should probably aim for substantially more than that in the good times.

INC.: You're saying, in effect, that this is not a good time to pile on unnecessary debt. But isn't it an awfully good time to be renegotiating existing loans?

TREPTOW: Yes, but that may not be so easy to do. If you, as a borrower, think rates are at a low point, you'll be looking to get a fixed rate at today's levels. But if your banker shares that view, he won't want to do that. Even so, it's certainly worth asking. Your banker's view of the future might be different from yours. That's what makes a market.

INC.: How confident are *you* that interest rates have bottomed out?

TREPTOW: Speculating on interest rates is a very tricky business. If I were really confident that rates were at their lowest point, I'd stop lending money to businesses and invest all the money we've got in the bond market. Granted, there are a lot of indications that we're pretty near the bottom. To begin with, you have the federal deficit. And if rates go much lower, consumers will have very little incentive to put money in banks. But I'm not prepared to bet everything on my interest rate forecast.

INC.: Do you have any tips for companies negotiating loans?

TREPTOW: To be successful, you have to exhibit as much strength as you can. In my judgment, you can do that best by having a very well-conceived business plan, which allows your banker to feel extremely comfortable about the company's credit quality. Once you've satisfied the bankers on quality, negotiating the price on a loan is no different from negotiating the price on nuts and bolts and washers. But there's no point even *trying* to negotiate rates or terms unless you've satisfied them as to your credit quality.

INC.: Overall, you're not sounding very bullish. In fact, you sound almost gloomy. Do your banking colleagues feel the same way?

TREPTOW: The unique thing about this period is that you can find bankers and economists to support almost any economic scenario you can come up with. I've never seen such a wide diversity of economic forecasts as we're seeing right now. It's almost chaotic. And maybe that should make everyone a lot more concerned.

SMART MONEY

If appearances were all that mattered, Oklahoma's twenty-third largest commercial bank would be much like any other small-town bank. On the street level, where the teller lines are, a dozen or so employees sit at dark wooden desks, stapling papers together and talking with customers looking for car loans or new checking accounts. Upstairs, in the commercial-lending department, the owner of a dress shop or hardware store might be dropping by to deliver a check or chat with a lending officer. Even the bank's boardroom, where a stately portrait hangs on walnut paneling, looks about as unusual as a Holiday Inn.

All this gives a visitor the impression of an elaborately constructed stage set, complete with well-dressed men and women sent down from central casting and told to act like bankers. It is hard to imagine, in other words, how Stillwater National Bank & Trust Company can be what it is and still look quite so ordinary.

Certainly the numbers by which banks are measured give quite a different impression. On 1984 assets of $165.9 million, for example, Stillwater National earned $2 million—at least 20 percent more than most U.S. banks its size. Those assets have quadrupled over the past decade, yet the bank's loan losses have remained low. A banker examining its balance sheet would spot something else right away: Where most banks depend largely on interest income, Stillwater National earned a hefty 80 percent of its profits from fees, inplying a level of operation a lot of banks haven't discovered yet. Once a sleepy, second-fiddle bank in a dusty Oklahoma town, it has made itself into the preeminent bank of a growing regional center, and it has done so through maneuvers as astute as those of any big-city financier.

Go-go banks, to be sure, are nothing new in Oklahoma. From Oklahoma National Bank to Penn Square Bank, high-riding moneylenders have risen and fallen with the fortunes of the oil business. But that only makes Stillwater National all the more remarkable. The bank has one picture of an oil rig on an upstairs wall. That is about as close as it has come to the industry.

So what's the secret? "We're not trying to be everything to everybody," says Bob McCormick, a trim fifty-year-old who has engineered the bank's remarkable growth. "But over the years, I guess we've done some pretty creative things for a little county-seat bank in Oklahoma."

A decade ago, admits McCormick's counterpart at the number-two bank in the town of Stillwater, "*we* were the biggest bank in town. But we haven't grown the way they have." Part of the reason, he says, is that they have "chosen a different strategy." But there's another factor, too.

"Bob McCormick," the banker adds, "is a very sharp guy."

When Bob McCormick was growing up in Oklahoma City during the 1940s and 1950s, nobody took him for the banking type. His maternal grandfather had dabbled in real estate and in oil and gas, with mixed success. His father, a hard-charging wholesale paper salesman, was so bothered by his boy's careless attitude that he packed him off, at age sixteen, to military school. Young Bob, explains a friend from that era, wasn't exactly lazy, "he just didn't do any more than he had to do.

"I saw him as a perfect salesman," the friend adds, "running a Chevy dealership. Definitely not a bank."

It took McCormick five years to get through the University of Oklahoma, where, he claims, he majored in finance and parties. It took him only four years to get through the Marines. By then he had a wife and three sons, and after a brief stint selling insurance, he jumped at an entry-level position with Fidelity Bank, in Oklahoma City. His eight years there would be his only on-the-job training for heading up Stillwater National, but he remembers the lessons some two decades later.

As a trainee, he was shuffled through a series of jobs. He worked as a teller, then with the credit department, where he was supposed to make sure that loan applications were supported with all the right documents. Ambitious, he dug out back issues of bank lending journals and studied the proper procedures for making loans. But the bank was growing rapidly, and a lot of his peers weren't going by the book; instead they were "shooting from the hip" and generating a lot of problem loans. Among the hip-shooters: Bill P. "Beep" Jennings, who later became the chairman of Penn Square.

So McCormick wasn't surprised when Fidelity reported big losses in 1963 and 1964. But despite the losses, he was impressed with some of the bank's positive aspects. Fidelity's president, Grady Harris, seemed to have a knack for making customers feel at ease. "After a session with Grady," McCormick says now, "they'd *want* to do business with his bank."

The contact with Stillwater National came in 1970. A commercial bank with $22 million in assets, it was controlled and managed by the Berry family, whose patriarch, James Berry, was a longtime lieutenant governor of Oklahoma. Now James's forty-nine-year-old son Frank, who had been heading the bank, was dead of a massive stroke, and a cousin of the family put the Berrys in touch with McCormick, by then a clean-cut and confident man of thirty-five. The Berrys figured he was just the type of fellow they wanted to manage their small-town bank. They weren't, after all, asking much. He wasn't expected to overtake the number-one local bank, which commanded some 57 percent of the market; he was only supposed to keep things sound. As George Berry, Frank's older brother, comments, "We didn't want him doing anything too racy."

When McCormick arrived that September, he found a pleasant enough place. Seventy miles from both Tulsa and Oklahoma City, Stillwater was a university town of some 31,000 surrounded by farms and cattle ranches. The bank itself wasn't so pleasant. Its officers "gave the strong impression," as one local businessman put it, "that they didn't want your business." Talking with customers—and a number of ex-customers—McCormick caught several earfuls about Stillwater National's aloofness toward the community.

"In those days," confirms Paul C. Wise, an eighty-year-old executive vice-president who is still active at the bank, "we rarely took the time to visit customers in their place of business." If they did, Wise adds, they didn't usually take the liberty of suggesting products or services. "It was a totally different atmosphere. If we were going to talk about the business, we waited for customers to come to us." With a high percentage of its assets invested in municipal bonds and other government securities, Stillwater National had the look of a bank that didn't *like* lending money.

McCormick, recalling the personal style of ex-boss Grady Harris, quickly tried to repair the bank's image. He put his own desk on the main floor and made a point of greeting customers. He spent time out of the bank, talking with people. But his main effort was to begin making bankers out of time-serving employees and wet-behind-the-ears recruits—a process that has since been dubbed the McCormick School of Banking.

When McCormick arrived, few of the bank's fifty-five employees had been trained or encouraged to make even small decisions on their own. "There was one guy," McCormick remembers, "who'd been here for twelve years and had to get approval to buy a few dozen *lightbulbs*. And there was only one person in the whole bank who could approve a loan for more than five thousand dollars." That, he decided, would change. He asked Jim Lovell, a man in his early forties who had been making consumer installment loans, to begin learning about construction and real estate lending. He assigned Rick Green, who had worked part-time printing custom checks while completing his undergraduate degree at nearby Oklahoma State University (OSU), to coordinate a new marketing effort.

McCormick also hired several enthusiastic young college graduates with no banking experience at all. Stan White and Tom Bennett, two graduates of OSU in their early twenties, arrived within a few months of each other in 1974. McCormick had them doing everything from keeping the Coke machine filled and locking up the premises at night to going after borrowers who were delinquent on their loans.

Being a student at McCormick's school wasn't easy or glamorous. White once drove back and forth on poorly marked back roads forty miles from Stillwater in search of a borrower who had moved away and was several months late on a car loan. When he finally located the deadbeat's mobile home, he walked up to the front door and told the man who he was. The customer reached for his shotgun and told the young banker he'd better leave. "I agreed with him," says White, who is now an executive vice-president. Chased to his car by two Doberman pinschers and the thought of a shotgun aimed at his back, White has to this day, he says, "no recollection of how I made it."

Bennett, a wide-eyed sociology major when he started at the bank, got another kind of lesson—less dramatic but equally important to a banker. Despite Bennett's youth, McCormick asked him to supervise the liquidation of a local jewelry store, which had defaulted on its loans. The bank, Bennett remembers, was hoping to recover as much of the money as possible during the Christmas selling season, and by Christmas Eve was "taking every reasonable offer." But even though the inventory was gold and silver, the bank still got less than 60¢ on the dollar.

"The thing I learned," says Bennett, thirty-five, an executive vice-president who is currently a White House Fellow assigned to the Comptroller of the Currency's office in Washington, D.C., "is that no inventory is worth as much as you think it is, especially on the downside of a business."

To McCormick, such slices of reality were the stuff of which great bankers were made. If you wanted to learn how to lend money, he told his trainees, you had to see the bad sides—like how miserable it was to collect loans based on collateral. "People promise you all sorts of things," he would say, "but they don't always make good on what they say."

Lurking behind the practical training was another kind of lesson. Every time McCormick sat down and talked with a job candidate, he spelled out his hopes for the bank and for the community. Stillwater, he told them, was going to be more than just a sleepy university town. It could be a regional shopping and medical center, an ideal place to raise a family. And an ambitious young banker could be a catalyst. When a banker made a loan, the impact was there for all to see: A building went up and people went to work. At other banks, job interviews might revolve around job descriptions and salary; here McCormick was selling a vision. "When you talked to Mr. McCormick," remembers White, "you talked about your own goals, and you talked about building a community."

Beyond putting forward the vision, beyond training his personnel, McCormick made sweeping changes in Stillwater National's operations and marketing. That was no small feat, particularly since banks in those days faced serious restrictions on what they could and could not do. They were prohibited by law from paying interest on checking accounts, and they couldn't pay more than 5¼ percent on savings accounts, which was a quarter of a percentage point less than competing savings and loans. Yet a bank's lending business, which was its bread and butter, depended on its ability to attract deposits.

In retrospect, McCormick's motto seems to have been "Find a new product and market the daylights out of it." For openers, he kept an eye on the nation's most aggressive S&Ls and mimicked their best moves. His Golden Passbook accounts, for example, paid interest on 90- and 180-day savings at the higher rates then allowed for certificates of deposit. And though rates were regulated, service wasn't. So when Golden Passbook customers visited McCormick's bank, they didn't stand in a teller line; they were invited to sit down and discuss their needs with somebody who had been trained to talk about the product.

To find new customers, Stillwater National blitzed OSU. Students opening accounts received coupons for free pizzas and movie tickets. "There were days when we were opening seventy-five or eighty accounts a day," says Rick Green. "None of our competitors had even attempted to capitalize on that market." In another move aimed at new customers, the bank became the first in town—the second in the state—to introduce a twenty-four-hour teller machine.

But McCormick's boldest move into consumer banking came on the lending side, when he began going toe-to-toe with the savings and loans on residential mortgages. At the time—the mid-1970s—it was a dramatic move. Most commercial banks in those days took for granted the traditional division of labor between thrift institutions and banks, and few were writing residential mortgages on any scale. But the provider of home mortgages, McCormick figured, got the opportunity to offer other profitable services. "In a town like this," he says, "you had to do what an S and L did. We wanted to be in a position to finance a person's home, his car, his business, and just about everything else."

Many commercial bankers, of course, either wouldn't have known how to enter the mortgage business or would have balked at the riskiness of using short-term deposits to originate twenty- or thirty-year loans. But McCormick had a card or two up his sleeve. He had lent money to some mortgage bankers back in his Oklahoma City days, and he knew that you didn't need to hold on to the actual mortgages to be in the business. All you had to do was understand the ins and outs of a then-mysterious entity called the secondary market. Executives of the thrift industry understood it. Commercial bankers, for the most part, didn't.

Essentially, the secondary market in home mortgages involves packaging mortgage loans and reselling them to investors all over the country. The trick is to follow the technical guidelines of the Federal National Mortgage Association (Fannie Mae) and the Federal Home Loan Mortgage Corporation (Freddie Mac), then pull together the complex appraisals and lengthy documents required. The time-consuming nature of the process only made McCormick more eager for the business. "He wanted us to learn the hard things," says Green, "because he felt they'd give us an advantage—fewer people would be doing them."

Besides giving the bank an important new product, the mortgages provided servicing fees that boosted the bottom line. During its first year in the business, Stillwater National underwrote $1 million worth of mortgages. By 1979, as people got the hang of it, the volume soared to about $10 million. The mortgage trade also brought in new customers. Rick Green stayed in steady touch with local employers and would call new people before they came to town to see if they needed a mortgage or anything else. Even today, he says, "we'll go out and meet the moving vans when they arrive at a customer's new home."

New approaches to consumer lending, of course, can take a bank only so far. The rest of a commercial bank's operation is its business lending, and in that department, Stillwater National may be one of the few banks even an entrepreneur could love. Lending officers working under McCormick are expected to turn people away if they have to. But before they do, they better have explored every possibility of a financial package acceptable both to the borrower and to the bank.

Not long ago, for example, the owner of a local hardware store came in looking for $70,000. He needed it to buy more inventory and to complete the buyout of his former boss. McCormick, after some discussion, agreed to make the money available, but in a way that was a lot more intricate than the method proposed by a banker down the street. Instead of one short-term loan, McCormick suggested three smaller loans, each with a different repayment schedule (ranging from ninety days to fifteen years). Why? A single loan with a one- or three-year maturity, explains McCormick, would almost certainly have brought about a cash-flow crisis.

Bankers trained under this approach are expected to be as imaginative and inquisitive as McCormick himself. But it isn't unusual for McCormick to spot problems the others miss. In a loan review meeting last summer, a forty-four-year-old lending officer named Scott Gregory proposed a working capital loan of $350,000 to the owner of an agricultural-equipment company some ninety miles outside of Stillwater. The business, recently spun off by a large Midwestern company, had experienced some difficulty, Gregory said, but it had also booked some large orders. To him, it looked to be on the rebound. He had brought along a dozen or so pages of information to support his presentation.

McCormick, however, wasn't satisfied. He wanted to see separate schedules to back up the company's balance sheets. He wanted to know if Gregory had visited the physical premises. (He hadn't.) Had he *talked* to any of the middle managers, or *seen* the way the books were kept, or *inspected* the alleged $188,000 worth of inventory? "Accountants," McCormick growled as he got up and walked away from his chair, "usually aren't tough enough about valuing inventory." That means that bankers have to do their own valuations.

Afterward, Gregory visited the borrower's plant. "They had a good product and operation," he says, but when he got there he found that some of the things McCormick had identified "didn't add up." So the loan application was turned down.

Over time, so rigorous an approach pays dividends measured in customer loyalty. Buster Simon, thirty-eight, who started a women's clothing store in 1976, has relied on the bank to finance his seasonal inventory ever since his first year of operation. But he has received, he says, more than just a series of loans. "From the beginning, McCormick asked questions that made me think. . . . He'd want to know how I decided how much inventory I wanted, how I knew that I was in line with my customers, how I chose when to take markdowns, and whether I was taking inflation enough into account when I thought about buying inventory for the next season." When the business opened a second store in 1981 and immediately ran into a working capital crunch, Simon says that both McCormick and a new lending officer who had taken over the account were able to understand the problem. "They rode along with us," he says, "and agreed to shift thirty-six thousand dollars of short-term loans into ten-year notes."

McCormick has also encouraged his bankers to develop market expertise and technical abilities ignored by competitors. One niche—health care professionals—has become a lucrative lending specialty. In the past several years, Green estimates, the bank has financed the professional and personal needs of more than two dozen doctors as Stillwater became a regional medical center for north central Oklahoma. Today, he adds, when the bank hears that a young doctor is even thinking of moving to Stillwater, "we'll call him up or go see him."

The Small Business Administration's guaranteed lending programs have provided another lucrative and often-ignored niche. "A lot of bankers turn their noses up at the idea of SBA loans," McCormick notes with amusement. "They don't like the red tape, and they say, 'We don't do marginal loans.'" But he and other officers saw SBA-guaranteed loans as a way of providing capital to customers they couldn't do business with on any other basis.

Here, too, McCormick figured out how to package and resell the guaranteed loans, just as he had with home mortgages. By tradition, commercial banks only sold loans when the total credit went beyond their lending limit. But a broader secondary market for SBA loans, allowing 90 percent of a loan to be sold, was just coming together in 1978, and McCormick wanted in. It made sense for borrowers because it allowed longer terms and, in some instances, fixed rates. It made sense for the bank because the loans would generate origination and service fees without tying up scarce funds or capital. And it made sense for the community. As McCormick saw it, selling a $500,000 loan in New York City was much the same as flying to New York and beating the bushes for deposits. But unlike the latter, the business wouldn't be based just on price; it would trade on Stillwater National's special skills. By 1984, the bank had made 120 SBA-guaranteed loans, totaling $19.3 million, and was selling them to investors all over the country.

One evening last August, Bob McCormick and his wife, Peggy, were at the dining-room table in their one-story brick house, talking about how Stillwater National Bank managed to escape the energy-loan problems that plagued so many other Oklahoma banks. To Peggy, it was simple common sense based on hard experience. "My father," she said, "was an independent oilman who lost everything he had. There was a boom one year and a bust the next. If you grew up in Oklahoma, you knew that's how the oil business was." Bob McCormick, relaxing with his tie off after a long day, concurred. "The guys from Penn Square showed us a bunch of oil deals they wanted us to participate in," he said. "But they didn't look right." The bank's board of directors didn't argue with him.

There are other ways, too, in which Stillwater National reflects Bob McCormick's sense of what's right. The bank has rigid—some would say puritan—policies on conflicts of interest. No officers are allowed to invest in local companies. Officers at the vice-president level and above aren't allowed to have loans from the bank. If an officer's spouse is in business, he or she is asked to bank elsewhere. An employee can't be related to another employee at the bank. If two employees marry, one of them must leave.

McCormick's bankers, moreover, *always* look the part. Even during the energy crisis, when another bank in town turned off its air-conditioning and allowed its employees to take off their coats and ties, McCormick said no, his bankers would dress like bankers and be warm. Nor does he like his people to live in fancy houses or drive fancy cars. "It's as if we're all here in one glass house," explains one officer. "Our customers are looking in."

For his part, McCormick is an avid golfer whose dining-room window faces the eighth hole of a golf course—but he seldom plays with customers. "If somebody wants to do business with the bank, we'll sit down and have a serious conversation, but they don't have to be my friend," McCormick explains. "We don't always have the best rates in town, but we'll be professional. We'll bust our rears to make the smartest deal they can find."

Today, in the wake of a lingering oil glut and a severe farm crunch, as many as one-third of the banks in the state are running in the red. "We've seen twenty banks go under since Penn Square," McCormick says, and Stillwater National itself has seen its loan defaults rise and its profit levels fall as the regional economy weakened.

Still, the bank has made some impressive efforts to sell money and expertise to a wider universe of customers than ever before. During 1984, for example, Stillwater National opened its first two loan-production offices, one near Oklahoma City and the other in Tulsa. Since the offices opened, the bank has made lots of conventional loans and thirty-seven SBA loans to small-business people, attorneys, and health care professionals. The bank traced some of its new customers—dentists and doctors, for example—from old student-account records, while other leads came from a director who is an ophthalmologist in Oklahoma City. Rather than staying home, says Stan White, "we'll go almost anywhere in the state to meet with professionals who need to talk about money."

The bank has also been using its SBA lending experience in creative ways. Designated as one of the approximately one hundred "preferred" lenders in the United States by the SBA in March 1985, it has hosted seminars for bankers from all over the state on how to structure deals, and has offered to travel anywhere in Oklahoma to help as the packager. "They are among the very best lenders in the whole country," says Danny Gibb, the SBA's director of the Office of Financial Institutions.

McCormick is evidently not one to rest on his laurels. The bank has recently upgraded its computer system, enabling its personnel to call up customer records for marketing purposes. It has moved aggressively into the student-loan area and has recently reorganized its credit-card operation. McCormick himself has become much more involved in employee training than he's been in several years. The bank, which today employs about 115 people, has a stated policy of promoting from within, and he has encouraged his senior managers to switch around their job responsibilities and learn parts of one another's areas. He goes to several meetings a week and often stays late to coach managers on ways to improve loan collections and upgrade their supervisory skills.

To McCormick, who spent several months a few years ago traveling around the country as president of the Independent Bankers Association of America, it's all part of an effort to create an effective financial-services company that can compete with the likes of Merrill Lynch, Citibank, and Sears. "You can hear them rapping at the door," he says. "They're doing deals and they're handling money. It means we'll have to be sharper and shrewder than we've ever been." Someday, he adds, Stillwater National may grow by acquiring other banks. But he doesn't feel that the substance of what he and his people do will change very much from what they've been doing for years.

"When people do business with us," McCormick says, "they get more than money. We take an interest in the business. A lot of our customers don't have anyone else to bounce ideas off of, so we try to respond. We won't tell a guy how to sell dresses, but we'll help him understand his business a little bit better.

"It ain't easy," he concludes in his best down-home manner, "to teach people to become better financial managers. But if you don't have quality customers, you won't have a quality bank."

Balancing the Risks

Running a commercial bank is like juggling several balls at once, with each ball a different kind of risk. Mishandle any one of them—too many bad loans, not enough stable deposits—and you can throw the whole system out of whack.

The system at Stillwater National Bank & Trust Company, so far, is very much *in* whack. Since Stillwater National, though privately held, is regulated by the Comptroller of the Currency, the numbers to support this judgment are publicly available. So are comparable data for other banks.

Using these data, Cates Consulting Analysts Inc., of New York City, compared Stillwater National's 1984 results with results for other institutions in the $100-million to $300-million asset class. Cates measured the bank's performance against industry medians for 1,688 banks across the United States and 318 in the Southwest.

Profitability

Return on equity		Return on assets	
Stillwater National	16.8%	Stillwater National	1.34%
U.S. average	13.6	U.S. average	1.02
Regional average	15.4	Regional average	1.15

The bank outperformed both its national and its regional peer groups in profitability by skillful management of two key variables. First, it invested more of its assets in loans than the average bank: 71 percent versus 62 percent nationally. Second, it has been able to get a higher loan yield while paying depositors competitive rates. That has produced a healthy spread between what it pays for funds and what it charges—nearly three-quarters of a point higher than the U.S. median.

Quality of Assets

Nonperforming loans as percent of loans		Loan mix (percent retail)	
Stillwater National	1.05%	Stillwater National	37.6%
U.S. average	1.60	U.S. average	41.4
Regional average	2.15	Regional average	29.2

If the bank had major problems lurking in its loan portfolio, they would show up on the books as nonperforming loans. No such difficulties are evident. In fact, says David Cates of Cates Consulting Analysts, Stillwater National has "taken its medicine in full" in the past few years by charging off loans as soon as they looked soft. The bank's mix of loans also points to a reasonable degree of stability, particularly by comparison with its regional counterparts. Statistically, says Cates, loans to individuals and households, known as retail loans, are more secure than those to businesses.

Stability of Deposits

Percent of demand and "core" deposits	
Stillwater National	84.7%
U.S. average	85.7
Regional average	73.1

The most substantial funding risk for a bank is large deposits. They can be pulled out at a moment's notice, forcing managers to scramble for other funds. But in the past four years, Stillwater National has strategically reduced its dependence on big, uninsured deposits from 24 percent to 15.3 percent. It thus has funded most of its growth with fully insured savings and time deposits, known as core deposits. The chances that these local deposits will be yanked out of the bank are negligible, analysts say.

Operating Efficiency

Overhead as percent of operating income

Stillwater National	48.5%
U.S. average	58.0
Regional average	54.5

Even though the bank's overhead expenses are roughly the same as those of the median bank in its peer group, the investment produces a bigger bang than it does for most banks. Stillwater National, explains Cates, puts its resources to work making higher-yielding loans. This accounts for the bank's relative efficiency.

Capital Position

Primary capital as percent of total assets

Stillwater National	8.19%
U.S. average	7.63
Regional average	7.59

Even if Stillwater National did have a sudden increase in problem loans, its strong capital position—equity and reserves set aside for loan losses—would provide an important cushion. The bank has boosted dividend payouts to shareholders significantly over the years, but it still manages to accumulate new capital (through retained earnings) at a rate that's around 50 percent greater than the national median.

McCormick's Rules of Lending

Want a loan from Bob McCormick and Stillwater National Bank & Trust Company? It's a bank that's eager to lend money, but you might be surprised at how deeply its loan officers will assess you, your top people, and your business before committing the bank's funds.

You and your executives. The "threshold requirement," says McCormick, is that your group have the ability and the discipline to do what you propose. Education and prior work experience will be taken into account—"but," he explains, "you really need to look at the whole picture, which includes a person's character."

McCormick investigates character in obvious ways like credit checks and talks with past employers, and in not-so-obvious ways like freewheeling discussions with loan applicants about their goals. He pays special attention to how applicants have organized themselves financially during their careers and whether they put their own money into the business. A former sales manager for a big Pontiac dealership in Tulsa, for example, greatly impressed McCormick when he came in looking for money to finance his own dealership. He was not only willing to take a big pay cut, he was sinking $80,000 of his own money into the new business.

Other signs make McCormick wary. If an applicant shows a tendency toward high personal debts, extravagant living, or speculative investing, he says, "you have to wonder whether the guy has good judgment and whether he can think about long-term goals." Indications of drinking or drug problems raise obvious red flags.

The business itself. Here there are fewer ironclad rules, says McCormick. Someone from the bank will, however, tour your facilities, review your balance sheets and other financial statements, compare your situation with that of your competitors, and in general try to sniff out your strengths and weaknesses. The most pressing concern is always how the loan will be repaid. Sale of inventory? Collection of receivables? Future earnings? "We look at the source of repayment," says McCormick, "and we ask, 'How assured is it?'" Nor will he accept unrealistically bullish projections. "We'll ask how they expect to double their sales or how they're going to collect from their customers so much faster than others do. If we're really uneasy, we might ask a guy to put in more equity."

Even if the source of repayment looks as solid as the Rock of Gibraltar, McCormick will ask for collateral or a personal guarantee without hesitation. Some 80 percent of the bank's loans are secured in one way or another. Don't businesspeople balk? Sure, McCormick concedes. "I say to them, 'We love you and we think the world of you, but we want our collateral.'"

Besides assessing a business's financial health, McCormick may offer blunt criticisms about the choices a business owner has made. "If a guy's paying himself eighty-five thousand dollars a year and leaving very little money in the business, I'll tell him he'd be better off paying himself half of that," McCormick says. "The guy who's going someplace is the guy who's grossing the same amount and paying himself a more reasonable salary. He's putting the rest to work inside the business."

AHEAD OF THE PACK:
How Some Banks Are Prospering Under Deregulation

With the U.S. financial-services industry in the throes of deregulation, bankers everywhere have been brushing away the cobwebs and looking for new ways to attract and keep customers. They have to; there isn't a chance that all of the nation's 14,000-odd commercial banks can survive, let alone flourish, in an era of nationwide banking and blistering competition from "nonbanks" like Sears Financial Network. But some will do very well—and the following, bankers and industry analysts say, are likely to be among them.

• *Morgan Guaranty Trust Company of New York*

J. P. Morgan, the legendary financier, may have said it best when he was asked in the 1930s to describe his distinctive approach to banking: "We do a first-class business in a first-class way." The bank's role in history on both sides of the Atlantic is testimony to its clout. Among its accomplishments: It played an important role in financing the Union side in the Civil War; it bailed out the U.S. Treasury during an 1894 run on gold; and it acted as purchasing agent for the French and British governments during World War I.

Today, the $68-billion (assets) Morgan bank, headquartered at the corner of Broad and Wall streets in New York City, is as powerful and as well respected as ever. Instead of pushing credit cards and other retail loans, as other big banks have done, it has focused entirely on the needs of governments, the *Fortune* 100, and wealthy individuals (minimum balance for checking accounts: $5,000). It also continues to take a leading role in the banking industry. In 1984, for example, it played a pivotal part in the rescue of Continental Illinois Bank.

The industry may be changing, but Morgan's focus isn't—for very clear reasons. Its customers are fiercely loyal, and its per-employee earnings are around three times those of other large banks.

• *The Bank of New Haven*

An aggressive young bank that tells most people to stay away sounds like a contradiction in terms. But to Joseph Ciaburri, the fifty-five-year-old president and chief executive officer of the Bank of New Haven ($115 million in assets), it makes perfect sense. Since he founded the bank six years ago, he has been aiming all of his marketing artillery at one niche: small business. And the strategy has been a big success. Today, says Ciaburri, "We have seventeen hundred customers, ranging from ma-and-pa's to companies with sales of forty million dollars." In 1984, the Connecticut bank had earned an average of 1.49 percent on its assets over a five-year period, placing it above most of its peers.

Decorated in an old-style manner, the bank is modeled after Morgan in more ways than one. In particular, it provides a level of attention and service unequaled by its local competitors, staying open one hour later and handling some transactions in private offices rather than at teller windows. "There is a bit of snobbery," Ciaburri concedes. "The customer is more than king. And as long as I'm president, we won't have any of those automated teller machines."

• *Wachovia Bank & Trust*

Some years ago, the late Robert Hanes, then president of Winston-Salem, North Carolina–based Wachovia, preached a radically new gospel of banking to a crop of young hirees. Bankers, he declared, could no longer afford to define themselves as clerks. In the new age, they needed to get closer to their customers, solve their problems, and sell them services.

Hanes's vision has paid off. Wachovia (pronounced wa-KO-vee-ah) has $8.8 billion in assets and 209 branches in North Carolina. It is an outstanding money-maker and, like Morgan, is regularly named by U.S. bankers as one of the best-managed institutions in the country. Much of what Wachovia does is standard fare among regional banks, but its unusually well-trained staff seems to handle the details better and more consistently than its competitors. "A lot of what we do isn't the sort of thing you can write ads about," admits a senior officer, "but our customers *expect* us to do the little things right. So we do."

• *State Bank of Cross Plains*

Ten miles west of Madison, Wisconsin, is an unlikely place for the headquarters of a shrewd financial services firm. But State Bank of Cross Plains, with $44 million in assets, is offering its customers a lot more than you'd expect from a small surburban bank. In one trip to the bank, a patron can invest money in an individual retirement account; buy property, casualty, and life insurance; get advice on personal financial planning; or do business with a travel agency located in the bank building and affiliated with the bank. This year, for the first time, customers will also be able to hire the bank to prepare their tax forms.

Helped along by such services, the bank has been extremely profitable; it earned 1.46 percent on assets in 1984. Its employees and directors, moreover, own half the stock. "Our goal," says executive vice-president Lee Swanson, "is to maintain and increase our customer base. And we're doing it."

—BRUCE G. POSNER

PART

II

VENTURE CAPITAL

Part II explains the world of venture capital—what venture capitalists want and why this source of capital is the right choice for
some but not for everyone.

A BRIEF HISTORY OF VENTURE CAPITAL

Venture capital is as old as capitalism itself. But organized venture capital in the United States has a relatively brief history. After World War II, several wealthy families, including John Hay Whitney's and the Rockefeller brothers, decided to set up partnerships to finance new companies in electronics, communications, and other fields. Their timing was perfect. The combination of rapid technological advances in many fields during the war and pent-up consumer demand for new products created a booming economy in the 1950s, largely fueled by the new technologies they backed.

Following the Whitney and Rockefeller leads, other wealthy families and individuals in New York, Boston, Chicago, and San Francisco also established venture partnerships during the fifties. In 1958, their efforts were given a substantial boost when Congress passed the Small Business Investment Act. This authorized the Small Business Administration to license and lend money at preferred rates to Small Business Investment Companies.

Within six years more than 700 licenses had been granted and half a billion dollars in private capital committed to SBICs. Many of venture capital's first generation of professional investment managers learned the ropes while working in these early SBICs.

Venture capital's first boom era peaked in 1969. During the succeeding eight years, new investment activity slowed and the professional community consolidated. During the same period, large institutional investors, particularly pension funds, became the dominant force in the stock and bond markets. By the late seventies, when lower capital-gains tax rates and a new wave of technologies combined to provide a fertile climate for renewed venture capital vigor, the financial institutions (pension funds, banks, and insurance companies) had begun to invest in venture partnerships as well. Major corporations also began to test the venture capital water, both by investing in established firms and by setting up their own venture capital subsidiaries.

According to *Venture Capital Journal,* at the beginning of 1987, there were approximately 590 venture capital pools: 328 private firms, 64 managed by banks, 73 managed by corporations, and 122 managed by other venture capital and SBIC groups. The funds were staffed by about 2,200 professsionals. Since most parent groups manage more than one venture capital pool, the number of investing entities is smaller. Organized venture capital is still concentrated in the cities and regions where it grew, although some branching out has begun.

In the forty or so years since its birth, venture capital has expanded from an informal art practiced by a tiny number of individuals into a formally managed business with carefully defined and controlled risks. It has also become a more active business. Most venture capitalists provide management advice and technical help as well as money to the companies in which they invest. It is still a very small community but, as the success of many of the high-technology companies and other small businesses it has spawned suggests, it is a vitally important part of the U. S. capital structure.

VENTURE CAPITAL:
Who Gets It and Why?

Inc. interviewed a leading venture capitalist to give its readers insight into the nature of the beast—how to approach him and how he's likely to respond to you and your proposal.

Frederick R. "Fred" Adler is a senior partner of Reavis & McGrath, a New York law firm. As a venture capitalist, he's widely known in industries such as telecommunications, medical electronics, data processing, and energy conservation.

Adler began his career as a trial lawyer, but he became bored with the routine practice of the law. As his case load in the venture area grew, he began to concentrate on the area. He was the major capitalist in the start-ups of Massachusetts minicomputer maker Data General and of Intersil, a major semiconductor firm based in California. In 1978, he financed Advanced Technology Labs in Bellevue, Washington, the ultrasonic imaging company that was later sold to Squibb for $60 million. And he was responsible for the financing of Loehmann's, the New York–based women's apparel retailer.

Adler bears no resemblance to the caricature of the venture capitalist. His manner is open and relaxed. His office, while it has a spectacular view from forty-two stories above Park Avenue, is a workplace. It has no desk—a large cabinet provides storage, and Adler works at a table. During the interview, associates and staff took advantage of his open-door policy to interrupt him with messages and phone calls, which he handled quickly, but with a friendly manner.

INC: Why do you think venture capitalists have a bad image among people in small companies?

ADLER: Probably because most people who apply for venture capital and get turned down have failed to put themselves in the place of the venture capitalist. Let's look at what a VC is: He invests his own and/or other people's money in a business, either at start-up or later, if that business shows recognized growth potential and able management. A VC usually assists in the management of the company after investment, helping with policy decisions and financial problems, recruiting new management staff, defining new areas of activity, and providing help and access to new or existing markets. He's a participatory investor, unlike the investment banker or ordinary stock buyer, so he wants to feel in tune with the company.

So we consider all proposals but accept very few. We try to keep our losers down to no more than one out of ten, maybe two at the most. Some firms work on the theory that one big one will bail them out of six mistakes. Our firm doesn't aim just for the big winners, though we've had our share of them. We aim for the best opportunities and people rather than for quantity of deals.

INC: What do you look for in a winning proposal?

ADLER: The ideal proposal has a business plan and a market analysis, with a full explanation of how and why the plan will work. It discusses the problems—every company has problems—and tells how they will be overcome. The plan should also contain an evaluation of the competition and show how and why the product and the plan have the competitive edge. A proposal should be an analytical business plan, not a sales pitch.

Most proposals we receive are poorly written and poorly constructed. You'd be surprised how many are just a one-page cover letter attached to a copy of a patent. But we also receive proposals that look like the *Encyclopaedia Britannica,* with endless but often meaningless statistical tables and graphs. They give the impression the applicant thinks we judge proposals by weight.

In short, we want proposals that give precise information and are concise and candid about the company's problems as well as its successes. Then we feel we can have confidence in the management of the company. And that confidence in management is the key. There *is* such a thing as the sweet smell of success. When that aura's there, you know the guy is going to make it.

INC: You say that you try to keep your losers down to one out of ten. Have you had any big losers?

ADLER: Sure. I really took a bath on a West Coast computer firm called Tenet. It started up in 1969 and ran right into a major recession. But more typical of the kind of mistakes you can make is the loss some friends of mine had in an upstate New York semiconductor memory systems company called Cogar Corporation. It started up in 1969, and before it went into operation it had put out hundreds of pages of publicity. Among other things, it mailed out hundreds of "ferrite donuts," components of the kind of computer memory system it claimed it was going to make obsolete. Trouble was, it never produced anything *but* publicity. I still have my ferrite donut—I keep it around to remind me to be sure a company can make the product before it launches the publicity campaign.

That's why I like to hear from an applicant about his mistakes and problems. Every company has problems, and if you ignore them, they can be fatal. Look at Penn Central. One of our successful companies, Intersil, got into trouble because we on its board failed to learn from past experience.

In 1974, Intersil began to lose money, so the board of directors took control and cut the staff by 40 percent. In January 1975, Intersil became profitable again and began to beef up staff and sales. But management repeated their mistakes because they failed to notice the negative signals the economy was broadcasting. They didn't know it, but some of their product lines were losing money on every item sold. By the fall of 1975, they were dropping $700,000 a month. The board again assumed control and elected me president pro tem. As we dug into matters, we found Intersil to be overstaffed, with significant over-capacity and poor allocation of resources. We reassigned authority to a few first-rate executives already in the company, who turned Intersil around. We reduced the staff once more, rid the company of unprofitable operations, allocated more assets to our higher-margin areas, restored profitability, and ultimately arranged a satisfactory merger. Because the company failed to learn from its mistakes, ignored its basic problems, what could have been corrected with a Band-Aid required surgery.

INC: Your taking control of Intersil saved the company, but it also calls up the fear many businessmen have—that they'll have to surrender control of their companies to the venture capitalist. How do you answer that objection?

ADLER: I took control of Intersil because the board of directors and the major shareholders wanted me to. And it doesn't make sense to worry about voting control if you're in danger of going out of business. I know of a drug company that has developed a "wonder drug." It's a small company, closely held by the president and a few employees. They want to keep total control, but they can't raise money without substantial dilution. They're not creditworthy, and right now they don't even have the money to run a clinical test. If they continue to refuse to dilute the ownership, they'll go under. On the other hand, look at the Watsons. They own only a small percentage of the stock of IBM, but look at how much it's worth. A 2 percent or 3 percent holding of a substantial company is worth more than 100 percent of nothing.

INC: In the case of Cogar, it's obvious that appearances were deceiving. Do you find that applicants often try to put on a good show for you?

ADLER: I'm always suspicious when an applicant tries to impress me by taking me to lunch at a fancy restaurant. I lunch at my desk, and I think three-martini business lunches are a waste of money, especially for an entrepreneur, who at start-up should apply every dime he has to the business. A tank car leasing executive used to insist on picking me up at the office in a limousine and taking me to expensive restaurants. It wasn't long before we found the company was in serious trouble. We should have taken the subway and eaten at McDonald's.

On the other hand, when Data General presented its proposal to me, the company's executives had to borrow money just to pay the air fare. There were no lavish luncheons or dinners, just straightforward business discussions. That company has grown on $800,000 of investment to $650 million of market value and over $500 million of sales in eleven years, and has returned a yield of over $250 to $1 to the original investors, all since 1968.

One of my "laws" [see box] is "The probability of success of a small company is inversely proportional to the size of the president's office." I once received a well-constructed proposal from the president of a small company, so I decided to visit the plant. In the parking lot space reserved for the president was a brand-new Cadillac. I was ushered into his office—enormous, impressive. But the plant was only twice as large as the president's office. So I asked about cash flow.

ADLER'S LAWS

Venture capitalist Fred Adler has condensed his experience into a few epigrams that could serve as guidelines for dealing with a venture capitalist.

1. The probability of a company's succeeding is inversely proportional to the amount of publicity it receives before it manufactures its first product.
2. An investor's ability to talk about his winners is an order of magnitude greater than his ability to remember his losers.
3. If you don't think you have a problem, you have a big problem.
4. Happiness is positive cash flow. Everything else will come later.
5. The probability of success of a small company is inversely proportional to the size of the president's office.
6. Would-be entrepreneurs who pick up the check after luncheon discussions are usually losers.
7. The longer the investment proposal, the shorter the odds of success.
8. There is no such thing as an overfinanced company.
9. Managers who worry a lot about voting control usually have nothing worth controlling.
10. There's no limit on what a man can do or where he can go, if he doesn't mind who gets the credit.

"Our projections—" he replied.

"I didn't ask for projections," I said. "What about cash flow?"

"Well, our estimates—"

"I didn't ask for estimates, either. What about cash flow?"

"Well, last month it was a negative three hundred thousand dollars."

"Then on the basis of the figures I've seen, you can stay alive another three months?"

"Yes."

INC: You put a great emphasis on cash flow in evaluating a company, then?

ADLER: With good reason. Loehmann's grew from a $6-million firm to a $160-million firm on internally generated cash—and from a four-store chain to one with forty-nine stores. And if you want examples of what negative cash flow can do, even with profitability shown on income statements, just look at the records in bankruptcy court.

INC: You say that a VC is a "participatory investor." What contribution, other than money, do you see as the most significant one you can make in running a company?

ADLER: One of the greatest assets a venture capitalist has is his little black book with the names and present locations of first-rate executives. We try to help locate good managers for our companies.

INC: What makes a good manager?

ADLER: I have five characteristics in mind when I evaluate a manager. First of all, judgment—the ability to think things through objectively and accurately. Second, aggressiveness—determination, courage, a refusal to accept defeat. Third, sincerity—a man who won't lie to others is unlikely to lie to himself. Fourth, experience—if you know the road you can travel it faster and more safely than someone who doesn't. And finally, something I can't define, but I'll call charisma. You can tell almost at a glance whether a manager has it. It's the strength of character necessary to attract and hold good people around you. The importance of a team of managers shows up when you're in trouble; then, two or three heads are always better than one.

INC: You have a "law" that seems to relate to the qualities of a manager: "There's no limit to what a man can do or where he can go, if he doesn't mind who gets the credit." Can you elaborate on that?

ADLER: Some years ago, I was in a protracted negotiation. Near the end of it, I was approached by one of my partners who said, "I can see what you're doing, Adler. You're rewriting everything to make it look as though all the ideas come from the CEO." Later my partner reported, "The CEO just told me, 'That fellow Fred Adler is really open-minded, very receptive to new ideas.'" We got the deal.

WHAT TO DO BEFORE YOU APPLY

Venture capitalism is a lot like banking: You can get the loan if you can prove you don't need it. Fred Adler advises prospective applicants to do the following:

1. Have a product or service with a competitive edge in a field with a recognizable opportunity for growth.
2. Surround yourself with a management team, each member of which has a demonstrable ability in his field.
3. Develop a business plan or a profit plan that includes an analysis of your market, an evaluation of the competition, a listing of the anticipated problems and how they will be overcome, realistic projections of the capital required, and a summary of how and why the plan is expected to work.
4. Make the plan clear and concise, emphasizing the key factors and supporting them with hard data; forget the wild estimates and sales jargon.
5. Admit your mistakes, but be sure you have learned from them. Growth covers up a lot of mistakes.
6. Most important, be able to prove you're entirely committed to the success of your firm, and that you're willing to put in not only long hard hours of work but also something of your available personal capital.

—BURTON W. TEAGUE

WHAT VENTURE CAPITALISTS WANT

Though the idea of venture capital is as old as capitalism itself, like the proverbial policeman, it's often hardest to find just when you need it. But it *is* there—if you know where to look and how to go about asking for it.

To help pin down the criteria that venture capital organizations require—and thus increase the chances of a needy company's striking a deal—291 high-technology venture capitalists were recently queried with a four-page questionnaire. (The survey results have been compiled into a directory of venture capital organizations with funds available for high-technology investments.) Although the questionnaire was directed toward venture capital funding of high-technology industries, only 10 percent of the respondents replied that they invested exclusively in high-tech projects. That means that nine out of ten are willing to consider *any* proposal—given the right circumstances. Here are some questions and answers derived from the survey. A company that is aware of such data before beginning its search for financing will be that much closer to finding it.

- **When do venture capital investors expect to show a profit?**

The majority of venture capitalists queried will invest in a company that is showing a loss. On the average, they expect to see a profit within two years. If profits are four or more years away, only 14 percent are interested. Only 4 percent insist that their portfolio companies show an immediate profit.

- **Is there a relationship between stage of development and profit expectation?**

Yes—but there are no standard definitions of "stages" within the industry. Generally, the pattern goes like this: Investors in start-ups—companies in the process of being organized—expect a profit in two years; in first-stage companies—very young concerns operating at a loss and projecting further losses—a profit in one year; in second-stage companies—young concerns approaching break-even and projecting profits in the near future—immediate break-even. (A third-stage company is one for which the investment likely will be its last round of private financing.) If you've been in business for two years but you think it will take another two years to show a profit, you're more of a start-up than a first-stage company in the mind of the typical venture capitalist.

• How important is the size of the company seeking capital?

Most venture capital organizations have no preference concerning annual sales of the companies in which they invest.

• How much money can you expect?

If you're looking for a small amount, the odds are against you. Roughly 75 percent of venture capitalists are not interested in deals involving less than $100,000. (Since each investment requires a certain amount of effort and expense, small sums are simply not cost-effective.) However, a number claim they have no upper limit. And there is always the possibility of a syndication for larger deals: Half of the firms will act as lead investors to raise more capital than they can invest singly. The average that venture capitalists prefer to invest individually ranges from $200,000 to $750,000 per deal; the average preferred ceiling for a syndicated deal is $6.5 million. The average individual Small Business Investment Company (SBIC) prefers to limit itself to $500,000; the average Minority Enterprise Small Business Investment Company (MESBIC) to $200,000. The average syndicated deal with an SBIC leader is limited to $4.5 million.

• What are SBIC and MESBIC governmental restrictions?

The amount that can be invested per deal is restricted to 20 percent of paid-in capital for SBICs and to 30 percent of paid-in capital for MESBICs. Further, companies in which they can invest must have a net worth not exceeding $6 million and average after-tax net income for the preceding two years of no more than $2 million. In most situations, both SBICs and MESBICs are precluded from taking a controlling interest in a portfolio company.

• How much management assistance is provided?

Almost two-thirds provide frequent assistance. Only 8 percent limit their help to "occasional" assistance or none at all. A large number stated that a quality management team is essential for the companies in which they invest. Without a team that is well rounded and experienced, a company will find it extremely difficult to raise venture capital. "But my company has a dynamite product," you say. "It can't help but be successful!" Don't be so sure. Most venture capitalists much prefer good management with a mediocre product to mediocre management with a good product. When you get right down to it, they're looking for both good management and good product.

• What regions are favored?

Geography apparently is not a critical factor in determining a company's chances of finding venture capital. About a third of those queried had no preference; among those with a preference, no particular region was clearly favored or disfavored. As for the venture capitalists themselves, about half came from only three states: New York (22 percent), California (20 percent), and Massachusetts (10 percent).

• What should a seeker prepare for a first contact?

Three out of four venture capitalists prefer initially to look at a short business plan or a description of the company and the deal being sought. Long business plans usually are not required initially—only 9 percent of those queried request them when first contacted.

• Are cities preferred over small towns?

No. Only 4 percent of the venture capitalists prefer that your company be in or near a major metropolitan area. It undoubtedly would be to your advantage, however, to locate in a region served by a commercial airline.

• How far should a company go to look for capital?

Keep in mind that most venture capitalists provide management assistance as well as funding, and that the younger a company is, the more likely they will insist on working closely with it. And the closer your venture capitalist is, the easier it is for him to provide assistance. Thus most newer companies and those who expect management help as well as funding are well advised to begin their search for capital close to home. But don't automatically rule out distant sources. If you can't find a venture capitalist in your area, you may find one somewhere else who is sufficiently interested in your company to recruit a nearby organization to sponsor the deal.

• How should a venture capitalist be approached?

Only a handful of those questioned preferred that the initial contact be made by a third party or another venture capitalist rather than by the entrepreneur himself. With that in mind, you'll probably find it cheaper and faster to call before sending a letter or proposal. Remember, "nothing ventured, nothing gained" is, in this case, a maxim that works both ways.

—RICHARD LOFTIN

WHY SMART COMPANIES ARE SAYING NO
TO VENTURE CAPITAL

It seemed, at first, like the logical next act in the classic entrepreneurial script. Having developed his new database software on his home-built Heathkit microcomputer, Wayne Erickson packed his bags and set off on a pilgrimage to the venture capital mecca of San Francisco in search of the help he needed to turn his creation into a multimillion-dollar enterprise.

It was a well-worn path, that route from the entrepreneur's garage to the investor's suite. It was part of an initiation rite through which hundreds, if not thousands, of dreamers and doers had passed before. On the surface, at least, Erickson seemed little different from the rest. He was thirty-five years old, a former bass player in a rock band who at some point had discovered that his real talent lay in computers. Going to work as a software programmer at Boeing Computer Services Inc., he had developed something called the RIM (relational information management) software system to help track missing ceramic tiles on the space shuttle. After leaving Boeing in 1979, he had done contract work for the National Aeronautics and Space Administration at the University of Washington in Seattle, and—in his spare time—experimented with adapting RIM for use on microcomputers, eventually developing a powerful database system that could quickly and easily organize data from as many as forty different files.

The system seemed to have commercial potential, so in 1981, Erickson and his older brother Ron, an attorney, formed Microrim Inc., to make and market the product, which they called R:base. Selling to a few large customers, Microrim enjoyed revenues of $360,000 in its first year, and the Ericksons began to think about broadening their horizons. They believed that with a little help, Microrim could become a major player in a burgeoning industry. What the company needed was capital and, equally important, the wisdom of those who had done it before. They hoped to find both in San Francisco's venture capital community.

And so, in late 1982, they traveled down from Bellevue, Washington, accompanied by Microrim's chief operating officer, Kent Johnson. Arriving in the city, they were as nervous as novices entering the Holy See. "We felt a little intimidated," Johnson recalls. "We were all small-town boys from Washington in big San Francisco. We

knew that the venture capitalists there had made fortunes and had
seen hundred of plans. We were the new guys on the block, and no one
knew us."

Over the course of three months, they made two trips to the Bay
Area and met with more than a dozen venture capital firms. Wide-eyed
and reverent, they were ushered into the very offices where some of the
greatest entrepreneurial successes in recent memory had been
launched. There they demonstrated their product, analyzed their competition, talked about themselves, their company, and their plans for
the future.

And something odd began to happen. As they moved from meeting
to meeting, their awe gradually dissipated, giving way to a different
emotion. They looked across the table at the people whose help they
were seeking, and they felt . . . disappointment.

Were these the venture capitalists they had heard so much about?
They could scarcely believe it. To be sure, these guys acted powerful
and important, and they undoubtedly had access to a great deal of
money, some of which they indicated they might be willing to part with.
But they were hardly the experienced sages that Erickson and the
others had been hoping to encounter, people who had built fast-growth
companies from coast to coast. Some of these venture capitalists didn't
even know very much about running a business, having only gradu-
ated from business school two or three years before.

"Just because they had MBAs from Stanford or Harvard, they
thought they knew everything about everything," Wayne Erickson
recalls bitterly. "Their approach was pretty much antagonistic. 'Why
don't you do this? Why don't you do that?' they would say. They wanted
us to redo everything we had done, and most of them didn't know
anything about writing software. I felt I had been nursing this baby
and they were telling me that they didn't like the way the baby looked.
But the fact is that we had done some things right."

In the end, several of the venture capitalists expressed interest in
backing Microrim, and one made a firm offer. The company sorely
needed the money: Erickson and his associates were well aware that
their meager cash reserves and their bank credit line would soon be
exhausted. Nevertheless, they decided to turn everybody down.

"I remember sitting in this high-rise in San Francisco, talking to
this young venture capitalist, and thinking, 'This guy is so precious,
he's such a nerd. I don't want him on our board, telling us what to do,'"
says Ron Erickson. "We were sick of haughty disdain. Maybe we
wouldn't go silk-stocking, but we didn't care. We were going to find a
different route."

There have always been young companies that, for one reason or
another, have preferred to grow without venture capital, but lately it
seems that more and more have, like Microrim, begun searching for "a
different route." The entrepreneurs in question cite a variety of reasons. Some share Microrim's complaint about the quality of the exper-

tise available. Others fear loss of control over key decisions. But perhaps the most frequent criticism—and, in some ways, the most devastating—is that venture capital, by its very nature, distorts the process of growth.

"Venture capitalists make you too 'now', too profit-oriented, instead of quality-oriented," say David Fast, president of Perennial Software Services Group (see page 101), a leading software service firm that has avoided venture funding. "You introduce factors with venture capital that don't really help build the company. We want to use our profits to do the things we want to do, not to please some investor who's screaming, 'Fifteen percent or you're out!' I'd rather have the steady, balanced growth that comes from pulling yourself up by the bootstraps."

That may be something of an overstatement, but it is also an increasingly common refrain in Silicon Valley and other centers of new business formation. It reflects a growing disenchantment with an industry whose successes have become synonymous with the resurgence of the entrepreneurial spirit in America. Since the late 1950s, venture capitalists have played a crucial, even heroic, role in launching some of the nation's most spectacular growth companies, from Digital Equipment and Federal Express to Apple Computer and People Express. At a time when the giant commercial banks, investment houses, and large corporations disdained small start-ups, venture capitalists were ready and willing to take the risks necessary to build their economic future.

But venture capital today may well be becoming a victim of its own successes. Once a collection of small firms run by brilliant, if often idiosyncratic, individuals, the venture capital business is developing into a large-scale, highly institutionalized industry. The main impetus has come from pension funds, investment banks, insurance companies, and the like. Lured by annual returns as high as 40 percent to 60 percent, they have poured huge amounts of money into venture capital funds. In 1977, just $39 million flowed into the pipeline. But in 1983, new capital shot to $4.1 billion, according to *Venture Capital Journal*. Another $8.9 billion was committed between 1984 and the end of 1986.

As the money has flowed in, the game has changed. "You have to understand this is an industry where people are not used to having a lot of money," observes Oxford Partners' Stevan Birnbaum, who has been a venture capitalist for fifteen years. "Then somebody gives you one hundred fifty million dollars, and you start to feel you can walk on water. You read in the paper that you're a genius, and you believe it. Some of the old constraints tend to get eroded away."

One manifestation of this tendency has been the recent emergence of so-called megafunds—venture capital funds of $100 million or more. The first one was established in December 1982 by the well-respected firm of Kleiner, Perkins, Caufield & Byers, which raised $150 million for the purpose. Since then, nine other firms have followed suit, including such pillars of the industry as T. A. Associates, Hambrecht & Quist, and the Mayfield Fund.

Those are big numbers for an industry in which, in 1979, the largest fund was about $40 million and the average fund was about $15 million. The problem of managing such megafunds, however, may be even bigger. "In this business, you don't multiply your talent with size," notes John Hines, president of Continental Illinois Venture Corporation. Stretched thin, the often illustrious general partners of the larger firms have had to depend increasingly on inexperienced subordinates for much of their investment decision making and due diligence. This, in turn, has had an impact on the venture capital process itself. From the entrepreneurs' standpoint, it means that they may not get the expert advice, or "intelligence equity," which they often value more than cash. From the investors' standpoint, it means that they are entrusting their money to people with limited knowledge of the business.

Part of the problem has to do, quite simply, with the dearth of available talent. Experienced venture capitalists are hard to come by, and their number has not kept pace with the explosion of the industry as a whole.

"It's like a large law firm," adds Hines of Continental Illinois Venture. "You can say you're with the greatest law firm in the world, but, if a junior person is handling your account, I'd say that's baloney. The question is: Who is your individual lawyer? This is not a profession for a lot of inexperienced young people in their twenties and thirties."

Then again, it would be unfair and wrong to blame most of the industry's woes on MBAs, whose role, after all, is more a symptom than a cause of the problems. Certainly, there were very experienced hands involved in many of the recent venture-backed fiascos—Osborne Computer, Fortune Systems, Victor Technologies, Pizza Time Theatre, Diasonics, and so on. What those cases reveal is a broad pattern of mistakes and misjudgments. "There's been a lack of tough-minded checking out of deals," admits one top Bay Area venture capitalist. "People get into situations with entrepreneurs or companies that they soon realize aren't going to work out, but once you start, you often find a deal takes on a life of its own."

Exacerbating this situation is the growing involvement of major financial institutions in the venture capital process itself—not just as suppliers of capital, but as direct participants in latter, or "mezzanine," round financing. As investment banks, insurance companies, and other large institutions have formed their own venture capital arms, they have added millions of dollars to the already huge pool of money available to companies on the verge of going public. The temptation is to pump these companies full of cash in hopes of increasing the appeal of their initial public offering. It is a temptation that some venture capitalists have found impossible to resist.

"A lot of our troubles started when the institutions began coinvesting with us," laments one prominent San Francisco venture capitalist. "It's a fundamentally unsound process. It's like believing in Santa Claus. The pressure is to shortcut the whole process. Instead of giving companies five or six years to grow, they try to do it in two years. Some companies have been rushed and grossly overfinanced as a result. The institutional involvement distorted everything. It's a process that will lead—is leading—to disaster."

Disaster may seem like a rather strong word, and *overfinancing* a rather strange concept—especially to young companies that are struggling to make ends meet. Yet that concept touches the root of the problems precipitated by the influx of new money and new players into the venture capital business. "The business has become very chic," says venture capitalist Don Valentine of Menlo Park, California, one of the deans of the industry. "Five or ten years ago, many of these same [institutional investors] would react to venture capital like venereal disease. Now they think it's the greatest thing in the world, but they have picked up none of the skills."

In their enthusiasm, says Valentine, the new players often fail to comprehend the fundamental difference between venture capital and conventional financing mechanisms. "They think it's an investment business, but that's wrong. Venture capital is not a business of trading stocks and investing for fast returns. I am not a banker. I am into building companies."

That is, indeed, what venture capital used to be all about—building companies—and Valentine's own record on the score is extremely impressive. The companies he has helped build bear names like Apple Computer, Tandem Computers, Altos Computer Systems, and LSI Logic. But the man whose work best exemplifies this approach to the business is a predecessor of Valentine, a French emigré by the name of General Georges F. Doriot.

Doriot, who died in 1987, was a highly influential professor at the Harvard Graduate School of Business Administration during the 1930s and 1940s. In World War II, he served in the U.S. Army, rising to the rank of Brigadier General. On his return from war, he decided that the business climate around Boston had become too stale for his taste. So, in 1946, he founded American Research and Development Corporation (ARD), a company dedicated to fostering new, exciting companies.

Backed by Yankee financiers, Doriot began scouring the depressed New England countryside, looking for business and technological talent. One of the high points of that search came in 1957, when he was contacted by a young engineer and entrepreneur named Kenneth Olsen, who had an idea for something called an "interactive computer." By that, he meant a computer with which a user could communicate directly via a keyboard or terminal, rather than punch cards. (This was, in fact, the forerunner of the minicomputer.) Olsen wanted to start a company to develop and produce the device.

On the face of it, his prospects seemed bleak. He had no prior business experience, and nobody but IBM Corporation was making money on computers anyway. But Doriot saw the opportunity and persuaded ARD's board to invest $70,000 in Olsen's fledgling company, which became known as Digital Equipment Corporation (DEC). Headquarters were set up in an old woolen mill in Maynard, Massachusetts, a Boston suburb—on the second floor, with a narrow stairway and no elevator. Such was Doriot's style. He believed that with too much money, a company's founders might "start buying Cadillacs, fifty-room mansions, go skiing in summer and swimming in winter." Then again, he himself never invested in his companies, fearing a conflict of interest.

Over the next fourteen years, Doriot worked to help build the company. He stayed in close touch with Olsen, advising him on a wide variety of matters, always pushing him to focus on long-term development. Doriot even became upset the first year that DEC reported a profit, because he feared the company was not spending enough on research and development. In the end, however, everyone profited. By 1971, ARD's initial investment of $70,000 was worth an estimated $350 million.

Doriot had similar successes with other companies, including Ionics, the water treatment company; Cordis, the manufacturer of pacemakers; Teradyne, the electronic test-equipment maker; and Cooper Laboratories, the pharmaceutical company. Throughout the low-inflation era of the late 1950s and 1960s, ARD consistently enjoyed a 15 percent annual rate of return. For Doriot, however, such returns were a by-product of his work, not a goal. "I don't consider a speculator—in my definition of the word—constructive," he once observed. "I am building men and companies." To do that required, above all, patience and loyalty, and Doriot often worked with a company for a decade or more, through good times and bad, before realizing any return at all. Small wonder that he came to refer to his companies as his "children."

In 1972, Doriot sold ARD to Textron Inc. and retired. But the Doriot tradition lived on in a new generation of venture capitalists, men who had themselves built companies and now wanted to help others do the same. Among them were Eugene Kleiner, a founder of Fairchild Camera & Instrument; Thomas J. Perkins, former director of corporate development of Hewlett-Packard; Burgess Jamieson, a onetime chief development engineer of Honeywell's Computer Control Division; and, of course, Don Valentine, who had been marketing director of National Semiconductor Corporation. What these venture capitalists and others like them had in common was a particular sort of knowledge and experience that was, and is, especially valuable to young, growing companies.

That knowledge allows the venture capitalist to serve, for example, as a kind of clearinghouse—a screen through which bad ideas, even bad business plans, cannot easily pass. It was just such a screen that Wilf Corrigan was looking for when he approached Don Valentine in late 1980. Corrigan had an idea for a company, LSI Logic Corporation, that would make semicustom integrated circuits. He believed that Valentine, as a veteran of the semiconductor industry, was particularly suited to assess the viability of the scheme. Indeed, Valentine relentlessly challenged Corrigan's theses, and he forced him to define his ideas more sharply. As a result, says Corrigan, LSI Logic started on a firm footing.

"Don is one of the world's toughest negotiators, but it's good to talk to someone who knows what he's talking about," Corrigan says. "He's very analytical, very unemotional. He does a lot of analysis before he makes a decision. He won't be rushed into anything. He's got the ability to turn deals down. A lot of venture capitalists are just parallel investors who follow what other people do. When Don went with us, we knew that the idea made sense."

Valentine performed a somewhat different service for Steven Jobs and Stephen Wozniak when they were trying to put Apple Computer Company together back in 1976. Their problem was that many of their potential backers felt the two young engineers lacked the necessary management experience to succeed. They turned to Valentine, who persuaded a friend and former Intel executive, A. C. Markkula, Jr., to serve as Apple's president. Markkula, in turn, played a central role in guiding the fledgling company through its initial period of rapid growth and into the public market.

But it is often later—after the company is up and running—that the knowledge and experience of a skilled venture capitalist becomes most important to the entrepreneur. In the case of Altos Computer Systems, for example, Valentine was able to contribute his substantial marketing program, as he had previously done at National Semiconductor. Beyond that, he served as a sounding board for Altos founder and chairman David Jackson. "Venture capitalists came to me, but I didn't see where I needed them," Jackson recalls. "I run a tight ship, and I didn't need the money. What I did need was somebody who could tell me what a big company is all about. I needed a strategist, and Don's a great one. He's not a witch doctor, but you tell him a problem and he sets the guidelines for you, so you can get a solution."

By playing such a role—by helping to build companies—venture capitalists of the Doriot school earned the loyalty of the entrepreneurs they served. "I think venture capital has been fantastic for the country," says James Treybig, founder and chief executive officer of Tandem Computers Inc., launched in the mid-seventies with $50,000 from Kleiner, Perkins, Caufield & Byers. "Without their help, there'd probably be a lot fewer new companies around today. And it wasn't just the money. The venture capitalists were always there to help."

In the early 1980s, however, the venture capital business began to change. Indeed, it is almost possible to fix the date—December 12, 1980, the day that Apple Computer went public. The initial offering price was $22. By the close of trading, Apple stock was selling for more than $34 per share.

The Apple Computer offering was, of course, a bonanza for the company's founders and backers, and it provided dramatic proof of the fortunes that could be made by entrepreneurs and venture capitalists alike. Beyond that, it showed how receptive the public equity markets were to new issues of technology stocks—a lesson reinforced by the subsequent initial public offerings of companies like Cetus, Pizza Time Theatre, ASK Computer Systems, Vector Graphic, and Altos Computer Systems. As the IPO market heated up, investors realized that, instead of having to wait five or ten years for returns on their investments, they could count on Wall Street to produce ten-to-one paybacks in as little as two years. It was a message heard loud and clear from New York to San Jose, California, and it set off a stampede to the public market, boosting the number of new issues from 281 in 1980 to an astounding 888 in 1983.

"People say power corrupts, but I think it's money that does the trick," observes San Jose venture capitalist Burgess Jamieson.

"We have the symptoms of the heightening of greed among venture capitalists and entrepreneurs. I suppose greed is okay up to a point, but it's like wine. A glass is pleasant, a bottle will have a different effect."

This particular form of inebriation produced a variety of effects and manifested itself in a variety ways. To begin with, it drew into the venture capital business a lot of people and institutions that were less interested in building companies than in scoring "quick hits"—that is, realizing enormous returns in a relatively short period of time. That was all right for entrepreneurs of a similar mind, but it posed a dilemma for those who were interested in something more than a fast buck.

A case in point is Mark Richardson, a former Hewlett-Packard engineer, who teamed up with three of his colleagues to found San Jose–based Structural Measurement Systems (SMS), a company that develops software packages for diagnosing such design-related problems as stress and noise. Launched in 1979, SMS got off to a fast start, with sales running at about $1 million per year, but it needed additional capital infusions to maintain that growth. So Richardson began contacting venture capitalists.

"One of the first things the venture guys did was to come in and ask, 'Do you want to be rich or president?'" Richardson recalls. "When he said that, I tell you, I had to wonder about whether I wanted to make that choice."

Richardson and his partners soon came to believe that taking venture money could have serious consequences for SMS. They had dreams of building a company like Hewlett-Packard, with a strong emphasis on product quality and a humanistic orientation. The venture capitalists they encountered tended to stress financial considerations and the prospects of going public. An obsession with "putting up big numbers," observed vice-president of marketing Ken Ramsey, could threaten not only their control of the company, but its fundamental character as well—something the partners were not willing to risk.

"We would have taken money from the right person, says Ramsey, "but we wanted a sympathetic party, someone who would help us out. We never got the sense that these guys wanted to be partners. They seemed like cutthroat types, and that isn't the kind of company we wanted to build."

But even if the new venture capitalists were not particularly cutthroat, they often had little to offer companies that were striving for solid, long-term growth—little besides money, that is. "If I could have had an experienced venture capitalist, I would have considered" taking venture capital, says Chuck Colby, who founded Colby Computer (see page 100) in 1982. "But the two venture guys who offered to invest in us were a completely different breed. One was a guy from New York who would show up every once in a while, and the other was a kid with no experience. They had all the money in the world, but there's no way they could help me build this company. There are things more important than money. I wanted people who would be real partners."

Another case was Ashton-Tate (see page 102), the software company based in Culver City, California, which was courted by more than fifty venture capital firms. "If we had found a partner who offered a high value added, we probably would have taken it," says company president David Cole. "But most of them represented cash, and the way we manage, that's not what we really needed. It just didn't click."

On the other hand, there were plenty of entrepreneurs who were happy to take the money. Indeed, the venture capital boom soon gave rise to a new phenomenon, what Oxford Partners' Stevan Birnbaum calls the "pseudo–growth company." These were companies founded by charismatic, charming, even brilliant entrepreneurs, whose rhetoric and salesmanship often exceeded their business skills. According to Los Angeles venture capitalist Richard Riordan, these super-salespeople succeeded in raising money partly because investors thought they "looked more like a CEO" than blander entrepreneurs, many of them engineers, who—although introverted and awkward—might nevertheless have sounder ideas.

It is an opinion often echoed in Silicon Valley. "In the last few years, it's gotten so venture capitalists felt they couldn't just invest in Joe Schmuck," says Duane C. Meulners, founder of Dymek Corporation, a $10-million-a-year manufacturer of alignment disks for disk drives. "You have to be a celebrity. Good solid growth isn't enough anymore. The venture capitalists are looking for wild, rampaging weeds."

Whether or not they were looking for weeds, that is what they found. All over Silicon Valley, companies began to spring up that were heavily promoted and heavily financed on little more than grand schemes. In place of expertise, the venture capitalists provided the companies with tons of money. The people who ran the companies often wound up spending it like oil sheiks on a weekend jaunt to Las Vegas.

There was, for example, the leading semiconductor start-up that added a totally unnecessary, albeit esthetically pleasing, sloping roof to its headquarters at a time when losses were running at more than $1 million a quarter. An elaborate management information services staff, elegant work stations, and a host of other extravagances helped boost this company's break-even point as much as $4 million above that of its competitors.

"Those types are still all around the Valley," says a former manager at the company, "the hip shooters, the guys with a good front who feel they can do anything. It's a lifestyle thing. They want to live like kings on other people's money. What amazes me is that the venture capitalists let them get away with it."

There was, in the words of one executive, "an atmosphere of false euphoria." But the spell broke along about the summer of 1983, with the collapse of Osborne Computer Corporation.

In some ways, Osborne Computer was the quintessential pseudo-growth company. It certainly had all the right elements—an exciting, breakthrough product; a charismatic and articulate founder; and a list of investors that read like a "Who's Who" of venture capital and investment banking. Jack Melchor, one of Silicon Valley's leading venture capitalists, sat on Osborne's board, as did Ken Oshman, founder of Rolm Corporation and a Valley maven of the first rank. They, in turn, helped to bring in additional millions from the investment community—including the investment banking firm of L. F. Rothschild, Unterberg, Towbin; New York's First Century Fund; and Hewlett-Packard's venture capital wing. "Melchor was the driving force in getting people to invest in the company," explains one knowledgeable source. "Some of the investors relied heavily on the fact that Melchor and Oshman were on the board."

But there were also those who let greed—and the prospect of a lucrative public offering—overcome their better judgment. "We invested in Adam Osborne and, looking back at it, I don't know how he did it," admits one highly respected venture capitalist. "He had a real good idea, and he's very articulate. If he could run a company, he would have made a lot of money. I knew in my gut he couldn't do it, but I guess I felt, you know, 'miracles can happen.'"

This was one miracle that wasn't going to happen, however. In April of 1983, the company's new president, Robert Jaunich II, canceled the widely expected public offering, citing problems of production, product quality, and cash flow. In August, the company started massive layoffs at its Hayward, California, factory. A month later, it filed for protection under Chapter 11 of the Federal Bankruptcy Code, amid a barrage of lawsuits.

The Osborne collapse sent shock waves from Silicon Valley to Wall Street. Blake Downing, an investment analyst at the San Francisco investment banking firm of Robertson, Colman and Stephens, states flatly, "Osborne was a symbol, and one of the factors which drove the 1983–84 IPO market away."

What happened at Osborne unveiled, for the first time, the fundamental weaknesses of many highly touted venture-backed companies, and that lesson was driven home as first Victor Technologies Inc., then Pizza Time Theatre followed Osborne into Chapter 11. To make matters worse, there is a growing tribe of what one investment banker calls "the living dead," companies that were once hot, some receiving as much as $20 million in venture capital financing, but that are now struggling just to stay alive: Diasonics, Fortune Systems, Vector Graphic, Xonics, Evotek, VisiCorp, to name a few.

The consequences of all this are already being felt throughout the venture capital industry. With the souring of the public market, many knowledgeable observers expect the returns of venture capital firms to plummet over the next few years, perhaps dropping by as much as half. That, in turn, will affect the supply of venture money available from institutions. "If [institutions] are making venture investments on the basis of the returns we've seen over the past five years, they are going to be disappointed," says Walter Cabot, president of Harvard Management Company, the firm charged with investing Harvard University's $2.6-billion endowment fund and a leading venture capital supplier for the past eight years.

Similar views are expressed by other top suppliers, including Robert Knox of Prudential Venture Capital Management Inc. They all say that, as a result, they plan to be far more selective in choosing the venture partnerships they subscribe in. "Every business has cyclical peaks and valleys," says Cabot. "In my opinion, venture capital is at a cyclical peak. A lot of companies and partnerships will have trouble."

The first casualties will probably be the industry's newer players, particularly those venture groups set up by investment bankers and other traditional financial institutions. At least three such funds were dissolved in the first half of 1984, including one that had been launched by Los Angeles–based California Federal Savings & Loan Association scarcely two years before. "When [Cal Fed management] realized this was not a short-term business but a long-term business, they pulled out," says Anna Henry, who had joined Cal Fed Venture Capital Corporation a few months earlier. "I think you'll see other institutions pulling out. A lot of people got unusual returns in the last few years, but now it's becoming clear that things aren't really that way. Venture capital doesn't fit easily with the mentality of large corporations."

But the ripples of venture capital's plunge are likely to spread far beyond the institutional funds. Some venture capitalists, in fact, fear a backlash similar to the one following the "go-go" years of the late 1960s and early 1970s. That era had seen a spectacular boom in young growth companies, many of which went public with great fanfare. Aggressively promoted by young brokers and underwriters, these hot new issues soared briefly across the investment horizon, until the fundamental weaknesses of the companies brought them, and their investors, crashing back to earth. "There was a binge, followed by a sharp hangover, in 1974," recalls venture capitalist James Morgan, managing partner of Boston-based Morgan, Holland Ventures Corporation. "There was much bloodshed and many losses. The whole structure came tumbling down."

Something like that could happen again, particularly if a significant number of the "living dead" don't survive. Indeed, it is by no means inconceivable that a series of massive failures of venture-backed companies could send a chill across the entire entrepreneurial landscape, affecting all kinds of smaller businesses, even those that might never have been candidates for venture capital themselves. After all, the rise of venture capital helped generate new interest in small, growth companies in general; so, too, its decline could have the opposite effect. To a certain extent, this is already occurring. "The number of unqualified companies going public is very detrimental to the capital markets" for young companies, notes an East Coast investment banker. "John Q. Public takes a bath, and that's bad for his willingness to buy into that market again."

But even if the worst doesn't happen, entrepreneurs will increasingly have to look elsewhere for the money and expertise that they have traditionally counted on the venture capital community to provide. That is, in fact, precisely what the managers of Microrim did after their disappointing experience with the young venture capitalists of San Francisco.

Microrim's "different route" opened up in the spring of 1983, when one of the company's Seattle-area investors introduced Ron Erickson to Gary Blauer, a young stockbroker from the Minneapolis-based investment banking firm of Dain Bosworth Inc. Blauer, himself a former software programmer, was intrigued by Microrim's R:base software program. "It was love at first sight," recalls chief operating officer Kent Johnson. "Gary didn't come off as arrogant. He knew what he wanted to do and took time to understand what we were doing. There was an immediate sense of partnership that I never sensed with the VCs."

Prodded by Blauer, Dain Bosworth eventually raised $7.8 million for Microrim in two separate private placements. The money has allowed Microrim to market aggressively its R:base product family. Meanwhile, the company's founders and employees still control more than 45 percent of the company's stock—two to three times the percentage they would have controlled if they had gone the venture capital route.

Microrim also managed to find the "intelligence equity" it was seeking—in the person of Larry Mayhew, a twenty-two-year veteran of Tektronix Inc., the Portland, Oregon–based instrumentation company. As luck would have it, Mayhew had left Tektronix in November 1982 in order to become president of Data I/O, a leading manufacturer of programmers for silicon microcircuitry, which was located just ten miles from Microrim, in Redmond, Washington. As president of a fast-growing company, and a man experienced in running a billion-dollar corporation, he offered Microrim's young management team a cornucopia of battle-tested wisdom and contacts. Mayhew, for his part, was intrigued by the opportunity to get involved in the burgeoning software business and accepted a seat on Microrim's board for an option to buy 20,000 shares of company stock, less than 0.5 percent of the company.

"It's an almost ideal situation," says Kent Johnson. "We have the money, we have the people, and we have the product. We also have a guy with great experience and insight who can give us all the counsel we could never get from a venture capitalist. And we still have control of the company. It just shows that it's possible to grow without having the VCs get their screws into you."

To be sure, other companies may not be as fortunate as Microrim, but then there are those who would argue that they might be better off without a lot of venture capital to assuage their growing pains. "Too many start-ups we've seen over the years started with too much money," says George Tate, cofounder of Ashton-Tate. "The key thing is you have to go through the pain. If you sense pain in the beginning, the chances are you won't have to deal with it later. We learned to be careful with everything in the beginning. If some VC just handed us five million dollars, it would have sucked the blood out of us. The only way to stay focused is pain—and not being able to make the rent if you screw up."

In the future, that observation may apply as well to companies that have already received venture capital. Consider Linear Technology Corporation, a semiconductor microchip company launched in 1981 with $4.5 million in venture backing. A year ago, says Linear Technology president Bob Swanson, he sometimes had difficulty convincing managers of the need to control costs. With millions of venture dollars in the bank, and millions more apparently available on request, thrift seemed like an unnecessary frill. But with the collapse of the IPO market and many venture-backed companies in deep trouble, all that has changed. "People around here now realize that whatever money is sitting in the bank may be all there is for a long time," says Swanson. "There's no substitute for squeezing the nickels and dimes. It's hard to get people to batten down the hatches when the sun is shining and the pot seems bottomless, but it all comes out in the wash. The guys who spend lavishly will go under, and those who spend carefully will survive."

Much the same might be said for the venture capitalists themselves. While the newer firms begin to fade, some of the more traditional venture capitalists are pulling in their horns. Sevin Rosen Partners, for instance, plans to make fewer new investments this year than in the past. "We're holding up for a while," says general partner L. J. Sevin. "We just aren't going to be seeing as many new faces. We have a lot of work to do with the companies we already have."

"There's a time to reap, and there's a time to sow," echoes Alan Ruvelson of Minneapolis-based First Midwest Capital Corporation, who has been in the venture capital business for a quarter century. "Maybe this is the time to plant seeds and get through the long winter. The opportunities are still there at the end of the cycle. Survivorship never has been easy, but that's the way this business has been from the beginning."

So, in the long run, the venture capital industry may yet emerge from its "Big Chill" stronger than ever. It will, that is, if venture capitalists follow Sevin and Ruvelson, put their shoulders to the wheel, and return—in the words of General Doriot—to the business of "building men and companies."

Different Routes

COLBY COMPUTER, 1984

When Chuck Colby set out to build a personal computer company, he knew he would need help. As a former Ampex Corporation executive, he had the necessary technical skills, but he lacked both cash and experience in the art of managing a start-up growth company. The venture capitalists he met had lots of money but little to offer in the way of expertise. So Colby went elsewhere.

One of the people he turned to was Al Hassler, a Swiss-educated engineer with a wealth of experience gained over the years as a top technologist at Memorex Corporation and as founder of International Memories Inc. (IMI), a highly profitable Silicon Valley disk-drive maker. Hassler agreed to serve as an unofficial godfather to Colby Computer, helping out in a variety of ways. Early on, for example, Colby had decided to have high-quality casings for his computers, some of which are intended for heavy-duty industrial and military use. It was Hassler who arranged for the frames to be produced at Western Diecasting Inc., a well-regarded local company, which agreed to accept stock in partial payment. As a result, Colby was able to reduce his start-up costs. Similarly, the man who paints the Colby microcomputers became a stockholder in the company.

Hassler also introduced Colby to attorney Michael Philips, from the prominent San Jose, California, law firm of Hopkins, Mitchell & Carley. Philips agreed to take Colby Computer on as a client, and to accept less than his usual fee during the early phases of the company's development. In addition, Hassler helped develop Colby's financial strategies.

Hassler's role will become increasingly important as Colby Computer reaches out for larger market share, going head-to-head against larger, better-financed organizations. Preparing for that challenge, Hassler has lined up various key executives at other companies who are planning to join Colby Computer when the time is right. Some are already pitching in as part-time consultants.

"Al's given me everything that I could ever want from an investor," Colby says. "Getting him to go on board was one of the best moves I've made. It was like beating the venture guys at their own game."

XICOR INC., 1984

At a time when heavily financed, venture-backed companies are failing right and left, Xicor Inc. president and chairman Raphael Klein has emerged as a new role model in Silicon Valley. A former process engineer at National Semiconductor Corporation, Klein launched the company in August 1978 without any venture capital at all. He did so, moreover, despite the conventional wisdom that any new semiconductor manufacturing company would fail without at least $50 million in start-up money.

Xicor, for its part, started with little more than an idea about a new kind of chip, known as a NOVRAM, which allows systems to retain and save data if power is lost unexpectedly. There was a real market need for such a chip, and that proved to be a major advantage for Xicor. "We didn't have the money for a technology trip," the Israeli-born Klein recalls in his Milpitas, California, office. "Not having money made us do everything right the first time."

Among the things Klein did right was to draw on the wisdom and experience of Julius Blank, one of the founders of Fairchild Semiconductor (a division of Fairchild Camera & Instrument Corporation), who now serves on Xicor's board. Klein also spent money carefully. He eschewed fancy offices, working initially at the home of one of his engineers, and he arranged to have Xicor's original manufacturing work done overseas, in Switzerland. "We wanted a product, not a fancy building," he says.

Today Klein continues to practice spartan management at Xicor, which last year enjoyed sales of more than $15 million and announced profits in excess of $800,000 for the first quarter of 1984. He still does his own photocopying and maintains relatively modest offices. But what Klein and his colleagues lack in amenities, they make up for in equity, controlling about 35 percent of the company.

"There's a simple lesson in all this," says Klein. "I see it all around me. We built this company piece by piece, slowly but with our goals in mind. A lot of people in the Valley think you need a fancy building or a Mercedes to get respect. But customers don't care about that stuff—about your press clippings or the decor of your office. That's not what gets you where you want to go."

PERENNIAL SOFTWARE SERVICES GROUP, 1984

For David Fast, the issue is quality of growth. Fast is the founder and president of Perennial Software Services Group, in Santa Clara, California, a leading software service firm, and he has seen many of his friends follow the same route—raising large amounts of venture capital, growing rapidly, then flaring out in a blaze of red ink. "There are lots of smart people doing things that are dumb," he says.

Many of the problems he believes, stem from having too much money, which leads entrepreneurs to ignore many of the fundamentals of sound business management. "I really believe that people cannot learn fast enough to grow two hundred percent—something like fifty percent is all I think most can handle," says Fast, whose company estimates 1984 sales of $4 million. "A lot of companies, like Atari or Victor, hurt themselves that way. When you grow that fast, you don't take time to choose your people or markets carefully. The pressure is more, not better. You end up making third or fourth choices instead of the first. You end up doing things because you have money to do them, not because they are the right things to do."

At Perennial, Fast and his sixty-member staff try to live within their cash flow, which comes steadily from such clients as Apple Computer, Atari, Intel, and VisiCorp. Instead of driving for high profits and hyper-growth, Fast keeps his profits low—about 5 percent of sales—and uses his capital to upgrade the quality of service, putting employees through intensive training programs and hiring top-flight software engineers. Using this method, Fast expects Perennial to reach $15 million in annual sales by 1987 without compromising its obligations to its customers—which he sees as more important than meteoric growth.

ASHTON-TATE, 1984

Software companies may be in a better position than most high-technology companies to avoid venture capital in the early stages of development. Largely dependent on the creativity of key employees, they can usually get by for a while on a shoestring. But sooner or later, every company needs money to grow and gain market share, and—at that point—it might do well to exchange its shoestring for a set of bootstraps to pull itself up.

Consider Ashton-Tate, which was launched in 1980 with a $7,500 investment from its founders, George Tate and Hal Lashlee, who—in building the company—eschewed every unnecessary cost. For example, they located their headquarters in an unfashionable section of Culver City, California, and outfitted it with surplus furniture. During the first year, they each received the princely salary of $1,000 per month. Meanwhile, their initial product (called dBase II) was on its way to becoming the world's largest-selling database management program. So in 1982, with sales running at a $20-million-a-year rate, then-president Tate doubled his salary—to about $2,000 a month.

"We didn't have any money at all, except for the seventy-five hundred dollars and a lease on the copier, until 1982," Tate recalls. "We thought it would be the worst thing to have too much money at the wrong time."

Eventually, Ashton-Tate's success caught the attention of venture capitalists. By that point, however, the company could afford to play hard to get. In the end, it did not accept any venture capital, but secured a $6-million line of credit from Bankers Trust Company. Since then, revenues have continued to soar, reaching $39.8 million in fiscal 1984—and the company still has $6 million of its bank line available.

Both Tate and his successor, David Cole, credit "bootstrapping" for the company's success. Large doses of venture capital can lead a start-up to become "unfocused and arrogant," says Cole, who became president in 1982. "People forget money's just a tool. For too many companies, it's become a game of 'My-venture-capitalist-is-bigger-than-yours.'"

—JOEL KOTKIN

PART
III

EQUITY FINANCING: GOING PUBLIC

In Part III we look at the equity market to raise money: What are the important considerations in going public? We include stories from those who favor this capital market and those who warn against it.

SHOPPING FOR AN INVESTMENT BANKER

Your company has come a long way in the last few years. So far, in fact, that you may have a cash flow problem. Your commercial banker has gone to what he considers the limit in your line of credit, and you've drawn down all of that money. Now you need a substantial infusion of new money to continue your growth, so you're considering a public offering of your company's securities.

Whether your contemplated offering will be your company's first sale of stock to the public or a subsequent sale, you face a critical decision: choosing an underwriter, an investment banker, to manage the offering. The decision involves a bewildering number of options. There are hundreds of securities underwriters, from the prominent national houses to local two-man firms down the street. You must also consider more than just the offering itself. Other financial requirements of your company in the future should affect your choice of an investment banker.

Which criteria should you use in selecting the investment banker best suited to your company and the offering you want to make? Here are some of the key factors that should be evaluated:

• **Distribution capability.** This simply means the underwriter's ability to sell your stock or, as underwriters say, "to get the deal done." The amount you're seeking in the public market will often be the determining factor. If you want to raise only $1 million or so, the offering can be handled by a small local firm with a single office and a dozen or so retail brokers—that is, brokers who deal with individual investors. Such a firm may be your only choice, in fact, because larger investment bankers usually prefer to handle larger deals.

If you need to generate $5 million or more from your public offering, your best bet may be a regional investment firm—one with retail offices in a number of cities in a particular area of the country.

Beyond the local and regional investment bankers are the national firms. They have the capability to sell your stock without any difficulty. The key question is will *they* be interested in *you?* If your company is in an industry that happens to be glamorous at the moment, your offering may be attractive to one of the national investment houses.

Potential stockholders are an important consideration in evaluating an investment banker's distribution capability. Chances are you'll want to establish a broad stockholder base, either throughout a wide

105

region or nationally. The largest firms have offices coast to coast that will enable you to achieve this objective. If you're considering a local or regional firm, find out about the firm's ability to form a national syndicate of investment bankers to sell your stock. If, however, you want to place your securities mainly with customers and potential customers in the geographic area where you do business, find out how the investment banker rates in your area. Does the firm have a strong identity and a good reputation for service? Ask its clients and other investors; check with your accountant and commercial banker.

• *Market-making capability.* Once your stock is in the public's hands, you'll want to have a ready and orderly market for it. This means that a stockholder wishing to sell shares should be able to find buyers quickly, should have a good idea of the price his shares will command, and should be able to sell lots of at least a few hundred shares without depressing the price. Conversely, a prospective buyer should be able to find a seller easily, and his order shouldn't make the market price jump several points.

To meet these conditions you need at least one securities dealer (and preferably several) who stands ready to buy or sell your company's stock. When your company and its stock have become better known in the financial community, you may find a number of securities dealers making markets in your stock without any solicitation on your part. But until you've achieved that recognition, you'll have to make a concerted effort to line up market-makers for your stock.

The best time to start that effort is when you're selecting an investment banker. He is the logical person to turn to because he should know your company better than any other market-maker. Find out what types of securities the firm's trading department makes a market in. Does the list include young, unseasoned companies like yours, or are the issues traded mostly those of longer-established, better-known companies?

Also, find out how committed the investment firm is to the issues on its list. Has it invested its own capital in those stocks? Talk to some of the companies on the investment banker's OTC list. Does the firm actually carry an inventory in the stock? Some securities firms say they make a market in a stock, when in reality they're in a "workout" situation. If a seller approaches them with, say, 500 shares, the broker will reply, "Give me a few days to find a buyer." That's not market-making in the true sense, because the securities firm has made no investment in and no commitment to the stock.

• *Research capability.* In order for your company's stock to become better known, it's important that your company be the subject of research reports written by qualified financial analysts. Many securities firms prepare research reports, but not all of them cover newly public companies. The larger national firms rarely cover smaller companies, and with good reason: Their reports are so widely circulated and have such an impact that they could drive the price of a stock with a small public "float" right through the roof (or floor, if the report were negative).

Regional and local securities firms are much more likely to prepare reports on emerging companies. Ask prospective underwriters how often they issue reports on client companies. You should expect that a report on your company will be made available soon after your public offering and that follow-up reports will be prepared every six months or so. There should be a strong tie-in between the investment firm's research department and its retail operation. A report is only as good as its distribution. Does the firm have an efficient system for distributing its research reports to its brokers and encouraging them to send the reports to customers and prospects?

Finally, check the credibility of the firm's research and the degree of its independence. To whom does the research director report? Are the analysts free to "call 'em as they see 'em" in writing a report, or does the firm's corporate finance department have the power to dictate what the report says or doesn't say? Naturally, you don't want your company commented upon unfavorably. But you certainly want to know that the firm reporting on you has the credibility that stems, in part, from a research department that is as independent as it is professional.

• *Service beyond initial offering.* In evaluating a prospective investment banker, find out whether the firm has a reputation for maintaining interest in its clients after taking them public. One of the services you should expect from an investment banker after your offering is financial planning.

If your investment banker talks with you regularly, he'll be in a much better position to advise you on how to finance the implementation of growth plans as you formulate them. Your plans may include raising more new money at some point or taking the merger and acquisition route to growth. Check the banker's record for finding suitable mergers and acquisitions for clients. Have the banker verify the number of deals that actually were consummated, and talk with several of the clients involved.

Another future need of your company may be to raise capital through private placement—selling equity or debt securities to insurance companies or other types of institutional investors. Many investment bankers claim they can arrange private placements, but you'll save a lot of time, money, and annoyance if you check a banker's achievements in this area before letting him try to put together a deal for you. Arranging a private placement requires a lot of connections and experience on the investment banker's part. Ask him to document the extent of his firm's expertise in this area.

If your company is going public, your costs are going to be roughly the same regardless of which investment banker you choose. Going public, however, could be the most critical step in your company's growth. Contact at least ten or twelve investment firms; then evaluate, compare, and confirm the differences to find the one best suited to your company's needs.

—FRANK L. BRYANT

WHAT I LEARNED FROM GOING PUBLIC

In 1970, when I took my first company public, the market was falling. We had to sell our stock for less than we'd hoped, and our expenses seemed astronomical. I ended up feeling that I had more people looking over my shoulder than a hot Las Vegas crapshooter does—hundreds of actual and potential shareholders, a couple of dozen investment bankers and analysts, the financial press, and the Securities and Exchange Commission.

On the other hand, going public did great things for the company. It helped us meet our corporate financial and growth objectives quickly. And my top managers, who had acquired stock at 25¢ a share early on, saw the value of their holdings increase more than 3,000 percent.

Should your company go public? Maybe my experience can serve as a guide.

I founded Time Industries Inc., a corrugated box and packaging company, in 1958, largely on borrowed money and my experience in sales management for a couple of large packaging companies.

The company was built with internal earnings and hard work until about 1964 when, with a net worth of about $250,000, we found an opportunity to buy a paper mill for about $5 million. To make the acquisition, we borrowed $3 million from Continental Illinois National Bank and paid for the rest with Time stock, which the paper mill's seller was willing to value at approximately $3 a share.

We began thinking about going public because we believed that selling shares on the open market would reduce our debt so we could obtain further conventional financing for growth. We also wanted to have tradable stock so it could be used for acquisitions. And we hoped to increase the value of management's long-held shares.

In 1968 and 1969, the stock market was rising. It was better for new issues than it's been since. By 1969 we felt the timing was right to go public.

Unfortunately, going public is an amazingly complex process, and you can't go ahead until you've done all the paperwork and obtained SEC approval.

First we had to find an underwriter (an investment banker who would market our stock). We settled on William Blair and Company because Blair had stature in the industry. He also had the ability to provide us with a "firm" (guaranteed) underwriting, rather than a "best efforts" underwriting. That meant that if our stock didn't sell, the underwriter would purchase the remaining shares. And on top of that, the chemistry was right: They were people we trusted completely.

We were attractive to William Blair because of our steadily increasing earnings. We had reached $500,000 a year, and Blair felt our growth could be attributed to skilled top management.

Although I have mixed feelings about my experience of going public, I know that the success we had was largely due to William Blair's expertise.

Working with Blair, we decided to sell 400,000 shares at $12 per share, which was ten times earnings. We filed to go public in mid-1969, but because the SEC was swamped with filings, we didn't get the go-ahead until early 1970. The market had begun declining in the fall of 1969.

Thus we learned another lesson about going public—you can't tell how much money you'll be able to raise almost until the day you raise it. William Blair called us in to tell us the market wouldn't pay more than $8.50 a share for Time Industries.

After a year's work we were going to receive 30 percent less than we had expected. We decided to go ahead, but to reduce the number of shares offered from 400,000 to 200,000. Managers would sell 53,000 of their own shares and the company would sell 147,000 new ones. The principals, including me, would retain about 60 percent of the company.

We went public on February 3, 1970. The experience demonstrated that for a company like ours, going public was a realistic way of reducing debt and making our stock more valuable, though it made me wonder if there weren't some easier way.

The stock sold. Almost all was purchased by individuals on the recommendations of brokers who assisted William Blair in the underwriting.

Time Industries' managers made money, and the company's debt was reduced. The successful stock sale helped us acquire eight other businesses over the next several years.

But there were problems.

A small company in an unexciting industry may find shareholders have a hard time selling their stock even after the firm has gone public. Our stockholders did not have an active market for their shares. Investors tended to think of Time Industries as just another over-the-counter company. A packaging firm is no glamor stock.

The company continued to prosper, but as a *small* publicly held company we had the same SEC reporting requirements and expenses as a *large* publicly held company. We had to prepare elaborate annual and quarterly reports, inform the SEC of important developments in our business, and conduct annual proxy mailings and shareholders' meetings. Moreover, to keep the new stockholders happy, I had to avoid doing anything that would cause even a temporary drop in the stock's price.

In sum, we had regrets about going public when we did. But as I look back at the 1970s, a poor decade for selling stock to the public, I believe that I made the right decision.

About five years after Time Industries went public, an Ireland-based firm named Jefferson Smurfit Group Ltd. acquired the company in two stages for an average of about $10.50 a share. I still sit on their board of directors.

My banker at Continental Illinois National Bank recommended I buy another company, Clark Products, a privately held restaurant and institutional food supplier in Chicago. I bought it with bank financing in 1975, when it had sales of $18.5 million. Its sales have grown to over $75 million today.

What have I been thinking about for the last two years? Taking it public.

I learned a few principles the first time around, however, that I'll pass on to you.

First, be realistic about your objectives. If your objective is to provide financing to acquire other companies, repay outstanding debts, or finance an immediate expansion, I'd suggest you consider other sources of finance first. Almost any other capital source is likely to be easier to deal with than the public market.

But if one of your objectives is to multiply the value of your equity, there is no other way—short of selling your company outright—to do it as well and as quickly as by going public.

Even if that is your objective, you shouldn't try to take an unglamorous company public unless you have earnings of at least $1 million a year. You need that much earnings to be able to sell enough shares to the public to create liquidity and to command a high enough price per share so that your offering won't be dismissed as "junky."

You should also be able to show substantial growth in earnings over the past five years, have top management in which bankers and others consistently demonstrate confidence, and honestly believe that you would buy the stock yourself if you were an investor.

In 1970, I followed some of these guidelines. The next time I go public, I'll follow all of them.

—DONALD J. HINDMAN

BE PREPARED

If you run a company in a quiet, behind-the-scenes industry like packaging or food service, you'll have difficulty attracting either an investment banker to underwrite the issue or investors to buy your shares.

Nonetheless, you can take a number of steps toward going public even if your company isn't sexy enough to sell stock right now. First, discuss the pros and cons with your legal and financial advisers and with business associates who have been through the process.

If you decide that going public is the best way to meet your corporate objectives, you should begin talking to investment bankers right away. Only an investment banker can give you a good idea of how the market is likely to value your firm. And if you begin working with an investment banker soon, you'll be in a position to proceed with the Securities and Exchange Commission filing when the market becomes more receptive.

From now until the market improves, these things should keep you busy:

- Finding an investment banker who will help you prepare and then take your stock to market. Your investment banker will organize a syndicate, including other investment bankers, to market your stock to their clients and others. A company with, say, $1 million to $2 million in earnings should probably look for a medium-size investment banker. You want to be assured of maximum attention. But it's a good idea to look for a "firm" or guaranteed underwriting rather than a "best efforts" underwriting. A "firm" underwriting means the underwriter promises to buy any shares that the public doesn't.
- Hiring legal and accounting counsel familiar with procedures for public offerings.
- Preparing your registration document for filing with the SEC.

All of this costs lots of money. The underwriter's fee, your largest expense, is generally 7 to 10 percent of the total price of the shares.

Legal fees for a multimillion-dollar offering can be $50,000 to $100,000. Accounting fees for a first offering ordinarily range from $35,000 to $75,000. Printing fees run from $35,000 to $100,000. Each

111

state where you will sell your stock will require that you register and pay another fee. These fees could cost you between $15,000 and $50,000.

For an offering of $4 million, going public could cost you $400,000 to $600,000. Add administrative and executive time invested by your own personnel, and you have a rather large expense.

Moreover, after you go public, there are legal, accounting, printing, and postage fees, as well as administrative expenses involved in annual and interim reports you must make to your stockholders and the SEC.

When you think about going public, you are thinking about a complicated, expensive process that can have great financial results but may add hours to your work week and many more responsibilities to your position.

—NEIL L. BERGMAN

TOO PUBLIC TOO SOON?

On Friday, August 13, 1982, Ferrofluidics Corporation, a manufacturer of high-technology products using magnetically controlled liquid, ushered in its second year as public company with a breathtaking surprise for shareholders: a loss of $2.2 million for fiscal 1982, ended June 30. Of course, this was hardly the first time a company had run negative figures in its first public year. The loss at Ferrofluidics, however, was notable not only for its magnitude in relation to sales of $7 million, but also for the extraordinary item that in large part caused it: a one-time write-down of $1.3 million on supposedly sophisticated inventory, much of which the company had purchased for cash a bare eighteen months earlier.

The gush of red ink undoubtedly would have escaped national notoriety had not the company gone public "far more prematurely than we intended," as cofounder and president Ronald Moskowitz admits. Had the company stayed private, the complications of this decision and other problems Ferrofluidics was to experience would not have arisen; there would have been only the board to contend with. To a professional capitalist, the write-down would be considered little more than an unexpectedly high cost of going into business. But now every move had to be taken under the scrutiny of the public eye—a not always well-focused instrument, Moskowitz was to learn. Some 300 calls from institutions, mutual funds, pension-plan holders, and just plain man-in-the-street stockholders flooded Ferrofluidics' Nashua, New Hampshire, switchboard in the two days following the announcement of the loss, each caller demanding to know what had gone wrong.

Similar demands were also coming, more ominously, from the Securities and Exchange Commission and the National Association of Securities Dealers, under whose auspices Ferrofluidics stock was traded over-the-counter (symbol: FERO). The rapidly shrinking stock price reflected the owners' gloomy realization that assets valued at more than $1 million suddenly had been deemed irrecoverably worthless, like so much caviar spoiling in the sun. In August, on volume of 2,370,000 shares—a sixfold increase from the previous month's level—FERO was sliced in half to a bid of $1\frac{5}{8}$, amid rumors that the company was in deep financial trouble. Ordinarily, such rumors might have been squelched by the sponsoring underwriter of the new issue. Unfortunately for Ferrofluidics, precisely one month after its public flotation in July 1981, the underwriter, John Muir & Company, had sunk into voluntary liquidation, leaving fresh-born Ferrofluidics without its primary market maker and financial-community mentor.

Ferrofluidics open-book troubles go back to early 1981, when Moskowitz, as any chief executive officer of a young company must on occasion do, was weighing alternatives for capitalization in order to continue expansion. Until that time, the company had been financed largely through four infusions of venture capital. With its rarefied technology (there are only 300 people in the field in the world, and half of them are at Ferrofluidics, says Moskowitz), it had opened domestic and overseas markets in computer peripherals and other industrial processes.

But twelve-year-old Ferrofluidics was still struggling. Back then it didn't matter. Investors like First National Bank of Boston and TA Associates, also in Boston, were sympathetic about the volatility of start-up situations, and were willing to be patient so long as the company's strategic plan remained intact. The trouble was that, although Moskowitz felt that "going public always was our destiny," Ferrofluidics' strategic plan didn't include a scenario for what happened next.

When the Muir salesman came knocking, Ferrofluidics was working on the state-of-the-art development of a huge computer-controlled silicon crystal–growing furnace that would sell for $500,000. To finance this grand instrument, Moskowitz, the scientist behind the fluid (together with cofounder Ronald E. Rosensweig), had been considering a few typical private sources, including tapping previous investors for yet a fifth round of venture capital. Alternatively, with a balance sheet still unsullied by long-term debt, he might have floated a loan. The last mode to be considered was going public. For one thing, there were losses still ahead, and for another, it would entail considerable expense and diversion at a pivotal stage when the company could least afford the time and money.

Then Ferrofluidics was contacted, out of the blue, as Moskowitz recalls, by new issue–hungry Muir. Public money would come in much more cheaply than a private placement or a loan, Muir argued. Stock dilution would be considerably less, and the underwriting fees would be lower than interest payments. "I said, 'Wait a second, we're not ready to go public,'" says Moskowitz. "But they made us an attractive offer. We weren't totally satisfied with the arrangement—the timing, the price of the stock, the number of shares, and a lot of other things."

The new-issues market was then showing signs of slowing down after its hectic pace of the previous year. Aftermarket prices of growth stocks had peaked and were declining. And while, shortly before, underwriters had been launching new companies at prices well over preliminary estimates, now such open-arm welcomes for initial public offerings were cooling. Moskowitz sensed the chill in the air. But "on balance, the pluses outweighed the minuses," he reasoned. "We fig-

ured, there's a window now, and a window is finite in duration. Who
knows when the next one is going to open? It could be a year, it could be
five." If no less a hotshot firm than Muir, then the country's fifth
leading underwriter (in dollar volume), was sure Ferrofluidics could
successfully make its debut at this juncture despite having no track
record to speak of, why cavil?

Ferrofluidics' board, however, thought otherwise. Moskowitz had to
plead with them to take the public route. Eventually the reluctant
directors gave him the go-ahead. "We didn't *advise* him to do it, but we
acquiesced," recalls Harvey Mallement, a board member from Harvest
Ventures Inc., a New York group that had invested some seed money.
"Going public too soon is fraught with risk," Mallement counseled.
"The public puts tremendous pressures on a company. With the amount
of capital available in the private market, there's really no hurry."
Mallement felt strongly that no company should consider going public
until it has at least $500,000 in earnings—about twice Ferrofluidics'
profits that year.

On July 16, 1981, Ferrofluidics became a public company. The
offering of 2 million new shares (plus another 500,000 from previous
holders), at $2 each, went off without a hitch. After costs and commis-
sions, the company netted $3.6 million—more cash, even, than could be
used at the time. The move cost Ferrofluidics $325,000—more, cer-
tainly, than the expense of a private placement. But if it hadn't gone
public, it would have received less money and given away more of the
company (perhaps twice as much, Moskowitz estimates) through a
private placement.

A born worrier, Moskowitz fretted that when Ferrofluidics began
to report steady earnings, the per-share numbers would be embar-
rassingly low and dissuade new investors. And by coming out through
Muir, with its reputation for obscure offerings, Ferrofluidics might be
considered a rank speculation—an appellation that made Moskowitz,
with his visions of Ferrofluidics becoming a respected international
conglomerate, most uneasy. As far as Moskowitz was concerned, Ferrofluidics already was becoming a blue chip—the chip in question
being the ubiquitous circuit etched on shiny slices of silicon wafers that
make electronic products smart.

Even if he had really wanted to worry, only in his wildest night-
mares could Moskowitz have imagined John Muir going down the
tubes a month later and taking with it a substantial inventory of
Ferrofluidics stock. (And he could have added an epilog: the demise
about three weeks later of another FERO market maker, M. S. Wien &
Company.) But the denouement turned out relatively happy. When
Muir did depart the scene after running afoul of the SEC because of
violations involving new-issue disclosures, FERO stock was the only
Muir issue that closed unchanged that hectic week. A Boston broker,
Fechtor, Detwiler & Company, took in the Muir inventory that threat-
ened to be junked into the open market. Moskowitz ascribes the rest of
the firmness to the Ferrofluidics employees and vendors who, in coming

in contact with the company's operations, wanted a slice of the action. They spoke for half the flotation and would have gone for more. "We didn't even need an underwriter," Moskowitz figures, with only a slight hint of hyperbole. "These people didn't know who John Muir was in the first place, so they could care less."

Sensing that there was bound to be apprehension about Ferrofluidics' impending market entry, Moskowitz had held a locker-room talk and informed his employees that they were going to remain a company oriented to the long term, despite attracting public stockholders who were accustomed to short-term results. "You can watch the newspaper every day to see what the stock price is," he coached, "but *I'm* not. The stock will follow the business in time." Sure enough, as Ferrofluidics' revenues soared (sales were up 60 percent in fiscal 1981), so did its stock. FERO was *Inc.*'s leading stock market gainer for 1981 in a bad year for many high-tech issues, and ran up to 4¼ bid early in 1982, more than doubling its price within eight months of the initial public offering.

And if he kept to his no-peeking pledge, Moskowitz was spared the horror that was to befall the rest of the stockholders after the August announcement. In similar situations, many other public-company CEOs might have deferred or chipped away at the extraordinary loss until the books could absorb it and management wouldn't appear quite so inept. But not Moskowitz. You have to be unswervingly objective, he insisted, just as if you were examining the books to buy the business. "My definition of *right* hasn't changed just because we have a few more shareholders," he declared. "Later on, we can always sell the inventory for more, and they won't get mad at you then."

His director of finance begged him to take the write-down more slowly, and the majority of his board complained that it was an exceptionally aggressive stance. But Moskowitz won out. "I communicate with my stockholders quarterly," he explains, "and I try to tell it as it is. We project ahead a quarter or two with clear visibility, and I had been telling them we expect to have losses all year long, even into next year. We don't try to cover up losses, we spotlight them. In dealing with any group—shareholders, employees, or bankers—there's nothing like candidness. You have a plan, you know where you're going, and you're taking steps to get there. The worst that can happen is somebody will disagree with you." Such disagreement was almost inevitable: On its now open-to-the-public books, the write-down looked like an expensive meal of crow resulting from a poor business decision.

The presumably smug seller of the now worthless hardware was a New England branch of Varian Associates, a Palo Alto, California, electronics company that was marketing a crystal grower of its own. But what couldn't be stated on the balance sheet was the intrinsic value of what else besides the obsolete inventory had been acquired from Varian. This included intangibles such as patents, a noncompete covenant, "low-tech" know-how of furnace assembly, and, most important, workers who could put everything together. "It's not high technology, but is it important! How can you inventory people?" Moskowitz asks. The self-contained team of experienced arc-welders, hardware designers, and other skilled laborers and engineers that came over from Varian helped Ferrofluidics pick up the pace toward production of its silicon crystal–growing system. Now it expects to have several evaluation systems installed by February and to be rolling shortly thereafter. The write-down can be considered to have paid for perhaps two years worth of time in systems development, Moskowitz calculates.

The acquisition of such intangible assets enabled the company to upgrade its technology and unexpectedly leapfrog over itself to a higher plateau in the state-of-the-art of ferrofluid-sealed growing chambers. Not only did it have one elephantine silicon crystal–maker, it now had two. Based on preliminary peeks, customers overwhelmingly preferred the new, fully automated system to a semiautomated one that would have incorporated the manual Varian hardware that was no longer state-of-the-art. Thus, argues Harvest Ventures' Mallement, it was a straightforward, if painful, business decision to scrap the latter. "One of the dangers of premature public offerings," notes Mallement, "is that decisions aren't always understood by the public." The decision was made in August. By accounting standards, the write-down had to be reported as part of the old year even though the fiscal year had closed on June 30. Trash-canning every cent of the obsolete inventory at once was a conservative accounting procedure, insists Mallement, himself a CPA. "I'm not happy with public companies that don't follow conservative practices. We had very little choice. It turned out that Ferrofluidics misjudged the cost of getting into business. That's not an unusual mistake for a small company when it's involved in a new product."

Most stockholders stuck with the company, according to Moskowitz's review of stockholders' names, even to the extent of buying more shares as the stock price plummeted. Despite Muir's forced silence on Wall Street, Ferrofluidics now has an impressive total of twenty market makers, including some major brokerage houses. "Every stockholder has come from brokers pulling in investors pulling in more investors. Not one has come from a corporate finance department. We're an anomaly of the process. It's the way it should work. There's nothing packaged, no one took it out there promoting bullshit. It was really a matter of that we needed some capital, and Muir got it for us." But Moskowitz also acknowledges that there is a cost in being public that is particularly penalizing in the early stages. "It takes more of my time, because ultimately people want to talk to the president of the company. That's what I mean by being premature. If it wasn't a public company, the time would be spent in looking at strategic opportunities or in building markets. In a small, emerging company, those are more critical needs."

Even so, not all was idyllic as a private company, either. Although the SEC wasn't looking on, Moskowitz's initial investors were. Some sat on Ferrofluidics' board. If expectations weren't met, as they weren't in the early years when the company fell badly behind, the investors wanted to know about it. "You could expect them to come visiting," Moskowitz puts it. "In many respects, the reporting requirements were even more rigorous. But the plus side is that they're a finite group. You call in three or four major stockholders, meet with them, and sort things out. And they're not afraid of losses, because that's what venture capital is all about."

There is a cash drain in being public as well, says Moskowitz, who estimates that the yearly costs exceed those of staying private by $100,000. When the quarter closes, there are forty-five days to file a 10-Q form with the SEC, and those financial results are also sent to stockholders and the financial community. At the end of the year, a formal, slick annual report has to be prepared, instead of a typewritten letter from the president, and proxies have to be mailed out for corporate elections. There are attorneys and stock transfer fees and stockholders meetings. And none of the cost includes the half of the director of communications' time that now goes toward responding to stockholders and investment analysts.

Even though the furnace is yet to be proved—and Moskowitz admits that a failure in the field could set the company back again—the company is on to the next project. Ferrofluidics suffers what Moskowitz calls an "antidilemma": It enjoys far more opportunities in the technology of magnetic fluids than it has financial resources to pursue. But twice-shy Moskowitz won't go back to the public well to water the next idea. This time around, he is studying a research and development limited partnership structure, in which a separate body of investors takes the risk. "Any product we're looking at can afford reasonable royalties," says Moskowitz of his high-margin markets. "And the shareholders are happy, because they have more products coming sooner. Besides," he adds, "I don't want to bury the company in red ink as we did last year."

—ROBERT A. MAMIS

WE TRIED A NEW APPROACH TO
DEBT EQUITY FINANCING

A year and a half ago, we needed capital at Texas American. Until our underwriter showed us how we could do better, offering high-yield debt with an equity kicker appeared to be the best approach.

But our underwriter suggested a novel move—one that would keep our debt/equity ratio from rising higher than we wished while minimizing our Securities and Exchange Commission registration cost, cutting our paperwork, permitting investors to buy stock, bonds, or both, and getting the capital into our hands quickly. They showed us how we could make a simultaneous offering of debt and equity without linking the two together.

We wanted to take on long-term debt that could be retired out of future production to finance our continuing gas and oil exploration. If we stayed with the bank, we would have to roll over short-term debt at increasingly higher interest rates.

We talked to five major brokerage firms in our search for the right deal, asking each of them to define our corporation's financial needs and to recommend methods of financing. We liked E. F. Hutton's plan best, although it was eventually revised. Hutton originally suggested offering high-yield bonds with warrants attached, but later concluded that at the time we wanted to make the offering, straight debt would have more appeal in the investment community. Investors were particularly attracted to lower-rated, higher-yielding bonds and were not interested in owning bonds with equity kickers.

Still, we wanted to maintain our ability to borrow in the future, so we didn't want to load up our balance sheet with too much debt. We considered making two separate offerings—one of long-term debt, and another, later offering of common stock. That would have meant two separate filings with the SEC, two separate prospectuses, and almost double the underwriting expenses of a single offering. It seemed like a waste of time and money.

That's when Hutton came up with the simultaneous offering plan. They suggested that we sell $20 million in subordinated debt and $5 million in common stock—separately, but at the same time.

A simultaneous offering sounded like a good bet for us. We would get our money all at once, and we would save on expenses, since much of the accounting, legal, and printing work for one filing can apply to the other as well.

But there are some drawbacks, and our underwriter was quick to point them out. A simultaneous offering requires stable markets for both debenture and common stock financing. If market conditions aren't favorable, there's no point in making a simultaneous offering, because sequential financing can often improve a balance sheet.

Up to the effective date of the offering, either deal could have been withdrawn or postponed. But the market stayed solid, and we decided to go ahead.

After increasing the debt from $20 to $25 million, to take advantage of a good demand, and adding 75,000 shares of stock (from a selling stockholder) to the offering, we made our deal. Hutton asked that we agree to issue an overallotment option of 10 percent of common stock, allowing the underwriter to cover a short position.

The stock, including the overallotment, sold well. The 12 percent debentures went at a small discount, raising the investors' yield to slightly more than the coupon rate, but still better for us than current bank rates.

Overall, we were pleased. There is nothing revolutionary about a simultaneous debt/equity offering, but it's just one more option a quickly growing public company can use to raise capital.

—WILLIAM F. JUDD

EQUITY MADE EASY

Until recently, small companies interested in raising cash through the sale of their own stock were almost always faced with the time-consuming and costly task of registering their offering with the Securities and Exchange Commission.

Recently, however, a new set of SEC rules, called Regulation D, has allowed small firms to enter the equity capital market with significantly less red tape. A company seeking up to $500,000, for example, can now sell stock through a brokerage firm to an unlimited number of investors without having to register the offering. A year ago, no broker would have touched such a deal because commissions on small private offerings weren't permitted.

Regulation D also has important advantages for companies needing more than $500,000 but less than $5 million. They, too, can sell unregistered shares as long as they follow the SEC's special rules on investor qualifications discussed below.

Wall Street professionals still see some obstacles in the practical application of the new rules, but nearly everyone agrees that Regulation D is good news for many companies that previously were shut out of the equity capital markets. The SEC has been receiving hundreds of calls from businesses asking for more details, according to SEC staff attorney Daniel Abdun-Nabi.

Here's how a company seeking capital may benefit from Regulation D:

Up to $500,000

Perhaps the biggest break for small private companies comes from rule changes that apply to securities offerings of less than $500,000. The SEC's commissioners think that some deals are simply too small to warrant Uncle Sam's involvement, so an exemption from federal regulation is allowed. Under previous rules, this advantage used to apply only to stock offerings of $100,000 or less.

The section of Regulation D, called Rule 504, that applies to private offerings in the less-than-$500,000 category permits equity and debt issues, limited partnership interests in oil and gas ventures, and any type of security to be sold without registration to an unlimited

121

number of purchasers. Prior to Rule 504, the number of investors was restricted to one hundred.

One of the most promising features of Rule 504 is that brokerage firms, which previously had no incentive to take part in such deals, are now allowed to charge as high a commission as the market will bear. (Observers expect those fees to be 15 to 20 percent of the offering.) In the belief that broker-dealer involvement provides safeguards for investors, the SEC chose to remove the ban on commissions on small offerings in order to bring the expertise and sales organization of investment bankers and brokerage firms to the aid of small businesspeople.

Yet despite the new opportunity, brokerage firms aren't rushing to underwrite Rule 504 offerings. They cite the economics of handling an issue as small as $500,000 as the principal deterrent. At 15 percent, the commission would be only $75,000, points out Mike Novom, a vice-president of Philips, Appel & Walden, a New York City brokerage firm. Out of this fee would come commissions to salespeople, the firm's overhead, and days or weeks of research time. Thus, few think that large or even medium-size Wall Street firms will hustle after Regulation D deals.

One drawback to Rule 504 is that securities sold under the Regulation D exemption are "restricted" securities. A warning must appear on each stock certificate stating that it was sold without registration and that its resale is limited. Investors must hold restricted securities for two years before selling them again. "People tend to wonder if the company will even be around after two years," comments Seymour Zwickler, an executive vice-president in the Miami office of Rooney, Pace Inc., a Wall Street firm. "So unless the restricted stock offers an outstanding venture situation or an excellent tax shelter, it's difficult to market."

Regulation D or not, any sale of stock must also meet the provisions of the securities laws of the states where potential investors live. Because these rules, known as "blue sky" laws, vary greatly from state to state, a company's attorneys would have to analyze the firm's proposed offering thoroughly before giving the go-ahead for the sale of securities that may draw investors from more than one state.

When Regulation D was first proposed last year, SEC chairman John Shad urged states to model their rules after those of the SEC, thus simplifying small securities offerings to investors across state lines. However, getting states to make the necessary changes won't happen overnight, and many experts expect it to take years.

$500,000 to $5 Million

Once you get over the $500,000 ceiling, a different exemption from SEC registration applies. Regulation D, under separate Rule 505, lets all companies, closely held or public, sell unregistered securities for up to $5 million as long as specified conditions are met. To begin with, as in the under-$500,000 category, shares can't be resold in the first two years. But unlike Rule 504, the number of investors permitted to buy Rule 505 securities is limited to thirty-five, unless some of them can pass a test as "accredited investors."

Who are accredited investors? In essence, they are savvy sophisticates who the SEC figures are able to fend for themselves without the protection provided by registration. Included in the commission's definition of accredited investors are banks, insurance companies, investment companies, pension plans and tax-exempt organizations such as college endowment funds with more than $5 million in assets, directors and officers of the company raising the equity capital, and individuals with net worth of more than $1 million or annual income of at least $200,000 for the last two years and an expectation of at least the same amount in the third.

Under Rule 505, a company can place unregistered securities with an unlimited number of accredited investors, and, as long as the total offering doesn't exceed $5 million during a twelve-month period, with thirty-five nonaccredited investors as well. Investment banker Zwickler believes that the strict definition of the accredited investor is one of the most important features of Regulation D. "The determination of whether an investor qualifies is no longer left to the broker's subjective judgment, so possible legal liability is greatly reduced," he notes.

Because accredited investors are expected to be able to take care of themselves and get investment information through their own research, there are no requirements for prospectuses, financial statements, or annual reports, provided the entire offering is sold to those who are accredited. But if just one of the investors fails the "accredited" test, the issuing company must provide a disclosure document listing financial and corporate information to all its investors.

What happens if, after the entire offering is sold, it turns out that an investor didn't qualify? Rule 505 has an escape clause for this purpose. If the issuing company and its underwriter "reasonably believe" that all investors meet the requirements at the time of the sale, nobody can be held liable for not making a disclosure document available.

—ANDREW C. SAXLEHNER

WHAT I DO IN PRIVATE
IS MY OWN BUSINESS

Going public. In some circles, it is considered the ultimate rite of passage for any company, the entry as a legitimate member in the nation's most exclusive business community. Companies that don't trade on Wall Street—or ones that don't plan to—exist in the dim netherworld of the national business consciousness, undiscussed and unheralded, even dismissed.

In 1986, with the market for initial public offerings as hot as it had been in three years, the pressure to take a company public and cash in for millions was all the more intense. In the first nine months of 1986, more than 400 companies opted to play under Wall Street's glaring lights, netting $12 billion for company owners, investors, and their minions of investment bankers. By now, you've probably read at least one of the accounts of Billy Gates' score with Microsoft Corporation's offering or heard the fantastic story of Home Shopping Network, which jumped from 18 to 42⅔ on its first day of trading. It's unlikely, however, that you've ever heard of Warren Braun or ComSonics Inc., which is precisely the way Braun prefers it.

"The problem is that people mistake Wall Street for business. You end up putting all the focus on impressing the folks in New York with short-term earnings," says Braun, chairman and chief executive officer of a $7-million cable-television equipment and service company in Harrisonburg, Virginia. "A private firm can focus on the more crucial things, like maximizing long-term growth and profits."

These are not just penny-ante companies that are choosing to stay private. Many have respectable sales, healthy profits, and histories of steady growth in attractive industries—just the sort of firms that make investment bankers salivate.

"We're hit up all the time, at conventions mostly, with propositions from investment bankers and business consultants," says Carlton Cadwell, president of Cadwell Laboratories Inc., a medical-electronics firm in Kennewick, Washington. "But I don't need them. To me, it would be like selling my soul. Having investment bankers on my board doesn't turn me on."

It's not hard to figure out why investment bankers swarm around

Cadwell's convention booth. Since its founding late in 1979 by Cadwell and his brother John, a physician and medical researcher, the company has established itself as a world leader in electronic devices that measure various brain functions. With sales now well over $10 million, Cadwell Laboratories has been growing at nearly 40 percent annually and has never had a year without a profit. Staying private, he figures, is the best way to continue the trend.

"The disadvantage to us, if we go public, is that we would no longer be primarily accountable to our customers and our products," says the forty-two-year-old dentist. "You become prisoner to a quick-hit mentality. I'm a long-term-planning kind of person."

Last year, for instance, Cadwell siphoned much of its double-digit profit margins to finance the yearlong development of a revolutionary new machine that evaluates brain functions. Using novel software developed jointly with New York University Medical Center researchers, the Cadwell Spectrum 32 can track brain-wave patterns that aid psychiatrists in diagnosing and monitoring treatments for such disorders as alcoholism and depression. Now, instead of selling his machines only to the nation's 8,000 neurologists, Cadwell has a big, new market: 30,000 psychiatrists.

"The Spectrum 32, I'm convinced, will be our leading revenue producer in a year," Cadwell predicts. "But would they—the stockholders, the investment bankers—have sacrificed much of last year's profit for this? I doubt it. I guess it boils down to the fact that these high-rolling types just aren't my kind of people."

Kenneth George, on the other hand, makes his living off high rollers. Still, as president of Birr, Wilson, a small brokerage and investment-banking firm in San Francisco, George has turned down numerous offers from other investment banks to merge or go public. Instead, he prefers the ambience of a comfortable regional firm that affords him and his 170 brokers the luxury of concentrating on providing quality service to local clients. George watches the public markets for a living, and he shudders at what their relentless need for ever-greater profits would do to his own firm.

"When you get hooked on the numbers, you tend to become mass merchandisers," explains George, whose $35-million firm has been growing 15 percent a year over the past decade. "You tend to stop doing what the client needs and start peddling whatever the company needs, just to keep the stock moving."

George says his decision to stay private is a matter of preference, not principle. But he adds quickly that even some of Wall Street's biggest and most profitable investment-banking firms, such as Goldman, Sachs & Company and Lazard Frères & Company, remain proudly private.

How large is this universe of private companies that are big enough to go public but don't? There's no way to tell exactly, but David Birch, Massachusetts Institute of Technology's small-business expert, estimates that private companies with more than one hundred employees now account for nearly one-fifth of the U.S. economy. By comparison, all public companies account for about twice that amount.

Some of these private firms are actually quite large and well known, like Bechtel Group, the world-class construction and engineering firm, or Ernest and Julio Gallo's wineries, or the Pritzker family's private conglomerate, which includes a law firm and divisions that manufacture everything from aluminum forgers to boxcars.

But by and large, this is a hidden economy, wedged unobtrusively between the boisterous giants whose shares are traded on Wall Street and the small shops, offices, and factories of Main Street—midsize firms such as those you might see on the annual *Inc.* 500 list of America's fastest-growing private companies. Only 17 of last year's 500 companies took advantage of this year's hot market. And in a recent survey, more than half the CEOs responding had little or no interest in even considering going public in the future.

Going public, of course, sometimes is more a matter of necessity than simply the desire to cash out. A start-up in the semiconductor industry, for instance, might require a capital investment as high as $30 million, which would be difficult to raise privately. But most firms find themselves in less capital-intensive industries, and they have found ways to finance their growth without surrendering control, whether from reinvested earnings, bank loans, industrial revenue bonds, or employee stock ownership plans.

At Computer Technology Associates Inc., in Englewood, Colorado, for example, Carmelo Elliott "Tom" Velez has financed the growth of a $36-million computer-engineering firm with retained earnings and a modest $5-million bank line, secured by accounts receivable. And although his government clients have begun to demand more cost sharing for research-and-development projects, Velez is adamant that he won't turn to Wall Street for financing.

"If the Department of Defense wants me to bid on something on Star Wars, it might cost me now, but it's key to my long-term business," Velez explains. "In this business, we can't serve more than one master—and that master is our client. If we have to spend a few dollars to make him happy, I don't want to have to spend my time dealing with investors who want to know why."

Of course, staying private does impose certain constraints and disciplines, particularly on a company that has been growing at a 64 percent compound annual rate since its launch in 1979. It has no huge corporate war chest, nor does it have any of the trappings of corporate grandeur that became *de rigueur* for much smaller companies during the last IPO gold rush of 1983—the speculative real estate purchase, the fleet of company sports cars, the elegantly furnished headquarters decorated with pricey art.

"I keep my expenses totally in line with my growth, and that's it," says Velez, who grew up in New York City's Harlem. "If I need another office, I rent it. If I need furniture, I rent that. I use the money to do what I need to do. I don't see where it helps just to have millions sitting in the bank."

Often, you'll find some of the largest and most successful private firms in industries that Wall Street now considers unattractive, either because margins are too low or there is too much competition from overseas. Consumer electronics, only a generation ago Wall Street's happy hunting ground, now is something of a no-man's-land among public companies. But the privately owned Bose Corporation, headquartered in Framingham, Massachusetts, a worldwide leader in stereo equipment, continues to thrive. Bose's sales have jumped an average of 30 percent annually, last year to $130 million. And founder Amar Bose credits much of his success to his decision to stay clear of the public equity markets.

"We win only by staying on the cutting edge of technology, and that can't be done by just following short-run goals," Bose says. "No one ever won a chess game by betting on each move. Sometimes you have to move backward to get a step forward."

Recently, Bose sank some $13 million into developing the prototype of a new car stereo system, in the hopes of a long-term relationship with General Motors Delco Electronics Corporation division. Although it was clearly a risky proposition, Bose believed that an eventual deal would provide a vital counterbalance to the company's traditional audiophile market.

"It would have been impossible as a public company," Bose says of the GM project. "I certainly would have lost my job." In fact, he's still there—and so is the car stereo line. General Motors started offering Bose's new system as an option on some of its more expensive car lines in 1982, and by 1985, the original $13-million investment had been fully recouped. This year, the General Motors partnership will account for more than 20 percent of Bose's sales.

Nowhere did IPO fever hit harder in 1983 than in California's Silicon Valley, where going public was the way to instant riches and respectability for hundreds of high-technology companies. Over the past few years, the fever has subsided as the industry slumped. And many of the founders and entrepreneurs who had decided to cash out now find themselves tossed aside like so much excess baggage, often by the same investment bankers who had fawned over them and convinced them of the glories of going public.

Jerry Rochte might have suffered the same fate. Back in 1983, his Cavro Scientific Instruments Inc., in Sunnyvale, California, would have been an ideal candidate for an IPO, a $5-million company with sales of precision liquid-handling instruments that had been growing 30 percent annually since 1972. But a year later, a disaster struck. The company's largest customer, Syva Company, a subsidiary of Syntex Corporation, cut its orders drastically, and sales dropped 50 percent.

Rochte envisions what this debacle would have done to a public company. "The demand from shareholders would have been to cut back the business," he figures. "With our sales down by half, the demand would have been to lay off workers or get rid of facilities." But as the CEO of a private company, Rochte's highest priority was not to boost the fading bottom line, but to find new customers. Cutting back key sales and development staff might have improved earnings for a few months, but at the expense of undermining the company's ability to bounce back from the doldrums.

"When you're public, the financial people take over," Rochte says. "You end up focusing on today's numbers as the be-all and end-all. Companies lose their identities; they are simply chips on a board. And you forget that profits aren't everything. Survival is everything."

To survive, Rochte covered his operating losses with $2 million from retained earnings and launched a new sales drive, which soon turned the company around. Today, Syva represents only 10 to 15 percent of total sales, down from 70 percent in 1984, while the number of other clients has increased sixfold. Sales this year are expected to climb to more than $6 million, a 20 percent jump from the predisaster period.

Richte's argument is that the head of a public company inevitably comes to look at his company as merely a financial asset. "You start laying off to make short-range financial goals, and in the process, you destroy the organization. In a private company, you're more apt to have the sense that the organization is an entity with a purpose—an organization of people with compatible skills who make a product and serve the customers. And that purpose is something worth protecting."

Warren Braun knows firsthand what it's like to be part of a financial asset. For fifteen years, Braun worked happily for a Washington, D.C., television broadcaster, rising from engineer to station manager. Then in 1957, the owner retired and sold off his group of stations to the first of a succession of corporate owners. Over the next eight years, Braun worked for four different managements.

"It was terrible," Braun, now sixty-five, recalls. "Wall Street guys come in and load up all the debt. That creates nothing but headaches for the guys doing the work. You don't have any stability on the staff. There's chaos at the top, and it runs through everything the company does."

Frustrated, Braun decided to go out on his own, opening a television consulting business. Slowly, as his client base grew, he saw an opportunity for a service company providing field repair services, system design, and testing for the emerging cable-television industry. He finally incorporated ComSonics in 1972, with a clear sense of what kind of business he wanted to run.

"I felt very strongly about staying private after all that I had seen," Braun says. "I couldn't just talk about it. I had to make it happen." And so every year, Braun has been slowly selling off his interest in ComSonics to company employees, who today own 99.45 percent of the company. In fact, Braun, who calls himself a "CEO without portfolio," is just about the only person in the company without any stock.

"I have a lot of faith in what employees can do if they are treated right and properly motivated," Braun says. "When I worked for other people, I saw colleagues work their buns off and get nothing out of it. I saw Wall Street rape employees. That confounded drive to make money quickly really does nothing for the whole company's performance."

Today, in an industry racked by pervasive merger mongering, privately held ComSonics has developed a reputation for steadiness. The annual employee turnover rate is less than 3 percent, about one-seventh the industry average. And an average 25 percent annual growth has been financed by reinvesting two-thirds of the company's gross profits. In addition, industrial revenue bonds helped finance a factory for manufacturing cable-TV-related products, which now account for roughly one-third of the company revenues.

As for Braun, he's planning to retire soon and walk away with about $1 million in cash, his proceeds from selling his interest in the company. He estimates that had he gone public or sold out to another firm, he might have wound up with two or three times as much.

"I'd be the first to admit I'm not making as much as I could," Braun says. "But I have more than enough to be comfortable. In spiritual and moral return—well, I'd say my satisfaction is simply far greater."

Staying private, however, does not require such a well-restrained passion for making lots of money. In fact, John Oren, president of Eastway Delivery Service Inc., in Houston, sees staying private as the best way to make the most, while still doing things his own way.

"It comes down to money, and when it comes to me, I don't want to have to ask anyone how I get paid," says Oren, who bought the company in 1979, when he was Eastway's general manager. "I pay myself a salary that shareholders would never give me, pay my taxes, and go down the road. Having total control of my life is where I'm at. The company is a reflection of that."

Like the owners of many other private companies, Oren believes that investing in his own company—which has been growing at better than 40 percent for the past six years—simply represents a better financial alternative than putting his money anywhere else. But that might not be true if Wall Street were calling the shots. Oren believes that he couldn't achieve the same quality of growth if he were pressured, as are his publicly owned competitors, to rack up the numbers by buying up other local delivery services willy-nilly—acquisitions that might not be compatible with Eastway's strategy.

There is about Oren the plainspoken, action-oriented aura of the archetypal Texan. So it should come as no surprise that he eschews memos, long meetings, and the other trappings of the publicly held corporation. "We want to be able to move fast," he says. "When I decided to move into Sacramento, we made the decision in a matter of a week. Hell, we make more decisions in the hallways here than most companies make behind closed doors. We like the freedom to make a successful decision, or even an unsuccessful one, without having to explain it to some analyst.

"Just screw those guys on Wall Street."

Mostly, personality and culture separate Wall Street—the analysts, the fund managers, the investment bankers, the New York business press—from the world of private companies. Wall Street cannot deal with the idiosyncrasies that provide the energy for so many entrepreneurial ventures. In its paint-by-number universe, there can be little appreciation for the technological artistry of a Carlton Cadwell or an Amar Bose, the survival instincts of a Jerry Rochte, the altruism of a Warren Braun, or the bite-your-neck egoism of a John Oren. Wall Street tends to see money as the only real commodity; how one generates it is not really important.

"We're not money hungry," explains Cadwell. "We're good at what we do, and we enjoy what we're doing. We feel we're making a big difference in people's lives, and that turns us on.

"I guess this is something those Wall Street guys can't understand," he adds. "Every year, I see them at the neurology convention, and they can't believe we're still in business. They can't believe we can make it without them. They think I'm a fool. Now we don't even talk to them. We just want them to go away."

—JOEL KOTKIN

WHAT I DO IN PUBLIC
ISN'T SO BAD, EITHER

It was one of the hottest months in the hottest year in the history of initial public offerings—June 1983. Tad Witkowicz took Artel Communications Corporation public, and now, three years later, he tells us he'd do it all again. So would Joseph Mooibroek of American Medical Electronics Inc. And Donald Steen of Medical Care International Inc. And Nigel Webb of Damon Biotech Inc.

In fact, so would the overwhelming majority of chief executive officers of the sixty-four companies that made their public debuts in June 1983, according to an *Inc.* survey. As a group, they are as enthusiastic about being public as so many private companies are about remaining private. Do they have complaints? Of course. Headaches? A bunch. What they lack, though, is the self-righteous smugness of some of their still-private peers who are quoted in the preceding chapter.

If putting themselves and their companies "under the thumb of Wall Street" was going to work out badly for any group, it would have been the Class of '83. They went public at a time when the lure of easy cash seemed irresistible, when investors and investment bankers were reaching for fruit not yet ripe. To any young business with a *tech-* or an *-onics* in its name, investors were saying, "Take our money, please."

About 680 companies did take the public's money that year—more businesses than had gone public in any previous year. They raised some $12.5 billion, which was also an annual record until it was surpassed in the fall of 1986. Were they unwise? Have they compromised their entrepreneurial virtue? Sold their souls? Lost their creative edge? Are they sorry now?

Not to hear them tell it. In fact, it's surprising how comfortably most of these companies seem to have accommodated themselves to the Big Three Bugaboos of Public Ownership: the loss of founder control, the financial reporting demands, and the dreaded shareholder pressure for short-term profit performance. "It's all been boringly simple," says Harold S. Schwenk, Jr., cofounder of BGS Systems Inc., in Waltham, Massachusetts. "Maybe the biggest surprise is that there have been no surprises."

Take control, for instance. Not one of the founding CEOs I checked in with complained about losing it. On the contrary, several see going public as a way of keeping control. Gabriel Raviv, president and co-founder of Bio-logic Systems Corporation, in Northbrook, Illinois, says he had a choice: He could either sell some portion of the company to venture capitalists, or he could take it public. He went public, he said, in order to distribute control "among many small shareholders, not one or two strong individuals."

That was much the same explanation I got from Tad Witkowicz, who desperately wanted to keep Artel from the clutches of "vulture capitalists," with their well-deserved reputation for dictating company policies and tossing aside company founders when the going gets a little rough. Unfortunately, since we talked, things have not worked out so well for Witkowicz. In September, his board of directors removed him as president and chairman. Although Witkowicz won't comment on the change, his experience proves the general point that there is always a risk of giving up control when you turn to somebody else for capital, whether the company is public or private.

Another common fear about going public concerns the reporting requirements. Not a single one of the CEOs I contacted complained—or not much, anyway—about providing financial information to stock-holders and the Securities and Exchange Commission. "Filing reports," says Joseph Mooibroek, president of American Medical Electronics Inc., in Dallas, "isn't really a big deal. The 10-K is a major event, but it only comes up once a year."

Some, in fact, see the reporting requirements as a plus. "Our numbers are out there," Bio-logic's Raviv says, "which means our customers feel better about doing business with us. There's nothing we can hide. I think it helped us with the bank when we went for an industrial revenue bond to build our headquarters." And Nigel Webb, vice-chairman of Damon Biotech, in Needham Heights, Massachusetts, argues that having the company's financial results talked about in analysts' reports and the financial press gives it higher visibility in its industry and therefore higher credibility—"even though it's just a perception thing."

Short-term performance pressure *is* an issue. "There is far too much pressure to pay attention to quarterly results," Witkowicz complained to me before his ouster. But most CEOs I talked to said that Wall Street analysts can only put pressure on a CEO; they can't dictate decisions. Raviv says he has followed his game plan without pressure. "We always low-ball our numbers to analysts," he says, "and we tell them we're going to have hiccups, but we don't know when. . . . There may be some pressure to do short-term things, but we've managed to stay out of that."

Granted, it might be a bit awkward for the president of a public company to criticize his stockholders or the analysts who help set the price for his stock. But I take on face value the assertion of CEOs such as Donald Steen of Medical Care International Inc., in Dallas, when he says, "We're not letting our being public influence the way we run the company."

So, yes, being public has its costs. But there are costs associated with getting a loan, too, whether it's from the bank or from Uncle Harry. Both will want to know what you intend to do with the money. Both will want progress reports. And both are going to charge you interest. The difference is that the bank is just a bank, but Uncle Harry is your mother's brother.

The bank or Uncle Harry? Public or private? City mouse or country mouse? We're talking lifestyles here, not moral choices. But in the debate as it is cast by the cheerleaders of privatization, the two kinds of issues get confused.

Privately held companies are not, as Warren Braun, of ComSonics Inc., seems to suggest, any better equipped nor any more likely than publicly held companies to be generous to employees. Braun has transferred ComSonics stock to his workers, but he could have done the same had the company been public. In fact, if ComSonics were public, employees could turn their stock into cash at the market price anytime they want. In a private firm, they don't have that option.

Besides, the vast majority of private-company founders do *not* share equity with their employees and wouldn't dream of it. Their attitude is much more likely to resemble John Oren's—it's *my* company and *my* money (Oren, you will recall, is the Texan who is president of Eastway Delivery Services Inc.). It's small *public* companies that are more likely to use stock and stock options to attract and reward employees. For them, sharing equity is not an ethical issue of choosing generosity over greed. It's a business issue: What's the best way to motivate employees?

I suppose it's true that many entrepreneurs don't trust Wall Street lawyers, consultants, and investment bankers. So what? I don't trust people who sell insurance or cars, but I do business with both. Entrepreneurs *shouldn't* trust investment bankers, but that's no reason not to buy their goods if their goods are what your business needs. "I needed money in 1983," says Lewis G. Zirkle, founder of Key Tronic Corporation, based in Spokane, Washington, "and with the market the way it was, going public was the easiest way to get it."

Don't get me wrong. The market is also one of the easiest and quickest ways for founders of growing companies to get filthy rich. For example, consider the case of Calton Inc., a member of the Class of '83 *and* the Class of '86.

Calton, a residential real estate development company, headquartered in Freehold, New Jersey, was part of a larger company until Anthony J. Caldarone and some of Calton's current officers bought it in a leveraged deal for $13.6 million in 1981. They put up just $90,000 in cash. Two years later during the hot IPO market, they took Calton public. Then in 1984, Caldarone and his partners sold most of their Calton stock to another developer for $8.3 million, but stayed on to manage the company. Caldarone took home $407,000 in compensation and profit-sharing during the following year, but he found he missed owning his own business. So in 1985, he and his partners did another leveraged buyout, then took Calton public again in 1986 while retaining 53 percent of the stock for themselves. Thus, in the space of five years, Caldarone and his partners have converted their $90,000 investment into at least $15 million in cash and $68 million in Calton stock.

The Calton story is a pretty good indication that greed thrives on both sides of the public-private divide. The same might be said for egotism and lavish spending. The Transamerica pyramid in San Francisco and AT&T's new Manhattan skyscraper are just bigger than the tasteless monuments that countless smaller-company entrepreneurs build to their own expanding vanities. Perhaps an extreme example is Edward Baker, whose Vanguard Groups International Inc., in Houston, was listed for three years on the *Inc.* 500. Baker was apparently so busy overseeing such matters as construction of a new headquarters building with a black marble bathroom for his personal use that he didn't even see that his company was sliding into Chapter 11.

Let's be honest: When it comes to lavish spending and converting company assets to personal use, owners of private companies take second place to no one. Gather a few together where they can brag candidly, and you'll hear some surprising stories of what's really behind some of the business expenses they claim on Internal Revenue Service forms. Home computers, cars, airplanes, vacations, lakeside cabins—it's all very creative.

Public-company CEOs can, and do, pull the same tricks, but they've got more people watching them—directors, investors, and the SEC. The chief financial officer of a just-gone-public company told me once that his biggest problem was getting the founding CEO to understand that it wasn't "his" money anymore. Terry Jacobs, founder of Jacor Communications Corporation, a growing media holding company based in Cincinnati, finds that he can sometimes increase a newly acquired radio station's profitability in the first year of ownership simply by not running the previous owner's boats and cars through the company books. That leaves him more money for, among other things, employee bonuses.

Of all the arguments for staying private, the least convincing is that the decision making is easier—or better. In the preceding chapter, John Oren says remaining private gives him the freedom "to make a successful decision, or even an unsuccessful one, without having to explain it to some analyst." He makes more decisions in the halls, he says, than most companies do behind closed doors. That's nice. But the reason the plainspoken, action-oriented Texan can practice his cowboy-style management has nothing to do with being private or public. He can do it because he's running a $9-million company with just a few hundred employees. Let him try making all his decisions in the hallway when Eastway Delivery Service is a $100-million company with several thousand employees.

That probably won't ever become an issue for Oren because, by choosing to stay private, Oren has probably decided that he really doesn't want his company to be that large. That's not a put-down. It's an assessment based on Oren's own self-proclaimed priorities: a desire for direct, as opposed to delegated, control; an aversion to notoriety and the discomforts of the financial fast lane; a predilection for privacy in personal affairs; a fascination with the quality of growth rather than its pace. These are the sort of issues that impel some founders to keep their companies private. But that's a matter of preference, not propriety.

—TOM RICHMAN

PART
IV

Financing Alternatives

In the summer of 1983, the CEO of a growing retail chain and his treasurer set out to do something that they'd been discussing for months—they began to search for long-term investors who would put up $2 million in equity under strict conditions. In order to finance the thirteen new stores they planned to open in the coming four years, they needed a cash infusion. But they were wary. "We didn't want anybody to interfere with the way we ran the business," reflected the CEO. "We wanted to grow at the rate we deemed reasonable."

Sound familiar? It's the customary rite of passage for growing companies—the debate on growth versus control. In Part IV of this volume, we look at some new and different methods of finding capital that can bring growing companies the money they need for expansion without always forcing them to trade off control to outsiders.

In "Equity Without Tears," you will see the retailers mentioned above getting the financing they needed—on the terms they wanted—from an unusual investment firm interested in investing in promising U.S. companies while maintaining distance. The money came from a group of British banks.

Banks, however, are only one source of capital. In "New Money," *Inc.* investigates a network of venture capitalists who roam about the country looking for people and projects in which to invest their money and their expertise. Unlike traditional venture capitalists, this new breed of investors, whom we dub "adventure" capitalists, are ex-entrepreneurs themselves. They seek to develop companies not only with infusions of capital, but with their hard-earned lessons and technical know-how as well. With the use of calls on stock, many new entrepreneurs find they can regain control of their companies once they are off the ground.

137

G. Albert Bourgeois is an investment banker who set up shop in Exeter, New Hampshire, even though he'd spent some time in Wall Street and had a Stanford MBA. He had also structured hefty deals in Japan and worked for a time in San Francisco placing hundreds of millions of dollars in computer leases with financial institutions. Bourgeois is a skilled deal-maker. In "A Rare Case of Bourgeois Values," *Inc.* profiles Bourgeois Fils, the company he set up to help businesses—and the people who run them.

Shopping around for capital involves a bit more than a quick trip to the bank. Among other options, entrepreneurs can borrow long-term money abroad ("Limiting Liabilities") or raise capital from a corporate partner instead of a bank or venture capitalist ("Big Deal" and "Strategic Alliances").

The final four articles in this section consider licensing, zero coupon bonds, asset-based loans, and factoring.

Financing growth is a creative endeavor. In this collection of *Inc.* articles, we attempt to illustrate a range of possibilities for finding capital and introduce entrepreneurs to some new alternatives.

NEW MONEY

Like every aspiring merchant, David H. Chung had an idea. Not only did he think his telecommunications box was very clever and worth presenting to the world, but, since it stood to save big companies large amounts of money in data transmissions, he was confident it could be very profitable as well. The only problem, as usual, was that he needed money to develop it. So Chung cast about in the plentiful pools of capital that had been gathering in California's Silicon Valley over the past several years, but he had little luck. For one thing, the venture community didn't warm to him: He hadn't even bothered to draft a business plan. And Chung didn't take to them, either. They wanted too large a share of the business.

Even 450 miles from the border, that is what is called a Mexican standoff, and it might have gone unresolved were it not for the arrival of Charles Ying, erstwhile part owner of Atex Inc., a text-processing computer systems business whose sale a few years back had left him with a good deal of cash to spend.

Ying, thirty-seven, was retired. But he was no ordinary retiree. Instead of lying on the beach or hanging out at the country club, he spent most of his time trekking about the country in search of investment opportunities. An engineer with a degree from Massachusetts Institute of Technology, he was looking for people with ideas that he felt could someday develop into technologically sound and sellable products. When he found one, he intended to play an active role in giving shape to the operation and bringing the product to market.

Chung was just the sort of person Ying was interested in, and he listened closely as the young semiconductor engineer explained his concept for an artificial-intelligence machine that squeezed redundancy out of data transmissions. As a result, said Chung, computers would be able to talk to one another over cables more than twice as fast as was currently possible. Such a device would be worth millions to any large company that rented expensive phone lines to handle data flow—provided Chung could come up with the product. "I need money to develop the thing," Chung told Ying, "only I don't want to give up half the company to raise it."

Ying couldn't fathom the tortuous learning algorithms Chung was demonstrating, it just didn't seem likely that the program could really

139

do all that he said it could. But this is often the case with technological breakthroughs, and such was the nature of Ying's quest: to discover a person with an idea that would bewilder ordinary venture capitalists. Ying decided it was worth the gamble. He told Chung he could have enough capital to construct a working model. Then, if Chung produced it by an agreed-on date, "I'll give you money to do some manufacturing with and get into business."

As it happened, Ying had used just such a pay-as-you-go financing technique to keep Atex afloat in its lean years, a decade earlier. He, too, had tried to peddle a complex notion without the benefit of a prototype or the rudiments of a business projection—and he, too, had had doors slammed in his face. Chung had an additional problem, moreover. He possessed "a personality that would not attract venture capital," says Ying. "If there was a venture capital checklist of reasons to reject a deal, David would be checked off on every entry."

To Ying, none of that mattered. He didn't even ask for the standard reassurances that usually go with obtaining seed-level capital. It was a bold, swashbuckling, risk-taking plunge into an amorphous business situation and an undefined market—a gamble for which *venture* is too tame a term.

Adventure is more like it. And Ying is not its lone practitioner. Indeed, quite a few well-heeled retirees have been taking up the sport lately. "Every successful engineer I've talked to—I mean those who intellectually know they don't have to work—is putting his money at risk to make a living," says Ying, who already holds cards in half a dozen hot high-tech hands and flies around the country scouting out investments. By "putting money at risk," Ying doesn't mean the Nolan Bushnell approach of bringing small businesses to a climate-controlled greenhouse where they can be watched over like fragile seedlings. Rather, he and his fellow adventurers actually get out among the rocks and clear the fields. Why? "Probably because that's the only thing we know how to do."

These are not, however, members of some dismissable, rag-tag band. Indeed, they include retirees, resignees, and executives still at work in some of the country's most successful high-tech enterprises. Many have already endured the same slow-moving, mistake-ridden ordeal that rough-hewn entrepreneurs like Chung expect to undergo—but may be spared, thanks to this high-rolling crew. With the confidence born of hard-knocks experience, "working" financiers like Ying are beginning to beat laid-back venture capitalists and investment bankers at their own game. They are able to deliver the goods precisely at the critical point where the old school is stretched thin—that is, they can supply both business and technological acumen in a hurry.

Once, of course, venture capitalists did supply that expertise, and new businesses welcomed it, but lately some entrepreneurs have grown cautious. "Venture capitalists sometimes are meddlers," says Federico Faggin, a physicist who left Intel Corporation ten years ago to start up Zilog Inc. with some $500,000 in venture money, then sold it to Exxon Corporation, and in 1982, founded Cygnet Technologies Inc. "If you have trouble, you should be allowed to get yourself out of trouble. But some venture capitalists want to 'help.' They get irrational and want to run the show." With dozens of companies in their portfolios, moreover, venture capital firms simply cannot know the particulars of each company very well. Their concern is natural enough, given the sums at stake, but it is often so misdirected, says Faggin, that "many companies go out of business merely because venture capitalists can't keep their hands off them." Moveover, the venture capital firms can *afford* to lose a few: Traditional venture capital has always assumed that enough investments will pay off to balance the inevitable failures.

Not so with adventurists: They expect to make *every* project a success, and not by vast infusions of capital, either. Many a start-up has taken in unneeded capital simply to get a big-name venture capitalist on its board, ostensibly tapping him for guidance, influence, and prestige. Ying operates the other way around, parceling out funds only when they are called for. The result is that businesses like David Chung's Chung Telecommunications Inc. (CTI) can be coaxed from soil that conventional capital would consider untillable.

And—with Ying's support—Chung did, in fact, produce a convincing prototype of his sophisticated machine. At that point, he was in the enviable position of possessing a product many people needed but no one could duplicate. Ying advised Chung to take the model to large businesses with communications networks, then, once they started salivating, he should get them to pay in advance for the product. If that didn't do the trick, Ying confidently pledged, "*I'll* write your business plan."

In effect, Ying already had such a business plan, the same one he had followed ten years earlier, when he, his brother Richard, and a third partner, Douglas Drane, founded Atex. Like CTI, Atex had been avoided by venture capital. Yet in 1981, Atex Corporation was shipping $53 million worth of editing systems. That October, the founders sold it to Eastman Kodak Company for some $75 million in stock—and, more remarkably, retained 80 percent of the company.

"We had heard the stories about how there were long directories of willing venture capitalists, but suddenly they weren't there," Ying recalls. "It was the winter of 1973–74, and we were told that, in the last twelve months, there had been only two private deals—and they were both second round. We didn't know what we were doing, which is probably why no venture capitalist ever called, but we had good *ideas*. Richard and I were experienced in minicomputers, and Doug had been selling systems. We told them, 'We have the technical and the marketing [know-how], so what more do you want?' They were probably just being polite by telling us it was hard times. I know why—now. I'm in that same position today, but once we, too, were just a couple of engineers and a salesman getting together without a product." These days, Ying admits, even he sometimes has to rein in aspiring founders shorter than they would like. "Look," he tells them, "you have no track record."

That was something they couldn't learn in school, as Ying himself knew from his own salad days. He had come to the United States from Hong Kong, having applied blindly to MIT, a college he had found listed in a catalog and applied to because it waived the application fee for foreigners. "MIT tried not to teach you about the real world. My kids would tease me, 'You went to MIT, and you don't know how to fix a TV?' And the *last* thing [MIT taught] was anything to do with practical business. They didn't tell us that [you need more than] a good product to be successful in business." Nevertheless, Ying made up for that academic oversight and went on to become one of MIT's more respectable graduates: Using only the interest on the interest on the interest of the Atex cash-out, he can afford to sent his TV *out* for repairs.

As ill-prepared as they were, the three Atex partners tried mightily to get outside financing, but—in the end—they had to make do with capitalization of a mere $2,500, curried from the founders' savings. Leading a hand-to-mouth existence, they figured out from day to day how to run a business on thin air. "We were too busy to ask for any advice," Ying remembers. Nevertheless, they quickly had to learn a new vocabulary, the pivotal word of which was *cash*. "What we relied on was a bank line. We always had a line of credit at the bank. That's just sound management." Because Atex "never operated with much of a cash balance," Ying was forced to plan for the worst. "What happens if sales suddenly drop? What happens if our software development is behind schedule and our customers stop paying us? How much of a cash cushion do we need?" As Atex grew, its cash needs got bigger. Ying aimed at having a month's worth of cash available just in case none came in. "The last thing you want to do is run out of cash," Ying instructs his current charges, "because that's when you lose the company. Ask Adam Osborne."

In building Atex's cash reserves, Ying had used the same tactic he later urged on David Chung: He got it from would-be customers. His own product had been a multiterminal text-editing system for editors and writers that, Ying promised, could instantaneously set pages in type. His first customer was *U.S. News & World Report*. The magazine was about to phase out of an old-fashioned typesetting operation, so Atex seemed to have come along just in time. Well, almost: The trouble was that, like CTI, Atex had nothing concrete to show. To help speed its arrival, *U.S. News* sent a check a couple of days before Thanksgiving 1973. But there was a catch. In order to get further payment, Atex was obliged to demonstrate a working prototype by the first week in January.

"It's so impossible to do," industry observer John Seybold consoled Ying at the time, "that if you pull it off, the rest of the financing will be a snap." On New Year's Day, Ying announced to his partners, "It's working!" Not even Archimedes uttered "Eureka!" more passionately.

Indeed, that type of seat-of-the-pants adventure might be called Ying's Principle. Following it, Chung got customers to finance his company's early growth. CTI's first products are now on the market, and the pleased founder has given up only a fraction of his company. "He built the box," says Ying, "and it's selling. I think he's going to

make a significant impact on the whole field of telecommunications."
And to this day, Ying hasn't had to help him write the promised
business plan that his new associate, David Chung, had disdained.

If Chung Telecommunications does make it, its success will be a
tribute not only to Chung and Ying, but to Richard Black as well.
Black is the former chairman and chief executive officer of AM International Inc. More to the point, he is part of "the Network," as Ying refers
to the word-of-mouth buddy system of investors who occasionally take
adventure-capital fliers and who help each other out when a flight is
struggling to gain altitude. Ying considers Black a kindred spirit: "He
doesn't have to work. He's running all over the country starting companies. He's basically doing the same thing as I am."

At the time Ying discovered CTI, Black was already involved in six
start-ups. Ying offered to share his discovery in exchange for Black's
special expertise. Using his contacts with banks and other large companies that could most benefit from Chung's technology, Black helped
to formulate CTI's marketing strategy. "The Network is alive and
well," Ying happily concludes.

Indeed, it is alive and well. Black himself is now on the board of
another Ying-assisted company, Verticom Inc. Ying and his brother,
meanwhile, have also started an investment company that has been
licensed by the Small Business Administration as a minority enterprise small-business investment corporation in Seattle.

So it goes. And if these capitalist-retirees hit the jackpot with the
businesses they are now seeding, *those* companies will spin off yet more
capitalist-retirees. Although barely begun, this spirited breeder reaction eventually could have enormous significance, not only for capital
investment, but for the economy as a whole.

All the more so, since there are indications that the adventuring
spirit is spilling over into low-tech and no-tech arenas. Consider
Michael Berolzheimer, who cashed in some chips and set up a program
for raising consumer-oriented businesses. In this case, the chips were
not silicon; they were wood chips that Berolzheimer salvaged from saw
mills and packaged into fireplace logs. The company he founded, Du-
raflame Inc., was started with about $35,000 of his own money, and was
acquired by a subsidiary of the Clorox Company in 1978 for more than
$9 million.

Berolzheimer found that the traditional venture capitalists "had
no personal experience with market-driven operations, so we decided to
do it ourselves." He and an associate gathered a $12.75-million capital
pool called The Early Stages Company, digging out businesses that
ordinary venture capital ignored, among them a shampoo maker in
Boston and a packager of snack foods in San Francisco. Like Ying,
Berolzheimer rolls up his sleeves alongside each entrepreneur. "I love
to work with these guys and help them avoid the mistakes I made." He
is already committed to half a dozen start-ups.

Robert McCray also struck out in a nontechnology direction after
cashing out of the value and control devices manufacturing business he

founded. With his new fortune, he decided to invest broadly, rather than launch a second company of his own, as is a current Valley vogue. "But I want to be part of the management of the companies," he insists, "not just a silent partner." In five years, he has fired up five companies. He got involved in one venture when his neighbor joined him on an evening stroll and announced, "I want to start my own business, and I understand you're the person to talk to." McCray put in $30,000. Today the company—a photocopier distributor called Offtech Inc.—employs more than sixty people. Departing again from venture tradition, Mc-Cray granted the founder a call on his stock, which was exercised.

By standing shoulder-to-shoulder with founders, as it were—rather than communicating sporadically from a distance—the adventure capitalists hope to spare greenhorn businesspeople-engineers even the slightest false start. For the most part, they are engineers themselves and they appreciate and tolerate, for better or worse, an engineer's singular sensibilities.

"Everybody makes mistakes," says Ying. "You don't run a business without making mistakes. But engineers have a disadvantage, because they tend to be too logical. To them, everything has to have a reason, but a lot of times in business, there is no reason—half is luck, half is common sense. There are definitely instincts you need to succeed in business that are different from those you need to succeed in engineering. But I've found that anybody can adapt to them." Harking back to his own pre-Atex roots, Ying genuinely feels that "these people that I come across deserve a break. It's good for everybody. Nobody loses. First, the entrepreneurs win, then if they succeed, I win—and the U.S. is maybe a little bit closer to Japan. That's why I'm doing what I'm doing, instead of sitting on a beach in Maui."

The same empathy can be an invaluable asset in dealing with delicate situations that involve investing in people and ideas. Ying and some associates recently made such a "person" investment in a twenty-seven-year-old engineer named Steven Kirsch.

After earning his master's degree from MIT a few years ago, Kirsch decided to go west. So he hopped a plane, crossed the continent, and, landing in the Valley, set out to fulfill his self-appointed mission: not to build a better mousetrap, but a better "mouse." The mouse in question, invented by Kirsch at age twenty-four, is a palm-size LED-equipped device that when moved around on a pad, "reads" a grid and correspondingly directs a microcomputer's cursor on the video display.

Kirsch's mouse was a very sharp animal, but Kirsch himself was an unfocused sort who could test the patience of an investment banker faster than four straight losing quarters. When it came time to raise working capital, Kirsch had only the barest bones of a business plan to pass around. If he had management skills, they weren't evident in the rudimentary mouse-making operation he was running out of his apartment. Nor did he understand the protocol of the search for capital. When a well-meaning friend advised him to trade in his 1972

Buick for something a little more presentable, Kirsch asked if that meant a 1973.

To sponsor Kirsch under such dubious conditions required a vision that could see well beyond the inchoate picture he presented to the ordinary world. His promise was not as a tactical businessman, but as a brilliant inventor whose social clumsiness could be overlooked and whose ideas could be harnessed. Were there not investors around willing to take such uninsured risks, Kirsch's clever seeing-eye mouse might have died aborning.

But, fortunately, there were such investors around, and Kirsch's Mouse Systems Corporation did get an early round of working capital—from an elite pack of twenty or so highly liquid Silicon Valley entrepreneurs who call themselves Summerhill Partners. The group has counterparts in other regions, notably New England, where some sixty-five executives from high-tech companies have pooled their pocket money into a venture fund managed by Eastech Management Company. Summerhill, however, is not so much a fund as a loosely organized "club" whose members meet monthly to review possibilities. The group was organized by Thomas Whitney, a former electronics engineer who cashed in an Apple Computer Inc. vice-presidency to devote full time to venture capital activities.

Ying is one of Summerhill's most active members and ardent advocates. "Everybody [in Summerhill] is 'busily' retired" says Ying, who has observed such capital klatches from coast to coast. "I haven't seen anything like it before." Besides Ying, the group includes such Valley denizens as ex–Apple Computer vice-president John Couch; Manny Fernandez, founder of Gavilan Computer Corporation; and L. William Krause, president of 3Com Corporation.

This roster is all the more impressive in view of founder Whitney's concern that "when we do find the situation, we try to have one or two of the partners take a very active role in the company." Any proposal that comes before the club is closely examined by partners proficient in the field; if it passes muster, it may then be recommended to the rest. Assuming the rest are receptive, the club performs its own due-diligence search and takes an equity position.

In making investments, Summerhill members also provide a "service" to stockholders of private companies, who, under Securities and Exchange Commission rules, often find themselves locked into positions, unable to sell their stock. The club will often absorb the block for an agreed-on amount. One of 3Com's founders, for example, was able to sell private stock in this manner last year, well before the company registered for a public offering. Of course, Summerhill doesn't provide this service out of pure magnanimity: Its coffers stand to swell substantially when the companies go public.

It was through Summerhill that Ying first met Kirsch. Like most Summerhill candidates, Kirsch had found the group by word of mouth, having been steered to a monthly meeting by the founder of a high-tech company with whom he had interviewed for a job. Before appearing,

"Kirsch had bounced around the Valley a bit trying to raise money," remembers Whitney, "and had been laughed off as a young kid with a little bit of nerve and possibly some design talents, but who had a long way to go to make a company."

The Summerhill adventurers, of course, did not read him that way. He made his Mouse presentation and, says Ying, "he was bright, bright, bright! The director of corporate engineering for Hewlett-Packard was there and listened to him. He said, 'This guy could be another Steve Jobs; he has the raw talent. This may not be the right *product,* but let's bet on the *guy.*'"

And bet they did. All told, Summerhill came up with $300,000 for Kirsch—$50,000 from the partnership itself, and $250,000 from individuals, who are allowed to participate on their own behalf as well. Having invested the money, the group then weighed in with expertise.

"We felt that as good as Steve Kirsch was as an engineer and idea generator and inventor," says Whitney, "he did not have the talent to grow a company into the size that we had in mind. . . . He needed someone to learn from." Summerhill placed three of its members on the Mouse board, which—Ying recalls to his dismay—had previously "consisted of nobody." As part of the package, Kirsch agreed to let an executive officer take over. Summerhill recruited a general manager of Zilog, who was soon at work hiring a management team. At the same time, the Summerhill members of Kirsch's board helped him negotiate a mouse deal with nearby VisiCorp. Not surprisingly, Mouse Systems showed a profit in its first year of operations.

"We found a diamond in the rough," Ying reflects. That diamond was very rough indeed: Not only did Kirsch lack a board of directors and formal business plan, "he had no financial projections, he had no idea how many units he was going to ship the next month, and he barely knew his costs. Yet he was already busily working on a next-generation product. Those were the symptoms that would scare a venture guy to the moon."

For Ying and his buddies, however, it was just another adventure.

—ROBERT A. MAMIS

A RARE CASE OF BOURGEOIS VALUES

One cold, wet Saturday morning in March 1982, three aspiring entrepreneurs from Arizona arrived at an early-nineteenth-century wooden house in Exeter, New Hampshire, for an 8 o'clock meeting with a man they had never met. Neither Mike Koether nor his two partners—his brother Bob and Joe Zavislak—knew what to expect from their weekend journey. Koether hoped they could return to Phoenix on Monday with an innovative blueprint for financing their new equipment-distribution business.

But the lengthy conversations that day and the next seemed to resolve very little. There was hardly any discussion of money matters. Instead, as heavy rains pelted the house, Koether and his partners were urged to reflect on their personal and business strengths and weaknesses, their values, and the financial and nonfinancial motivations for wanting to start a business. Even when the talk shifted more directly to the equipment-leasing venture itself, they were asked to describe the basic concepts and factors they felt would make the business work rather than to focus on more explicit facts and figures. "We were there for two days and it was awfully hard to tell what was going on or if anything would come of it," recalls Koether. "We knew we were being tested."

The scrutiny Koether and his associates received wouldn't have been the least bit surprising if they had been soliciting money from a venture capitalist in exchange for equity in their business. But, although they were in desperate need of money, they had no interest whatsoever in giving up ownership or control of the business they were founding.

Mike Koether, who had spent fifteen years selling copiers for Xerox Corporation, and a team of four other ex-Xerox marketing specialists were planning to sink a total of $150,000 of their own money into a new office-copier dealership that would sell Japanese-made Ricoh machines in a market dominated by Xerox, IBM, and Eastman Kodak. It would be difficult to succeed, because of the established and well-financed competition. To have any hope of competing for the most lucrative leasing and rental customers, Koether, who is now thirty-nine, and his partners knew they would need more money than they had and a lot more than banks seemed likely to provide. In the early years, the financing requirements for the leases and rentals would

147

expand with the growth of the business. Yet the business would also need to invest substantial amounts of both money and management time in building a quality sales and service organization so it could begin carving out its place in the market.

Although he had been a successful marketing man at Xerox, Koether's early encounters with bankers on behalf of his new business raised substantial doubts in his mind that adequate financing could be found. "I was pretty bad at articulating how the business would work and what our financial needs would be," he admits. "But even if I had explained things better, it seemed pretty clear that we weren't the kind of new customer the banks were looking for. We didn't have enough equity to justify the money we would need."

Koether's problem wasn't atypical for a new equipment distributor short of equity. One unappealing option Koether knew of was to sell his leases to a third-party leasing company and minimize bank borrowings by staying out of the rental business. But before he even began to pursue such a solution, he learned of an intriguing start-up strategy that seemed to require very few compromises. It was an aggressive financial battle plan that had already enabled an East Coast Ricoh dealer to launch his business with ample capital and to compete broadly against its big-gun competitors.

Relying on an unusual approach, the Eastern dealer had been able to achieve a presence in the leasing and rental business during its first year that might otherwise have taken several years. In effect, the dealer's leases and rentals were treated as two distinct businesses, with different methods of financing then selected for each. The plan had been designed by a New Hampshire investment banking firm that Koether hadn't heard of before, Bourgeois Fils & Company.

While the whole dealership functioned as a single entity under a holding company Bourgeois Fils (pronounced BOOR-JWA FEECE) had created, the investment banking firm had also set up a wholly owned leasing subsidiary so that the dealer could receive cash advances from its bank whenever it booked three- to five-year leases. And for the capital to buy the fleet of copiers required for the short-term rentals—the activity Arizona banks seemed most unwilling to support—G. Albert "Bert" Bourgeois, the mastermind behind the strategy, had chosen a different technique: He structured and sold a $300,000 limited partnership to own the rental equipment and receive income from it, but without any equity interest in the business. The overall solution, Bourgeois says, had been the result of the type of analysis his young and innovative firm has attempted to bring to every client it works with. "We looked at the business, exploded it into its pieces, and then put it back together."

As exciting as this offbeat approach was to Koether, what appealed to him most was the fact that Bourgeois Fils was facilitating more than just capital. For fees over and above those associated with structuring the business, tapping investors, and managing the partnership, the New Hampshire firm also served, in effect, as the company's treasurer and controller, permitting the dealership's owners to focus on building the rest of the organization during the start-up period. Bourgeois and the handful of others who worked for him would even handle the dealer's relationship with his local bank. "It was almost a turnkey package," Koether says. "It would enable us to do what we knew how to do. We could hit the street and sell."

If Koether had been calling the shots, he would have hired Bourgeois to put together an identical start-up package almost immediately. But before Bourgeois would make any sort of commitment, he wanted to assure himself that Koether and his partners had both the talent and the personal dedication to make the business work. Initially, Bourgeois says, "I was disturbed by Mike Koether's offhand style." Indeed, it was only after their two-day encounter in Exeter that Bourgeois felt confident enough about Koether's abilities to bet on the success of Koether's new venture, Infincom Inc. As with any client, Bourgeois Fils was putting its own credibility and the prospect of future fee income on the line. And early signs seem to show that the firm chose wisely. In its first year, Infincom had revenues of about $1.5 million and was gearing up for a second limited partnership of as much as $1 million to get under way in the summer of 1983 to support its booming rental business. Based on its rapid progress, Bourgeois now expects sales to double, at least, during the second year. "And we'll make money while Koether gets there," he says.

The man Mike Koether and his partners had traveled nearly a continent to see, Bert Bourgeois, is a thirty-four-year-old financial strategist who has built his own risk-oriented business out of designing non-venture-capital options for entrepreneurs. Rather than seeking an ownership stake for himself or other investors, Bourgeois, who cut his financial teeth on Wall Street and at two large companies during the 1970s, specializes in helping businesses raise enough money to support rapid growth without diluting the equity positions of the entrepreneurs.

Bourgeois formed his investment bank four years ago as the vehicle for his financial services to private businesses. While part of what Bourgeois Fils does involves structuring and placing deals as small as $500,000, what makes the business go is its orientation toward ongoing relationships with clients (currently numbering fifteen to eighteen) who, as long as things work out, will need to do several financings over the space of a few years in order to keep pace with business expansion. "We don't get involved unless we think it will lead to bigger and better things," says Bourgeois. By design, the firm's clientele consists of companies in growth markets, many of which are start-ups, where the profit outlook is attractive and where the appetite for capital equipment is substantial. The current financial needs of such enterprises may not be sufficient to invite the attention of Merrill Lynch, or even smaller investment banking firms, looking for large transaction fees to cover their high overhead, but it hasn't lessened the appeal for Bourgeois. "We're in a market Wall Street doesn't want," he says. "This means we can have the pick of the lot."

In addition to tailoring transactions to fit the specific needs of a business, such as financing purchases of costly equipment through limited partnerships, Bourgeois Fils has shown a knack for placing the deals it structures with private investors and persuading commercial bankers to back the businesses with the necessary credit. In many instances, moreover, the firm has gone so far as to assist client companies in their day-to-day operations by furnishing a wide-ranging set of fee-generating management services, such as preparation of financial statements, cash management, planning, and even acting as the liason with the client's local accountant and bank.

Since at least some of the fees Bourgeois Fils earns from such client services are tied to the ongoing success of the business, the firm, like a venture capitalist, actively bets on its clients' success in order to get paid. "If things go badly, then we do badly," Bourgeois explains. "But the more value we bring to a business, the greater the potential there is for us." For this reason, a major component of Bourgeois Fils' evaluation of prospective clients involves the capability of management. "For us to bring in money of any kind," Bourgeois says, "we have to be satisfied [the client] knows his business inside and out. That's orders of magnitude above everything else." But beyond the firm's financial interests, each deal also requires that Bourgeois Fils risk a bit of its own credibility in the market. In order to line up the pieces of a puzzle to make a complex financing plan work, notes a Boston banker, "people really have to believe in Bert." A miscalculation, Bourgeois concedes, would mean that "future deals would be harder to do."

The idea of setting up a new investment banking firm so exposed to risk wasn't even on Bourgeois' mind when, after graduating from Harvard College, he got his MBA from Stanford Graduate School of Business in 1974. At that point, motivated to prove himself in an established environment, he joined First Boston Corporation's corporate-finance department. For the next three years, in New York and Tokyo, he worked on structuring project financings of $40 million and more for *Fortune* 500 clients. But soon after beginning his next job, at Itel Corporation in San Francisco, placing hundreds of millions of dollars of computer leases with financial institutions, Bourgeois began to think about using his deal-making skills on small, private transactions in which he felt there were significant opportunities for creativity. The idea simmered even after he moved back to his native New Hampshire in 1978 to become the financial vice-president of Wheelabrator-Frye Inc.'s energy division.

Having worked mostly on large debt transactions, Bourgeois admits, "I didn't know what the actual products would be for small companies, or even who the most likely clients were. But I was pretty confident there would be opportunities for integrating what I knew about credit and markets with the tax, legal, and accounting skills necessary to create financial options for private business." On this gut feeling, Bourgeois, at age thirty, quit his $80,000-a-year job in 1979 and started assembling a network of bankers and accountants who could lead him to his first clients.

Almost immediately, Bourgeois began to do deals. And while the deals relied on fairly standard techniques, they often showed a creative flair. As a way of financing a $1.3-million Portsmouth, New Hampshire, nursing home, for example, Bourgeois arranged a conventional long-term mortgage with an insurance company, a guarantee from the Farmers Home Administration, and a partnership to enable the investors to own and depreciate the real property while their company operated the nursing home. A local bank, which kept a small piece of the deal, had introduced Bourgeois to the investors. But on its own, he says, "the bank couldn't have done anything that large." In another deal, Bourgeois used his computer-leasing background from Itel to arrange a $2.7-million leveraged lease for a private Massachusetts-based company in need of tax shelter. The company he found to lease the computer, as it turned out, was based in California. "All our client really knew was that he wanted tax benefits," Bourgeois explains. "It would never have occurred to the company to get them by owning a computer."

Even as Bourgeois Fils has grown from one person in 1979 to twelve people today, an enduring theme in its financings has been the preservation of ownership for entrepreneurs. "I have an intense conviction that the people who put their sweat on the line ought to be able to reap the rewards," Bourgeois says. In late 1980, for example, he succeeded in persuading a local bank and a small business investment company to provide $1 million of working capital and subordinated notes to enable two managers to do a leveraged buyout of the New Hampshire footwear-manufacturing company they worked for. Originally, the bank had turned down the managers' request for a loan. But later, with Bourgeois' intervention, they succeeded in getting 60 percent of the business with only $10,000 of their own money.

Since 1981, however, the firm has tended to specialize in creating financial strategies for financing new ventures that Bourgeois deems both promising and apt to require multiple infusions of money during the early years. Even before establishing its first relationship with an office-copier dealer, for instance, Bourgeois Fils became involved with Atavar Corporation, which was gearing up to enter the nascent semiconductor-testing industry in Scarboro, Maine. To enable the capital-short owners to obtain about $1 million of testing equipment to launch their new business, Bourgeois Fils put together and sold a limited partnership of $500,000 in early 1981 and then a second one for the same amount five months later. But even though Atavar was a risky start-up of the type conventional venture capitalists might back, the investors received no equity in the company. Instead, Atavar leased the equipment from the partnerships, who, in exchange for their investment, got tax benefits and income designed to provide an after-tax yield of more than 20 percent on their money.

"In order to bring investors into a deal like this, you needed to offer a significant return," explains Bill Nyhan, the number two person at Bourgeois Fils. But, as usual, the firm also had to risk some of its own credibility. Before taking Atavar as a client, Bourgeois Fils had done an extensive analysis of the business the entrepreneurs were entering and its management team, which was headed by a former executive from Fairchild Camera & Instrument Corporation. "No bank wanted anything to do with it until we found additional equity," Nyhan says. However, the type of equity Bourgeois Fils found from thirty private investors didn't require Atavar's founders to give up any ownership, the partners' interest was only in the equipment.

Bourgeois Fils' ability to add value by structuring and placing creative deals has been enhanced by its growing credibility in the marketplace. "Lots of other people advising small businesses seem to bring us every deal that occurs to them," notes a bank executive who has lent money to a series of Bourgeois Fils clients. "Bert Bourgeois understands what a bank needs, and he doesn't waste our time."

While Bourgeois Fils has walked away from a number of chances to provide its services to other office-copier distributorships in which the management didn't measure up to Bourgeois' standards, the firm now has formed relationships with Ricoh dealers in ten cities, including Phoenix, Los Angeles, Denver, Chicago, and Boston.

To cater to the needs of these and other clients, Bourgeois Fils has been assembling a staff that now consists of nine financial professionals, among them Bourgeois' wife, Marsha Francis, the firm's treasurer, who oversees internal operations and planning. Three other staff members handle data processing and communications at the Exeter office.

For the professionals, the firm has relied mostly on recently minted Harvard and Stanford MBAs who have been willing to start at base salaries in the low thirties, substantially less than they could earn at better-known investment banking firms. "It's exciting to work on transactions from beginning to end, and there's a real challenge in managing a client relationship," says Carlyle Singer, a recent Stanford MBA. Her job, like others at Bourgeois Fils, combines investment banking and selling of partnership interests with the hands-on duties of a chief financial officer. To ensure quality control while promoting the risk-taking spirit on which the firm is based, employees are encouraged to put their own money in deals they work on. "This isn't Morgan Stanley and it's not Hambrecht & Quist," says Bourgeois. "But it's a place where you can get your hands dirty and learn some things."

Yet even as the firm becomes more established, Bourgeois doesn't expect it to stray very far from where it began. As its clients mature, Bourgeois says, the firm may start doing somewhat larger transactions on occasion and may even act as underwriter for their initial public offerings. What is more, the firm may soon open its first branch office— not in New York City, but in Newport Beach, California. The new location, like Exeter, would help keep overhead costs down, permitting Bourgeois Fils to operate much as it has from the start. "Our business isn't really numbers and analysis," says Bourgeois. "What we sell isn't dependent on five or ten basis points but on whether a guy will be able to keep his whole company or have to sell a piece of it. It's a very personal, emotional business, and you can't really institutionalize it. We try to do things a little bit differently, and we really believe in the deals we do."

Says Alex Bernhard, a senior partner at Hale and Dorr, the prestigious Boston law firm that advises Bourgeois Fils, Bert Bourgeois "knows what's economically viable, and he's constantly testing the parameters of what's possible." Happily for Mike Koether, his equipment-leasing venture in Arizona fell within those parameters. "If we hadn't been able to strike our deal with Bourgeois," asserts Koether, "I don't think we would have gotten started in this business."

Without Nickels and Dimes

Bourgeois Fils & Company invests substantial amounts of time evaluating management and market prospects before deciding to take on new clients. But what keeps the dynamic young investment firm humming are its capital-raising and management services for the some fifteen businesses already on its client roster. The level of activity within its Exeter, New Hampshire, headquarters is reflected in the surging volume of deals Bourgeois Fils has promoted. During the first six months of 1983, the firm sold nearly $6 million worth of partnerships for companies—half of which had done prior financings—compared with $3 million for all of 1982 and $750,000 for 1981.

For a typical limited partnership, Bourgeois Fils looks for twenty to thirty investors willing to put up $10,000 to $20,000 apiece. While the prospects, mostly professionals and entrepreneurs on the East and West coasts, are found through a network of accountants and financial planners, the complex nature of the deals makes them difficult to sell without a great deal of explanation of their tax and income features. "It's not uncommon to spend up to ten hours on the phone and in person with one investor," notes Bert Bourgeois. Fortunately, he says, nearly half of the 250 partners the investment firm has recruited to date end up putting money in subsequent partnerships in which less selling is required. For debt financing, meanwhile, Bourgeois Fils cultivates relationships with major regional banks around the country.

In its role as off-site chief financial officer, Bourgeois Fils performs a variety of financial services for client businesses, including basic record-keeping, billing, and cash management. To carry out these functions, the firm relies heavily on its Data General Nova minicomputer, which has already become inadequate for the firm's needs. Almost daily, moreover, Bourgeois Fils employees communicate with clients by phone, generating bills of upwards of $5,000 per month.

In keeping with Bourgeois' approach to his business, neither telephone expenses nor other costs are ever directly billed to clients. Since the payoff Bourgeois looks forward to comes with the fees for syndicating future financings, managing partnerships, and even business activity, "we don't want to put things on a nickel-and-dime basis," he says. The no-billing policy even extends to larger expenses such as airline tickets and lodging. "We want our clients to know we're willing to do whatever's required to make things work out, and that we'll even pay our own way," he explains.

For some busines trips, however, Bourgeois and his associates have no need for hotels. As houseguests of clients, they not only keep travel costs down but also foster the kind of personal bonds that Bourgeois thinks are important to the success of his business. "Bert has become a friend of my whole family," says Mike Koether, president of Infincom Inc., who hosts Bourgeois and others from the firm when they visit Phoenix. "And even though I've technically hired him to work for me, we're really in business together. I want to do well, but I also don't want to disappoint him."

—BRUCE G. POSNER

LIMITING LIABILITY

The grass, as they say, is always greener on the other side of the fence, but money may be greener on the other side of the ocean. Such, at any rate, was the conclusion of Knogo Corporation of Hicksville, New York, when it recently set out to find new debt financing.

Knogo is an eighteen-year-old, publicly held maker of electronic article-surveillance systems—the devices that set off alarms when, for example, a shoplifter tries to leave a store with merchandise under his coat. Last year, the company had revenues of about $25 million, much of which came from sales of large-store systems costing $50,000 and up. At such prices, Knogo has found that in order to grow, it had to be able to provide customers with attractive lease financing. "In our industry," says vice-president of finance James R. Dellomo, "the financing is really part of the product. We need to give buyers the lowest rates possible."

In the past Knogo has supported its growth by, in effect, gambling on interest rates: When customers needed financing, the company boosted its borrowings from U.S. commercial banks. This approach entailed obvious risks, since Knogo generally offered its customers fixed-rate loans over a period of several years while its own cost of this money floated up and down with the prime rate. Nevertheless, the company felt that it had to provide such fixed-rate financing in order to remain competitive.

Last summer, the company seized an opportunity to pay off its burgeoning bank debt with the proceeds of a $14-million equity infusion. "The market was strong," notes founder and president Arthur J. Minasy. "So it was the cheapest way to go." But, shortly thereafter, Minasy and Dellomo began looking for a new way to bankroll Knogo's future expansion without piling up more floating-rate debt. "We figured that our needs would be thirty million to forty million dollars over the next two or three years," says Minasy. "So we started talking to our investment bankers about financing possibilities."

One possibility was to sell long-term bonds that would be convertible into Knogo stock. Says Minasy, "We were quoted fixed rates of nine and a half to ten percent, which compared quite favorably to our eleven percent borrowing costs." Then, last December, the fifty-seven-year-old

155

president came upon an even more favorable option. While on a business trip to Europe, he met with bankers at Banque Gutzwiller, Kurz, Bungener S.A., a private bank in Geneva, and learned that Knogo could borrow long-term in Switzerland at rates that were as much as four percentage points lower than those in the United States.

Minasy responded quickly, hammering out a deal within days. Banque Gutzwiller agreed to lead a syndicate of Swiss banks in raising 75 million Swiss francs (then the equivalent of $35 million) for Knogo at a fixed rate of 6½ percent. The eight-year subordinated debentures would be sold to private Swiss investors, who would get annual interest payments on the 5,000-franc bonds in Swiss currency.

The danger for Knogo was that the dollar might weaken in relation to the Swiss franc, making the whole deal increasingly costly. As protection against such foreign exchange risks, Minasy obtained the right to pay off the bonds in a fixed amount of dollars. "We didn't want to have to worry about whether the dollar was losing ground," he explains. "We paid a little extra, but we limited our total liability to thirty-five million dollars."

Then again, Knogo may *never* have to pay off its new Swiss bondholders in hard cash, thanks to a special conversion feature. If, at any point, the company's stock trades at a price exceeding $21.04 (a price that is about 20 percent over the trading price at the time the deal was signed) for twenty consecutive days, Knogo may ask investors to convert their 6½ percent bonds into common stock. "Each bond would be worth around one hundred twenty-seven shares," says Minasy.

Whether or not the company ever does convert the bonds, Minasy is confident that Knogo has solved its major financial problem. "We think we've found an awfully good way to lock in our borrowing costs and reduce our exposure," he says. "We can sleep a little more peacefully. And now that we don't have to spend so much time looking for money, we can go out and build up the business."

What does a privately held research company do when it wants to bring a new product to market but cannot afford to tie up its own precious capital? Flow Industries Inc., of Kent, Washington, pondered this question back in 1982 and came up with an interesting strategy.

Flow Industries is a $14-million-a-year research and development company that has been doing government-sponsored research in a variety of technical areas for more than a decade. In 1981 and 1982, Flow raised $800,000 from an R&D limited partnership to develop an innovative wind turbine for generating low-cost electrical power. Flow's turbine—which rotates on a vertical axis like an egg beater—had been fine-tuned and tested, and Michael Pao, the company's forty-nine-year-old founder and chairman, thought it was time to launch full-scale production. "Our long-term plan was to develop and operate wind-power facilities all over the world," he says.

Toward that end, Pao had already created a separate company named FloWind Corporation, which generated some cash in 1982 by selling a handful of its $300,000 turbines to various customers, including a utility on the island of Antigua. Pao had big dreams, however, and so he decided to speculate on the development of a $14.9-million project at Altamont Pass, California. He drew up plans for a sixty-turbine "wind farm," and worked out an arrangement to sell whatever power it generated to Pacific Gas & Electric Company under a thirty-year contract.

FloWind began to develop the Altamont wind farm with money advanced from Flow Industries, plus $4.6 million in secured bank loans, but it soon became evident that the company would need a lot of new capital to grow as quickly as Pao wanted. So he met with some investment bankers from A. G. Becker Paribas Inc. in New York City to talk about bankrolling FloWind's expansion plans through limited partnerships. "It was a way to raise money without giving up equity in the company," he says.

FloWind later sold its Altamont Pass wind farm to a group of limited partners for $14.9 million. The partners, who put up $100,000 each, get regular investment tax credits and additional federal and state credits for investing in solar energy. They also get income from the sale of wind power to the utility. FloWind used the proceeds to pay off the bank debt and to replenish capital that had been advanced by Flow Industries, and FloWind will continue to manage the wind farm for an annual fee.

Meanwhile, FloWind is already planning to develop other wind farms in New York, Oregon, Guam, and other places. Pao says the company will also be designing some new products for storing wind energy. As FloWind grows, its capital requirements will be enormous. "We'll be doing a series of limited partnerships over the next few years to move this company forward," says Hugh Rose, FloWind's senior vice-president.

But that may not be the only way the company raises money over the next couple of years. "Once we're earning one million dollars after taxes, we hope to do an initial public offering for FloWind," says Pao.

These days, the term *venture capital* conjures up visions of electronic gadgetry and software and annual investment returns of 35 percent or more. But if you believe that *nobody* is interested in making plain old loans for machinery and buildings, you haven't met Gerald Grossman.

In 1982, Grossman took $1 million of his own money and established a new small-business investment company (SBIC) in New York City, called American Commercial Capital Corporation. Under the terms of his license from the Small Business Administration, Grossman is allowed to use a wide variety of investment vehicles, ranging from secured debt to equity, but he has decided to play things cautiously. "I'm not very comfortable with equity risks," the fifty-one-year-old former finance company executive explains. "So I lend against the hard assets of a business. Since I don't try for big hits like a lot of venture capitalists, every transaction has to stand on its own."

To date, Grossman has made fixed-rate loans at 17 percent or 18 percent to one California company and about a dozen New York City–area companies. Typically, the businesses require $100,000 to $200,000 to buy expensive equipment or to solve basic cash-flow difficulties. American Commercial Capital looks for ways to lend on a secured basis, even in cases where banks have said no. "Before making a loan, I listen to the story and look at the numbers, much the way a banker would," explains Grossman. "But I'm less concerned about the overall condition of the balance sheet than a typical banker. I'm interested in how the proceeds of a secured loan can *strengthen* the business."

A recent loan of $150,000 to a troubled meat-processing company in upstate New York is a case in point. The $12-million business was attempting to reorganize under Chapter 11 and needed new capital to buy equipment and expand its marketing department. The company's commercial banks had shied away from advancing any new money, but, says Grossman, "the plan for putting the business on its feet seemed realistic." Grossman's SBIC made the seven-year loan at 18 percent and has protected itself heavily on the downside if the turnaround fails. "If it doesn't work out," explains Grossman, "I'll own a building that's been appraised at about one hundred sixty thousand dollars."

Grossman is the first to admit that there is nothing terribly glamorous about his style of investment. Indeed, his goal for return on capital is a modest 15 percent. Nevertheless, he believes he fills an important gap in the marketplace. "A lot of the things we finance simply aren't bankable," he says. "But with the money we provide, businesses can take the steps they need to become more profitable." To be sure, he admits, "we won't be investing in the next Apple Computer. But when a supplier to U.S. Steel needs a machine to remain competitive, we think we can be part of *that* package."

—BRUCE G. POSNER

THE COMMERCIAL PAPER CHASE

When a company like Gulf Oil Corporation or Coca-Cola Company needs short-term cash, it rarely turns to a commercial bank. For a well-known corporation with a good credit rating, there is cheap money available—not at the banks, but in the commercial-paper market, where institutional investors are quite willing to lend at rates well below the prime. The maturity for the paper is as short as 7 days and as long as 270 days. Depending on market conditions, the interest-rate savings may range from one percentage point to three or more.

Altogether, there are about $180 billion worth of IOUs floating around the commercial-paper market (including those of financial institutions), but virtually none of them come from smaller companies. The reason is that institutional investors are reluctant to gamble on the creditworthiness of companies with which they are unfamiliar, no matter how solid the underlying business may be.

Now, however, a New York City company named IDBI Managers Inc. is trying to remedy this situation. IDBI, a bond-insurance underwriter, has been negotiating with a large insurance company to provide a new type of coverage against commercial-paper default. With such insurance, small but creditworthy companies with annual sales of less than $10 million would be able to issue unsecured commercial paper on the credit of the insurance company. They would thus be able to finance their working capital needs by selling short-term IOUs—just as the giants do.

If all goes well, the insurance could be available as early as this spring, according to IDBI president Michael Curley. It won't be cheap. Curley estimates that, to cover the cost of IDBI's detailed credit analysis and the insurance, corporate borrowers will have to pay a total of about one percentage point on top of the prevailing commercial-paper rates for the highest-rated companies. But even with an extra point, says Curley, "commercial paper will usually be cheaper than borrowing from a bank."

Bankers, of course, aren't apt to be overjoyed by the appearance of commercial-paper insurance. The obvious worry is that some of their most profitable lending business may disappear. But for many banks, says Curley, the new insurance may actually help. "A lot of the smaller banks have lending limits of less than two million dollars," he points out. "So commercial paper could be a way for the bank to hold on to a growing customer."

In any case, Curley says that IDBI, which has been insuring industrial revenue bonds since 1982, plans to design other products aimed at giving smaller companies more financial flexibility. "We're not a bank," he notes, "but we think small companies should be able to do most things that big companies do. You might say that we're interested in bringing Wall Street to Main Street."

The Securities and Exchange Commission has good news for companies gearing up to do an initial public offering (IPO). Beginning March 31, 1984, first-time equity issuers will be able to raise up to $7.5 million by registering under S-18, a route that requires less disclosure and, generally, less time and money than a standard S-1 filing.

The SEC introduced form S-18 back in 1979, in order to streamline the requirements for small companies wishing to go public. Under the 1979 rules, a business was entitled to raise as much as $5 million in an IPO once it had obtained the green light from one of the SEC's nine regional offices or its national headquarters in Washington, D.C. In addition, application requirements were simplified. With a regular S-1 filing, for instance, a company has to furnish audited financial statements reflecting the preceding three completed fiscal years. But S-18 demands only two years of audited financial statements.

The net result was to speed up the application process, in part because the regional offices may be able to respond faster than the Washington, D.C., office, and also because there is less information to review. "By using S-18, a company can cut two to four weeks off its processing time at the SEC," says Peter M. Rosenblum, an attorney with Foley, Hoag & Eliot, a Boston law firm.

Now the SEC has made the S-18 route even more attractive by raising the ceiling on offerings to $7.5 million. Investment bankers expect that the total number of S-18 filings will increase dramatically as a result. With the $5-million ceiling in effect, the SEC says that nearly one-third of the 1,967 initial public offerings in fiscal 1983 were registered under S-18. But "there's a material difference between five million and seven and a half million dollars," says Thomas J. Shields, a limited partner at Bear, Stearns and Company. "In addition to obtaining more money, the larger issue size permits a company to sell more shares. Investors and underwriters like that because it means that there will be a broader market."

For that reason, if no other, it is likely that more and more prospective issuers will be taking the S-18 path to the public market in the future.

What do you do when your multiproduct company is barely breaking even and the most profitable part of the business needs lots of cash? Albert W. Ondis, founder and president of Atlan-Tol Industries

Inc., grappled with this very question last spring. And, with the help of accountants and investment bankers, he found an unusual solution.

Atlan-Tol is a fifteen-year-old, $14-million-a-year public company in West Warwick, Rhode Island. Although organized as a single company, it has been involved in two distinct businesses from its early days. Through one, it supplied the electronics industry with metal-plated plastic film and plating equipment. In its other business, the company designed and manufactured graphic recording instruments used in such applications as electrocardiograms.

Last year at this time, the graphic recording equipment business was going great guns, acounting for about 70 percent of overall sales. Orders flowed in from such customers as IBM Corporation and American Hospital Supply Corporation, and there was a need for additional capital to support the growth.

But recent losses from the plating operations were causing problems. The losses had seriously sapped Atlan-Tol's earnings and depressed its stock price. "Selling more [Atlan-Tol] stock would have been very unappealing," says Ondis, who owned 47 percent of the company's shares.

So he was in a quandary. The company needed money, but, if he waited for the price of Atlan-Tol's stock to rebound, business would suffer. In an effort to find a solution, the fifty-seven-year-old marketing specialist approached Baker, Watts & Company, a Baltimore investment firm, which suggested an intriguing alternative: Why not spin off the graphic recording business into a new company and then take *its* stock to the public market? The offbeat approach, dubbed the "equity carve-out" on Wall Street, had already been used successfully by, among others, Cooper Laboratories Inc. and Trans World Corporation. For Atlan-Tol, notes Ondis, "it seemed like an ideal way to finance the business."

To set the ball rolling, Atlan-Tol brought in a team of auditors from Arthur Andersen & Company, the national accounting firm. Over the next two and a half months, the accountants spent hundreds of hours piecing together separate financial statements for the new company, called Astro-Med Inc.

When all the costs and revenues had been allocated, the audit showed that Astro-Med was even more profitable than Ondis had assumed, having earned $634,000 on sales of $7 million in the fiscal year ended January 31, 1983.

Such numbers certainly did the company no harm when Astro-Med went to market with an initial public offering last May 25. Shares sold for about twemty-three times the previous year's earnings. By selling only 18 percent of its shares (the remaining equity was retained by Atlan-Tol), the new company still managed to raise about $3 million, even after deducting underwriting costs and a whopping $137,000 accounting bill.

As for the proceeds, they have been used to pay off about $1 million of long-term debt, expand working capital, and double the research and development budget of the graphic recording business. A new type of recording device was introduced in November 1983.

Meanwhile, Ondis, who is also chairman and chief executive officer of Astro-Med, has been besieged by requests for offering prospectuses from companies and underwriters considering similar financings. He credits the innovative financing technique with putting his business back on track. "Around here, we call it a pretty good idea," he remarks. "If we hadn't found some new money, we would have been forced to put most of our plans on hold."

—BRUCE G. POSNER

RENTING MONEY

As interest rates soared out of control in the early 1980s, the ambitious growth plans of Arkansas Waffles Inc., a chain of family restaurants, might well have been shelved until better times arrived. The business, based in Jacksonville, Arkansas, had opened its first twenty-four-hour restaurant in 1971, and the owners were eager to continue penetrating their market by constructing a network of similar units throughout their statewide franchising territory. But by 1981, rates on long-term mortgages for commercial properties were creeping to 17 percent and higher, far more than most businesses would even dream of paying.

"The cost of financing should never be out of line with the economics of the business you're in," says R. Bert Alexander, president of Arkansas Waffles.

Yet even in 1981, when commercial mortgage rates reached their high-water mark, Alexander and his partner, Charles Menser, Jr., the company's secretary/treasurer, managed to open two new restaurants without a hitch, thanks to a creative financing technique that kept the rate they paid—and their own capital requirements for the business—to a minimum. Through a series of sale-leaseback transactions, the two entrepreneurs have built Arkansas Waffles into a chain of fourteen restaurants with combined 1982 revenues of about $7 million.

While four of the company's properties are owned by Alexander and Menser, the remainder have been sold to private investors with whom Arkansas Waffles has negotiated twenty-year leases at fixed rates several percentage points below the prevailing mortgage rates. When rates hit 18 percent in 1981, for instance, "we signed lease agreements for at least seven points less," Alexander says.

By definition, the use of sale-leasebacks limits the amount of equity the company will build in the land and restaurants. But this doesn't bother the principals, who see their primary business goal as running a chain of restaurants featuring "good food fast," with enough profits to support growth of at least three new restaurants a year. "Doing that," says Menser, "is worth more to us than accumulating real estate."

The sale-leaseback technique is hardly new. For decades, many businesses, including service and manufacturing concerns, have used the mechanism as a way to conserve working capital or perhaps cash in on real estate holdings when money is needed elsewhere. And while it is true that periods of high interest rates and inflation often provide added incentives for businesses like Arkansas Waffles to sell property and then lease it back, financial experts say that the arguments for sale-leasebacks continue to be compelling when rates are down for businesses that are growing. With lower rates, the sale-leaseback still lets owners of capital-intensive companies sink their limited equity into working capital needed to run the business, where the anticipated return on assets is more attractive.

"The sale-leaseback is a way of renting money," explains Menser. "We see the restaurants and the real estate as two separate businesses. We've left our credit lines open to finance equipment and other things." Without having to tie up capital—amounting to about $250,000 per restaurant—in land or buildings, Alexander adds, "we can concentrate on becoming a bigger operating company."

Alexander, a former savings and loan executive now living in Memphis, and Menser, an Atlanta-based certified public accountant, got started in the restaurant business in 1971 when they purchased a franchise to operate Waffle House restaurants in Arkansas from Waffle House Inc. of Atlanta. As a franchisee, Arkansas Waffles receives the specifications for constructing the 1,800-square-foot restaurants, along with management advice for running the business profitably. But when it comes to sources of capital, Alexander and Menser, who own some 90 percent of the Arkansas company, have always been left to their own devices. From the very beginning, notes Alexander, "we knew we could rely on the sale-leaseback."

Arkansas Waffles didn't waste any time before arranging its initial sale-leaseback to finance its first restaurant. A commercial landowner in Hot Springs, Arkansas, was interested in repurchasing the half-acre parcel complete with the new building, and he agreed to offer a twenty-year lease. Four subsequent properties were retained jointly by Alexander and Menser for themselves. While those properties generate attractive personal tax benefits, the decision to sell the others to private investors wasn't difficult. To begin with, the company needed outside capital, and, says Alexander, he and Menser "didn't need all that depreciation."

On a typical sale-leaseback deal, Arkansas Waffles seeks an appropriate site and develops the restaurant with a total budget of about $250,000. Prices for commercial half-acre parcels in prime locations, notes Menser, sometimes run as high as 40 percent of total costs. An investor—usually an individual, a family, or a trust—is identified and committed even before construction begins. And unlike a financial institution, which is apt to finance only about 75 percent of the cost of a property, Arkansas Waffles has found investors who have been willing to purchase the properties outright, resulting, in effect, in 100 percent financing.

"The investor knows exactly what he's getting," says Menser. "We build it and sell it to him at a prearranged price." The cash proceeds are used to pay off the construction loan and all other costs. A major objective throughout the process is keeping development costs as low as possible and making sure the sale price is not higher than the expenses Arkansas Waffles incurs during development (including financing, legal, and engineering fees). That way, says Menser, rent payments can be held to a minimum.

At each restaurant, the rent Arkansas Waffles pays varies according to what the commercial mortgage rate may have been at the time the lease was signed. But in each instance, Alexander and Menser claim, there are monthly cash-flow benefits amounting to hundreds of dollars versus what the mortgage payment would have been if the property were owned by the company. Whereas a 10 percent lease on $250,000 would require monthly payments of about $2,100, a 14 percent, twenty-year mortgage, for example, would cost $2,590 monthly, Menser explains.

As far as taxes are concerned, leasing has consequences that are different from ownership. Instead of deducting the interest expense of the mortgage and depreciating the cost of the building (without the land) over fifteen years, as it would if it were the owner, Arkansas Waffles, as a tenant, treats 100 percent of its rent payment as tax-deductible business expenses. Since the long-term leases aren't unlike debt obligations, the company describes them in a footnote to its audited financial statements.

For investors in the properties, the key incentives are twenty-year leases paying relatively attractive fixed yields, depreciation on the building cost, and whatever future value there is in the property. But, at times, Arkansas Waffles has offered another lure, too. A few years ago, to keep its lease rates low when mortgage rates were going through the roof, the company offered investors a sweetener, consisting of a small percentage of restaurant revenues over a fairly substantial volume. The company, in effect, agreed to pay investors a bonus if the location was a real winner. In the future, Menser notes, the company would like to find willing investors without having to offer such extra benefits.

For the next several years, Arkansas Waffles wants to continue to add at least three new restaurants a year. And although the company evaluates its financing alternatives each step of the way, the chances are that at least one or two of the new restaurants planned for 1983 will be financed with sale-leasebacks. Beyond that, the future game plan, Menser says, will be influenced fundamentally by the level of commercial mortgage rates and whether they fall below 12 percent or so. "While we can't expect to get money as cheaply as General Motors," he concedes, "we're always looking for the best deal for Arkansas Waffles."

—BRUCE G. POSNER

EQUITY WITHOUT TEARS

There comes a time in the life of almost every vigorous, privately held company when it has to face up to a difficult choice—one between growth and control. It is a choice forced upon the company by the need for equity capital to finance future expansion. In order to get the money, the company usually finds that it has to offer investors some degree of control over its destiny. Alternatively, it can scale back its expansion plans.

This was more or less the dilemma faced by the owners of John S. Cheever Company of Hingham, Massachusetts, back in 1983. Unlike many others, however, they found a way to eat their cake and have it, too.

For most of its ninety-one-year history, Cheever had been a small, family-owned wholesaler of specialty paper goods. Then, in 1968, the company changed hands, and in 1971, Paul E. Cullinane, son of the new owner, decided to try his luck at retailing. He began by opening a discount store in a room off the warehouse, where the company sold a limited assortment of bulk paper items—bags and pizza boxes, for instance. Before long, the cash-and-carry business started to take off; Cheever's annual revenues grew from about $700,000 in 1971 to $4 million in 1975. This success encouraged Cullinane (who became president and chief executive officer in 1975) and executive vice-president Jack Allegrini to invest the company's profits in two new outlets south of Boston.

While Cheever's wholesale paper business saw little or no growth in the next few years, annual sales of the three discount stores, named Paperama, climbed to about $7 million in 1981. By then, the stores were carrying a broader selection of merchandise, ranging from party supplies and stationery to aisles and aisles of such seasonal items as rakes, snow shovels, and holiday decorations.

Cheever's future clearly lay in retailing. Over the next year, the company opened two more stores, and Cullinane, Allegrini, and treasurer Stephen Dreier began to explore long-term options for Paperama. Retained earnings, they figured, would be adequate only for bankrolling slow growth, perhaps one or two new outlets per year. But what if the company wanted to expand the chain more quickly? Where would the capital come from?

Fortunately, the company was in excellent financial condition. It had financed seasonal inventories with a revolving credit line from its commercial bank, repaying the borrowings in full at the end of each selling season. What's more, there was almost no long-term debt. On the other hand, management had thoughts of opening thirteen stores over the next four years—a move that would require new sources of capital. "We realized that unless we got some new equity, the bankers would get nervous," says Dreier.

At the same time, however, they were determined to retain full control of the company. "We didn't want anybody to interfere with the way we ran the business," explains Allegrini. "We wanted to grow at the rate *we* deemed reasonable."

So, in the summer of 1983, the company set out to find long-term investors willing to put up about $2 million in equity under certain strict conditions. Cullinane and Allegrini—the principal share-holders—made it clear from the start that they were quite prepared to walk away from any deal unless they were assured of continued control. "Frankly, we didn't think we'd find anybody," Allegrini admits. Nevertheless, a few months later, their attorney introduced them to a Brit-ish-based investment company that seemed to find Cheever's condi-tions quite reasonable.

The investment company was called Investors in Industry, or 3i. Its shareholders included the Bank of England and eight British banks. It had recently opened offices in Boston and Newport Beach, California, and was looking for promising U.S. companies in which to invest. In the summer of 1983, it opened discussions with Cullinane and Dreier, during which the latter spelled out their conditions: They didn't want to give up a majority of Cheever's equity; they didn't want the investor in a control position on the board; and they didn't want to be forced within any set time span to sell the company or to go public. Much to their surprise, the British investors voiced no objection. Rather, 3i did a thorough analysis of the business and listened closely to management's goals, then proceeded to suggest a series of mechanisms for meeting Cheever's terms.

To enable Cheever's owners to retain as much control and equity as possible, 3i proposed investing the $2 million in two types of nonvoting preferred stock. The first type would function more or less like an eight-year fixed-rate loan: Cheever would receive $1.5 million and would have to pay the investors an annual dividend of 6 percent. Eventually—in years six through ten—the company would redeem the $1.5-million principal in equal installments. The second part of the deal called for 3i to invest an additional $500,000, in return for which it would receive a 3 percent slice of Cheever's after-tax earnings. Unlike the fixed-rate preferred stock, this participating preferred stock would not be redeemable, and thus the investment would remain in the company indefinitely. When and if management ever decided to sell the company or take it public, the participating preferred would convert into a minority percentage (something under 30 percent) of the com-mon stock.

After considering the proposal, Cheever's management decided to accept. To date, the British investors have agreed to remain passive observers, with no representation on the company's board. "They've told us that we control the reins," says Allegrini. "They want us to keep doing what we've been doing."

And what if Cheever had wanted the opportunity to buy out its investors entirely? Well, says 3i president David Shaw, that flexibility could also have been structured into the deal—for a price. In fact, 3i recently participated in a leveraged buyout of a Massachusetts apparel company whose new owners insisted on an option to repurchase the participating preferred stock after the eighth year. The put-call feature doesn't have to be exercised. If it is, the redemption price will be based on a multiple of earnings from the previous two years.

"We're in the capital gains business just like other venture capitalists," says Shaw, a thirty-six-year-old Scotsman. "But we can be a very flexible investor. If we think an opportunity is attractive, we can attempt to solve any problem."

How many "angels" can dance on the head of a silicon chip? An enterprising group of New Hampshire businesspeople is hoping that the answer is up in the hundreds—maybe even higher. "Angels," of course, are those well-heeled individuals, found in every area of the country, who like to invest in promising young companies. What the New Hampshire group has done is to put together a new type of computer "dating" service, whose purpose is to match up New England–area angels with local entrepreneurs seeking modest amounts of capital.

The idea for the new service, called Venture Capital Network Inc. (VCN), grew out of a 1981 study on the availability of risk capital in New England. The study—conducted for the Small Business Administration by William E. Wetzel, Jr., a professor at the University of New Hampshire's Whittemore School of Business and Economics—showed that entrepreneurs and angels were locating one another by largely random methods. "It was all very informal," says Wetzel, "and the investors were essentially invisible."

As one might expect, the entrepreneurs Wetzel interviewed felt extremely frustrated by the situation: Their capital needs were often too modest to interest venture capitalists, yet it was very difficult to find other potential investors. The research suggested that the pool of money available in the informal private market was at least as large as the more organized venture capital market.

That informal market was made up of thousands of business angels looking for companies that needed as little as $30,000 to $50,000 in capital. As it turned out, the angels were as dissatisfied as the entrepreneurs with the random nature of the search process. "The information needed to support a *real* market for smaller investments— anything from fifty thousand to five hundred thousand dollars—simply wasn't available to them." The obvious challenge, then, was to develop a way to bridge the information gap.

In 1983, the Business and Industry Association of New Hampshire, a private business organization, decided to meet this challenge, setting up VCN as a nonprofit corporation. The new organization spent the next year designing its service. In May 1984, it began sending out confidential questionnaires to entrepreneurs and investors in New Hampshire and nearby states. The entrepreneurs were asked to supply a two-page business summary, as well as information on their financial performance, their growth projections, and their estimated needs. A $100 filing fee was established to discourage frivolous proposals. Potential investors, meanwhile, were asked to describe their areas of interest and their personal investment criteria, including their geographic preferences.

VCN plans to begin doing regular computer match-ups this summer. "When we get a potential match, we'll send them along to the investors," says executive secretary James K. Hoeveler. To avoid potential legal liabilities, VCN will not act as investment adviser or broker-dealer, but will limit itself to making the introductions.

Wetzel is the first to admit that VCN is only experimental. Even so, he has already fielded inquiries from people in other states—including Florida, Nebraska, and Louisiana—who are contemplating the creation of similar services. "The market we're trying to serve revolves around the entrepreneur who needs more than he can get from his Uncle Charlie and less than what it takes to interest a venture capital firm," explains Wetzel. "That's the hole in the market that the angels fill."

—BRUCE G. POSNER

TALES OF EQUITY

The Real Over-the-Counter Market

How do you finance growth when you are already up to your eyeballs in debt? That was the challenge confronting the owners of Photogenesis Inc. of San Antonio, a $7.2-million-a-year photo and video equipment retailer that ranked number 205 on *Inc.*'s 1983 list of the 500 fastest-growing private companies in the United States. Last April, the company found itself with four bustling camera stores in San Antonio, Austin, and Midland, Texas, and plans to open at least two more. But with a debt-to-equity ratio of eight to one, the company was in no position to bankroll the expansion through further borrowings. "We needed to raise two hundred thousand to three hundred thousand dollars to reach our near-term goals," says Roy Graham, the chairman and cofounder. "We knew that the best way to support our growth would be to beef up the equity."

As it happened, Photogenesis had raised $80,000 of equity in 1982 by selling 5 percent of its common stock to two key employees, but Graham and his two partners, all in their early thirties, were reluctant to go that same route again. In particular, they wanted to avoid any further dilution of either their ownership or their control.

So they came up with an alternative. They would raise the new equity by selling nonvoting preferred stock in a private offering to a group of selected investors—their customers. "In the early days, each of us spent a lot of time behind the counter," says Graham. "We got to know several customers who were interested in our business. They bought cameras from us, and they like to follow our growth."

A former division controller of Church's Fried Chicken Inc., Graham knew that the deal had to be structured to compensate investors for the risks involved. "We put ourselves in their shoes; we figured that the returns should be several points above money market rates," he explains.

In the end, the company decided to offer monthly dividends based on an annual rate of about 16 percent, and beyond that, a 3 percent share of net earnings, thereby allowing the investors to share in the success of the business. If an investor ever wanted to cash out, moreover, the company would "simply buy seven percent of his preferred shares each month at par value," says Graham. The investor could thus liquidate his entire investment over a period of about fourteen months.

Graham contacted several people about the investment opportunity last spring. Within three or four months, the company had raised $250,000 from two San Antonio investors—a retired construction executive and a well-heeled professional in his early thirties. That money has enabled Photogenesis to pursue its expansion without a hitch. Last October, the company cut the ribbon on its third San Antonio outlet and a second store in Austin.

Graham is understandably pleased about all this. Although the costs to the company associated with preferred stock are not tax deductible (unlike interest payments on debt), the deal has filled a critical gap in financing the company's growth. "We needed a way to enhance our borrowing power," Graham explains. With the new equity, Photogenesis has access to a larger bank credit line and more liberal trade credit terms from equipment manufacturers.

At the same time, the company has carefully reserved the right to buy the investors out at any point in the future. It simply has to give them thirty days notice and pay a premium of about 20 percent above the amount of their investment. "This gives us a lot of flexibility if we find alternative financing sources at a lower cost," notes Graham. Down the road, for instance, Photogenesis might try to refinance the deal with a second class of preferred stock, which would be tied to a less costly formula. For the time being, however, there are no such plans. As Graham puts it, "As long as we're generating income in excess of what this money costs, we see it as a plus situation."

Public Offerings for Start-ups

There is a new twist in initial public offerings, and it may just open up a whole new source of capital for start-ups. Called a "public-private" deal, it involves going public at a stage when most companies are still trying to demonstrate a market for their products or services.

A case in point is Office Solutions Inc. of Portland, Oregon, which was formed in January 1983 to sell microcomputers and telephone systems to businesspeople in the Pacific Northwest. Last May, the company began looking for approximately $1 million of equity to cover the expenses of opening its first three sales centers. The original plan, says president and chief executive officer Ralph D. Lockhart, called for a private equity placement with a dozen or so wealthy individuals. But instead, the company wound up selling $1 million of stock in an initial public offering that was fully registered with the Securities and Exchange Commission—this despite the fact that Office Solutions had yet to generate any revenues or earnings.

The deal was underwritten by Paulson Investment Company, a Portland-based securities firm, and required the founders to give up slightly more than 50 percent of their ownership. Unlike most public offerings, the issue was aimed specifically at investors with annual incomes over $50,000, or net worths over $150,000. Indeed, the stock could be purchased only in 1,400-share units (of which there were just 408), and each unit was priced at $2,450. The prospectus made it clear, moreover, that there would be no market for anything but the units during the following twelve months. "We stated from the very beginning that this was a high-risk, venture capital–like investment," notes Lockhart. "The idea was to discourage widows and orphans."

The Office Solutions underwriting was similar to a previous offering that Paulson Investment had managed for another start-up, Schuchardt Software Systems Inc. of San Rafael, California. Using the "public-private" approach, Schuchardt had sold 40 percent of its stock and raised $1.4 million for the company to develop and market a line of business-applications software compatible with the IBM Personal Computer. "So many investors seemed to be interested in software opportunities," says president and founder Fred Schuchardt, a former executive with MicroPro International Corporation. "We saw this as a less costly alternative to venture capital financing."

Lockhart took a similar view, and today his company has four stores in Oregon. Meanwhile, Lockhart is already looking well down the road. He hopes that the young computer retailer will soon be able to expand into other parts of the West without major additional financing. "We'll have a real advantage in being a public company," he notes. "Our strategy would be to acquire established operations with our stock."

Of course, there are pitfalls involved in going public so early in a company's life. Nevertheless, the benefits make it likely that other young companies will soon be folllowing Office Solutions and Schuchardt to the public market. Paulson Investment president Chester Paulson, for one, thinks that is just fine. "There's nothing wrong with selling big opportunities as long as you sell them for what they are," says Paulson, who expects to do future deals of this type for companies in growing industries. "There are certain types of investors who can take certain types of risks. And for us, it's a matter of matching the two."

—BRUCE G. POSNER

THE EQUITY PARTNERSHIP
AS A SEED FOR START-UPS

Venture capitalists have invested more than $1 billion in each of the past two years, but very little of the money has found its way to start-up companies. In fact, many of the newest and biggest suppliers of investment dollars, notably pension funds and large companies, instruct venture fund managers to invest only in more mature enterprises needing second- or third-stage financing. Yet however scarce true "seed" capital may be, a small but growing number of venture capital groups are gearing up to meet early financing needs of at least some entrepreneurs through a vehicle rare in money-raising circles: equity research and development partnerships.

Equity R&D partnerships are cousins of the more straightforward R&D limited partnerships that recently have been in the spotlight. But instead of providing investors with a current tax shelter and a future royalty interest in a single product, the equity R&D deals are designed to launch not just products but entire new companies. In the early years, investors get tax benefits as limited partners in start-up (and money-losing) enterprises. Under the Tax Reform Act of 1986, however, the losses can generally only be used if there is income from other passive investments. Later on, as the initial losses disappear, investors are asked to convert their partnership interests into an equity stake in the company.

Venture capital experts based on the West Coast expect several new equity R&D partnerships to be up and running by year-end with newly raised pools of capital earmarked for start-ups. And many believe that the timing couldn't be better. As some of the more established and well-funded venture capital pools chase after second- and third-stage multimillion-dollar investments, "there's been a real hole in the marketplace for smaller deals in newer companies," says Nicholas Moore, an equity partnership specialist in the San Jose, California, office of Coopers & Lybrand, a Big Eight accounting firm. Indeed, unlike the big funds, which aim at relatively riskless investments on behalf of pension funds and corporations, managers of the new-style equity partnerships say they want to put their cash principally into attractive—and risky—young companies seeking less than $1 million.

One fund moving aggressively to capitalize on the dearth of seed capital is Crosspoint Venture Partners of Palo Alto, California. Having already assembled more than a dozen equity R&D partnerships under the name of Crosspoint Financial Corporation, for its own founders, it intends to expand on the approach with the money it raises from outside investors. While previous deals have involved only one company at a time, by year-end, says John Mumford, a managing general partner, the group expects to have $15 million for investment in many start-up businesses at once. Crosspoint, however, is not the only venture capital player doing equity R&D deals. Among the others in the field are Bay Partners II of Mountain View, California, and Alpha Fund of Palo Alto.

Mumford characterizes Crosspoint's perspective and role as "that of both the entrepreneur and the venture capitalist." Having worn both hats, he is convinced that the approach offers important advantages for each. "For the manager, the key is that he gets to retain the maximum amount of equity in his company," Mumford explains. But the tax benefits of the limited partnership, he adds, enable the investor to commit less money on an after-tax basis than other equity investments not eligible for tax write-offs.

The mechanics of equity R&D partnership investments are relatively simple. Since the $15-million Crosspoint Venture Partners Fund, which will invest in as many as forty separate deals over a three- or four-year period, is itself set up as a partnership, the investors—for the most part, individuals in the highest personal tax bracket of 50 percent—can use the early-year losses of the businesses as deductions against other ordinary income. Later, when profits loom or a product is ready for commercialization, the limited partnership interests in a particular business—held by the fund and the company founders—are converted in a tax-free exchange for equity in a new corporation based on a formula set when the deal was negotiated. (The managing partner in each investment of Crosspoint's fund will be Crosspoint Financial Corporation or one of the general partners.)

Unlike conventional venture capitalists seeking only an equity position, an equity R&D partnership is structured to lure investors willing to settle for somewhat less in the way of up-front ownership. Investors demand less because the tax deductions from early losses reduce the economic risk of the investment.

In today's market, according to Mumford, a conventional equity venture capital investment in a start-up business with a good product and marketing plan but with an unproven management track record might require founders to hand over 50 to 65 percent of the equity. But by using an equity R&D partnership under similar circumstances, he says, "investors would look for thirty-five to fifty percent of the equity." In a recent deal involving a company started by scientists and engineers from Stanford University, Mumford notes that the founders gave up just 35 percent of their ownership in the $1-million start-up.

In addition to the tax features, investors also are often willing to take a smaller share because they expect the eventual appreciation in the equity interest they do get to be substantial. "We are targeted at the highest risk/highest reward sector of the business," says Mumford.

While he won't be specific about earlier deals—most venture capitalists look for after-tax earnings of 30 to 40 percent per year—Mumford says, "after-tax returns on our own equity R and D partnership investments have been significantly higher than conventional venture capital returns."

The ability to generate such lofty returns stems, in Mumford's view, from his own experience as an entrepreneur and general manager and the expertise and training of the other principals. With a background in both accounting and law, Allan Anderson has been running an electronic-controls company. And Jim Willenborg is an engineer who has worked at Hewlett-Packard, Rolm, and Data General. Before establishing Crosspoint Venture Partners, the three were putting together equity R&D deals one at a time. Among the dozen or so new ventures they have financed are RoBind Corporation of Palo Alto, a start-up that merged with 3M; and Inmac Corporation of Santa Clara, California, a leading supplier of mini- and microcomputer accessories.

In early October, Mumford says, Crosspoint was studying about ten possibilities for the new pool of money, including a maker of medical lasers, a computer software developer, and several companies in communications and electronics. The emphasis is undeniably on high tech, but Mumford says, "We're open to any company with a proprietary product or marketing concept." Geographically, the fund will focus on California, Arizona, Colorado, and the Pacific Northwest.

But no matter what their business or location, all of Crosspoint's investments will be in early development phase. "Many venture capital pools now are so institutionally oriented that they don't have the management background to handle start-ups,' Mumford believes. "We like to get involved with the entrepreneurial/technical team." To Mumford and his associates, that means helping to structure the business, marketing, and financial strategies, and to select the proper management—"functioning like one of the founders."

While royalty-oriented R&D limited partnerships, built around the financing of a single product, have existed for some time, equity R&D partnerships have been slow to catch on, despite a Supreme Court ruling in 1974 that clarified the deductibility of R&D expenses for limited partners. But as advantageous as the more established R&D limited partnerships may be for financing development of new products, Mumford says, "the royalty arrangement doesn't work very well in an early-stage financing because most start-ups don't have the cash flow needed to pay a royalty." Furthermore, he notes, many venture capitalists would be reluctant to get involved with later-stage financings of companies committed to royalty payments.

Given such drawbacks, Coopers & Lybrand's Moore is one expert who expects interest in equity R&D deals to rise. "They offer a high level of support to entrepreneurs," he says. But thanks to the way the tax benefits work, Moore adds, "they enable founders to keep more of their companies."

—MICHAEL GECZI

BIG DEAL

About two and a half years ago, the founders of Sytek Inc., a young consulting firm in Mountain View, California, gave some well-known venture capitalists a look at their ambitious plan: They wanted to move from consulting to manufacturing. Specifically, they wanted to manufacture local-area networking systems—both hardware and software—which would allow large companies to transmit data, voice, and video to multiple facilities. They had already built prototypes, using profits from the $2.5-million consulting business. But finding the money to make and market the new products would be another matter. "At a minimum," says Sytek president and chief executive officer Michael S. Pliner, "we needed about eight million to ten million dollars. There was no way we could come up with that kind of money without major outside investment."

As it happened, major outside investment was available from such discerning venture capitalists as Hambrecht & Quist of San Francisco and Continental Illinois Venture Corporation of Chicago, both of which appeared ready to ante up the necessary equity. Says the thirty-seven-year-old Pliner, "They were willing to pay a price which we found entirely acceptable."

But, in the end, the company went elsewhere for the capital—to General Instrument Corporation, a New York City–based company with a commanding presence in the cable TV equipment business and a keen interest in Sytek's communications expertise.

The financial terms of the General Instrument deal, says Pliner, were substantially the same as those offered by the venture capitalists. General Instrument, a company with annual sales in the $900-million range, agreed to provide Sytek with an initial investment of about $9 million. In return, General Instrument would obtain about 37 percent of Sytek's equity and rights to buy more. Yet even if the money was the same, the Sytek founders saw other possible benefits in hooking up with a known supplier of cable TV equipment. Sytek's networking systems rely heavily on cable TV technology, an area in which General Instrument is an acknowledged leader. "We had no interest in being folded into General Instrument, and we told them that up front," says Pliner. "But we viewed General Instrument as the IBM of the cable

176

industry. Besides money, we thought it could add value to a lot of the things we wanted to accomplish."

To be sure, Sytek is not the first small company to obtain capital from a well-heeled corporation. During the 1970s, many large companies—including Exxon, Xerox, and General Electric—entered the venture capital arena with buckets of cash and high expectations. By and large, the giants were interested in forming relationships that could give them "windows" on new technologies. Some also hoped to find diversification opportunities by investing in and, later on, acquiring the more promising businesses in their portfolios.

General Instrument, however, launched its investment program in 1981 with more limited aims. "We found that most of the big companies which had moved into venture capital were failing badly at meeting their goals," explains vice-president Frank Sterling. "Most of them were such large and complex organizations that they couldn't find ways to bring the benefits home." Moreover, corporate investors often tried to monitor their investments too closely, triggering management defections that undermined their overall goals.

In light of these experiences, General Instrument chose a different approach. Rather than going out on a shopping spree for acquisition candidates, Sterling says, "we decided to invest in companies which were doing things close to what we were doing in our own operations. That way, we'd have opportunities for commercial relationships which could bring benefits to both companies."

Sytek was the first major investment prospect General Instrument approached, and Pliner and his associates found the possibilities intriguing. "Traditional venture capitalists could have provided management support and some very good contacts," notes Pliner, "but they couldn't give us access to some of the things we knew we'd be needing." General Instrument could, for example, help Sytek provide customers all over the country with product maintenance and support services. In addition, recalls Pliner, "we felt that an affiliation with an equipment maker as well known as General Instrument could give us market credibility quickly."

On the other hand, Pliner and his cofounders worried that the relationship might force the company to abandon its entrepreneurial business style. In a data-communications market that was changing almost weekly, "we wanted the freedom to make quick decisions, and we worried about having to go through lengthy approvals," says Pliner. Aside from operating control, the Sytek executives wanted to retain their right to raise money in the future from other sources. "When the time was right," says Pliner, "we hoped to do an initial public offering."

Following preliminary talks on the West Coast, Pliner and Sytek chairman Jack Goldsmith flew to New York, where they discussed their worries with General Instrument's top management. They said that they wanted to control a majority of the seats on their company's board of directors. General Instrument could name two of the five directors and would be permitted to hike its equity interest from an initial level of 37 percent to 51 percent later on. But even if their stake reached that level, Pliner says, "we asked them to promise on paper that once our sales reached twenty-five million dollars, we'd be free to go public." In addition, Sytek insisted that a 90 percent vote of shareholders be required on major issues—"to insulate us from capricious decisions," says Goldsmith, and to prevent General Instrument from changing the company's basic direction or divesting its assets.

Such stipulations might have scared away other investors, but General Instrument's executive—from the chairman on down—agreed to them. They believed an attempt to drive a harder bargain might backfire. "We didn't want to muscle them into any agreement they weren't comfortable with," says Frank Sterling. "We felt that the key to making the relationship work would be to let them run their own business. If we didn't do that, they wouldn't be happy. And we might end up with an empty shell."

A thick legal document was prepared, spelling out the finer points of the deal, but Pliner realized that no contract could be written to protect Sytek or its management completely. As a result, he and Goldsmith did extensive reference checks on General Instrument and its executives with business contacts and suppliers. "We had to believe in the credibility of the people," Pliner says, "and we wanted to make sure that their goals could be compatible with ours."

General Instrument's references checked out, and the deal went through. Since then, Sytek has hammered out a series of other business deals with its new equity partner. Early in 1982, for example, the company arranged for General Instrument's data-systems division to provide Sytek customers with on-call repair service in about sixty cities. By setting up third-party maintenance through General Instrument, Sytek avoided the expense of building an operation of its own from scratch. The ability to offer service is critical from a marketing perspective, notes Pliner, "but from a profitability standpoint, it's usually a loss leader."

A second deal involves a "multimillion-dollar" contract with General Instrument's Jerrold Cable Division, under which Sytek will develop a more powerful local-area network system, called MetroNet. Unlike Sytek's current hardware and software-based systems—which are sold to corporations or universities interested in linking entire office complexes or campuses—MetroNet is designed to operate on a citywide basis, from both homes and businesses, through cable TV facilities. According to the plans, both Sytek and General Instrument will be manufacturing components for the new systems, which will be sold jointly to cable operators.

In addition, discussions are under way on a manufacturing agreement that would make General Instrument a key supplier of electronic components to Sytek. By purchasing such items as circuit boards from General Instrument's offshore plants, Pliner says, "we hope to take some costs out of the products we sell in a competitive marketplace."

Clearly, these deals cover a lot of ground, but Pliner insists that each of them has been negotiated on an arm's-length basis—and only after Sytek has explored its other options. In any event, the complex relationship has been a smashing success—judging from Sytek's overall growth, that is. Since General Instrument's investment in late 1981, Sytek's sales have increased from about $2.5 million to more than $16.7 million for the years ended May 31, 1983. The number of employees, meanwhile, has surged from 75 to more than 250. "We've had all the benefits of being part of a larger company," says Pliner, "but we've been able to control our destiny and build an independent company."

Sytek's independence was especially evident last year, when the founders raised another $10 million through a private equity placement arranged by Hambrecht & Quist. Although some of the new money came from General Instrument (which upped its interest to 50.5 percent), most of it was raised from institutions, including the IBM pension fund and the University of Rochester's endowment fund. Nevertheless, Pliner indicates that an initial public offering may be necessary sometime in 1984, in order to raise capital for Sytek's product-development efforts in the years ahead. For this, Sytek has already obtained General Instrument's blessing.

Indeed, General Instrument's Sterling believes that his company will benefit handsomely from such a development. He also believes that General Instrument and Sytek will retain their commercial ties even after the financial stake is liquidated. "We'll be doing deals with Sytek just as long as they're of benefit to both companies," says Sterling.

Pliner, for his part, takes a similar view. "Only part of this relationship has been based on money. If money were all we wanted, we would have gone with the venture capitalists."

—BRUCE G. POSNER

STRATEGIC ALLIANCES

In the spring of 1983, Richard Sebastian, armed with a Ph.D. in physics, dreaming entrepreneurial dreams of lucrative contracts with the Pentagon, journeyed to Cleveland to see how he might be useful to a venerable machine-tool manufacturer, founded in 1916, called Acme-Cleveland Corporation. It was a speculative trip, to put it mildly. Sebastian, after all, had little in common with his hosts. He was a James Bond outfitter from outside Washington, D.C., who could sell you a gizmo that could detect a security guard nodding off to sleep or the presence of passengers hidden in the trunk of a car. So what was he doing in Cleveland, talking up his wares to a roomful of Rust Bowl managers and engineers who, for all he knew, were one step from the scrap heap of history?

As it happened, he was there precisely *because* Acme-Cleveland, like so many other machinery companies, was in very serious trouble. The company needed to retool its manufacturing operation, and its executives thought that Sebastian's spy devices might help. They wondered, for example, whether the sensor signal–processing technology that could alert you to a body in a car trunk might not also be able to tell you whether metal tools were cutting correctly and when the blades were wearing out. The meeting lasted for around two hours. When it was over, the Acme-Cleveland executives invited Sebastian to come back soon, this time bringing a business plan with him.

Over the next few weeks, the discussions grew earnest, focusing on just what sort of deal was most beneficial to both parties. Sebastian wanted money—to get his new company off the ground, to do research—but he also wanted to retain his independence. His ambition encompassed more than a lifelong devotion to refurbishing the Rust Bowl. He remembers being somewhat surprised that Acme-Cleveland appeared to understand this. "It seemed enough to them that we were interested in their problems," he says. "They said they didn't want to control us; they didn't want to be our Sugar Daddy." So a deal was struck: Acme-Cleveland put up $250,000 in seed money, and another $100,000 for a research and development contract to be spent during the following year; Sebastian agreed to help the company apply sensor technology to factory processes.

It was not the first such deal between a high-technology start-up and an old-line manufacturer, but the idea was new enough that both entered into the arrangement with a sense of experimentation. It was a venture that offered something to both companies—a partnership, really, based on mutual needs. For lack of a better term, it was called a "strategic alliance."

All across the heartland of American industry, such antique companies as Acme-Cleveland are scouring the countryside for business innovators who can help them bring technological changes to their markets and retool their factories for the future. Their motive—survival—is as basic as their industries. The pulse of the heartland, pressed by low-cost foreign competition, is slowing down. Plants are out of date; products are being rejected as irrelevant or inferior; layers of management, once thought indispensable, now stand revealed as so much cotton batting. Competition has turned the gaze of these giants outward and downward—to the world of small companies, sometimes to copy their procedures, sometimes to harness their genius, always to find the spark that will enable the large companies to live and grow.

The effort takes many forms. One of the most talked-about is intrapreneurship, as when such industrial behemoths as IBM Corporation and 3M Company discover that product innovation thrives best when employees are turned loose to function like independent entrepreneurs. Another is the corporate start-up, as when such companies as Control Data Corporation and Tektronix Inc. offer capital and support to restless employees eager to go out on their own. The trend can be seen as well in the changing relationships between large manufacturing companies and their small suppliers. And even General Motors Corporation is rejiggering its legendary bureaucracy in hopes of fashioning a more nimble, decentralized operating system. Indeed, GM chairman Roger B. Smith himself has appeared on "The Phil Donahue Show," explaining to the nation's housewives why executives of the new Saturn subsidiary will have total freedom to invent new ways of manufacturing automobiles.

All these maneuvers reflect an apparent change in big-company attitudes toward small enterprise. The giants, to be sure, have long recognized that smaller companies offered things they wanted. Historically, however, their approach has resembled that of a sultan in search of a new favorite for his harem. Acquisition was the goal, whether in the short run or the long, and as often as not the acquired company didn't protest. But funny things happened on the way to the seraglio. For one thing, the small-company founders tended to take their money and run, leaving little more than the shell of a business behind. Then there were the cultural conflicts—notably the attempts by large companies to impose highly developed management systems on entrepreneurial ventures. A case in point was Exxon Corporation, which bought or spawned several new businesses in the late 1960s and early 1970s, smothered them with management, then watched them expire one by one. Other big companies learned similar hard lessons, which put a temporary halt to their search for small company "windows on technology."

But along about 1980, a new kind of relationship began to appear, primarily in the computer, telecommunications, and pharmaceutical industries. In these relationships, the large company would buy a minority stake in a small company without seeking to acquire or even control it. Thus, for example, Memorex Corporation, a leader in computer-memory storage, bought 4 percent of a young disk-drive company called DMA Systems Inc. General Instrument Corporation, a big force in the cable TV equipment industry, settled for less than half of Sytek Inc., a computer networking company. Such companies as Abbott Laboratories took minority interests in young, avant-garde medical research companies.

These deals had two things in common. In each, both parties were intimately involved in research and technology, and the focal point was new products. What the large company wanted was a leg up on products and markets it felt would be important to its future. The alliance was a way of extending its internal research and development effort at relatively low cost, while protecting its approaches to potential new markets. What the small company wanted was money, without giving away its freedom and incentive to create a viable business.

And the newfangled arrangements worked, or at least some of them did. They certainly became very popular. During 1984, the number of minority investments by big companies in small companies financed by venture capitalists soared to 200, almost three times the level in 1981, according to Venture Economics Inc., in Wellesley Hill, Massachusetts. There was also a wave of deals between young technology companies in the United States and more established European and Japanese companies, and this was paralleled by another wave that linked big American companies and smaller ones abroad. Meanwhile, some growing companies began to explore alliances with each other. Cullinet Software Inc. and Lotus Development Corporation, for example, worked out an agreement to develop software links that will provide users of 1-2-3 and Symphony with access to mainframe-computer databases. Then there was the deal between Jack Eckerd Corporation, the $2.6-billion Florida drug retailer, and a California start-up called HomeClub Inc., which is developing a chain of home-improvement centers. In addition to acquiring about 20 percent of HomeClub's stock, Eckerd agreed to have its chairman, Stewart Turley, serve on the smaller company's board.

But perhaps the most startling development has been the appearance of such alliances in the industrial heartland, where some of the wooly mammoths of American enterprise have begun teaming up with hot, young technology companies in an effort to rejuvenate their operations and adapt to changing environments. The incongruity of such partnerships aside, these new industrial alliances represent a significant broadening of the trend, for their goals are quite different from those of the earlier technology alliances. Unlike Memorex, General Instrument, and Abbott, the large companies involved in these heartland deals are generally not looking for new products. Rather, they are seeking ways to streamline and upgrade their manufacturing processes, in hopes of competing better in international markets.

General Motors is perhaps the foremost example of the heartland's new outreach policy. For generations, the auto giant chugged along on a proud tradition of internal R&D. Almost overnight, it has struck up operating alliances with six small companies, all but one of them in the fast-emerging area of machine vision, which uses computer-controlled cameras during manufacturing for such activities as quality- and process-control. Besides providing the companies with equity capital (it owns about 10 percent of each of them), GM has signed multimillion-dollar R&D contracts.

Another example is Caterpillar Tractor Company, which is looking to alliances to restore its overseas competitiveness. Last February, its venture capital arm put $2 million in a three-year-old Arlington, Texas, company that develops systems for factory robots. Caterpillar is now considering other, similar deals.

So, too, is Rockwell International Corporation, the $9.3-billion defense and aerospace giant. It paid $1.2 million for a 5 percent interest in Micro Linear Inc., a young San Jose, California, company with expertise in the design and manufacture of semicustom linear integrated circuits. Rockwell expected to be one of Micro Linear's major customers during its first year of operation.

It remains to be seen, of course, how these relationships will work out, but already new questions are arising and new issues emerging:

• How, for example, should a deal be structured to maximize the chances of success? How much ownership is too much or too little? Companies are experimenting with different equity percentages, development contracts, and licensing deals. A few big-company partners have discovered, to their dismay, that the wrong deal can present entrepreneurs with the same irresistible temptations to maximize short-term over long-term objectives that the big company executives are so often accused of falling into.

• How do you cope with the inevitable cultural differences between industrial giants and small, entrepreneurial companies? Robert J. Eaton, a vice-president at General Motors, remarked recently that he had been meeting with guys in jeans and sneakers who rode to work on ten-speed bicycles. "They don't wear suits," he said. "I'm not sure some of them even *own* suits." On a more serious level, skeptical observers wonder whether big companies will be able to restrain themselves from imposing their own decision-making structures, their compensation policies, their very language, on smaller, more fragile partners.

• What about the independence that lies at the heart of the relationship? To what extent should the small company be allowed to set its own agenda? How much latitude should it have? As a minority owner, the big company can try to persuade; it can't order. On the other hand, its persuasion can be mighty persuasive, and this has already made for some interesting discussions between large and small partners. The chief executive officer of a GM-allied machine-vision company, for example, recalls a dispute over the responsibilities of the man whom GM wanted to sit on his board. He insisted that the director's duty, first and foremost, was to foster the small company's interests, not GM's. "We went round and round on that issue, before they saw our point of view," he says.

- What sort of commitment is needed from the big-company partner? Will deals initiated by high-level corporate managers be accepted in the operating divisions? Maybe not, or so some companies have discovered. Their experience suggests that the most successful alliances are those that speak to the particular needs of line managers.

Questions like these drive home the point that alliances are no magic bullet, no instant cure for the ills of basic industry. Rather, they constitute an experiment to try to tap the very different resources and cultures of large and small companies. Like most experiments, they proceed by trial and error, on a case-by-case basis, through the gradual accumulation of knowledge and experience. And therein lies the advantage to companies that have begun acquiring such knowledge and experience—companies like Acme-Cleveland.

In the summer of 1982, the principal question was whether or not Acme-Cleveland had a future at all. The recession was spreading through the Midwest like the plague, and the sixty-six-year-old machinery maker was in serious jeopardy. Only a year before, Acme-Cleveland had been a profitable $400-million company. But when the slowdown hit the shores of Lake Erie, everything unraveled at once. Orders suddenly collapsed; sales went into a dramatic free-fall; profit margins were deteriorating rapidly. Acme-Cleveland quickly shrank to less than one-half of its former size. The workforce—once 6,500 strong—was slashed to 2,600. To be sure, the company's competitors were also hurting—the total market declined from $5.5 billion in 1981 to $1.5 billion in 1983—but none quite as badly. And nobody knew where the bottom would be.

None of this was especially surprising to B. Charles Ames, Acme-Cleveland's tough-minded fifty-nine-year-old CEO and chairman. He had anticipated the difficulties almost from the day he joined the company in January 1981. Chuck Ames, a veteran consultant with McKinsey & Company, had been the CEO of Reliance Electric Company, a large manufacturer of electric motors and components, until shortly after its acquisition by Exxon. He had spent his early months at Acme-Cleveland skeptically touring the facilities. Nothing he saw pointed to a very optimistic future.

The problems, in Ames's view, went beyond the specifics of any economic cycle. Rather, it seemed that the company was all geared up to conquer a world that didn't exist. Many of its products were based on outdated technologies that took no account of the changes its major customers were going through. The most profitable division, for example, made dedicated transfer systems that the Detroit auto companies were in the process of abandoning. Ames thought they were "absolute dinosaurs," but Acme-Cleveland hadn't developed newer, more flexible systems. Another division made high-speed steel drills and other tools for cutting through metal but had no tools for cutting holes in the increasingly popular plastics and ceramics.

But it was the central research facility that most disturbed Ames. To begin with, the building itself was several miles from the nearest production plant. He soon learned, moreover, that there was very little dialogue between the research people and the marketing staffs over what customers really wanted. "Walking around that R and D center," recalls Ames, "I got this sick feeling in my gut. We had a bunch of guys in lab coats doing showcase research. And my reaction was, 'Holy Christ, is this a commercial operation?' "

Ames quickly concluded that some of Acme-Cleveland's operations needed to be reorganized. He had too many managers at corporate headquarters: He got rid of some and dispersed the rest. Production facilities were poorly designed: He reduced the working floor space by more than 1 million square feet with no change in productive capacity. But beyond that, the company had to acquire new kinds of expertise. In factories all over America, new technologies were revolutionizing the way products were designed, assembled, and inspected. They involved robotics, lasers, and other dazzling applications of computers. Bigger machinery manufacturers, like Cincinnati Milacron Inc. and Cross & Trecker Corporation were moving in those directions, but Acme-Cleveland knew almost nothing about them. All the company knew, notes Ames, was old-fashioned metal-bending and -cutting techniques. "If I had brought our very best machinists to IBM or Xerox," he says, "they wouldn't have had a thing to talk about."

But how could Acme-Cleveland explore a lengthy list of new areas quickly enough? The company didn't have much money for acquisitions. What's more, Ames had learned at Reliance that acquiring 100 percent ownership of smaller businesses didn't always work; Reliance had purchased several owner-managed service businesses during the 1970s, only to see the spark go out once the owner had the money. So over the next two and a half years, Ames embarked on an ambitious course, negotiating one strategic alliance after another.

With one deal, he sought to introduce Acme-Cleveland to the powers of robotics. The corporate planning staff looked at prospective partners and settled on a robotics consulting firm in Detroit. At the same time, Ames also wanted to align himself with a partner that understood laser applications. The search led to a company in Santa Clara, California, named XMR Laser Systems Inc.

Sometimes, Ames simply identified an area of expertise that looked promising. He knew, for example, that computer-aided design and manufacturing (CAD/CAM) was becoming important to manufacturers all over, so an alliance was formed with a CAD/CAM time-sharing business in Dayton. There was yet another deal with a company in St. Paul, Minnesota, that licensed a Soviet technology for surface coatings on metal, using a chemical process that made tools and parts more durable.

Just as Ames was hustling to get the company involved in new technologies, he was experimenting with new forms of deal-making. The structure of the alliances varied greatly, depending on the circumstances. With the robotics company, for example, Acme-Cleveland invested $500,000 in exchange for 35 percent of the equity and a seat on its board. But the arrangement with the CAD/CAM company was different: In addition to investing $2 million for 40 percent, Ames negotiated an option to buy the rest, based on a multiple of earnings five years down the road. In light of his experiences with acquisitions, he thought this approach was less risky than buying the whole company at once. With the coating business, there was still another approach: Acme-Cleveland didn't invest in the company itself, but agreed to become a 50/50 partner in a new joint venture. Together, they would operate metal-coating service centers all over the country. Acme-Cleveland's sales force would push the new service.

There were other types of partnerships to fill other types of needs. A Rochester, New York, factory automation software company had a series of quality-assurance products in the works; Acme-Cleveland became a 10 percent owner. There was a small industrial-consulting and software house in West Lafayette, Indiana, named Pritsker & Associates Inc., which Ames hopes would help on big-ticket development contracts; its cofounder, Alan Pritsker, a leader in computer simulation of manufacturing processes, agreed to sell around twenty-five percent of the business.

And then, of course, there was Richard Sebastian's Springfield, Virginia, company, Digital Signal Corporation. Ames hoped that Sebastian, forty-two, and his colleagues could apply their laser sensors to such elements of manufacturing as noncontact gauging and inspection.

To be sure, Ames didn't know what the future held with any of the alliances. The road ahead had nothing but blind turns. It was almost as if Ames was attempting to create a different sort of company.

To date, Acme-Cleveland has invested more than $10 million in eight partnerships and joint ventures. It has been three and a half years since Ames negotiated his first alliance. Sitting in a leather wing chair in his office about fifteen miles from downtown Cleveland, Ames, a square-jawed, balding Illinois native, says he never expected all of the relationships to result in benefits for Acme-Cleveland, and indeed the process has been a series of trials, errors, and surprises.

The robotics consulting business in Detroit, for instance, never really got off the ground. The founders weren't very good at marketing their expertise, says Ames. "They had too much substance and not enough veneer." Acme-Cleveland suggested possible customers, but to no avail. The investment was sold.

The experience with the quality-assurance software company was just as frustrating. New programs haven't been developed, and Ames laments that the founders frittered away their money on lavish over-head expenses. "I think it's been a simple case of poor management," he says. "But when you own a minority, there's not much you can do about it."

Even when the young companies have done well, Ames has learned some important lessons about the subtle art of structuring deals. The CAD/CAM company, for instance, is growing and making money. But Ames thinks that it would be growing faster if there were no buyout formula. He says that the purchase option has had a chilling effect on the way the founder has managed the business. He plans to rethink his approach to purchase options in the future.

Other relationships, however, have taken interesting turns. The deal with XMR, the California laser company, has spawned a whole new laser business within Acme-Cleveland. About two years after the alliance was formed, Ames sold the XMR interest and set up his own laser subsidiary south of Cleveland. The new subsidiary licenses tech-nology from XMR, which was offered a 10 percent stake; it has recently sold several large systems, including one to General Electric Company. "We're not in the dark ages anymore," offers Ames, "which is more than we could have said a couple years ago."

There are other sources of optimism for Acme-Cleveland, too. In the year and a half since the metal-coating venture was formed, it has become an $8-million business. Within the decade, Ames thinks it could be ten times that big—rivaling Acme-Cleveland's entire metal drill division. Acme-Cleveland's systems-design people, moreover, have recently been working more closely with Pritsker & Associates. And Richard Sebastian's company is in the final phases of testing for a new laser measurement device. Ames is hopeful that the technology (which Acme-Cleveland would license from Digital Signal) will provide the basis for some breakthrough inspection products. "I think we're going to be one or two years ahead of our competition," he says.

Not that Acme-Cleveland has always agreed with its partners about the best way to do business. The managers of the metal-coating venture, for instance, recently wanted to hire about ten new sales specialists to drum up more business. Acme-Cleveland people argued against it, saying that the added expense would be too harmful to profits. In another instance, Pritsker wanted money to develop an elaborate $3-million factory-control system. Ames advised him to seek outside funding, which Pritsker is doing.

Such back and forth has been common in Acme-Cleveland's rela-tionships. Last year, for example, Sebastian approached the company for a guarantee for a computer lease, which his bank would otherwise have refused. Ames had told him at the time of the company's founding that Acme-Cleveland would guarantee only up to its percentage of ownership. "There's a real danger in being too helpful . . . in being seen as a deep pocket," Ames believes. Thus, last spring when Acme-Cleveland indicated its willingness to make a bridge loan of $260,000 to a Digital Signal subsidiary, Ames insisted on a tough penalty. If the loan isn't repaid on time, Acme-Cleveland will take a majority interest. The threat, says Sebastian, is more than sufficient to assure that it won't happen.

While many of the more blatant clashes have been over money, the most fundamental difficulties have involved communication. Ames confesses that several of the relationships have suffered from lack of attention by him and other managers throughout Acme-Cleveland. Most of the alliances were initiated from the top. With all the turmoil the machinery company has experienced, it has been difficult to set aside the time or the people to make things happen. In fact, there has been an almost constant swirl of restructuring and reshuffling of people.

Yet some of the difficulties, Ames feels, are living proof of how hard it can be for any old-line company to learn new approaches to doing business. He says he had no idea how important it is to be comfortable with entrepreneurs as people, as well as with their businesses. In the future, he will set aside more time with founders before deals are signed, to assess whether the respective interests seem compatible. "I'm not looking for a best friend," he says. "But it's important to talk about values and goals."

The company is beginning to change in other ways, too. Over the past three years, several dozen newly hired managers are hastening what Ames calls a cultural transition. No one is expecting overnight miracles, but there are signs that the new people are willing to approach things with more open minds. Last spring, for instance, the company was considering three new partnerships, all of which were being championed by divisional managers, not by Ames or his corporate staffers.

For all of the questions that Acme-Cleveland still has about its future—the company still hasn't seen any profits, although the losses have been abating—there are other questions being asked about strategic alliances by large and small companies all over the United States. It has yet to be seen how many of the larger companies will succeed in their attempts to become more in tune with the marketplace. Nor is it clear how many of the smaller companies will find the advantages they hope for—or what the longer-term consequences will be. There are no guarantees that the relationships will continue or, for that matter, that the large companies won't ultimately try to control their partners or compete with them.

But if the stakes are high for companies, they are just as high for the nations' basic industries and for the economy at large. Alliances, to be sure, offer promises of greater efficiency, and even survival. But for anything to happen, independent companies will have to learn new forms of interaction and interdependency. Corporate managers and entrepreneurs will have to stub their toes before they can do new dances. The long-term benefits of this painful learning process may be a new ability to compete.

—BRUCE G. POSNER

IT'S WHAT'S UP FRONT THAT COUNTS

B right and airy as it may be, a third-floor walk-up is not the sort of estate business owners picture as home. Eljenn International Corporation's Mark Weissman *almost* got to move out of his a couple of years back, except that just as he was on his way to pick up nearly $4 million for his UltraSwim line, the sale was called off. Well, the prospective buyer was not exactly backing out, but technical questions had come up, and more research was needed. If they were to make the summer marketing season, they would have to radically restructure the deal—downward. "I didn't quite get rich," Weissman philosophizes, "but at least it was a learning experience."

What the expensive B school of hard knocks taught the forty-eight-year-old chief executive officer was a familiar curriculum: (1) A bird in the hand is worth two in the bush; (2) do not count your chickens before they hatch; and, (3) hire good lawyers. Since larger corporations often enhance their product mix by acquiring the patents and brands of others, this is a course that any small business with proprietary property might audit. In this particular instance, what Weissman learned was that in dealing with a big corporation, especially in a licensing deal, a small company is well advised to insist on getting its cash up front. And, Weissman further discovered, the nuances of licensing are so complex that a negotiations team with clout is not enough. Because the patents and trademarks involved are themselves extraordinarily complicated instruments, a savvy patent attorney is a good investment as well.

The seventy-plus-page typewritten tome that eventually granted exclusive world rights to Shulton Inc.—a subsidiary of American Cyanamid Company, best known for Old Spice toiletries and, in scalp circles, for Breck Shampoo—to manufacture and market Eljenn's UltraSwim brand of hair and skin care was signed on February 16, 1984. Shulton did not acquire the brand and its patent outright under the terms of the renegotiated license, but instead built in an option to buy later. To seal the contract, Eljenn pocketed an initial, nonrefundable fee of $450,000—a far cry from the hefty lock, stock, and barrel payment the Eljenn board had been toasting just a few weeks before. To help bridge the gap, Shulton raised starting royalty rates from the original 2 percent of net UltraSwim sales to 7 percent. With that boost,

Weissman felt he was looking at a return to Eljenn of as much as $3 million over five years, if all went well. And, if all went *exceedingly* well, UltraSwim might yet fetch its multimillion-dollar lump sum, since the purchase-option price was pegged to a liberal percent-of-sales formula.

Sad to say, however, after only twenty-four months Shulton threw in the towel. Its first-year sales of the line, which features a chlorine-removing process Weissman coinvented in 1979, amounted to almost $4 million, less than half of projections. Second-year sales dropped to less than $2.5 million. Even more disheartening, Shulton wasn't much more successful than Weissman had been on his own. Though he started Eljenn in 1979 primarily as a product design-and-development operation, Weissman had subcontracted out the manufacture of Ultra-Swim and had made some inroads in marketing the line. Sales had passed $1.5 million by 1983, the year Weissman decided to "get out of the marketing business" and let a seasoned pro properly exploit the brand in drugstores and supermarkets around the world.

What with gearing up for production and promotion, Shulton may well have poured as much as $2 million down the UltraSwim drain over the two years it had the brand. While such write-offs may be standard operating procedure among big corporations that willy-nilly acquire licenses on the assumption that one will pan out, the fallow years almost did little Eljenn in. Counting on royalty payments of a good $500,000 for the first year alone, the young company blissfully spent revenues that the postman never brought. Eljenn's two remaining products—Inner Sense Permanent Wave (still in development) and Purifying Shampoo (just going on the market)—nearly died aborning. To stem the slide toward extinction, Weissman had to pledge $300,000 on his own signature against the accounts-receivable financing that kept him afloat.

How had the once-lustrous deal turned into dross? Weissman blames the mass-retailing company's stubborn inability to market a specialty item. "They had been reading *In Search of Excellence*," he speculates. "Everyone was into aggressive niche marketing, and this was 1984, the year of the summer Olympics—a great chance to kick it off into the swimming niche." Shulton tried to get UltraSwim out in time, but with the late start and a tidal wave of competing new products all aimed at the same date, it was unable to establish beachheads on retail shelves. So Shulton jettisoned its advertising—but little matter: There were great plans for the next summer season.

For starters, Shulton would offer the trade an early-buy special, to be backed up with glossy floor displays and national print and television ads. "Fine," said Weissman, a consultant under the terms of the agreement, "but what are you going to do over the winter to keep some shelf movement going?" Essentially nothing, was the answer. As a result, Weissman relates, goods stayed on the shelves, and retailers didn't place new orders. When Shulton turned to such soap-selling ploys as money-off coupons and sweepstakes, Weissman sniffed disaster. It confirmed the uneasiness he had felt earlier when Shulton removed the slick marketing expert he had been working with and replaced him with an assistant product manager borrowed from one of the company's fragrance lines.

In a letter to Shulton dated June 14, 1985, a frustrated Weissman chided: "People will buy UltraSwim because they need it, not because it's fifty cents off. . . . Frankly, I don't understand [your marketing approach]. I'd save all my coupon and contest money," he advised, "and spend it on telling people I had a product they really needed." Not only did UltraSwim have outstanding credibility, he had always argued, but its profit margins were considerably greater than most shampoos. Shulton, not yet tuned into the art of specialty sales, spurned both features, "and kept selling it as if it were Old Spice. Big corporations tend to think they know everything, and that little guys who built the product from nothing are rubes."

But Shulton could well afford to dabble in the market. By reducing its initial payment to Weissman from $4 million to $450,000, it also had drastically reduced any fiscal motivation to recover the fee. Nonetheless, the smaller sum had bought Shulton the right to do with the products whatever it wanted (short of fiduciary negligence) until the day the UltraSwim patent expires, October 20, 1998. So there was little legal basis for Eljenn's objections. The only performance standard that had been specified in the agreement was the section that required Shulton to commit from 25 to 40 percent of actual sales to promoting the brand over the first two years. Section 15, Weissman came late to realize, was, in fact, a Catch 22: As sales declined, the *less* Shulton was obliged to spend on trying to spur them back up.

Why had Eljenn not required dollar-sales floors, below which the license would automatically be forfeited? It was getting late and he was getting nervous, Weissman explains. "They were asking, 'Are you going to run with us?' We couldn't have done the deal if we tried to lock them into guarantees, so we went along with it. Anyway, the royalties were such nice percentages we thought whatever minimums we put on would be far surpassed." To that he adds unerringly, "We were naive."

And then some, adds businessman Jerome Goldstein, a veteran licenser who served on the Eljenn board at the time. "They had to trade in the guarantees for a bigger up side, but it was totally unnecessary. Management's inexperience allowed it to happen. Once they took it so far into the selling, they were committed to doing a deal regardless. That's a bad situation."

Indeed, the alternatives were few. Time was running out on a summer-oriented product, and both sides considered the summer Olympics an essential marketing peg. The larger up-front fee would have required the approval of several layers of Shulton's top management, an uncertain, time-consuming process; only an immediate few, however, were needed to endorse the smaller payment. The higher sum also was contingent on clearing up the legal technicalities that concerned Shulton's lawyers, another potential delay. Even then,

Weissman couldn't be certain that Shulton would remain interested or that a competing brand might not pop up in the meantime. Finally, the fact that other big companies such as Johnson & Johnson, Vidal Sassoon, and Olin had already rejected Weissman's licensing proposition dictated playing out the hand then and there. "Besides," Weissman says, "we were enthusiastic, they were enthusiastic. We figured they'd do a great job. The main difficulty we had was, it went from the money in the bank to almost all the money on the come." But the come never came.

Even if Eljenn had insisted on written guarantees to protect against such misfortune, there is little it could have done in practice. As is often the case, licensees like Shulton don't *have* to pay the guaranteed minimum just because it's written in a five-pound document. They have to pay it only if they want to keep the license. So when a product falls disappointingly short of sales projections, most would just as soon dump the license as throw good money after bad.

For a small company, there is, however, at least one effective alternative to cash guarantees: Make the licensee's performance a matter of pride. That, for instance, is the strategy of Moleculon Inc., a small Cambridge, Massachusetts, developer of transdermal patches that has begun to license patented products to large companies. Moleculon insists that the acquiring company promote the product under one of *its* own brand names, rather than Moleculon's. Shulton, it follows, would have worked harder on behalf of Eljenn's hair rinse had it been marketed under, say, the Old Spice trademark.

In any case, after the second summer's flop, Weissman raised the possibility to Shulton of bringing his baby back home, and in September 1985, Shulton agreed to open negotiations for return of the brand. At the time, Weissman says, "we considered whether we wanted to get back into it ourselves or whether we wanted to find another big brother to license it to. We decided that for the same reason we licensed in the first place, we wanted to license it again—we didn't feel we had the financial resources to manage a mass-merchandised brand." Shulton, it turned out, was holding over a million dollars' worth of inventory that it planned to let dribble out to retailers over the next several years. But Weissman felt his only chance of saving UltraSwim was to get it all back immediately for resale. That, however, would require a bit of cash—"an amount equal to Shulton's factory cost," according to the licensing agreement. After the persistent Weissman got through, though, Shulton agreed to let him have the lot at discount.

With timing as dramatic as the U.S. cavalry's, to the rescue came Chattem Inc., niche-marketer of such emollients as Mudd facial masks and Corn Silk cosmetics. The $64-million Chattanooga company's researchers studied the UltraSwim brand and became "very excited." The retail market had not been injured, they found, and with two years of proper marketing, UltraSwim sales could be built into the $6-million range. Weissman immediately sensed the specialty-marketing kinship he never had with Shulton. "Their products had stories to them," he says. "Salespeople and marketing people *love* products with a story."

Even at only 5 percent royalties (versus Shulton's 7 percent), the notion was so irresistible that Weissman struck a handshake agreement with Chattem before he had gotten the inventory back from Shulton, and for the next three months, he paid for attorneys negotiating *both* deals. Although the service comes high (about $50,000 per deal), a good lawyer, he insists, "can get you back several times what he's charging you over what you could have done on your own." Case in point: The attorneys Weissman tapped to do the deed, both MIT alumni who had gone on to specialize in drafting hard-nosed licensing arrangements, were able to place the orphaned brand with unpredicted advantage. The license was reassigned to Chattem, and the deal was sealed with a solid $1.25 million up front, paid as a nonrefundable advance against royalties rather than a simple fee. "We were fortunate," says Weissman, a striking understatement for one who not only had just executed the rare fiscal feat of reselling a defunct brand, but got more for it the second time around.

The royalty rates on net sales are less, but, boilerplate for boilerplate, the arrangement with Chattem is essentially the same as the Shulton deal. Chattem, too, was unwilling to commit to performance minimums, but it made the up-front considerations attractive. Eljenn was able to post the advance on its books as revenues, instantly turning a potentially disastrous 1985 into the black. The profit phenomenon is likely to be short-lived, however, since that revenue represents royalties on $25 million of future UltraSwim sales that Eljenn will have to wait out before it can dip into a fresh revenue stream.

To Weissman there is no question of the relative quality of the new arrangement: "A deal where you get the money and it's there is the best deal of all," he concludes. That, of course, is yet to be seen. And it's possible that even the Shulton deal eventually would have been rewarding, inasmuch as the original Shulton marketer put in charge of UltraSwim went on to roll out a cockroach product successfully. But one thing is for sure, as Jerome Goldstein succinctly sums up the bottom line: "No deal with Chattem, the company folds."

—ROBERT A. MAMIS

A DEAL FOR ALL SEASONS

The zero coupon is to bonds as the Mexican hairless is to dogs. It looks like the traditional design, but one fixture common to the species is disturbingly missing. Why the dog evolved as bald as Telly Savalas (or vice versa) is anyone's guess, but the absence of periodic interest payments, or coupons (a term derived from the old days when you literally snipped payable drafts from the certificate itself), is all too explainable: this era's high cost of money. A zero, as the curious debt instrument came to be called in its heyday only a few years back, is designed so that the borrower does not have to service the debt through periodic cash payouts. Instead, the original loan is discounted from par (in bond biz, "par" equals $100) such that when the borrower pays it back at par on the due date, it yields the equivalent of the missing interest. In addition, kickers can be attached to the zero to make it even more enticing to otherwise timid lenders. These can include warrants that provide for buying more stock within a given time period, options for buying yet more—and cheaper—stock, stock in another corporation, interest-bearing preferred stock, and dinner at the Four Seasons.

A freewheeling zero is the kind of ingenious win/win financial showpiece that only capitalists could dream up. The borrower gets money interest-free, while for the lender the locked-up nature of the zero cements the rate of compound interest for the duration of the bond (which can be twenty-five years or more). When the bond is redeemed, some of the income might be reported as a long-term capital gain. With all that going for them, zero-based packages became hot brokerage-house retail items in the tight-money Carter regime, when lending rates were approaching the batting average of the Atlanta Braves. Even large and responsible public corporations seized the chance to unshackle themselves from expensive debt service, and to cast their lot with possibly better borrowing terms next century. So did marginal operations that could barely meet their Coffee-mate budgets.

The no-tickee no-money concept is neither new nor necessarily suspect. Certain federal obligations have been auctioned at original-issue discount (OID, to your accountant) for decades; you lend the federal government $900, say, and in a year the U.S. Treasury (if it's still around) will give you back $1,000, paying 11 percent interest. Now that the cost of capital somehow has Laffer-curved back into single digits, however, zero coupons have shed much of their service-free cachet. And a 1982 Tax Equity and Fiscal Responsibility Act (TEFRA) provision that holders of zeros and other OIDs must pay taxes as if they had collected the interest payments has put the kibosh on the retail market as well.

That might have been sufficient to maim an ordinary capital scheme like, say, the research and development partnership. Not so the flexible zero. An inventive application of OID financing recently emerged as an early-round font of working capital for a start-up enterprise. The business—Air Atlanta Inc.—was incorporated in May 1981 by Georgia native Michael R. Hollis, a twenty-seven-year-old lawyer and investment banker. In an industry noted for its swift consumption of cash as well as gas, one of deregulation's newest airlines has been issuing zeros for the lion's share of its money. Although more than $5 million was raised in common stock, as of year-end 1985, interest-free debt instruments—in this case, convertible debentures—accounted for roughly $19 million Air Atlanta's total funding of $54 million, exceeded as a single source only by a capital lease on its fleet of jets.

The company's reliance on a zero coupon convertible debenture for its very sustenance is thought to be unique not only in the annals of the airline industry, but among start-ups anywhere. Nor do the contributions come from kinfolk taking fliers. Air Atlanta's lenders are such demanding investors as Aetna Life Insurance, Equitable Life Assurance Society of the United States, and General Electric Credit, which together have loaned $13.6 million via zero coupons to the still-profitless carrier.

How were traditionally conservative asset managers persuaded to take on unsecured debt, payable no sooner than five years from issue, by a fledgling carrier that had only four routes and five planes; had been forced to cancel a public offering due to lack of Wall Street sponsorship; owned few assets (and those pledged as security under other instruments); was knocking heads with Eastern and Delta out of Atlanta by promoting deluxe service (including gourmet meals, free drinks, wide seats, and shrunken margins); had to enlist a big-name airline to feed in passengers; and was trying to take off vertically in a sector where no airline has made a profit in its first year and in which other haulers were dropping like—to be discreet—flies?

Keep sweetening the deal, answers Daniel H. Kolber, a corporate attorney who worked with founder Hollis on designing the zero vehicles. Saddled with the title of vice-president of communications and industry affairs for his efforts, the diminutive executive insists that rounding up wherewithal is mostly a matter of being able to answer skittish investors' objections.

"It's the same as closing any sale," avers Kolber, who helped coax the deal around a New York statute prohibiting insurance companies from owning voting shares by an on-the-spot redefinition of the preffered stock as Class B nonvoting, amendable to Class A voting at the lender's, if not the state legislature's, discretion.

Like apricot jam in a Sacher torte, the tastiest layer of Air Atlanta's debentures is their potential transmogrification into a generous chunk of ownership. But why not peddle common stock in the first place? For one thing, it would have been tough to convince venture capitalists to back a couple of buddies only a few years out of the University of Virginia School of Law, one black, the other white.

"We would love to have done common," Kolber admits, but as an alternative, borrowing appealed to their sense of fiscal adventure. "We got in the mood to put out paper," Kolber recalls with youthful insouciance. "We didn't want a demand note, though: In sixty to ninety days we'd have to come up with the cash outlay. If worse came to worst, we could always ask for deferral, but we wanted deferral built into the structure. Companies were starting to sell junk bonds and putting a lot of juice on them—you know, commissions; but we couldn't afford a lot of commission, so how could we sweeten it? Sell it at a deep discount!

"Back then, the zero was getting a lot of press, and it seemed a perfect way to get money without paying interest. It would still be accruing the interest, but we wouldn't have any cash outlay. We would have a current liability, yet it wouldn't impact our cash flow," says Kolber. For Air Atlanta's purposes, since it lacked a revenue stream, convertibility sprouted naturally: First, get the money; worry about dilution of ownership later.

The resulting instrument could not be taken for a Stradivarius, yet the complicated tune it played coaxed coins from deep and normally tight pockets. Among the covenants: what circumstances would constitute default; restrictions on additional borrowing and stock sales; lenders' access to company financials; and provisions for Air Atlanta to be able to force conversion should, God willing, the value of the company increase beyond the per-share conversion price.

The zero coupon debt debut—a five-year debenture for $4 million that netted the borrower $2.5 million—was signed with Equitable on February 23, 1984. Starting three years from that date, the note was convertible into common stock at prices ranging from $10.04 per share to $10.52. "And we sweetened it more," admits Kolber. "In this particular transaction, we gave them some options at a very low price."

Low is hardly the word: Forty cents a share is what investors expectantly refer to as the "quid." The attraction for Air Atlanta was that although it received only 62.5 percent of the note—a discount based on compounding 12.5 percent annually for five years—it would not be obliged to reserve even a dime for debt service. "Ordinarily, we would use ninety-six percent of it for working capital, and the other four percent for backing debt. Instead, they were telling us to *keep* the four. We got more than we asked for!"

Since its cash requirements were projected toward the lump-sum net, rather than on the face value of the note, Air Atlanta met its working capital budgets without giving anything away—for the time being. The lenders, bent on protecting their prodigy from capital burdens, didn't even formally require a "sinker," or sinking fund, in which cash must be amassed to guarantee the borrower's ability to pay at maturity. If by close of business on February 22, 1989, Air Atlanta has become profitable with its net worth expanding briskly, the debenture holder will convert to common, and early-stage funds will have cost little save dilution of ownership five or so years later. By then, few stockholders will be the sadder, since in converting, the erstwhile bondholders will have wiped debt off the books and turned it into paid-in capital. No rich uncle could have treated a deserving nephew more kindly.

Its unorthodox zeros aside, a student of start-up techniques tracing Air Atlanta's tireless search for capital would uncover an intriguing (yet aboveboard) maze of cross-default provisions and cross-collateralization of such fluctuating assets as accounts receivable. For example, the company's airport gates, on long-term lease from the city of Atlanta, were recently mortgaged—a bold leveraging tactic. But not even the company's bank, the National Bank of Georgia, which itself is keeper of several convertible Air Atlanta notes, has raised an eyebrow. The bank is the only Air Atlanta creditor to insist on a minimum cash balance, yet, reports Kolber, "they view the zero as a basically conservative debt instrument."

But that's not the way other lenders are playing it. For their unsecured exposure, the funds managed by Equitable, many of which also hold well-rated, long-term, paying securities of established airlines, get to speculate on a start-up—a capital position they would not explicitly take via raw seed capital. "To them," explains Kolber, pointing north toward the money managers who ultimately bought into the offering, "zeros look and taste and smell like *regular* subordinated debentures. They're used to dealing in deep discounts; they buy each other's paper. It's only when you put the thing together and shake it up that ours is unusual. It's a ticket to play the game without looking like a venture capitalist."

In corporate finance, though, tickets don't come with rain checks against risk. A zero debenture like Air Atlanta's might literally be worth zero before it could be flagged as a loser. Even if the struggling company was on the verge of going under, a zero would be carried in the books as debt in good standing and would appear respectable enough to an insurance company regulator probing the books. There would be no missed payments, and thus no provisions for a write-down.

To avoid catastrophe if a company were seen to be in danger of going under, the creditor would do well not to accelerate the note and cause trouble, but instead to write yet another large check, and then another. With a company capitalized mostly through debt, lenders who draw working-capital purse strings too tight can kiss previous investments goodbye. Even though a bond provides a measure of leverage beyond ordinary stockholdings, an unsecured zero can easily send a portfolio manager into an unemployment line.

"Doing a zero with start-up companies *is* a high risk," agrees Slivy

Edmunds, Equitable's pivotal zero-voter as assistant vice-president of corporate finance—but not an unexpected one. "You use it where you're willing to take an equity risk," explains Edmunds, disclosing the true timbre of Air Atlanta's odd instrument. "You should not evaluate the investment as debt. The determination would be whether or not you would take equity in the company. And to be comfortable with an equity risk, you have to be prepared to lose all your money."

Still, do you have to be prepared to lose more than all your money? This startling possibility was brought about by 1982's TEFRA tax provision. With a zero that is convertible into common, you pay taxes on the uncollected interest and then hope for the best; with equity straight out of the starting gate, you merely hope for the best. If the best ends up in bankruptcy, it might come about that the investor who has been dutifully paying taxes can get nothing back from a worthless zero, and will be out the levies as well as the loan itself. Whether a sympathetic Internal Revenue Service review of the case would allow recovery of the taxes has yet to be tested.

Although by its nature a debt obligation with restrictive covenants places something of a cushion under the equity play, in bankruptcy court it could turn into a Whoopee Cushion. A zero convertible debenture's standing in a Chapter 7 or Chapter 11 is still untested. If it comes to that, the judge will have to rule whether an unsecured convertible zero debenture is true debt or thinly disguised equity. The bondholder, of course, would plead the case for debt, and thus rank it senior to common stock. But real-interest-bearing unsecured debtholders would argue that the start-up company, what with its liberal conversion factors and the assortment of options and warrants that also reek of equity, never intended to pay back the loan. Yet Equitable and other long-term zero holders will have been paying taxes on interest accrual. Thanks to the IRS, that's undeniable proof—however layered with options, warrants, and convertibility—that the instrument constitutes a loan. Moreover, by the same argument, a *secured* zero convertible would have equal license with any other secured note to go after available assets.

So far, Air Atlanta has been able to borrow nearly at will. To do so, it must secure waivers from its creditors, but, says Kolber, "that has never been a problem, because we are adding value to the company." But unforeseen snares could yet develop, not only for the investor, but for the beneficiary. What if, when in five years the note matures and it comes time either to convert or to be paid back in cash, the deal is a wash—that is, the value of the stock is exactly equal to the face value of the note? An uneasy lender might opt to get its money back while the opportunity was there, instead of taking the common and chancing a still-clouded future. In that case, even though Air Atlanta had enough cash to meet its debt obligations, it still could be grounded.

But Equitable and other lenders are not asking for a parachute. "If we needed a secured position," Edmunds admits, "we would not consider a zero. There has to be upside potential. If we went for current return, the upside participation would normally be reduced."

Surely one wouldn't want anything so passé as current return to blemish an idyll in which management owns less than 1 million shares of common—far less than Equitable and others control through conversion. On top of lending over $10 million in zeros—convertible into nearly 5 million shares—Equitable holds such other modes of convertible debt as secured demand notes, plus warrants and options to load up on yet more common. Equitable already is about 15 percent owner, based on outstanding shares. If everything is exercised before convertibility expires (even if the other lenders make all their conversions) it will come close to owning half the company (on a diluted basis). This is a far larger chunk of the corporation than they would have had through early-stage equity alone.

That happy event will occur only if the new airline soars into the wild black yonder. If it continues to cruise in and out of the red, however, yet another complication could arise should Air Atlanta again attempt an initial public offering, either to raise more capital or to establish a market price for its stock. Convertible holders would want to cash out as well, but the days of capitalizing profitless companies merely by tapping the public market have passed, and no underwriter could be expected to sell stock from debt-laden balance sheets. Equitable and other lenders would have to cooperate, cleaning up the liabilities by converting to common. They would then hope to "piggyback" on the offering and dispose of at least some of their holdings. Unfortunately, Wall Street has come to frown on IPOs that seem designed to favor individual holders. The idea of an IPO is to let the public in on a good thing, the Securities and Exchange Commission agrees, not to bail an institution out of a flat investment.

In the end, the beauty of a zero convertible is in the eye of the holder—it *looks* like it's a performing asset, such as revolving debt, but it's really not. It reflects the tacit intent of both parties to structure debt that accrues interest but which the borrower has no intention of redeeming. Still, even the borrower's highly explicit willingness to bathe its creditors in equity surely is not the sole reason big money came to Air Atlanta, whose management in any event is worth betting on. However, Kolber reckons, "they invested *more* because of it. We were able to go to the well again, where we wouldn't have gotten a penny if they could say they were maxxed out on the equity side, and you're not going to get any more. Now we can answer, well, this isn't *really* equity."

If it's so magical a device, why don't more start-ups use it? There's no apparent reason, Kolber concludes. "The only argument against a zero coupon is its lack of an income stream. It's not an instrument for traditional venture capitalists. They have to have dollars coming in. Yet it's such a flexible creature—you can keep layering and layering it, and fine-tune the covenants and the restrictions, and play with the cross-collateralization. At first it seemed like there had to be something wrong. Were we being naive? Were we missing some tax thing or accounting standard? Is it really this simple?"

The jury may still be out, but so far, so good. After the concept and its various sweeteners were scrutinized by the company's accounting firm, Peat, Marwick, Mitchell & Company, and given official blessing, "that's when the phones started ringing," Kolber says. On the other end of the line were cash-hungry start-ups, wanting to know how to do it themselves.

—ROBERT A. MAMIS

LENDER OF LAST RESORT

An asset-based lender (ABL) may not be the first place a cash-starved small business would look for financing, but it shouldn't be shunned as a source of working capital, either. In the past decade, commercial finance itself has evolved, and with it the reputation of ABLs, which use borrowers' assets to underwrite risk. Once derided as a bunch of bearded buzzards, asset-based lenders have earned a modicum of respect. After all, anyone willing to finance high-risk leveraged buyouts, as asset-based lenders have been doing by the dozens, can't be *that* bad.

Most of the independent ABL operations have been acquired by banks, and some banks have even started their own divisions. But some independents remain. Foothill Capital Corporation, for one, is self-described as the nation's largest independent asset-based lender. The Los Angeles company originated in 1968 as a venture capital firm and gradually evolved to its present status.

Independent ABLs such as Foothill can lay claim to filling an important gap in capital structure by extending credit—especially to small and midsize businesses—in the face of *pro formas* that horrify traditional lenders. And they can accept as collateral tangible assets that would give the willies even to banks' own ABL divisions. Foothill recently made a substantial loan to a small business that rebuilds automobile carburetors. The company's most valuable possession was something only 1978 Camaro owners could love: grease-caked old carburetor housings. Although there was no immediately apparent market for them, Foothill ventured a number. So what if the appraisal fell well short of the owner's estimation—with empty carburetor shells, who could argue?

Rushing in where other financiers fear to tread, aggressive "hard-money" lenders often find themselves standing bravely between a shaky business and its extinction. If the liquidation value of the collateral doesn't build in a substantial margin for error, a secured lender can take a mighty cold bath should the fiscal climate change. Indeed, just such an unexpected reversal badly reddened Foothill's income in 1982 and 1983, when hard times in the oil-patch states decimated what once was rock-solid collateral. The freeze was so severe that Foothill's own credit rating wilted in the commercial paper market.

In consideration of gambles that could wipe out their own business, ABL money comes relatively dear. Four to six points over prime is common—and that's not to mention a litany of fixed and variable add-on fees (loan origination, collateral management, packaging, auditing, and closing among them) that can effectively tack on several more points. An ABL's annualized target yield for a risky deal is apt to be in the high twenties, all told.

Not that it can't be advantageous for essentially healthy businesses to use high-priced capital from time to time. The Los Angeles Lakers Inc. and Los Angeles Kings Inc., whose ephemeral assets, like those of many professional sports, confound traditional lenders, recently tapped Foothill's understanding for $12 million. The advance helps tide them over barren cash-flow cycles until the turnstiles click again in season. And when MacGregor Sporting Goods Inc. needed cash recently to acquire a manufacturer of souvenirs, Foothill spotted them $6 million.

But lest we get overly rapturous, it should be understood that working-capital financing such as Foothill readily performs can also hasten a sickly business's slide into default. Usually, some creditor or other has legal divvies on the struggling company's checkbook, grabbing incoming cash just when it's needed for servicing the high-ticket loan. And that purse-holding creditor, of course, can well be the ABL itself.

The maximum Foothill is willing to go is calculated on the price at which its team of liquidators estimates the collateral pool can be quickly moved (less costs for insurance, rent, and other handling charges). If the asset is clearly going to be hard to dump on the open market, as a large computer or a CAT scanner might be, Foothill will try to get a put, an arrangement by which a prospective buyer is entitled to purchase the item at a predetermined bargain-basement price, if and when it is liquidated. In MacGregor's case, the collateral consisted of receivables and inventory, part of which was some 12,000 souvenir baseball hats. "If the company were to go out of business," explains Peter E. Schwab, president and chief operating officer of Foothill Capital, the lending subsidiary of The Foothill Group Inc., "we'd call every concessionaire in the country and tell them, 'We've got your hats.' We're in [the hats] at so low an advance rate against their real value that we could say to the customers, 'If you'll take them tomorrow, we'll sell at our purchase price.' Of course," he acknowledges, "it might not be so easy right after the World Series."

One ABL is known to have accepted unbagged charcoal briquettes as part of a collateral pool, and Foothill itself has been willing to rent freezers to store the perishables that one client was able to put up as security. "The hardest asset [to evaluate] is inventory; you're guessing on its resale value," says veteran loan maker Alan Jacobs, a Foothill vice-president and western regional marketing manager. "One of my prospects is a winery—what do I know about wine?" Partly for that reason, a loan secured by inventory alone is deemed too risky; ABLs feel better when a pledge of receivables goes along with them.

Foothill is comfortable not only with exotic collateral, but also with unorthodox business setups. The resale value of for-profit hospitals, for example, has to be determined through formulas that don't apply to conventional structures, leaving potential for error. The standard for evaluating a medical facility presently is around $120 per bed—provided the bed is legitimately filled. A lender was recently confronted with an enterprise that, when the ABL's appraisers came to visit, stuffed its empty beds with staff members posing as patients, so that the occupancy rate would appear reassuringly high.

When a bank couldn't put a package together for one legitimate health-care establishment, Foothill didn't hesitate to loan $12 million—at prime plus four, plus three points. Secured by real estate and equipment, the obligation was interest-only for the first year, then amortized over a seven-and-half-year average life. Needless to say, Foothill gave itself plenty of recovery room, discounting the per-bed formula by 50 percent to $60 each, for starters. The entire package was structured and signed within three days.

While bankers are used to knowing exactly with whom and with what they're dealing, the trench-fighter heritage of independent asset-based lenders seems to goad them into taking on tougher challenges. Foothill marketing manager Jacobs tells the story of when he was working for another ABL and accepted new cameras as collateral for an advance to a company that ran retail photo-equipment concessions in department stores. The Nikons and other top-of-the-line cameras were "real good stuff—a cinch as a collateral pool," he remembers thinking smugly. "I was in for only fifty percent of cost—how could I lose?" Yet some Mean Street instinct told him to move the inventory into a public warehouse where he could keep an eye on it. He instructed the people there to count the cameras as they came and went, and to send him a computer printout every month. Sure enough, one day the owner left town, literally never to be seen again. Jacobs rushed over to the warehouse armed with his latest list. The crew had dutifully counted every camera; all were there, as reported. The hitch was, not a single one had a lens.

A rude awakening for you and me, maybe, but to a hard-bitten ABLer like Jacobs, no catastrophe. He rounded up "the cheapest lenses possible," and personally screwed them in. "On some of those cameras," he recalls with unexpected remorse, "it was a crime." Be that as it may, he placed the lot on distress sale, and the loan was recovered within a year.

Time is money to many an ABL applicant. Because lenders are a breed who don't say no quickly, usually a lot of time has been spent in shopping among prime-plus-two or -three loan possibilities before a needy borrower is willing to go to prime-plus-four and beyond. By then, circumstances have likely worsened. "Ninety-five percent of the time, we've got to get going quickly," says Jacobs, who has wrapped up many a deal in one weekend's nonstop work. "We're used to it; the rush atmosphere goes with the territory."

Not infrequently, that territory is staked out within a few feet of the bar, Foothill being among the few staunch lenders knowledgeable enough to escort a company into and back out of Chapter 11. One of its most notable round-trip tours took place in 1983, after Foothill's original $4-million line of credit to United Press International Inc. (UPI) was eaten up by continuing losses. At that point, as a major creditor Foothill could have elected to liquidate the company and recover its well-collateralized loan. Instead, it opted to let UPI file for court protection and reorganization, and to continue to finance the company through its travails once new management was installed. The procedure was agreed to by UPI before going in, and endorsed by the court. Explains Schwab, "If there's a reasonable possibility of the company surviving, as a lender it's always better to finance. We had faith in the new management. There was a chance for this company to emerge, either through a turnaround or by selling it."

The fresh financing—at about five points over prime—allowed UPI to pay back salaries and benefits to thousands of employees, and to be able to negotiate new contracts with unions. Emerging from Chapter 11, the wire service was, indeed, sold, and in 1986 Foothill's loan was paid back in full. "It shows what asset-based lending really can do," beams Schwab, who put Foothill on the line. Nonetheless, it can never make *everyone* happy. "Someone had to get a haircut somewhere," Jacobs suspects. "When a company goes into Chapter Eleven, even if it emerges, the old creditors usually don't get a hundred cents on the dollar."

A high-risk lender appreciates dealing with the debtor-in-possession businesses that operate under Chapter 11, says Jacobs, because nothing is hidden. "You can see how much fat has been pared off the bone, where the real operating efficiency level is. The debt has all been pushed back below the line or forgiven or turned into stock, and you get a brand-new baby. That's not to say the first bump that comes along isn't going to kill it again, but you start out with an item that is unspoiled by human hands."

When housing starts sagged and a Tacoma, Washington, lumber company got into trouble, it sought Foothill support from within Chapter 11, to which its nervous primary banker had sent it scurrying by calling a $3-million loan. By definition, all creditors were stopped from exercising their rights, but the lumber company told the court it meant to hide only from the bank, not the suppliers; the company intended to replace its general manager, find a new lender "real quick," and thence to carry on. For six months it sought financing, but was turned down until finally Foothill's Jacobs trekked up to the Washington woods. There he determined that the situation looked turnaroundable, that new financing could be safely covered by lumber stocks, and that the fluctuating commodity-market value of the inventory could be watched closely. So Foothill agreed, in loan maker's parlance, to "take the other lender out." Cutting sales expenses by 10 percent, within ten months the lumber company was released from Chapter 11 and on its way toward paying off all the creditors.

The opportunity to grab significant ownership from grateful businesses must be tempting, but Foothill turns it down on the grounds that as a lender it's not proper also to be in de facto control. But, admits Schwab, "if we see we have the opportunity to share in the upside, we might take a little equity kicker—maybe slightly less than one percent, maybe slightly more. That's only as a sweetener. It doesn't replace collateral. If we're not collateralized," he insists, "we will not take equity in lieu of collateral." But if the loan is defaulted, Foothill will step in. "Let's face it, at the level we deal, there is a high degree of failure," says Jacobs, "and the lender has to know how to run the business."

Death's-door rescues are, understandably, the most expensive of all. To shore up the lumber company, Foothill granted a five-year equipment loan, a ten-year real estate loan, and a revolving line of credit that enabled the lumber company to borrow on receivables and inventory when needed. The price was prime plus six, payable monthly, plus a substantial onetime funding fee. Not exactly charity, but the cash-flow reversal has been so dramatic after Foothill's refinancing that, Jacobs predicts, "After a year they'll go to another bank, and that bank will take *us* out."

Even a growing business, expanding so rapidly that its working-capital needs outstrip income, can be let down by banks' cautious standards. Lacking ready capital, the business might have to forfeit opportunities such as an LBO acquisition, in which a bank might argue that the new debt-to-equity ratio would be too high when laid across both companies. No such worry plagues an outside ABL: "From our point of view," reasons Schwab, "the two businesses together might be even stronger."

Foothill will go as far out as fifteen years with term loans secured by fixed assets, at a rate of three to six points over prime "all in" (a phrase that signifies that origination and other fees are included in the yield). On revolving lines of credit against receivables, interest is charged only on the portion that actually is used. But that portion is subject to being held open for a period of collection days after the invoice is paid—a throwback to the old manual check-clearing system that today gives the lender free use of interest-bearing money for a week or more. Unlike a factor, who primarily buys invoices outright at deep discount (see "Factors to Consider," which follows), an asset-based lender doesn't stand behind the credit; the business itself bills and collects directly, so that its customers are unaware the receivables are pledged as collateral. But high interest is not necessarily the cash-flow drain it may seem: A company borrowing on receivables to build inventory can use the early cash to take advantage of prompt-payment discounts from vendors and thus pare a point or two from the effective rate.

Foothill claims it normally advances up to 80 percent of total receivables, but occasionally that ceiling is lowered. Even though textbooks teach that they're the asset closest to cash, receivables have a tendency to shrink through trade discounts, returns, and other unseen forces. One persistent drain comes when otherwise straight-shooting creditors find out an ABL has come on the scene. "Even the best companies will try to compromise the balance," a dismayed Jacobs has found. "To them it's good business practice to beat up on the lender."

Still, asset-based lenders are elbowing their way up the pecking order of respectability. Their unsavory reputation as lenders of last resort has been assumed by new loan makers, at whose basic 5 percent monthly charges even old-line ABLs now cringe.

—ROBERT A. MAMIS

FACTORS TO CONSIDER

Among the oddities of the present state of the economy is that in the midst of plenty, commercial lenders are losing ground. Not only are their loans going sour, but so is the collateral behind them. When BankAmerica Corporation reported a record $640-million quarterly loss, one strategy to cut losses was to begin monitoring its loan decisions more carefully. The customers of one of the country's mightiest financial institutions were forced to work harder for short-term working capital, or to look elsewhere. Some need only look to one of the country's humblest financial institutions, the hundred or so firms that constitute the ancient, and for the most part honorable, community of factors—presuming, of course, the businesses understand that in many cases even a healthy operation can adapt factoring, once considered the loan of last resort, to its short-term advantage.

And there's the rub: Factors remain underappreciated, even after three dozen centuries. A survey last year by Dun & Bradstreet Credit Services of 1,060 companies of various sizes disclosed that only 7 percent dealt with factoring firms—or admitted to it. The aloofness of the other 93 percent was no doubt tinted by the popular view of factors as a pack of usurious Indian-givers who prey on desperate, capital-needy enterprises for quick profit. Some years ago, this appraisal was warranted to a degree, but as such reputable institutions as Manufacturers Hanover Corporation and the Fuji Bank opened aboveboard factoring divisions as a complement to conventional banking, factors have regained some respectability.

One reason for widespread ignorance of the financing technique of purchasing a company's receivables is that until recently most domestic factoring rode the coattails of the apparel trade, a sector whose growth was in large part spurred by factor underwriting. Another reason is that formulas for filtering capital through a factor are not standardized; the terms of a standard collateralized loan are often easier to pin down. Third, some so-called factors add to the confusion by selling themselves as factors even though they really do accounts-receivable financing—a similar but separate service (see box, "Accounts Receivable Financing," at the end of this chapter).

None of this ought to stop a business from at least considering a factor to solve short-term cash-flow bottlenecks, especially now that the core of the factoring industry is looking to expand beyond the patch-work clothing trade. Indeed, the financial force that kept garments from folding through the years applies to any enterprise that accumulates receivables. And though the terms may sometimes seem outrageous, they can foster growth better than traditional borrowing. "If you use a bank, you can do volume of six to eight times your capital; factored, you can do ten to fourteen times capital," says Barry M. Pearl, vice-president and director of marketing of BT Factors, a $1.6-billion (in 1985 factoring volume) adjunct of Bankers Trust Company in New York and among the ten largest factors in the nation. How is this minor miracle wrought? "You're getting a much better cash flow," explains Pearl. "You can buy better, pay your bills faster, and get more credit." Furthermore, by committing only its receivables, the other assets of the firm remain as possible collateral for additional borrowing.

The factor issues credit at shipment, based on the amount of invoices cut by the borrower; on any given day, the greater the dollar amount of the receivables, the higher the credit line. At a bank, however, to enhance a similar credit line based on receivables pledged as assets, the line and the paper behind it would have to be reconsidered periodically—if at all. "The more I talk to my banker friends, the more I am convinced that the banks really don't care about the smaller borrower anymore," observes Walter Kaye, founder of Merchant Factors Corporation, a $40-million New York City firm begat of garments in 1985 and now moving into other small businesses. "They can't make any money. Their overheads are huge. It takes the same officer, the same time, the same policing, to put on a million-dollar loan as it does a quarter-million-dollar loan. They want it collateralized by outside assets they can touch and feel. They love real estate."

His conclusion is not entirely self-serving. Banks are not in the collection business and would be unlikely to take on asset-based financing as their sole function to a customer. They would expect the rest of that customer's banking business as well. But not factors, who exist comfortably enough outside banking regulations and are thus free of the strictures of the system; factors want *only* that function, and the borrower need not mortgage its soul. "If an account is marginal, in tough times he won't get a bank to loan him anything," observes BT Factors' Pear. "We are more liberal." Which makes a factor sound a bit like Santa Claus. Fat chance! A factor takes risks, and with risk there must be compensating reward.

Factors make their profits by acquiring a company's invoices and collecting on them, charging the company a fee. Simply put, there are two variations. One derives the fee by discounting up front the face value of the invoices; the other by lending against the receivables until they are collected, charging daily interest on the open amount plus a one-time commission. Either way, the essential point is that, unlike a bank, the factor buys, pays for, and *owns* the receivables outright. The risk is that if they go bad, the factor suffers the loss.

If they don't go bad, the reward is that a factor's return on investment can exceed conventional lenders' returns. To cement that happy ending, factors execute thorough credit checks on each debtor before buying the invoice from the issuer. Indeed, unlike banks, to some factors the financial condition of the latter hardly matters. "We do not look toward the business that comes to us selling its receivables, but to the strength of the receivables it is selling. The capitalization of the business is not crucial," says David B. Clark, founder and partner of a West Coast group of independent financial firms doing $200 million a year.

A wide-ranging financier with specialties in oil, aerospace, importing, and transportation, Clark currently discounts his purchases by about 6 percent. That is to say, for every $1,000 in receivables, the seller receives $940, and the deal is done. While a few scattered factors discount according to a schedule, paying a smaller percentage up front and throwing in more depending on whether the receivable is collected within thirty, sixty, or ninety days, Clark's is a onetime charge. The factor then takes over the entire collection process, including mailing out the invoices. Each customer is notified that the account is owned by and payable to the factor. If the factor gets the check in forty-five days, essentially the client has been charged 4 percent a month. If the businessperson continued to sell his receivables on the same basis, over the course of a year, he would be paying 48 percent for the early use of money.

An unconscionable rate, perhaps, but factors aren't bankers, nor is that transaction a loan. It's an outright purchase, and a factor's client gets the cash immediately. "Maybe it sounds high in comparison to bank rates," admits Clark, "but remember *we* bear the risk. No banks are going to bear risk. They don't like to get involved with anything administratively burdensome. Yet that's where we shine. Paperwork is our forte." Of course, if the factor doesn't collect promptly, the return is not so attractive.

From the client's point of view, the arrangement is akin to a guarantee that his customers will pay *all* his invoices at once, and he doesn't have to rely on a bookkeeping clerk to perform credit checks and pursue laggard payers. And a debtor is apt to pay a factor faster than he would pay an individual vendor, if only to keep his reputation in good standing among credit watchers. On the other side, if some abstract entity is doing the collecting, the client business feels more comfortable selling goods to a customer while not at the same time trying to collect on the last sale. Let the factor be the bad guy.

An alternate school, taken from the garment industry, varies the basic setup, but the end advantage turns out much the same. As the process is executed by Merchant Factors, the factor likewise buys the receivables, but rather than discounting them up front, this method treats the advance as a loan. A Merchant client must agree to sell the factor all of its invoices on a continuing basis and pay a one-time commission of up to 2 percent of the value of the invoices. He is entitled to an advance of 70 to 80 percent of all the invoices he can create, and daily interest at 3.5 points over prime is charged by the factor until the bill is paid. Merchant's rates tend to be slightly above prevailing factoring levels because, like originating banks that resell the mortgages they buy, the ten-man Merchant operation refactors its receivables, turning around and selling them to a prime factor and then arbitraging the difference in costs. "We're entitled to, since we're taking small accounts and bundling them to [the clients'] advantage," explains founder Walter Kaye. "Their accounts are treated as if they're doing forty million dollars." Without its united-we-stand posture, argues Kaye, Merchant's sixty small-business clients, typically manufacturers capitalized at $60,000 to $150,000 selling $500,000 to $2 million worth of goods to retail stores, undoubtedly would fall outside the purview of the factoring industry's mainline firms.

The factor does all the administration and collecting under this structure as well, but the client has some exposure to the quirks of collection, inasmuch as if he takes the advance, he is obligated to pay interest until the invoice is closed out. This way, the factor is protected against collection bouts that may drag on unpredictably. However, a borrower ought not to be overly concerned with the extra interest expense if receivables exceed predicted aging, since the money—which otherwise he wouldn't have at all—can instantly be put back to work. Let's say, with the prime at 8 percent, a manufacturer taps his 70 percent allowance by borrowing $1,000 at 11.5 percent, and the receivables remain open for forty-five days. Interest plus 2 percent commission on $1,428.57 (the amount of which $1,000 is 70 percent) comes to about $43. That's the equivalent of straight interest at about 34 percent per annum, but factors would be quick to point out that the expense is negligible in relation to the cash-flow benefit of being able to count on the money coming in. "That's the attractiveness of factoring," says Kaye. "It takes a small-business man with limited capital and enables him to compete in the marketplace."

A somewhat larger business can get better terms from such large firms as BT Factors, which, after decades of apparel and related industries, has added toys and shoes, and is looking toward housewares, electronics, paper, and, Pearl pledges, "anything we can get credit information on and that creates an invoice." As of this summer, an average client was paying 1 to 1.25 percent commission, plus two points over prime on advances. BT likes to see a client doing sales of "five million to fifteen million dollars, but we can go from there upward to one hundred million, no problem." But, says Pearl, BT would consider as little as $1.5 million in sales if there were growth potential. "When we find someone is going nowhere, we don't have much interest. Generally, if there's no growth, the firm dries up. You go one way or the other; in business, it's hard to stand still."

Beyond quick access to revenues, a factoring client is also buying insurance against bad debt. Factors' credit checks are so painstaking that few receivables are uncollected (and most of those not due to credit unworthiness but to other complications). For that reason, some companies elect to sell their receivables, but not to be paid until the factor receives his payment—an interest-free process called maturity factoring. For a commission of 1 to 2 percent (depending on the average amount of the invoices), the client is acquiring both a bookkeeper and a crackerjack credit department. And its principals can sleep as soundly as General Motors. If a financial catastrophe such as a Chapter 11 sullies the receivables, the factor pays the client immediately. Short of that, the client gets paid after an interval that both parties agree constitutes a bad-debt situation. Considering savings in overhead, payroll, and collection inefficiencies, a business doing, say, $10 million may actually come out *ahead* for its $100,000 fee. Besides, the fee is an expense and comes off taxable income, so Uncle Sam kicks in as well.

In addition, a client gets free business advice whether he wants it or not, since it's to a wiser factor's advantage to help the business run smoothly. "A distribution problem? How to write the other partner out? How to set up a buyout? We charge nothing extra for consulting," says Kaye.

When the chips are down but the cash isn't, an independent factor can customize financial services to fit the peculiarities of a business beyond the pledge of its receivables. This flexibility stems from the old days in the apparel industry where, based on the mere promise of a big order, factors might back a production run while the invoice was but a gleam in the hard-pressed garment-maker's eye. Merchant's Kaye claims he makes advances against some invoices that normally would be rejected because credit couldn't be verified "on the theory that if the businessman is willing to take the risk, he knows the customer. I have to go along with it and make money available." And Clark has set up a cash service devoted to assisting transportation brokers in contracts with carriers. Clark covers gas and breakdown costs stop by stop as a hired truck crosses the country, and pays off the driver as soon as a receipt is signed at the destination. Doling out funds en route enables him to track the truck and prevent chicanery. As to rushing the driver's pay before the invoice is issued, "it promotes stable truckers," is Clark's rationale. "Once you go into an industry, you better know about it. Asset-based lenders will take other forms of collateral, but then you get into the business of collateral liquidation. The last thing I want to do," says Clark, "is liquidate some man's home."

Find a bank so kindhearted.

ACCOUNTS-RECEIVABLE FINANCING

Some companies would do better to borrow against their accounts receivable rather than to factor them.

Asset-based lending—the generic term for what basically is accounts-receivable financing—has many of the earmarks of factoring and is often confused with it. The critical difference is that in the former, the borrower keeps the receivables, pledging them as collateral rather than selling them outright. Consequently, another difference is that the borrower's own operating condition is scrutinized more carefully than in traditional factoring. While banks are steering away from asset-based lending due to the unpredictable nature of the underlying collateral and difficulties in liquidating it, such independent factoring firms as Merchants Factors Corporation, to whom receivables are the *sine qua non*, are warming to it.

When a borrower assigns his receivables to an asset-based lender as collateral for a loan—perhaps an advance of 70 percent of the bulk of the receivables at eight points over prime—the borrower's customers may be notified to remit payments to the lender, as in factoring. With A/R financing, however, the credit risk remains the borrower's, who sends out the invoices and is responsible for seeing that they are paid. As the receivables are collected, the lender credits the borrower's loan account. The lender does not perform the usual factoring services of credit-checking and bookkeeping. In some cases, though, the lender administers the account to the extent of providing periodic statements of aging, along with individual remittance statements. The borrower thus knows what bills remain unpaid and can mail the preprinted remittance statements for collection.

Businesses concerned with cash flow but not with collection might choose A/R financing over factoring. A temporary-employment agency that deals with law firms, for example, wouldn't worry about its customers' credit, but would need a flow of funds to pay part-time personnel. A busy manufacturer selling to known creditworthy retailers might turn to asset-based loans to pay for raw materials and capital equipment.

—ROBERT A. MAMIS

PART

V

VALUING, BUYING, AND SELLING A BUSINESS

"**I**f you've ever started a company and haven't yet sold it, rest assured, your day will come." This statement, which opens our article "With a Little Help from Your Friends," describes the focus of "Valuing, Buying, and Selling a Business," Part V of this book.

A merger may be the only way to introduce needed capital into the company for expansion or survival purposes. Or perhaps it's simply time for you to move on. The right merger could help you diversify, reach a new market, hire more employees, or gain a new image. The wrong one could bring disaster.

We begin with a story in which common vision and compatibility—rather than price—were the seller's first priorities. In "Finding a Merger That's a Perfect Fit," James Ruben, founder and former owner and president of ShopKo Inc., speaks frankly about his concerns when his $31.5-million chain of discount stores approached negotiations with Super Valu, a large wholsesale food distributor. ShopKo needed an influx of outside capital to support its rapid growth. Could Super Valu supply the necessary resources, both financial and managerial? After careful consideration, Ruben was convinced that the two companies were compatible, and when ShopKo and Super Valu reached the negotiating table, closing the deal was surprisingly swift and easy.

How can you "cash in" your company for the top price? Victor Niederhoffer, of Niederhoffer, Cross & Zeckhauser Inc., recommends that the seller actively pursue potential buyers. Unconventional? Yes. Effective? Yes! In the second article, "Getting Top Dollar for Your Company," Niederhoffer describes how the small companies ($1 million to $50 million annual sales) that turn to his firm for advice choose their buyers instead of being chosen and how the resulting competition secures them excellent prices. Niederhoffer encourages his clients to publicize their availability and actively seek a mutually beneficial deal. Telling them to "sell their companies like they sell their products," Niederhoffer's approach gives the edge to the smaller businesses.

"With a Little Help from Your Friends" and "Brokers for Hire" provide invaluable tips and advice on the dos and dont's of negotiating the sale of your business.

An immediate buyout is not always the most profitable or desirable way to transfer a company. "Sell Your Company on the Installment Plan" describes an attractive alternative in which both buyer and seller profit from an extended transfer. In his early sixties, Al Alden wanted to secure his own future and the future of his hydraulic manufacturing business after he retired. But he didn't want an outright cash or stock sale. Consultants from the Independent Business Institution crafted a solution in which his company was bought over several years to Alden's, the buyer's and the company's financial advantage.

Foreign acquisitions are becoming more common (nearly 20 percent of all private companies will receive offers this year), but Bob O'Brien, former president and part owner of American Cleaning Equipment Corporation, was nonetheless surprised when he was approached by the West German equipment corporation Hako Werke. "The New Owners Speak German" explains why O'Brien accepted their offer, although he had never previously considered a foreign merger.

"The Smart Way to Sell Out," details the experience gained by George Fricke during the three-year search for the right buyer for his established and profitable yarn factory. Bartlett Yarns Inc. required a buyer with not only experience and capital, but also the willingness to maintain the rural Maine location and the company's relationship with the town. The article concludes with nine steps to a solid sale strategy.

Knowing the value of your company is essential to making an educated decision. Valuation can be one of the most complicated and painful steps of a merger. Buyers and sellers rarely see eye to eye about the "real" worth of a business. However, valuation is a necessary first step. There are many approaches to valuation. In "What's Your Business Worth?" lawyer and CPA Irving L. Blackman describes one approach and a list of important factors to consider. "What's It Worth to You" provides a detailed step-by-step plan, including charts and a worksheet, for establishing your business market value. "Valuing a Business: More Than Numbers Alone" gives four reasons why smart buyers look beyond financial statements.

"Appraising Business Worth" and "Something of Value" offer some practical advice and warnings on dealing with professional appraisers. Should you opt for the do-it-yourself approach, or be merely curious about the value of your business, we offer two different models to help you establish an accurate valuation of your business. Finally, "How Are You Doing?" will help you measure your company's performance.

As with anything, there is more than one way to sell a company, and the articles "Preselling the Company" and "Going with the Flow" aptly illustrate this point. Both articles look at some unorthodox, if not ingenious, methods of selling a company. "The Leveraged Buyout Boom" and "The Dream Makers" explore the popular leveraged buyout.

"He Took the Merger Route" addresses the considerations of long-term versus short-term growth. Here, the choice between a merger and going public was a crucial one for Jerry Casilli, president of Millennium Systems Inc. Millennium needed capital to maintain its growth curve in a rapidly expanding market. Too heavily dependent on a single distributor for its primary product—a universal microprocessor development system—and in need of an expanded product line, Casilli knew his $5-million-a-year company had reached the point of decision. On the brink of going public, Casilli instead accepted an offer to merge with American Microsystems Inc., and he firmly believes that he chose the best solution.

Not all mergers guarantee success. The possibility of a company failing as a result of or despite a merger is the devil in the ear of potential buyers and sellers. Despite good intentions, both parties must be aware of the legalities of agreements and the sometimes intangible "situation" in which they are getting involved. "Anatomy of a Merger" describes Bard and Shirley Heavens' optimism about the future of their $750,000 shim manufacturing company, American Shim and Die Inc., with C.E.M. Company. In a merger that initially looked so promising that Bard Heavens said, "I was having my cake and eating it," the founders lost their company, their jobs, and their self-confidence as the relationship with C.E.M. soured. The offer was sweetened with attractive incentives, but when the transfer was complete the Heavenses suddenly had to contend with some factors no one had mentioned at the negotiating table. The lesson: Never assume more than is actually written down.

The closing article in "Valuing, Buying, and Selling Your Business," "Breaking Away," addresses an often overlooked aspect of selling one's company: the emotional stress involved in parting with the business, its employees, and loyal customers.

Is it time to sell, to expand beyond your immediate means, to enlarge your product line, increase your facilities, open another branch? Is it time to start a new venture? Whether to gain cash or long-term security, to find the perfect partner or the right price, merging a business is a decision that has both personal and financial ramifications. In "Valuing, Buying, and Selling a Business," *Inc.*'s best articles will provide you with concrete advice and food for thought, whether you're in the middle of negotiating a deal or just considering those "what-ifs."

FINDING A MERGER
THAT'S A PERFECT FIT

Finding a merger partner you can live with isn't easy. I know, because I've been on both sides in merger negotiations. From my experience both in selling the company I helped to found, ShopKo, and in acquiring companies for General Mills, I've learned at first hand that the seller of a small company should concentrate above all on one thing: how much its goals and attitudes are shared by the buyer. Nothing, not even getting the right price, is more important.

In 1962, twenty investors started ShopKo in Green Bay, Wisconsin, by pooling about $225,000. I owned a 20 percent interest, as did two others. We were convinced that discount department store chains were ignoring markets in communities with less than 100,000 people. We were right, and by 1971 we had opened eleven stores in Wisconsin, Minnesota, and Michigan. Our sales were $31.5 million and were growing by more than 40 percent a year.

We couldn't grow as fast as we wanted to, however, because we couldn't generate capital fast enough. That created a problem for us because bigger competitors, especially K Mart, had discovered our strategy and were beginning to open stores in smaller communities. We wanted to beat K Mart, and the rest of the competition, to the punch by opening as many stores as possible in our geographical area. To do that, we decided to go public to raise expansion capital.

We soon found out that we couldn't have picked a worse time. By 1971, the new-issues market, especially for small, capital-intensive companies, had collapsed. The outlook for going public was so bleak we decided to consider selling out.

Because ShopKo's sales and earnings record was good, I felt we were in a strong position to sell. But I wanted to be sure we had done our homework before we put the company on the market. I didn't want any surprises. I needed the answers to a lot of questions: How much was ShopKo worth? Should we sell out for stock or for cash? What kind of company should we sell to? By the time Super Valu Stores came calling, we had some hard answers to those questions.

With the help of an investment banker, we worked up a statement that we felt fairly reflected the company's value. We also agreed that the acquisition medium should be a tax-deferred exchange of stock. We didn't want cash, not only because we wanted to avoid paying immediate capital gains taxes but also because we wanted to participate in the appreciation of our acquirer's business as well as our own.

Super Valu is a large wholesale food distributor based in Minneapolis, about 300 miles away from ShopKo's headquarters. It operated in our geographical area, and it had a reputation as a strong, dynamic company. My first contact with the company came in late 1970, when I received a telephone call from Morris Lewis, Jr., then Super Valu's chairman. Lewis wanted to visit Green Bay and talk about a possible merger.

My major concern, even before I met Lewis, was whether the two managements could get along. We wanted to continue to manage ShopKo after a merger. If there were any potentially serious personality conflicts, I wouldn't sell out under any conditions.

When I met Lewis, my fears were alleviated. Our initial talks were cordial and open. We had both owned our own businesses, and we were both veterans of low-margin retailing to mass consumer markets. Since Super Valu was in a somewhat similar business, Lewis understood some of the risks and complexities of ShopKo's industry. Fortunately, Super Valu met another of our criteria: It didn't know too much about our business. I told Lewis that we wanted to invest our assets in a partnership; we didn't want an employer. ShopKo had developed a decentralized management style, and we certainly didn't want another company's managers jumping into our business and trying to manage it differently.

Most of our talks concerned each company's goals and strategies and postmerger relations. I wouldn't discuss price until I was certain the two managements could work together. The big questions I asked Lewis were, where is Super Valu going, and how is it going to get there? If Lewis was uncertain, uncommitted, or uncommunicative about Super Valu's long-term plans, I would break off talks.

Lewis was frank and forthright. He said that Super Valu had great stability and reasonable growth, but that it needed to acquire businesses that had more rapid growth and higher margins than the wholesale grocery business, in which average industry after-tax profits were only about 1 percent. He was concerned that Super Valu's maturity and low-margin business were depressing the company's stock price. He wanted a price-earnings multiple comparable with those of Super Valu's top competitors.

I told Lewis that ShopKo investors wanted a merger partner that would commit capital to the long-term development of our business. Supplying him with specific figures, I told Lewis that ShopKo could open a certain number of new stores a year using internally generated capital, but that with a contribution from Super Valu it could open a greater number each year and increase earnings much faster.

Lewis replied that he couldn't commit any specific amount of capital to ShopKo. But to show that Super Valu would meet its commitment to provide capital and other support to its acquired companies, he shared with me some internal operating figures. Those financial figures convinced me that in terms of capital base, credit support, and cash flow, Super Valu was sufficiently large to provide the support we needed. And since it was logical that Super Valu couldn't grow more quickly and increase its own earnings without committing capital to its faster-growing businesses, I knew that Super Valu's and ShopKo's objectives were closely linked. Once I understood Lewis's motives, I knew that the chances for a good postmerger relationship were greatly enhanced.

Like ShopKo, Super Valu took a realistic, conservative approach to business development. It had financed much of its growth through internally generated funds. It had also increased its dividend payments proportionate to earnings increases, a major selling point where we were concerned.

I also admired Lewis's openness. He encouraged me to talk privately with members of Super Valu's board of directors and with other Super Valu managers. In return, I tried to convince him of ShopKo's openness and good business practices by explaining that we had managed the company with the discipline of a publicly held firm. Procedures we had imposed with a view to going public were advantages when we decided instead to sell. They included job descriptions, a formal appraisal program for all employees, management by objectives, a results-oriented incentive plan, and long-range strategic, operational, and financial planning. More and more, Lewis and I were becoming aware of how compatible our management objectives and practices were.

Even though we knew the quality of our company was high, we had to convince Super Valu's board. I pointed out to Morris Lewis that we had paid for our earnings as we grew. We had spent money on fringe benefits, accounting costs controls, facilities, and so forth. We had even spent $50,000 the previous year in management training and development.

By the time Lewis and I sat down to talk price, I had a pretty good idea of what terms he had been thinking about. Members of Super Valu's management team told me that Super Valu had been burned once in an acquisition outside its basic business, and that the board, which was more conservative than Lewis, wouldn't be happy about taking an earnings-per-share dilution. In other words, if I asked for too much, the deal would die.

I had no intention of asking an outrageous price. Even if we didn't sell at the absolute best price, I felt that our shares would appreciate as Super Valu's sales and earnings grew. At that time, Super Valu's stock was selling at twelve times earnings. I wrote that figure on a piece of paper and held it in my hand as Lewis began to propose terms. He offered an exchange of stock equal to exactly twelve times earnings, or about $8.4 million. I thought he had offered the best price right away. I knew that if the merger wasn't completed, it wouldn't be because of price. The whole price negotiation took about thirty minutes.

Since the merger, which was completed in the spring of 1972,

ShopKo's earnings have increased tenfold and its sales have soared to about $236 million, partly as a result of new capital infusion. Super Valu's stock price has quadrupled and its dividend has increased by more than 267 percent. A number of our original investors have retained all of their acquired stock and have yet to pay capital gains tax. And the merger has given me the opportunity to pursue a new management career at General Mills.

My views on acquisition criteria haven't changed much in the past eight years, even though I'm now in the buyer's role. I still believe that price shouldn't be the all-important factor. My one message to small-company owners who want to continue to manage their firms after a merger: Consider very carefully how your company fits into a future parent's plans.

—JAMES H. RUBEN

GETTING TOP DOLLAR
FOR YOUR COMPANY

S mall-business owners sell their companies for many reasons: to save on taxes, to create an estate, to provide continuity and succession in the business. Some, because they lack the capital to expand, sell their businesses so that their companies can grow or diversify.

But the best reason to sell, Victor Niederhoffer believes, is to cash in. "After all," he says, "the owner of a successful business has strived for a long time. He's paid a lot in wages, made profits for his suppliers, given customers a better product for a lower price. It's time he was rewarded."

Niederhoffer's firm, Niederhoffer, Cross & Zeckhauser Inc., brings together small companies with sales between $1 million and $50 million and larger companies interested in acquisitions. According to the Federal Trade Commission, over 90 percent of the companies acquired in 1978 had assets of less than $50 million.

Niederhoffer started NCZ as a consulting firm for large industrial companies in 1967, after completing his doctorate in business administration at the University of Chicago. Niederhoffer soon became aware of how vulnerable the sellers of small companies are, which led him to develop NCZ's present specialty: corporate finder.

"We saw buyers step in and make fantastic offers in the funny money—restricted stock, convertible debentures—of the early seventies," Niederhoffer says. "Then, when the deal seemed closed, the buyer would hesitate. For six months, while the buyer studied the deal, the seller would wait in limbo."

Niederhoffer realized that sellers, who are typically hesitant to talk about their desire to sell, are at a disadvantage in the marketplace. When NCZ began arranging mergers in the early seventies, it pioneered what it believes is an unconventional but effective way to sell a company: to step out and contact buyers rather than sit back and wait. NCZ encouraged its clients to proudly proclaim their interest in a mutually beneficial arrangement.

Since its first mergers, between small toy companies and large food conglomerates, NCZ has arranged more than a hundred acquisitions. Recently, *Inc.* visited Victor Niederhoffer in his New York City

221

office to discuss the problems that owners of small companies must confront when they decide to sell.

INC.: What kinds of companies do buyers find most attractive?

NIEDERHOFFER: There's nothing a buyer wants more than to sink his teeth into a small, fast-growing company that hasn't reached its full growth potential and that promises a 20 to 25 percent return on investment. No buyer is going to invest in a company that offers less return than he would realize by putting the money back into his own business.

Buyers are also very interested in companies that sell something unique, a proprietary product. Or they may be looking for ways to expand their product bases. If they can take a product that's been sold through manufacturers' reps and hand it to their direct sales force, they can increase sales without increasing selling costs.

Large companies are particularly interested in good regional products they think they can take national. Beatrice Foods has been famous for this. They see a nice little company like Dannon Yogurt that's marketed exclusively in the East (Boston and Philadelphia) and they leap at it. Because they can expand the capital base, the marketing force, production facilities, inventory on hand, and advertising, large companies can do what small companies just can't afford to do.

Johnson Wax took Stim-u-plant out of plant stores and is trying to turn it into a nationally known plant food. Pillsbury bought Burger King when it had about 250 restaurants; now there are over 2,500. It's companies like these—or companies that can boast a fantastic technology—that can write their own tickets in a merger.

INC.: How does a seller determine what price he should put on his company?

NIEDERHOFFER: If you put it into a formula, you can expect the premium a company receives above book value to increase by one-half book value for every percentage point over 3 percent (net after-tax) earnings on sales.

For example, the selling price of a company earning 7 percent on sales would be three times net worth. For a company earning 6 percent on sales, selling price would be two and a half times net worth; 5 percent on sales would draw two times net worth. At 3 percent, you can't expect much more than book value.

Our figures show that a seller can expect to receive, on average, three times the net worth—book value— of his company in the year before acquisition.

INC.: That sounds fairly cut and dried.

NIEDERHOFFER: It's not. The formula is only a guide. A buyer is looking for a company that's going to keep growing, but I've never met a seller who doesn't think his business won't be three times bigger five years down the road. And they'll tell you that with unlimited capital their businesses would be tenfold larger.

There's always a lot of judgment and emotion in valuing a business. Sellers always believe their companies will grow, but only half of them will. So they have to be able to prove it. If sellers can't show a record of growth, buyers won't be interested.

One company projected $800,000 in earnings for the year ahead, when it had three years of $100,000 earnings. A prospective buyer asked them why they didn't just wait a year to show the $800,000, and then sell. It was a reasonable question. But all sellers believe their geese are swans.

INC.: You're saying that sellers have an inflated sense of their company's worth?

NIEDERHOFFER: More deals than you could imagine die on the vine because of the closed-mindedness of the seller. One seller we worked with was convinced his company was worth $5 million. It was an emotional valuation rather than an analytic judgment. Offers ranged from $3 million to $4.6 million, but he held out for $4.8 million. The extra $200,000 wasn't important; it was the emotional attachment to the company he created and built. Unfortunately, it killed the deal.

INC.: But what if he was right? Maybe it was worth $5 million.

NIEDERHOFFER: Our view is that a company is worth what the market will bear, what the maximum bidder will pay at the time you're selling. That's why it's important to be flexible. It could work the other way, you know. If you've fixed irrevocably on $5 million as the selling price, you'll take $5 million when it's offered. Unless you've exhausted the universe of possible buyers, you may have sold your company short.

It's very threatening to sell your company, perhaps harder than getting married. Some sellers get neurotic and kind of flip out. They let emotion get in the way of facts and analysis.

We're working with one guy who has probably ruined his chances of selling his company. Two years ago, he was approached by a company that wanted to pick up his company at book value. Out of fear of getting taken, he picked a price out of the air, three times the company's worth. He's left for Germany. I don't think he'll ever sell his company.

INC.: Then how can a seller be sure he's getting the best possible price for his company?

NIEDERHOFFER: Timing is critical. Buyers want to know why you're selling, because most of the time there are clouds on the horizon of a company up for sale. If they can't figure out why you're selling, they're going to assume there are problems.

It's hardest to think about selling when things are going well, but that's the best time. It's like borrowing from the bank. When you need the money, the banks won't lend it to you; when you don't need it, they're happy to give you a loan.

An ideal time for an owner to sell is five to ten years before retiring, because the owner is often a critical part of the business. He's an invaluable intangible asset. Typically, the buyer will offer the seller some portion of the selling price as a down payment and will keep him on salary until retirement.

Say a company with a $2-million net worth is earning $500,000 a year. As an ongoing entity, the company is worth $3 million to $5 million. If the seller waits five or ten years, until he retires, before he sells, the business will be worth only marginally more than its $2-million net worth, because without the owner the company is *not* an ongoing $3-million to $5-million company.

But if the seller takes $3 million now and invests it in real estate, he could watch it double over six years. Meanwhile, he would be earning a salary and bonuses—often quite generous—if profit goals were exceeded. But sellers are often offended that they have to "earn" the purchase price of their companies.

INC.: How does a seller go about selling his company?

NIEDERHOFFER: We got into the merger field because sellers have traditionally been reticent about publicizing the fact that they are interested in selling. They worry about key employees leaving, about what effect it might have on their suppliers, and so on. But as long as the seller is afraid to admit that he's interested in selling, he's put on the defensive. He can entertain only those offers he receives, and if he does get a bid, it's difficult to evaluate it.

We encourage our clients to take direct action. We tell them to sell their companies like they sell their products. The customer never beats a path to your door, so we encourage our clients to make it widely known that they want to sell. Our competitors denigrate us by saying we market companies the way Colgate markets toothpaste, but our philosophy is that you shouldn't be ashamed of selling your company. It's the only way to get the kind of deal you want.

INC.: But what about those fears of business disruption—the effect on employees and suppliers you were talking about?

NIEDERHOFFER: Compare the risks. If he hides the fact that he's out to sell the company, the seller may actually extend the period during which he's vulnerable to business disruption. What he doesn't realize is that it takes anywhere from three months to a year to complete a merger once it's agreed on. During that period, the seller can't do anything, because there is a potential new owner. He can't make any major plant acquisitions or market thrusts. And if the buyer gets cold feet after six months, the seller is like a bride-to-be whose fiancé has taken a walk. That's more disruptive than having it widely known that you're in the market to sell your company.

There's always a risk of business disruption, but it's not necessarily minimized by skulking around in dark alleys. Selling a company is the most important financial decision you'll ever make.

INC.: What is the acquisition marketplace like?

NIEDERHOFFER: It's a buyer's market, of course. There are about 2 million to 2.5 million companies that file active tax returns in the United States. Let's say you focus on companies that generate sales of at least $1 million. That would give you a universe of about 200,000 companies, of which about 10,000 are public companies. So about 95 percent of that 200,000 company universe is privately held. I would guess that in any given year, about half those businesses—about

100,000 companies—are interested in selling, but in fact there are only about 1,500 to 2,000 mergers each year, public and private. So the chances that any company that wants to be bought *will* be bought are very slim.

The best fish swim deep. We try to search out those buyers who are least eager to purchase a company. We work to develop competition among buyers, so a seller can choose the best company, with the best deal. The period when a company can command the highest multiple of earnings is not infinite. We try to bring several buyers together as the company is peaking, because that's when the offers begin to pyramid.

Nothing creates a sense of urgency like the feeling that other buyers are looking over your shoulder. We try to create an atmosphere like that of a girl who has been proposed to but is still undecided— suddenly all her other suitors come rushing forward. The fear that the bride will be taken forever gets a board of directors off its ass. There's nothing like the pressure of competition in negotiating.

INC.: What should the seller do during the negotiations?

NIEDERHOFFER: It's very important for a seller to create a sense of being genuinely interested in the buyer. For example, it's a mistake to nickel-and-dime a buyer. If you jack up the ante and shave the margins too close, the buyer will send the deal around to committee, and you'll fall into limbo. Some buyers will simply delay the deal until the company increases in value to balance off that extra $100,000 you're after.

Finders can be helpful here, too. It's far more plausible for us to tell a buyer that the seller doesn't have to sell than for the seller himself to say that. You can't pretend to be terribly interested in a buyer at the same time you're telling him you really don't have to sell.

INC.: Can't a seller go it alone?

NIEDERHOFFER: A seller gets a realistic perspective from being out in the marketplace, but the dangers—especially of setting an unrealistic price and ruining your chances—outweigh the benefits. After all, buyers are more experienced at buying than sellers are at selling. And a seller is best at running a company; if he's out for several months trying to sell it, it's likely the company will suffer. And if the company suffers, its value falls.

The biggest mistake sellers make is thinking they can pull a fast one on a buyer. Selling a company is like playing golf. It's better strategy to play conservatively and not make mistakes than to try to make spectacular shots. An owner of a successful business has already done the spectacular—created a company out of thin air and built it into an ongoing success. There's not much more a seller can do to make his company more valuable than it already is. On the other hand, it's pretty easy to make it less valuable than it could be.

WITH A LITTLE HELP
FROM YOUR FRIENDS

If you've started a company and haven't yet sold it, rest assured, your day will come. As sure as there are catfish in Georgia, you'll get an offer. And when you do, take my word, you'll need some special help. I know; I've been there many times. After completing the sale of a subsidiary a few months ago, the lead lawyer for the other side asked me, "How many of these sessions have you been in?" I counted and found to my amazement that over the past three decades I have been involved in more than sixty acquisitions, mergers, or sellouts. That may or may not qualify me as a specialist, but in any case, I'd like to pass along to you some thoughts for which I have paid dearly over the years.

When your day comes, there is one question to get out of the way before you meet with anyone. Ask yourself, "What am I willing to sell?" If the answer is company assets, that's one thing. But if you are selling yourself, which is usually the case, then you have some homework to do. And I literally mean *home*work. At my first opportunity to sell out, I came within a gnat's hair of making a really stupid mistake.

It was in the late sixties, when stocks were selling at incredibly high multiples. Out of the blue, I was contacted by the people at Booz, Allen & Hamilton Inc., the management consulting firm, who told me they had a client who wanted to purchase my company for forty times after-tax profits. That would have meant 20 million bucks to me personally. I couldn't believe my ears. I went rushing home, all excited, and told my wife, "We're rich, we're rich. Just think, we can buy tax-free municipals and have a lifetime income of over a million dollars a year." My wife, who is British and about as flappable as Churchill, said, "Well, I suppose that makes you very happy, old boy, but tell me, where will we live?" I thought for a moment and told her that we would probably live in Philadelphia, since that's where the acquiring company was located. "Do you really want to live in Philadelphia?" she asked, which caused me a moment of hesitation.

"Well, not really," I replied.

She was quiet for a minute and then asked me the kind of profound question that only wives think of: "Tell me, Wilson, what will we have then that we don't have now?"

I looked out our window at our yacht, parked at our dock on the beautiful Saugatuck River in Westport, Connecticut, and sheepishly answered, "Well, I can't think of anything right now, but what about all of that security?"

My wife nodded, smiled, and handed me a bomb: "To whom will you report?"

I took a deep breath, slowly exhaled, and said, "I didn't ask." Absolute silence. "But think of all that money, twenty million dollars."

"I am," she said. "I am also thinking about how hard you have worked to reach this point where we do pretty well what we want to do, when we want to do it. I am also thinking of me and our four children and all the difficulties we are going to have trying to live with you working for someone else, living where you don't want to live, working with people you don't even know."

I bowed my head and raised my hands in surrender. The next day I went back to my office and informed Booz, Allen that I was not interested in continuing the sellout conversation. They thought I was nuts and said so. My bankers agreed, as did my accountants and my lawyer. But I have never regretted the decision I made that day.

Of course, some owners may not have the luxury of saying no. There comes a time in the life of most companies when the owner must face the reality that the company won't continue growing unless he either sells out, goes public, or takes another mortgage on the old homestead. So let's assume that you have decided that you should sell everything, including yourself. You have some important considerations to make before you start the negotiations.

First, who will negotiate? I suggest you eliminate any thought of letting your lawyer negotiate for you. Chances are he has never owned a business or sold one. Nor should you turn the job over to investment bankers. In order to make commissions, they will sell you out for anything, including Confederate money, which may turn out to be better than some of the junk paper they will try to palm off on you—at least there's a chance the South will rise again.

A number of business-broker organizations specialize in evaluating and then negotiating the sale and mergers of companies for various fees and commissions. The competent ones can be helpful in restructuring your financial statement and determining values, but I would not let them handle the actual negotiations. I don't believe that they care a hoot about the person they are selling along with the business or about what happens to him right after the sale or merger.

So, if we eliminate lawyers, investment bankers, and professional business brokers, who is left? You? No way. Remember, you are selling yourself, which means that you are too close to be objective. The chances are you'll blow the whole deal over some insignificant detail. Let me suggest an alternative: Find another company owner and ask him to handle the face-to-face negotiations for you. You can still call the shots, but you can do it better from the next room. I've tried this, and it works beautifully.

The first time I used this technique, I was not selling myself or the whole company, only the name, sales, and distribution of a single product, but the sale was to a major corporation. I knew with absolute certainty that if I were a principal in the meetings, I would probably blow my cool and the deal right along with it. Entrepreneurs weren't very popular at large companies in those days. Admitting that you were one was about the same as confessing that you were a piano player in a house of ill repute. So, rather than take a chance with my ego and their attitude, I called an old friend and fellow chief executive officer and asked him if he would handle the negotiations for me. It took a lot of persuading, but he finally agreed. I knew he could and would be objective, and I had been around him enough to know that he was smart as hell and that nobody was going to outnegotiate him. During all of the negotiating sessions, I was in the next room, wiping off sweat and praying. My friend would come in once in a while and hold my hand while he briefed me on what was going on. Occasionally, he even asked my opinion. And he worked out a fantastic deal. In later years, when I was in the business of acquiring companies, I employed a full-time negotiating team, but I wasn't on it—I was still in the next room.

Regardless of whom you select to handle things for you, your negotiator should try to settle all the important points directly with the opposing principal. The whole process will run much more smoothly if you agree to tell the lawyers from both sides to keep out of the negotiations. Inform them in no uncertain terms—it may help to curse a little—that their sole responsibility is to reduce to legal terminology the agreement you reach. When they give you the first draft, just glance at it and hand it back, saying something like, "You lawyers were told not to try and negotiate this deal, so take these papers back and do what you were told." You just may get back the second draft bearing some resemblance to your agreement.

All merger and acquisition negotiations have a certain life of their own, but there are some statements and promises that will always be made by the acquiring company—for example, "We want you to continue running your company just the way you have in the past." That's a bunch of hooey, and don't believe a word of it. Ask them if you'll continue being CEO. The answer will be no. If you're lucky, your new title will be chief operating officer of your division, which means that you will report to someone, somewhere. If you are selling out to a large company, the chances are that you will be reporting to someone who reports to someone who reports to someone. When you meet him—if they let you—don't be surprised if he looks like your son or grandson and knows absolutely zero about your business. You may have no choice but to accept him as your boss, but at least you should know just how much fun you're going to have in your new life.

You can also expect to be told, "We won't require you to make any important personnel changes." More hooey. Within ninety days you are going to have a financial person assigned to you, and he or she will disapprove of almost everything you want to do. Again, there may be nothing you can do about it.

Finally, there's your employment contract. The buyer's principal concern will be the noncompete clause, which says that for a specified period you can't leave the company and restart the same kind of business. That's fair, but you'd be wise to make the period as short as possible. If things go well, it's not an important point. If things go sour, you'll kick yourself for not having negotiated a little bit harder. Another thing to insist on is that the employment agreement spell out as many details as possible—vacations, automobile, insurance, country club dues, and all those other little things that you have been writing off all these years.

Above all, be sure your specific duties are outlined and a clause added ensuring that you will never be asked to perform any duties that are inconsistent with your present position, like being a janitor or, worse, administrative assistant to grandson. Nail down specifics about the buyer's ability to transfer you to another location, like Nome, Alaska, or Beirut, Lebanon. If you have been offered a bonus program, insist that the buyer put all the details in writing. As to the length of your employment contract, make it as long as possible. Remember, they can't force you to work, so if you want to leave you have an edge; but you don't want to give them the option of picking the time. Also, be very careful about the conditions under which your contract can be terminated. Look out for vague expressions, such as "so long as you are effective" or "by action of the CEO or board of directors." Insist on their spelling out valid reasons. It's okay to have words like "gross misconduct" (wait until they try to prove that one) or "deliberate and continued refusal to follow the directions of the CEO." Of course, you should be willing to agree not to steal, ride a motorcycle in the office, or murder grandson. But be careful: Words can come back to haunt you.

As I said, these kinds of negotiations have a life of their own. The buyer is acquiring a company, a thing. But to you and your family, it's your lives that are being sold. Take your time, and remember: If you don't protect yourself, nobody else will.

—WILSON HARRELL

SELL YOUR COMPANY ON THE
INSTALLMENT PLAN

Nearly half of all owners of closely held businesses eventually sell
out. Another 10 percent seek a buyer when their interest fades or
their health fails but are finally forced to liquidate for whatever they
can get. But whether they sell willingly or reluctantly, most owners are
disappointed in the aftermath, and some are very bitter.

Buyers, on the other hand, tend to be satisfied once they've survived the drain of time, energy, and cash involved in an acquisition.
Even they, however, would do it differently a second time.

Much of the dissatisfaction can be traced to the inevitable conflict
over price: The seller wants a high one, the buyer a low one. But there
are other pitfalls in the acquisition process. For example, sales, profits,
and cash flow may not live up to the seller's forecasts—especially after
a sale, when the company's managers are preoccupied with the transaction. If the seller stays on, he may disappoint the new owner by
failing to work as hard as he did when he was the owner.

The buyer, meanwhile, discovers that the smoothly running company he purchased is riddled with problems nobody discussed until
after the papers were signed. Top men from the buyer's company spend
too much time with the acquisition, and their other duties suffer.

Moreover, the buyer wants to take money out of the business—why
buy a business, after all, if doing so is not profitable? But he finds it
hard just to create the cash necessary to pay off the seller. If he takes
out too much, and volume or profits drop, a cash flow crisis may result.

Can these problems be avoided? Yes, but not by conventional
acquisition techniques.

One alternative is an arrangement I call a contract buyout—
essentially an installment purchase of the company over a number of
years. This arrangement demands very careful preparation, but properly used, it maximizes benefits to both the seller and the buyer.

To illustrate a contract buyout, take the case of a Chicago entrepreneur I'll call Al Alden, who had built a very successful business
manufacturing hydraulic valves. As he moved into his sixties, Alden
realized that managing the firm had kept him so busy he hadn't
cultivated a suitable successor. He decided to sell.

Alden didn't want a deal that required him to stay on as president; he wanted to get back to designing valves. He didn't want cash for his company, either, because he had doubts about his ability to invest the proceeds wisely. And he was skeptical about accepting payment in a buyer's stock.

When Alden found an attractive buyer in Joe Johnston of Johnston Hydraulics, a growing cylinder maker, he was uncertain how to proceed.

My firm worked out a deal that let Alden hand over management of the company and go back to his drafting board and laboratory. Payments for sale of his company are made in installments, so he doesn't have the burden of managing a large lump sum. The total payment will be more than he would have received in a cash transaction. The buyer, Johnston, is happy, too, because his cash investment is small. And the company's health is safeguarded as well.

Under the terms of his sale, Alden retains the title and authority of president, but Johnston assumes responsibility for finding and training a successor and takes over interim management. Alden can keep an eye on the operation, but he is free to return to his design work. His payment for the company comes in the form of an annual payment amounting to 150 percent of his former salary. After age seventy, he'll get half of that for rest of his life. Should both he and his wife die before the ten-year contract ends, the payment continues to his heirs. A modest salary accompanies the payments and is increased each year by an amount equivalent to a cost-of-living adjustment on the payment. The total projected payout to Alden is twice the company's sales volume, with inflation adjustments.

The benefit of such a scheme to the seller is obvious, but the buyer, if he is patient, benefits equally. Here is how it works:

• Alden agrees to have Johnston Hydraulics, the buyer, assume responsibility for successful continuation of the firm for a period of ten years. During that period, most of the business profits flow to Alden.

Initially, the zero down payment may make Alden nervous, but contracts protect him from voracious, dishonest, or incompetent buyer management, and after the first year this nervousness wears off. And if, after five years or so, Johnston's ability to properly operate the business falters, these safeguards return the business to Alden, who has already received more than the business was worth, and yet still owns it!

• Meanwhile, since Johnston puts very little money into the business, he needs to take out only a nominal amount.

He forgets ideas about improvements because there is no money for them unless the seller agrees to this investment on the profits. That limits improvements to those that have a fast payoff and are inexpensive. That's likely to be good for the company—too many buyer "improvements" are for ego satisfaction rather than the benefit of the company.

The buyer doesn't worry about forecasts, either, as long as the business meets the conservative minimums already established, and that, barring total catastrophe, should be easy to do. His responsibility is simply to see that the business operates profitably far beyond the seller's productive years. In return for doing this, he eventually becomes the owner of a successful business.

• Johnston hires, and he and Alden jointly train, a general manager. This manager's loyalty is to the buyer. He is responsible for making the forecasts come true. Alden stays on to help train this manager, then returns to his own specialty. Thereafter, he is available for ideas or advice and to go to conventions.

• The purchase "price" is a large percentage of the net profit after taxes, as estimated by a conservative straight-line projection from the sales volume of the last five years to the next ten years. As such, the adjustment for inflation is built in (it is added if the last five years were erratic). If the profits exceed the projection (which they are expected to do), a part of the excess after taxes goes to Alden, the seller, as a bonus; the balance stays in the business. After the ten years are past, 10 percent or so of the next after-tax profits go to Alden as consulting fees for life, and to his widow after he dies.

• The buyer, Johnston, makes a straightforward contract or installment purchase of the seller's assets and liabilities. Under the terms of such an agreement, Johnston can put all assets into his books at fair market value and get the full tax benefit of depreciation, amortization, and writeoffs, but title to the assets is not transferred until the end of the ten-year contract period. This maximizes the amount passed to the seller, effectively repaying Alden for the higher taxes he must pay because proceeds from the sale are taxed as ordinary income.

• Alden retains his old corporation (and any hidden liabilities it may contain, such as incipient government, employee, or customer lawsuits) and liquidates it at the end of the ten-year period.

What have we achieved? A happy result for both parties.

Alden can brag about a sale that will ultimately earn him fifteen, twenty, or more times earnings. His advice on how he arranged that coup is good for free drinks as long as he lives.

And Johnston will have a good story for his friends about how he bought a nice business for nothing. That, too, is good for free drinks.

Of course, this is a quick sketch of a process that is somewhat complicated. The sales and profit projections must be drawn with great care, and both parties must agree that they are not only obtainable but should easily be exceeded. The profit, tax shielding, tax liability, and cash flow must be projected to all sorts of levels to see what payout can safely be made to the seller.

The procedure for finding and training the manager must be carefully laid out, including who has final authority for hiring, evaluating, establishing compensation, and firing.

The seller's safeguards must be worked out to protect him from a buyer who would raid or remove the assets, make adverse changes in supplier or customer arrangements, or pad the payroll. Generally this is done by having such activity trigger a "fine" paid by the buyer's parent corporation—or by a default, the same as missing a payment. The entire assets would then be returned to the seller. Because the price must be fixed in order to qualify for installment treatment by the IRS, the seller's bonus for growth beyond the projection is passed to him as an increase in his salary; sometimes this is paid with stock in the buyer's company, with some redemption limitations which prolong and thereby increase the total payout.

Many details must be worked out—including a separate buyout of the inventory, how to retire (or maintain) existing indebtedness of the seller, settling with minority stockholders, employee stockholders, major changes the buyer wants to make (how and by whom), brokers to be paid off, and so on. You should not attempt to structure this kind of deal without the help of your attorney and accountants.

Still—wouldn't you prefer to sell your business for four times what it's worth? Wouldn't you like to buy your next company for nothing? Seldom in business can both parties to a deal benefit so handsomely.

—FRANK BUTRICK

THE NEW OWNERS SPEAK GERMAN

B ob O'Brien went to the 1978 International Sanitary Supply Association trade show in Atlanta determined to write some big orders for his fast-growing cleaning equipment company. The big orders came in as expected, but one buyer handed O'Brien a surprise—an offer to buy his whole company.

Almost as surprising was the buyer himself. The distinguished, impeccably dressed stranger who approached O'Brien was Tyll Necker, president of a West German cleaning equipment firm that was in the market for a healthy North American subsidiary.

The next day, O'Brien and Necker got down to some serious talk. O'Brien's American Cleaning Equipment Corporation was certainly for sale, but the idea of a foreign buyer hadn't occurred to him until Necker walked up to his trade show booth.

Two years later, the deal with Necker's company, Hako Werke, went through—and Bob O'Brien had learned more than he ever thought he would about how to deal with the overseas buyers who are becoming increasingly interested in acquiring smaller American firms.

By the time Necker chose American Cleaning as his acquisition target, a hired consultant had studied over a hundred potential candidates for the German firm. "He knew who he was talking to. He knew a lot about the company," says O'Brien.

For American Cleaning, O'Brien says the experience was almost totally positive. During their first year of ownership, Hako Werke pumped more than $500,000 into the U.S. subsidiary and plans to spend several million dollars more in the next few years to expand the facility for manufacturing the entire Hako line in the United States.

Equally important, O'Brien adds, the new owners haven't spent all their time tinkering with the basic products, since their satisfaction with the quality of these products is what drew them to the firm in the first place.

For Hako Werke, a manufacturer of floor sweepers, scrubbers, and other maintenance equipment, the attraction was in an established marketing network and a complementary product line. The companies' product lines dovetailed nicely, with Hako tending to specialize in somewhat larger equipment than American Cleaning. The German firm had been exporting its products to the United States via a marketing subsidiary, but a major entry into the U.S. market required a manufacturing presence here. At the same time, the Germans were looking for a company whose products might find applications in Europe.

Founded in 1950 by Jim McSheehy and Mat Zmudka, American Cleaning had evolved from a seller of blowers to a manufacturer of a full line of industrial scrubbers, sweepers, and vacuums. This year's sales are expected to be more than $6 million.

O'Brien credits the company's growth to the founders' decision to sell to industry, rather than competing head-on with larger firms seeking such commercial accounts as hotels and office buildings. In 1952, as part of its industrial slant, the company introduced the first vacuum attached to a fifty-five-gallon drum. American Cleaning was also one of the first firms to build a critical filter vacuum, which is aimed at laboratories, hospitals, and nuclear power plants where even the smallest particles must be captured. O'Brien estimates that American Cleaning holds about 50 percent of the market for critical filter vacuums and smaller shares of other floor-care markets. "A small company can live on a specialized market. But for a big company, that market is meaningless," O'Brien says. "That's what I was counting on. Our competitors couldn't afford to pay attention to it."

O'Brien had bought into the company in 1974. An engineering graduate of Purdue University, he worked for Chrysler Corporation, Continental Can, and Lockheed before becoming a consultant. After several years in consulting work, the most recent heading up a Cleveland subsidiary of Booz, Allen & Hamilton, O'Brien got the itch to own his own company. In 1972, he left Booz, Allen for Chicago in search of a company to buy.

McSheehy had died a few years earlier and Zmudka wanted to sell the firm, but the McSheehy family, which owned the majority interest, balked. O'Brien worked out a deal to buy half the firm, including Zmudka's share, and took over as president on the first day of 1974.

Less than five years later, there were enough reasons to sell the firm for both O'Brien and the McSheehys to entertain inquiries. Interest rates were high and rising, the company was completing a year that would produce a marginal loss, and expansion was simply not affordable. So selling to a larger firm became a significant possibility. O'Brien recalls that for his company the timing of the West German overture was a major factor in the decision to sell.

"We could see that with the finances and the power that Hako Werke could bring into it, the whole name of the game would change," he says.

Tyll Necker visited the company's plant in Addison, Illinois, a Chicago suburb, in December of 1978 to study the facility, and O'Brien visited Hako's facilities in Bad Oldesloe, West Germany, the following month. While Hako and American Cleaning were negotiating, two more firms—one foreign and one American—began talking with O'Brien about a possible sale.

All three of the firms were in the cleaning equipment field, but Hako was special, O'Brien says. Besides being a sound company with people who impressed O'Brien as highly competent, Hako's size was attractive. At around $70 million in yearly sales, Hako was large enough to add capital to American Cleaning, but not so big as to swallow the firm without a gulp. One of the other suitors was about the same size as Hako, the other much larger, but neither was as aggressive in seeking a deal as Necker.

One advantage of selling to a foreign firm in that period, O'Brien recalls, was that exchange rates gave the foreigners a cheap purchase in their currency while the Americans could still recover a healthy amount of dollars. But that didn't mean that the Germans were willing to pay any price for the company.

"It was a real tough negotiation. We had a lot of arguments, a lot of discussions, and we both walked away dissatisfied and came back satisfied several times," he says.

When 1979 earnings came in at a record amount, O'Brien was encouraged to call his suitors to announce that "it's a whole new ball game." Oddly, the Germans didn't complain. "When I laid it on them, they were pleased," he says. "It meant that what they were buying was a good thing."

In that negotiation, price was the biggest factor. Smoothing out the process was the realization that the principals on both sides were truly interested in reaching an agreement—not just sparring. "Once we reached agreement on price, we had lots of discussion of details," O'Brien says, "but we all realized the essential thing was behind us."

When Hako took over the company in June 1980, its top management moved into Addison for a few weeks to coordinate budgeting systems, bookkeeping, and operations. The experience was necessary in order for both firms to understand the other's position—and it was a new experience for Hako in spite of its previous foreign ventures. "This was the first major international acquisition they had made," O'Brien says.

After the takeover, Hako poured its money into product support—advertising, public relations, promotion sheets—boosting that budget item tenfold, O'Brien says. Putting money into promotion pleased the Americans, who took it as a vote of confidence in the product line itself.

One reason that Hako didn't change the product is that the firm was satisfied with the goods before the acquisition. "They placed a major order with us for a sample of our equipment," says O'Brien. "They weren't arguing from ignorance. They knew what our equipment was, because they had it and were examining it."

That kind of knowledge was another factor that separated Hako from the other suitors, each of which dropped out along the way. "Nobody got as deeply into it as this company," O'Brien says. "The others were nibbling at the periphery, playing twenty other games."

Because Hako's only game had been American Cleaning, they knew how to spend money effectively, first in improving promotion and then in modernizing the production facilities. "They put their money where it would do the most good. If I had to spend the money, I would have done it the same way," O'Brien says.

Not everything went smoothly, of course. Hako had been exporting to the United States through its Hako North America subsidiary and, when American Cleaning was bought, the consultant who had conducted the takeover search, James McGee, became president of Hako North America. O'Brien, still president of American Cleaning, reported to McGee and he now says that the intermediate layer between him and Hako Werke proved troublesome at times.

"Whether you're with General Electric or any other company, when there's somebody between you and the boss, there's a problem. There always is," he says.

Communications were improved recently under a new structure that merges the Hako North America operation into the larger American Cleaning subsidiary and puts American Cleaning's president back into direct contact with the West German headquarters.

The new structure also includes a new president—O'Brien turned down a three-year contract, saying it was "time to find a new adventure."

He says he needed to stay through the first year under foreign ownership, both to learn how he would respond to being second banana and to help ease the transition for employees. "I owed it to myself and to my people to smooth the thing out," he says. "If it had been bad, I'd have stayed. If this had been a real bunch of stinkers, I'd have said, 'Yes, I'll stay and fight it out with them.' But they're good guys.

"We never questioned the wisdom of the decision to sell," O'Brien says. "We sometimes questioned the structure they had, because we weren't getting information back and forth quick enough to operate. When that intermediate layer went, we were delighted."

O'Brien adds that rivalry is standard for human interactions, and it would have been no different for two divisions of an American firm. In fact, he says, the care with which the German owners tried to minimize friction—both in the assumption of power and in the operation of the firm—might be the major distinction between acquisitions by U.S. firms and by foreign ones. "The Germans were much more careful and much more considerate than an American company," he says.

Dismissing most of the problems as minor, O'Brien says the disagreements on structure played no part in his departure from the helm. It was simply time for him to move on.

In leaving, O'Brien remains enthusiastic about the new ownership. The company's visibility is greater, operations are more efficient, productivity is up, and growth prospects are much improved over last spring. If a company has to sell out, he says, this certainly is the way to go.

WHAT TO EXPECT IF A FOREIGNER MAKES AN OFFER

The next takeover that you receive has a 15 to 20 percent chance of coming from a foreign suitor, says Jerold Morgan, a Chicago-area consultant who arranges and coordinates acquisitions and divestitures. While patriots may object to the idea of selling out to a foreigner, there are a number of reasons you might want to consider the offer seriously, as Bob O'Brien discovered when he negotiated and finally sold to Tyll Necker of West Germany.

When the dollar is weak, people begin to notice a flurry of foreign firms and individuals buying up assets in this country. When the dollar is strong again, foreign investment will slow down. But trends are partly coincidence. David Bauer, who prepares a quarterly report on investments for the Conference Board, says exchange rates affect investment in stocks and bonds and other liquid assets much more than purchases of companies. The purchase of a business by a foreign firm is a long-term activity, designed to produce profit for a lengthy period of time. Likely cause of an investment slowdown: weak markets here, weak economies (and profits) there.

In many respects, being bought by a foreign company is just like being bought by a U.S. company, but Morgan and other experts suggest a few distinctions that make the international acquisition special:

- *Sprechen Sie English?* Chances are good that the new owner will speak English. National origins most likely for foreign suitors: England, Canada, Germany, Netherlands, Switzerland, and France. What about the Japanese? They tend to open their own marketing subsidiaries, exporting their product from across the Pacific.
- *Bankers need not apply.* For the most part, foreign firms are interested in manufacturing companies, which can be used to extend or duplicate their own product lines in the United States. Small banks and other regulated groups, marketing firms and other service organizations are not prime targets.
- *A vote of confidence.* The tendency is for a foreign company to invest substantial effort in examining takeover candidates before selecting the one it wants. If a foreign firm comes knocking, it means they have faith in your product line or management expertise. While many American firms look for bargain takeovers in turnaround situations, it is very rare for a foreign company to take that kind of risk. At the same time, most are willing to pay the premium required to buy a quality firm.
- *The match game.* Many foreign firms seek companies whose products have a good match-up with their own. Rather than diversifying into another industry when buying a U.S. firm, the foreign company is likely to seek one whose marketing channels could accommodate the buyer's products. Likewise, the foreign suitor often has hopes that the U.S. firm's products can be sold overseas through the new parent's sales network.
- *Don't worry about the guillotine.* While U.S. firms often buy a firm and quickly engage in wholesale management shuffling, overseas buyers are less likely to chop heads. If the management was good enough to create an attractive acquisition, it probably has the expertise needed to stay on the job after the takeover. However, if the overseas firm has more than one subsidiary here, it may want to create a U.S. management team to coordinate operations in this country. Such a team would be in addition to—and would oversee—the existing management.
- *A capital idea.* A quality firm might not be one that is particularly profitable. Sometimes, an attractive candidate will be vulnerable to takeover as a result of its need for capital— and a foreign firm is often willing to cure the capital anemia.
- *Funny, you don't look French.* American firms tend to resemble American firms after a foreign purchase. There might be a new flag or two over the company parking lot, but that's about it. The reason, says a Commerce Department official, is that the firm that gets sold must still compete in the U.S. market, so the new owners do little to disrupt Yankee tendencies.

—MICHAEL ROSENBAUM

BROKERS FOR HIRE

Business brokers—deal makers in buying and selling companies—are for the most part an unregulated lot. Fourteen states require that they have a real estate broker's license, hardly a credential at all. In the remaining thirty-six states, anyone with a telephone and a glint in his eye can hang out a shingle. Complaints about brokers' ineptitude and questionable tactics are widespread, and it's not easy for prospective buyers and sellers to separate the good from the bad.

Some business brokers are the first to acknowledge that their reputation isn't so great. In recent years, for example, brokers in Texas and Florida have formed self-accreditation services to improve their image. They still have a ways to go, says Wally Stabbert, president of the Institute of Certified Business Counselors, a nationwide business brokers association in Walnut Creek, California. The 150 members have passed competency exams and subscribe to a code of ethics. "A large percentage of business brokers in this country I wouldn't consider for membership," Stabbert says.

And rightly so, says Chicago businessman Matt O'Connor, a thirty-two-year-old former Big Eight certified public accountant. O'Connor started looking in 1982 for a small manufacturing company to buy. Over the next year, he spent countless hours jawing with more than fifty brokers. O'Connor wanted a leveraged buyout of a company with sales under $5 million that would generate enough income to finance loans to cover the purchase price. When he called on several large business brokers, they told him his proposed deal fell below their minimum limit (see box, "Who'll Do Your Deal?" pages 242–243). Many of the smaller brokers O'Conner spoke to seemed baffled by his idea. "I got the feeling that some of them didn't understand leveraged buyouts," he says. In 1984, O'Connor did arrange a leveraged buyout of the twenty-employee Jebco Screw & Rivet Manufacturing Company, in Chicago—without a broker. Now he observes dryly, "There are a lot of brokers, and there are a few excellent ones."

Just how many brokers there are and how many deals they do in the course of a year is open to conjecture. Thomas L. West, president of the 400-member International Business Brokers Association, estimates that brokers operate 2,000 offices nationwide and that full-time brokers sell up to 75,000 companies a year. The great majority of these companies sell for less than $300,000, and it's in the low end of the market that most brokers earn their bread and butter. Numbers aside, though, the real question for most people who are contemplating buying or selling a business through a broker is how to tell the "few excellent ones" from the rest.

Beyond the obvious inquiries—what deals has the broker done? what is his or her personal background? references?—there are a few other areas you can investigate. One is a broker's record of sales as a proportion of total listings, says Shannon P. Pratt, a former business-school professor who heads Willamette Management Associates Inc., a Portland, Oregon, business-appraisal firm. "A broker who can document a successful track record of sales to listings is preferable to one that can't," says Pratt. If a broker averages below a 50 percent sales rate on listings offered for six months to a year, both buyer and seller should look elsewhere.

Pratt suggests a further test: How frequently does the broker's listing price correspond to the eventual sales price? Where a wide divergence is common, the broker is apt to be misleading the seller about the true value of the company and wasting prospective buyers' time. "I'd be much more favorably inclined to work with a brokerage," says Pratt, "if its average selling price is within at least twenty percent of the average listing price."

A broker's academic degrees and business experience have less to do with competence, says Pratt, than affiliation with such industry groups as the International Business Brokers Association. If a broker has dealt specifically in the industry or geographic area of the company for sale, that's a plus.

Good brokers can be the key to structuring the elements of a deal—advising a stock or assets sale, for example, and mediating disputed points. Some even help out in finding sources of financing.

As a buyer or seller, once you have located what you hope is the right broker, must you then rely entirely on good faith to see you through the deal? Well, not exactly, say the experts. In dealing with brokers, beware of these common pitfalls:

• *Bait and fish.* One device employed by brokers is what could be called bait and fish: The broker offers a seller the bait of a supposed buyer's interest in the company when the broker actually has no particular buyer in mind. If a seller takes the bait, the broker begins fishing around for a buyer. The same ploy can work in reverse if a broker approaches a buyer pretending to have a seller in the wings. Besides being deceptive, the bait-and-fish tactic can waste a lot of your time. If a broker's overtures smell fishy, you can ask for enough specifics to determine if the client is for real.

• *Premature disclosures.* In some cases of brokers' indiscretion, leaks about a company being for sale leave it vulnerable to losing employees and customers overnight. In the more flagrant cases, brokers will even court the seller's competitors as potential buyers without the seller's authorization. If you are selling your company through a broker, you should be explicit about the limits of the broker's authority to solicit buyers and divulge details of your business. When a broker does show the specifics to a prospect, insist that the prospect sign a nondisclosure agreement.

• **Bogus listings.** Some brokers will accept listings no matter how inflated the asking price or how reluctant the present owner is to sell. As a buyer, you can waste hours investigating patently overpriced companies. Matt O'Connor recalls slogging his way through numerous exorbitant listings while making the rounds of Chicago brokers. Often these listings are the result of an owner's unrealistic expectations about the company's worth. And while brokers are free to decline a listing, there's a bias at many brokerage firms toward obtaining listings at any price. At VR Business Brokers Inc., the nation's largest franchised business broker (number 127 on *Inc.*'s 1985 list of the 500 fastest-growing private companies), for example, a new salesperson's first duty on reporting to work is tracking down a dozen companies for sale. "Now, if you have to have twelve listings before you answer the phone, how fast are you going to do it or how carefully?" asks Wally Stabbert. "The motivation isn't there to do it, right?" Such pressures tend to pad brokers' inventories with illusionary listings.

If a sale actually goes through at an exaggerated price, it can boomerang against the seller in seller-financed transactions. These are commonplace in the sale of small and midsize businesses because the buyer is often short on assets. Buyers who are overburdened with debt tend to default, dumping the company back in the seller's lap. "A large proportion of these are never paid off," says Shannon Pratt. "The same business is sold three and four times."

• **Advance fees.** Brokers increasingly are charging sellers "packaging fees" for preparing a company's profile and appraising its worth. Up-front fees range from as little as $200 for a simple valuation to as much as $20,000 for an elaborate report. For a full appraisal costing $3,000 and upward, the work ought to accord with American Society of Appraisers (ASA) standards, Stabbert says. You can question whether you must pay for a broker's report on top of a sales commission. Brokers often will agree to deduct the packaging costs from their commission if they close the sale. (Commissions are typically 10 to 12 percent of the purchase price, with a minimum of $5,000 to $10,000.)

• **Valuation games.** In pricing a company, brokers routinely adjust a company's income statement to show earnings in their most favorable light—"recasting the financials," one broker calls it. Recasting is entirely legitimate if the company is, say, paying for the owner's Jaguar when a basic car would do just as well. But buyers should beware of recasting excesses. According to Pratt, "There's a tendency to take off things that ought not to be taken off, primarily a reasonable salary for the one who's doing most of the work. That's not profit." What's more, says Pratt, earnings are commonly figured before depreciation. That's perfectly logical if the asset is real estate or something else that's not declining in value. "But if it's a company that's using machinery and it's wearing out," says Pratt, "you should recognize that depreciation. It's a genuine cost of doing business."

Another bit of legerdemain involves the multiplier, or capitalization rate, that brokers factor into their valuations. A company's worth is usually calculated as the firm's earnings times a presumed multiplier for comparable businesses in that industry. If, however, the multiplier is derived from businesses that are more solidly established than the company for sale, the buyer should insist on a higher rate of return for the risk.

Not surprisingly, considering that business brokerage is a largely unregulated industry, competence in pricing varies widely. Many brokers say that standards are rising because buyers have greater corporate experience and business expertise and are demanding more professional service. Others say that franchised brokers are helping to raise standards by offering systematic, albeit limited, instruction to their employees. Still, the credentialed appraisers with alphabet tags like ASA are probably right when they say that most business brokers have a long way to go before they can be considered expert appraisers.

• *Sign first, look later.* A new ploy used by some brokers is what one attorney calls, "Sign 'em up, suck 'em in." The tactic is aimed at buyers, who are asked to sign an offer before looking at a company's detailed books and records. After looking at the documents, perhaps within fifteen days, the buyer has the option of reneging. "This new trend in brokerage is to psychologically suck in the buyer before he's intellectually committed," says Arnold S. Goldstein, a Brookline, Massachusetts, business attorney. "You shake hands, and you tell your wife and your mother you bought a pizza parlor. It's very difficult to back out psychologically at that point." A buyer who is pressured to sign an offer before seeing the books has a safe recourse: Simply refuse to sign.

WHO'LL DO YOUR DEAL?

If the company you want to buy or sell is a barber shop or a rural gas station, you are not a candidate for the mergers-and-acquisitions department of a Wall Street investment banking firm or a large brokerage company. Only if your company's sales exceed $10 million are you likely to interest Wall Street behemoths such as Goldman Sachs & Company or Drexel Burnham Lambert Inc.

For midrange companies with sales between $1 million and $20 million, you qualify for most of the large business brokers around the country. Chicago's W. T. Grimm & Company, also known as a leading scorekeeper for merger-and-acquisition deals, sets its minimum at $2 million. At Geneva Corporation in Costa Mesa, California, it's $500,000. Some brokers, such as First Main Capital Corporation in Plano, Texas, split their operations to handle different-size transactions. If your company has sales between $1 million and $50 million, First Main Capital's M&A intermediaries will gladly consider your deal. If your company's sales are below $1 million, First Main Capital will refer you to brokers in its Associates Business Xchange division.

The great majority of businesses sold through brokers are those that go for less than

$300,000. VR Business Brokers, the nation's largest franchised business broker, with 300 outlets, claims up to 7,500 sales a year, 80 percent involving companies with sales below $300,000. The nation's ten franchised brokerages operate about 500 offices, and they stress the geographic reach their computerized listings allow. Yet some fifty independent brokers have a cooperative exchange of their own through a network called NationList Network of Business Brokers Inc., in Denver.

—JOE ROSENBLOOM III

THE SMART WAY TO SELL OUT

George Fricke had owned Bartlett Yarns Inc., a knitting yarn manufacturer in Harmony, Maine, for five years when he started to think about selling out. He had known from the beginning that no one in his family was interested in taking over the company, so his strategy had been to "build up the business and then take a capital gain on it," Fricke, now sixty-three, says.

Although Fricke had anticipated that selling Bartlett could take as long as five years, he ended up completing the process in three. He feels he handled the sale well, in part because of significant advance planning. For example, when he first bought the business after leaving a career with a New Jersey pharmaceuticals manufacturer, he hired a Big Eight accounting firm, Ernst & Whinney, to keep records that would demonstrate his company's growth.

Then after Fricke decided it was time to begin the actual search for a buyer, he approached several customers and suppliers and "let them know I was available," he says. He opened the field to additional candidates by advertising in the *Wall Street Journal* as well as answering ads placed there by prospective buyers. He also contacted regional brokers.

At the end of two and a half years, Fricke had no serious candidates. None of his suppliers was interested enough to make an offer, and advertisers in the *Wall Street Journal* who said they wanted to acquire a manufacturer were not particularly drawn to a woolen-yarn maker. Hundreds of people had responded to Fricke's own *Journal* ad, but many were more interested in touring a Maine factory on a Sunday afternoon than in making a serious proposal. Most regional brokers were either unhelpful or too busy to give Fricke much time. And, though numerous out-of-state brokers answered his ad, Fricke suspected they were high-pressure salespeople rather than professionals concerned about his welfare. Several demanded thousands of dollars in advance payment before they would take his case.

At that point Fricke encountered a large regional broker, Country Business Services (CBS) in Brattleboro, Vermont. In CBS ads in the *Wall Street Journal* Fricke noticed a useful but by no means foolproof clue that CBS might be right for him: "They were appealing in their ads to the disaffected executive, and that was the type of person who was a candidate to buy my business," Fricke recalls. Successful but unhappy big-company executives might have both the means to buy a profitable yarn factory and the desire to relocate to rural Maine.

Moreover, Country Business Services gave Fricke satisfactory marketing help. They appraised his business at about 10 percent more than his asking price, and then introduced him to three buyers willing to pay that amount. Though one offered to pay 90 percent in cash, Fricke chose another who agreed to make a large down payment and pay the balance over a few years. Fricke thought the second buyer showed more aptitude for the business. "I felt I had an obligation to the town," Fricke says. "This is one of the oldest wool-yarn mills in the country."

Fricke believes few business sellers can avoid talking to dozens of unhelpful people before finding the right purchaser. Even if a seller decides to rely on a broker, it is difficult to find a truly professional one who will understand your company and how it should be packaged.

To minimize the frustrations of selling out, most businesspeople should try to map out a coherent strategy when they first contemplate a sale. Consider the following steps:

- Try to compile your own list of likely buyers from your personal contacts. Customers, suppliers, competitors, and larger firms with related operations are among the best candidates.
- Keep scrupulously honest books for a couple of years before a planned sale, even if this costs extra in income taxes. And reconstruct the profit-and-loss numbers for a few years to present the company in its best light. "You should add in off-balance-sheet items such as perks, bonuses, profit-sharing and pension contributions" that were kept high to minimize profits reportable for tax purposes, notes John F. Creamer, a Darien, Connecticut, consultant.
- Look for hidden value in your business. Are you carrying real estate on your books at less than market value? Is your customer list worth money? Could the right buyer expand your sales to reach a wider market? Is the business relatively free of strong competition?
- Prepare realistic projections of sales and earnings.
- If the business depends on a lease, cement the lease well into the future. Many businesses lose any value if their lease is about to run out and is not renewable.
- Talk with others in your industry and in related fields, including trade association officials, to learn which of them have been happy with business brokers they've known.
- Watch the advertising of the brokerage firms you are considering for perhaps three weeks to see if they advertise sufficiently and if they advertise different businesses over those weeks. A good turnover tends to attract more potential buyers, many of whom may decide to buy businesses quite different from the kind they originally planned to buy.
- Compare commission rates, and avoid brokers who try to charge a fee

up front for their marketing help. Sellers usually pay all commissions, and high rates don't guarantee service. As a rule, brokers handling companies worth a million dollars or more charge fees ranging from 3 to 7 percent of the sale price. Brokers handling smaller businesses charge up to 12 percent.
• Be flexible when discussing financing. Most sales—including Fricke's sale of Bartlett Yarns—are financed to some degree by the seller, particularly in times of high interest rates.

WHAT'S YOUR BUSINESS WORTH?

Sooner or later every closely held business must be valued for either sale or tax purposes. You can do it while you're alive, or the Internal Revenue Service will do it for you when you're dead. The process of valuation, however, is the hardest task in taxation. The primary reason is that the rules of the game aren't very well defined.

Valuation is an art, not a science, but there are disciplines to follow, lying mainly in approaches and techniques. The IRS outlines its approach in Revenue Ruling 59-60, a document that is must reading for any owner of a closely held company.

Ruling 59-60 lists eight factors to consider in a valuation:

- The nature of the business and its history from its inception
- The economic outlook in general and the condition and outlook of the specific industry in particular
- The book value of your stock and the financial condition of the business
- The company's earnings capacity
- The company's dividend-paying capacity
- Whether or not the business has established goodwill or other intangible values
- Past sales of stock and the amount of stock to be sold now
- The market price of publicly owned and traded companies in the same or a similar line of business

The ruling further requires "all available financial data" and other "relevant factors affecting the fair market value" to be considered.

To see how an approach to valuing a business might work, refer to the accompanying sample valuation. Remember that the real value of the company—the amount on which you must pay taxes—will probably be determined by a combination of approaches. The IRS itself emphasizes that the eight factors listed above do not have equal weight and that valuation is a matter of judgment and common sense. Two companies in the same business, with almost identical numbers, could have substantially different values because of a change in just one factor. No set of general rules or volume of regulations can account for the importance of unique facts.

However you solve the valuation puzzle for your business—and it's a process to be left in the hands of professionals—there will always be one important factor to consider. The courts call it "general lack of marketability." The problem is simple to explain. If, for argument's sake, you own 100,000 shares of a stock currently selling for $10 a share, you can call your broker and receive $1 million in about four days, less commissions and, in the long run, taxes. If your company, on the other hand, turns out to be worth the same $1 million, you're unlikely to find a buyer who will pay you the full amount in cash as of the date of valuation. To account for this fact, a discount from the "real" valuation of 10 to 30 percent is frequently allowed by the courts in tax cases. Of course, that presumes that you or your heirs would have to go to court to dispute the IRS over valuation of your business. It's more likely than you might think.

A SAMPLE VALUATION

The value of any business is usually determined by using a combination of approaches. The following example is one of many that can give proper valuation results. It is not, however, the "best" or the "ordinary" way to value your company.

Procedure	Assumption
1. Determine the average after-tax earnings of the company for the past five years.	$ 360,000
2. Determine the average annual net tangible assets used in the business for the same five-year period.	$2,000,000
3. Apply a fair rate of return, say 15%, on the amount computed in # 2 (15% × $2,000,000).	$ 300,000
4. Subtract #3 from #1. This equals excess earnings attributable to goodwill.	$ 60,000
5. Capitalize the excess earnings in #4 at a selected rate, say 25%, to yield the value of goodwill (4 × $60,000).	$ 240,000
6. (a) Determine net tangible assets (adjusted book value) of the company as of the date of valuation;	$2,500,000
(b) add capitalized excess earnings from #5.	$ 240,000
7. The fair market value will be:	$2,740,000

—IRVING L. BLACKMAN

WHAT'S IT WORTH TO YOU?

With few exceptions, our business is our most important asset. Most of us who own a successful small business have important reasons for wanting to know how much it is worth, even if it is not, at present, for sale.

It is wise to start thinking about and planning for succession long before you *need* to transfer ownership—whether to the next generation or to another company.

In most industries, there are frequently used formulas that may help you figure the rough value of your business. For instance, a motel may be worth three times present annual room income. An accounting practice may be worth from two to three-and-a-half times retained annual fee income. A contract metal-working company may be worth book value of assets plus one year's earnings.

Such formulas are useful starting points but virtually useless for marketplace valuation. Recognize them for what they are—rough indicators for an "average" business in a given industry.

The basic approach of this evaluation method is similar to that used by some professional appraisers of small businesses. It assumes that a business is worth the value of its assets, plus a premium for goodwill when earnings are sufficiently high.

What is unique about this method is that it establishes a precise format for the redefinition of earnings as well as a discipline, through the use of a detailed form, so that the method can be followed by anyone familiar with basic business accounting.

There are seven basic steps in preparing an accurate valuation of your business:

1. Prepare a stabilized income account.
2. Determine the value of tangible assets.
3. Determine the "cost of money" (annual investment cost of tangible assets).
4. Determine "excess earnings" (earnings as determined in Step 1 less "cost of money").
5. Calculate a multiple for excess earnings.
6. Calculate value of excess earnings (excess earnings as determined in Step 4 times the multiple derived in Step 5).

7. Determine total business value by adding asset value (Step 2) to value of excess earnings (Step 6).

Step 1. Calculate the "real earning power" of the business by preparing a *stabilized income account.* Real earning power is defined as what you think earnings will be over a twelve-month period beginning on the date of valuation. Do not simply estimate your entries that may have been distorted by such factors as accounting techniques used, nonrecurring circumstances that have affected earnings positively or negatively, and so forth. This "stabilized" or "adjusted" earning figure cannot be based on wishful thinking or used to disguise basic problems in a business (such as a chronically high cost of production due to inefficiencies). This statement of real earning power will be scrutinized carefully in the event of an actual sale, and it is best if all of the assumptions used to adjust income and expense entries are stated in writing in the evaluation.

Chart 1 shows a summary of *reported* earnings for a fictional company alongside the *stabilized* earnings. At the bottom of the chart are notes that explain why the adjustments were made (in a careful evaluation, the notes will be much more detailed, and possibly supported by other data, depending on the purpose of the valuation).

Other adjustments include replacing owners' salaries—which fluctuate greatly in real-life circumstances—with an owner's salary calculation based on what it would cost to hire a paid manager. Depreciation expense, an item that is often meaningless in past financial statements, is replaced with an expense called "replacement fund." Think of this as a sinking fund sufficient to build savings to provide for normal replacement as equipment wears out.

Note that stabilized earnings do not reflect interest expense, since interest expense can fluctuate according to the structure and the special circumstances of the owner. Instead, at a later stage we use a "cost of money" calculation following the procedure outlined below.

Step 2. Calculate the *value of all tangible assets.* A well-qualified appraiser may be needed to do this. This appraisal will cover value of land, buildings, inventory, furnishings, and equipment of all types needed to conduct the business.

Chart 2 summarizes the value of tangible assets of the company we are using for an illustration.

Step 3. Step 3 involves determining the *cost of money.* As used here, it is a specialized term defining the annual investment cost of owning the tangible assets of the business (as defined in Step 2). It is a substitute for interest expense. The rate used may differ from the current prime rate or the actual interest rate that may have to be paid under any particular set of circumstances. If we were to base the valuation process on prime rate, it would lead to a situation where business values went up and down as wildly as the prime rate does; and the market just doesn't work this way. So we settle on a figure that is somewhat more stable. It is also somewhat lower than prevailing inter-

CHART 1: SMALL BUSINESS INC.
Stabilized Income Account

	Actual, 1981		Stabilized 12 months	
Sales[1]	$650,000	100.0%	$700,000	100.0%
Cost of goods[2]	(197,600)	30.4%	(212,800)	30.4%
Operating labor[3]	(187,000)	28.8%	(201,600)	28.8%
Gross profit[3]	265,200	40.8%	285,600	40.8%
Sales expense*	(86,750)	13.3%	(92,400)	13.2%
Administrative expense*	(52,650)	8.1%	(42,000)	6.0%
Executive salaries[3]	(40,000)	6.2%	(49,000)	7.0%
Replacement fund or depreciation[4]	(11,700)	1.8%	(21,000)	3.0%
Maintenance and repairs*	(5,200)	0.8%	(7,000)	1.0%
Unclassified*	(5,200)	0.8%	(7,000)	1.0%
Total overhead expense	(201,500)	31.0%	(218,400)	31.2%
Indicated pretax profit	63,700	9.8%	67,200	9.6%

Assumptions:
1. Sales will increase at inflation rate assumed to be 7.7 percent.
2. Operating cost will remain at constant percentages.
3. Executive (owner) salary should be increased $9,000 to reflect current salaries offered in comparable businesses.
4. Replacement fund of $21,000 will be substituted for depreciation expense. This is ample to replace assets as they wear out.
* Minor adjustments were made through a detailed analysis of each line item or expense and reflect best estimates.

CHART 2: VALUE OF TANGIBLE ASSETS

Land	$ 20,000
Buildings	120,000
Inventory	60,000
Equipment	60,000
Working capital required	40,000
Total tangible assets	$300,000

est rates when most of the assets involved offer considerable tax shelter, as they do in this example. This may be called "the underlying interest rate." To keep it simple, we generally use a rate that is about four points above the inflation rate. In our example, we are using a rate of 12 percent.

This "cost of money" figure applies only to the tangible assets of the business, as calculated in Step 2.

Chart 3 shows how we have made this calculation in our example.

CHART 3: COST OF MONEY

Value of tangible assets	$300,000
"Underlying" interest rate	12%
"Cost of money"	
(.12 × $300,000)	$ 36,000

Step 4. Step 4 is to determine a figure that we call *excess earnings*. This figure represents how much the business can be expected to earn *after* the cost of money (as defined in Step 3) is deducted from stabilized earnings (as defined in Step 1). It is a simple calculation, as shown in Chart 4.

CHART 4: EXCESS EARNINGS

Stabilized earnings (from Chart 1)	$67,200
Cost of money (from Chart 3)	(36,000)
Excess earnings	$31,200

Step 5. Step 5 is to determine an *excess earnings multiple* that is appropriate for the particular business being examined. This multiple will be used in the following step to determine what value to place on the excess earnings as calculated in Step 4. This multiple reflects the risk, stability, and other factors inherent in the business.

Chart 5 is the tool we use to arrive at a correct multiple. It incorporates, in shorthand, the basic values that the market places on the quality of earnings of a particular company.

CHART 5: CALCULATING THE MULTIPLE

Key to Rating Scale

Risk rating (from 0 to 6)

0 =	Continuity of income at risk
3 =	Steady income likely
6 =	Growing income assured

Competitive rating (from 0 to 6)

0 =	Highly competitive in unstable market
3 =	Normal competitive conditions
6 =	Little competition in market, high cost of entry for new competition

Industry rating (from 0 to 6)

0 =	Declining industry
3 =	Industry growing somewhat faster than inflation
6 =	Dynamic industry, rapid growth likely

Key to Rating Scale

Company rating (from 0 to 6)

0 =	Recent start-up, not established
3 =	Well established with satisfactory environment
6 =	Long record of sound operation with outstanding reputation

Company growth rating (from 0 to 6)

0 =	Business has been declining
3 =	Steady growth, slightly faster than inflation rate
6 =	Dynamic growth rate

Desirability rating (from 0 to 6)

0 =	No status, rough or dirty work
3 =	Respected business in satisfactory environment
6 =	Challenging business in attractive environment

Rating formula (showing values used for Small Business Inc.)

Risk	4.0
Competitive situation	3.0
The industry	3.5
The company	5.0
Company growth	4.0
Desirability	4.0
Total	23.5
Excess earnings multiple (Total ÷ 6)	3.9

Step 6. The multiple developed above will be used with the excess earnings figure, as shown in Chart 6.

CHART 6: VALUING EXCESS EARNINGS

Excess earnings (from Chart 4)	$ 31,200
Multiple (from Chart 5)	× 3.9
Value of excess earnings	$121,680

Step 7. Finally, we are in a position to determine the value of the business. We do this by adding the value of the assets (Chart 2) to the value of excess earnings (Chart 6).

CHART 7: TOTAL BUSINESS VALUE

Value of assets (from Chart 2)*	$260,000
Value of "excess earnings" (from Chart 6)	+ 121,680
Total business value	$381,680

*Note that the $40,000 used in Chart 2 for required working capital has not been included here. A new owner will have this amount available in addition to the purchase price.

The steps above, if followed carefully, offer a commonsense approach to valuation. They suggest (accurately) that a business is worth the market value of the assets that are necessary to conduct the business, plus, where appropriate, a premium if the business is especially profitable.

A closer examination will reveal that the methodology used to determine the premium to be paid for particularly high earnings is quite conservatively calculated. In the example used above, we arrived at a multiple of 3.9. This means that if the business is sold at the same price as the valuation suggests, the purchaser will receive a return on investment of 25.6 percent on the portion of the purchase price that is not backed up by tangible assets (payback in 3.9 years equals an annual return of 25.6 percent).

"Negative" excess earnings. Many businesses may have no excess earnings. In this case, the business is likely to be worth no more than the value of the tangible assets. After all, a seller cannot expect to charge a premium (known in accounting terms as "goodwill") if the business cannot generate more than enough funds to pay for the assets.

In some instances the figure arrived at for excess earnings may be a negative or minus figure. In such a case, the business is not even worth the value of its assets, and the best course may be to liquidate.

Every business is unique, and these comments must be qualified according to the circumstances of each. An example would be the business that provides an exceptionally nice lifestyle for a retired couple—in a sense, a combined part-time job, home, and hobby. Placing a value on such a business is quite difficult and subjective. How much is lifestyle worth? This article will not solve that problem. However, this method will be helpful in understanding some of the basic principles on which an agreement might be reached.

Summary form. The summary form below can be used to follow this methodology to determine the value of a particular business. In all probability, an owner who follows this approach carefully and objectively will arrive at a conclusion of value that is quite close—within 5 to 10 percent—to what the business should sell for, given adequate time and effort to find a qualified, arm's-length purchaser.

It will be obvious that many of the steps involved will require quite a bit of knowledge and judgment about the particular business being examined. For example, a buyer and a seller, each using this method, may arrive at quite different opinions of the rating to be used for something so intangible as the "desirability" of a particular business.

However, if the method is followed closely, differences in judgment will generally lead to quite small incremental differences in overall value. Perhaps even more important is the process of getting all of these judgments, opinions, and assumptions written down in the disciplined form we have followed here. Then, a buyer and a seller (if they are not playing games with each other) can compare all of the instances where these judgments differ. This leads to a very important discovery—that when the negotiations and discussions relating to a purchase and sale are focused on particular, defined items, it is usually not difficult to reach agreement. A buyer and seller *should* discuss the differences in such judgments and *should* arrive at a middle ground. Often this is the only way to arrive at the facts behind a particular assumption.

SHORT FORM FOR VALUATION

1. **Sales,** estimated for 12-month future period. _____
2. **Operating expense,** stabilized as outlined in article to eliminate all anomalies. Include cost of goods and operating labor. _____
3. **Administrative expense,** to be prepared after close examination of normal expenses required that are not included in Line 2. Do not include owner's salary, depreciation, or interest expenses. _____
4. **Owner's salary.** Should be what would be paid for competent hired manager. _____
5. **Replacement fund.** This is a "sinking fund" that replaces the book depreciation expense. It is "charged" to earnings so that funds will be available to replace assets as they wear out. _____
6. **"Stabilized" earnings** (Line 1 less Lines 2 through 5). _____
7. **Value of assets plus necessary working capital.**
   A. Land _____
   B. Buildings _____
      Inventory:
         Raw _____
         Work in process _____
         Finished _____
         Resale inventory _____
   C. Total inventory _____
   D. Equipment _____
   E. Furnishings & fixtures _____
   F. Other tangible asset value _____
   G. Total tangible asset value (A through F) _____
   H. Working capital needed _____
   I. Tangible assets & working capital (G & H) _____
8. **"Underlying" interest rate** (use current inflation rate + 4 points). _____
9. **"Cost of money"**
   A. Reenter tangible asset value + working capital from Line 7-I. _____
   B. Reenter underlying interest rate from Line 8 (use decimal). _____
   C. Multiply 9-A by 9-B. _____
10. **"Excess Earnings"**
   A. Reenter stabilized earnings (Line 6). _____
   B. Reenter "cost of money" (Line 9-C). _____
   C. Excess earnings (Line 10-A less 10-B). _____
11. **Calculate multiple** (Refer to Chart 5 in text. Ratings are 0-6.) _____
   A. Risk _____
   B. Competitive _____
   C. Industry _____
   D. Company _____

E. Growth   _____

F. Desirability   _____

G. Total   _____

H. Total ÷ 6   _____

12. **Value of excess earnings**
    A. Reenter excess earnings (Line 10-C).   _____
    B. Reenter multiple (Line 11-H).   _____
    C. Value of "excessive earnings" (Line 12-C).   _____

13. **Total business value**
    A. Reenter asset value (Line 7-G).   _____
    B. Reenter value of "excess earnings" (Line 12-C).   _____
    C. Total business value (13-A + 13-B).*   _____

*If this figure is used by a purchaser, he or she will have to provide any extra working capital to operate the business. The total business value as shown here *includes* inventory.

This figure *does not apply to a stock purchase*. The stock purchase value will be this figure (13-C) less total liabilities to be assumed. In addition, other adjustments may need to be made in the event of a stock sale if tax benefits are lost as a result by the buyer.

Effect of terms. Finally, the *actual* price to be paid for a business will often differ considerably from its *value* as defined here if there are special terms available as part of the transaction. For example, it is worth paying a much higher price than indicated if a very low interest rate is available, the owner will carry a lot of "paper," etc. As a rule, a little work and help from a qualified CPA will help to place a value on the benefits of such special terms. Then a correlation between the value as indicated by this method and the value of the special terms can be established, and appropriate adjustments made.

Real problems are emotional. The real problems that generally arise in negotiations are usually emotional ones. One party does not trust the other. Opinions of one party are so vague and general that they arouse suspicion. Such problems will almost always arise unless a careful, step-by-step approach to valuation such as this one is followed.

Exceptions

There are several exceptional cases in which this approach to valuation will not work, or in which it has limited value. The following are some of the instances in which this method must be modified:

- **High-tech businesses.** These are generally valued by the condition of the acquisition market—exceptionally high if the market is "hot."
- **"Information" businesses.** Very difficult to value. Often based on an initial payment plus future payments depending upon sales and earnings.
- **"Hobby" businesses.** These so-called lifestyle businesses are part business, part fun. See comments above on negative excess earnings.
- **High-leverage businesses.** Such businesses have special qualities that make them worth more than this method would indicate. An

example would be a business that has exclusive rights or lines that might be expected to generate much higher earnings if fully exploited.

- **Professional businesses.** Medical, accounting, legal practices, and other professional businesses are generally governed by prevailing practices. Consult with appropriate professional organization or consultants. Valuation is often based on percentage of future billings.
- **Start-ups.** Start-ups are hard to value. Some, especially those with exciting technical qualities, can be worth much more than asset value or immediate earnings prospects would suggest. The price will be negotiated, and will depend on the needs of both parties.

—JIM HOWARD

VALUING A BUSINESS:
More Than Numbers Alone

While the "rule of law" is important in valuations, so is the "rule of fact." Whether you're fixing a value on your own company or thinking of acquiring another, it's vital to remember that facts, not law, ultimately determine 99 percent of all business valuations.

No set of rules can make clear the importance of unique facts as well as a few examples drawn from real life. Those that follow show that knowing the ins and outs of Revenue Ruling 59-60 is important but is only a first step.

Example 1. A retail clothing store had shown a 100 percent increase in both sales and earnings during the five years preceding its owner's death. Initially, these facts gave the impression that the business was booming and that it should command a premium valuation. The first impression turned out to be wrong. Analysis showed that each year's sales growth was directly related to expansion of floor space. Sales per square foot had not increased at all. In short, the former owner had doubled his investment to double his sales and his earnings. A buyer, therefore, would have to invest more than the cost of acquiring the business to continue the upward trend. The business was probably worth less than face value, not more.

Example 2. A manufacturing company with a long history of steady earnings was initially valued at $1.1 million on a federal estate tax return. Based on history, the valuation made sense. Inspection of the plant, however, revealed severe physical deterioration—not to mention the fact that the building was condemned. Remaining management had already made plans to acquire a new building elsewhere, but the cost of the new plant, the cost of the move, and the salvage value of the old plant had not been factored into the value of the company. An estimate of $500,000 in net costs to the business as a result of the move led to a reduced valuation of $600,000 ($1.1 million minus the $500,000). The logic was simple: No buyer would pay the full value knowing that an additional $500,000 had to be invested immediately for the company to keep earning at historic rates.

Example 3. A restaurant, the building and land where it was located, and an adjacent parking lot owned by the same person were valued separately at $400,000 for the restaurant and $70,000 for the parking lot. On the surface a total valuation of $470,000 seemed correct. But further analysis revealed that the restaurant was worth the full $400,000 only if the parking lot was available. So despite the real value of the parking lot as a piece of developable land, it couldn't be used for anything other than its present purpose if the restaurant was to hold value. The parking lot's $70,000 value was eliminated from the final valuation for tax purposes.

Example 4. The task was to value a 60 percent interest in a successful closely held company. When the lawyers, accountants, and other advisers met to do the valuation, they assumed that the 60 percent interest was made up of common stock. Then someone pointed out that the holding actually was in the form of a voting trust certificate that entitled the holder to receive 60 percent of the common stock at a fixed date in the future. Since the holder of a voting trust certificate has no voice in running the company (such power resides with the designated trustee), the 60 percent interest, while real, was no more powerful than a minority interest. The value of the 60 percent interest was reduced by 25 percent to account for this fact.

In each example, a simple numeric valuation would have overstated the value of the business. Of course, there is nothing magical about the conclusions reached above. Common sense is the guide in almost all cases. Yet each example points out the critical importance of the appraiser's role in a valuation. The lesson: Don't leave business valuations in the hands of amateurs. Whether you're fixing the value of your company now to save taxes later, looking at a potential acquisition, or dealing with an estate after death, who prepares the valuation makes all the difference.

—IRVING BLACKMAN

APPRAISING BUSINESS WORTH

Ask some owners what their business is worth, and they are likely to show you the latest balance sheet. But ask any good appraiser what *your* business is worth, and his first question will be, "What do you need the appraisal for?" That's because the method he chooses to value your company, if he's looking out for your interests, will depend on the purpose behind your request. I can do an appraisal of assets in an acquisition, for example, and come up with a hefty figure for depreciation on federal taxes. Then, unblushingly and legally, I can turn around and recommend to the new owner that he appeal the property tax on his major manufacturing plant because an appraisal for that assessment may be only half the value appropriate for federal tax reporting. The fact is, federal and local statutes, regulations, and legal precedents all have different standards for evaluating what a business is worth. And when you think about it, so do you.

At a given moment you might ask any of the following questions:

- What is my business worth to a competing company that could increase its market share if it acquired my product line?
- What's it worth to my banker, who might have to sell the assets if I default on my loan?
- What value would be put on it if I gave significant amounts of stock to my children, or if I set up an employee stock ownership plan?
- What should the value be for property insurance or for key executive insurance?

Obviously, the answers would all be different. The bank appraiser, for example, would assume a quick sale and consider only the liquidation value of your tangible assets. The value to a competing company that saw product synergies, on the other hand, would likely be much higher.

The question that interests most business owners, and the one I'll focus on here, is how to figure what a company is worth if you are considering its sale. There are three main ways to arrive at an estimate of value, and the choice of which methods or combination of methods to use is what makes the practice of appraisal as much an art as a science.

One of the most widely used ways to determine a company's worth is to compare it with similar businesses. In formal appraisals, smaller publicly traded companies usually are used for comparison, since good information about them is available. The theory behind this method is that an investor will pay no more for your company than he or she would for a similar company whose stock is traded in the public market. The measure of comparison is usually some form of price-to-earnings ratio. Other relationships that can be compared include price (or market value) to book value or dividend-paying capacity. In the simplest terms, we know ratios for the public company, we know your earnings, and by analysis we can derive a price.

It's never quite that easy, of course. Even though you know the earnings for your company, it's almost always necessary to adjust the figures so they will be comparable to the earnings of the publicly traded company. The appraiser may adjust for differences in executive compensation, for example, or in dividend policies, or in how non-operating assets are entered on the books. Adjustments also may have to be made to compensate for differences in accounting methods, such as accelerated versus straight-line depreciation, or LIFO (last in, first out) versus FIFO (first in, first out) inventory valuation. Even after your earnings have been adjusted so that they are comparable to those of the public company, there's still one more step before coming up with a value. That's an adjustment that takes into account the difference in the value to an investor of ownership in a private versus a public company. Majority control, which the buyer of a private company will get, adds to a company's value. Lack of liquidity, the downside of investing in a private company, detracts from the value.

The market-comparable approach to valuation can be used even when there is no way to compare your company with a publicly traded one. Rules of thumb, frequently multiples of gross earnings, often are used to assess service businesses, dealerships, retail establishments, and professional practices. An insurance agency, for example, might use a formula that puts its selling price at 125 percent to 150 percent of annual commissions. Or a funeral home might take its tangible net market value and add to it a bonus for intangible assets, such as a dollar figure for each burial in an average year, to come up with an estimated selling price. And access to data bases is available from some business brokers that document earnings multiples of actual sales. Rules of thumb are no more than generalizations, however, and should be used with extreme caution. If you're serious about wanting to know the value of your company, you'll want the estimate to be tailored to your specific circumstances.

In general, rules of thumb or actual sale prices of companies are useful for retail operations, such as stores, restaurants, auto dealerships, and service businesses. The comparison to public companies is useful for larger, closely held companies where a comparison can be made.

A second common method of valuation is to look at a company's assets. Assets are entered on the books at their historical cost to the company. You want to stress the current market value of the company's assets. And that's only the beginning. You'll also want to stress the worth of intangible assets, such as goodwill, that do not appear on the balance sheet. The spectacular headlines we've seen in recent years, with purchase offers of 50 percent or more over book value, tell a lot about the value to a buyer of intangible and undervalued assets. Baxter Travenol Laboratories Inc.'s acquisition of American Hospital Supply Corporation, for example, brought it the best distribution network in the business. United States Steel Corporation purchased Marathon Oil for its oil reserves, which may prove to be worth a good deal more than the price paid for Marathon.

Your own intangible assets may include your business software, patents, unpatented proprietary technology, your customer list, your distribution network, or even your lease if it's below current market rates. Goodwill, a less specific intangible asset, is a company's reputation in the marketplace, and might be gauged by the amount of repeat business or the ability to make an above average return on equity. Since goodwill is hard to define and harder to put a price on, however, identifying and valuing specific intangibles provides more persuasive support for values that exceed book.

Asset-based valuations are particularly appropriate for real estate holding companies or companies with significant tangible and intangible assets.

If you are interested in selling a start-up company or one that is growing and changing rapidly, the market-comparable or asset approaches may not reflect your company's potential value. These methods, oriented as they are toward past or present performance, can be rather static. With a fast-growing company, it makes more sense to look at projected performance.

Appraisers use a method called the discounted future cash flow, or earnings, approach to calculate a selling price based solely on the present worth of future earnings. The mechanics go like this. We project earnings over a time period we feel comfortable with, say five or ten years. That's the first component. However, we need to take into account the fact that your business will be capable of producing earnings beyond those five or ten years. That's the second component. So we discount these two components—projected earnings and future value—to a present value, using a discount rate competitive with other capital investments of comparable risk. In addition, some appraisers have rather elaborate computer software models to refine key variables—such as working capital needs, capital expenditures, and depreciation—in their projections.

The strength of the discounted future earnings approach is that it looks at your business the way many prospective buyers would: It looks to the future rather than to the past. The weakness is that its reliability depends on the quality of the appraiser's crystal ball to estimate future prospects.

An appraiser should use as many methods as are appropriate to value your business, just as sailors use more than one star to estimate their position. If you are considering the sale of the sort of business that changes hands often, such as a service or retail firm, a business broker's suggested price may be adequate for your purpose. But if you are considering various planning options or want to sell all or a partial interest in any other sort of business, a professional business appraiser can really earn his keep. You worked hard to build value in your company. Don't sell it short.

—MARGARET SINGLETON

SOMETHING OF VALUE

Business appraisal is nothing new, but what *is* new is a sharp upward swing in both the quantity and the quality of practitioners. Five years ago, it took some legwork to find an appraiser. Today, just let your fingers do the walking. The business valuation expert is here—and there, and everywhere.

"Business valuation has made quantum leaps in the past few years," says Allan Lannom, director of operations at Lloyd-Thomas/ Coats & Burchard, a ninety-year-old general appraisal firm based in Calabasas Park, California. Patrick Hurley, in his seventh year at Howard & Company, a Philadelphia firm engaged in corporate financing, publication, and valuation, agrees. Hurley, mincing no words, says, "We've seen a lot more potential, and decided consciously to market directly instead of waiting for referrals. Now, instead of waiting for an attorney to call up and say, 'You do valuations, right?' I tell everyone I see, 'We do valuations.'"

A sign of the times, notes James H. Schilt, editor of the American Society of Appraisers' *Business Valuation News,* is the emphasis in the financial press on targeting business appraisal as a money-making venture. And membership in the business section of the ASA has grown more than 300 percent since 1980, making it the association's fastest-growing category of accreditation. Attendance at the section's increasingly ambitious and sophisticated annual educational seminars has multiplied just as dramatically.

Why the sudden ascendancy of a discipline that for years has been largely ignored? Since every private company with an employee stock ownership plan must have an annual valuation for tax purposes, the rise in popularity of ESOPs alone would account for quite a bit of the boom. "The banks are going crazy trying to put these things in," says Lannom. "The tax laws make ESOPs so desirable that anyone who doesn't have one looks like an oddball or a redneck." If the prospect of diminished tax advantages under President Reagan's proposed tax amendments has had any chilling effect, Lannom hasn't noticed. He gets as many client calls for ESOP-related valuations as ever. Business valuator Brian Napier, of Greensboro, North Carolina, gets more. "Some people don't think there's going to be any dramatic change," he says, "and some who do want to get in under the wire." Rising demand for valuation experts also has come from private companies choosing to include equity in their employee-compensation packages.

Voluntary transfers of equity, however, are not the only transactions that call for the appraiser's stamp. Divorce—which more and more often features a closely held business as one of the most hotly contested properties—requires his-and-hers stock valuations. And the Internal Revenue Service, long an inadvertent fee generator for lawyers and accountants, is now performing the same service for valuation experts. "About seventy-five percent of our business is tax-litigation related," says John E. Bakken, who heads up his own business valuation firm in Denver. The hefty proportion of litigation-bound clients explains why the agenda of the ASA's fourth annual business valuation seminar this past November featured a session on "The Business Appraiser as Expert Witness."

Finally, there's the trickle-down effect of the media's current love affair with entrepreneurship to be considered. Small-business owners are eager to explore the dimensions of their starring roles in the age of the entrepreneur. "A number of my clients don't have a transaction at hand when they bring us in," says Napier. "They want to know the value of their companies, for whatever might arise in the future. They know they've got something of value, and they want to know what that value is."

Whether or not they find out will have a lot to do with which of the current crop of valuation "experts" they end up picking. The appraiser's art—recent gains in respectability notwithstanding—remains, as Patrick Hurley puts it, "a judgment call based on knowledge of how a company really works." And uncovering that information is no easy task for even the best of appraisers. Detailed and sophisticated examination of the books is necessary, but hardly sufficient. The conscientious value expert will also have to assess a barrage of information ranging from personal, financial, and legal relations among founding/owning families to game plans of prospective successors to whatever local, national, and worldwide conditions exist that affect the company.

"Anyone can call himself an appraiser," states Lexington, Massachusetts, attorney Dennis O'Connor, who believes that the new-wave valuation professionals, whatever codes of ethics guide them, are usually little more than the eternal guessers and assessors. "I think that the ASA is driving out the charlatans," counters Bakken—but even he admits that the battle is far from over. Clearly, the business owner should be cautious when selecting an appraiser.

Unfortunately, that warning is about the only definitive statement that can be made on the issue. When it comes to appraising the appraiser, there are no rules and few guidelines. Fee comparisons, often a helpful selection standard, fall short in this instance. At Howard & Company, for instance, says managing partner Joel S. Lawson III, a simple valuation might cost under $2,000, while a "high-end" job—"involving, say, a large, noncontrol block of stock in a closely held company, in the hands of the estate of a person whose name is the same as the company's, with many millions of dollars at stake and several groups of interested parties"—can run as high as $40,000 to $50,000. The vicissitudes of most projects—the standard ESOP valuation being an exception—often make it impossible to charge on a flat-fee basis, or even to give a responsible estimate of hourlies.

"How much you ought to be paying depends entirely on the specific circumstances of the transaction in question," says Sherwin Simmons, senior tax and estate-planning lawyer with the Tampa law firm of Trenam, Simmons, Kemker, Scharf, Barkin, Frye & O'Neill. "A fee that looks outrageous could be reasonable, a modest-looking fee could be highway robbery." Time estimates? "Two weeks is probably suspect, even for a tiny business," says Simmons. "A month might be more like it—but depending on the circumstances, one to three months wouldn't be all that unusual. In certain special circumstances, eight months to a year wouldn't be unduly long." Credentials? Maybe. The ASA's testing and practice requirements for certification do establish a quality floor. But assuring a business owner that he is hiring neither a neophyte nor a fool is far from saying he has bought the best service.

Experience? "I'd say that anyone who isn't a CPA or an MBA and hasn't been out on the street for twenty years or so is going to have a hard time telling what a company's really worth," says Bakken. Sherwin Simmons agrees: "No amount of formal education will make [an appraiser] worth a tinker if he hasn't had the experience, learning every day. To be really good, he's got to be battle-scarred." Essential, maybe, but no guarantee. Some of the charlatans have been at it for years.

Given ambiguous directions through uncharted territory, a business could use a simple word of advice. Sherwin Simmons has it: "Network," he says. "Ask around, and then ask around some more. Talk to people in your geographical area, even if their businesses aren't just like yours; talk to people with similar businesses, even if they're not in your geographical area. Appraisal is a fraternity, and once you know who's in the fraternity, who's respected, you'll know who to go to. And, very importantly, if the reason you're looking for a valuation has anything to do with taxes, or is likely to somewhere down the line, find out who's respected by the Internal Revenue Service—who do they use to do their valuation work? You've got to remember at all times why you're doing this in the first place: Sooner or later, there's a player on the other side, and if the other side doesn't buy your valuation, then you wasted your money."

The latter point would raise little debate these days at *U.S. News & World Report*. For the better part of the past two decades, the staid and respected publication has offered a series of benefit plans that ended up making stockholders of employees on their fifth anniversary of employment. The plans required that each participant, upon retirement or termination, sell his shares back to the company at the current stated value. This, in turn, called for an annual valuation of the privately held company, whose stock was appraised by American Appraisal Associates Inc., a national valuation firm based in Milwaukee.

As of December 31, 1983, with the stock's value exceeding $35 million, the magazine was put up for sale. Some six months later, it had a new owner, Boston real estate magnate and *The Atlantic* magazine chairman Mortimer B. Zuckerman, and a new value—Zuckerman's winning bid of $176 million. The "fair-market" value came as something of a shock to former employees who had cashed out at lower figures. Eager to cash back in, some 230 of them filed suit, alleging, among other things, collusion between the company and its appraiser, and asking for a chunk of the company's present value to be distributed among them. As of August 1985, numerous legal maneuvers and amendments later, the damages sought topped $90 million. Current equity-holding employees—their overnight enrichment in danger of vanishing overnight—are fighting back. Ten law firms, representing hundreds of plaintiffs and defendants, are now dueling it out.

As for the company's true value, a respected appraisal firm has been heard from. So has an actual buyer. Chances are good, however, that the final answer is going to come from a federal judge.

—NELL MARGOLIS

HOW ARE YOU DOING?

Someone once said that if you have one clock, you always know what time it is, but if you have several clocks, you are never quite sure. I often get that feeling when I calculate financial ratios. This is because the dozens of financial ratios I use seem to provide different answers to the same simple question, "How'd we do?"

So I've been on the lookout recently for financial models that summarize one general aspect of overall company performance. An example is the affordable-growth rate, which tells you the maximum rate your company can afford to grow without having to increase its debt ratio. Another is the Z score, which, though developed to measure the likelihood of bankruptcy, can be used as a handy measure of overall financial performance.

The original Z score was created by Edward I. Altman in the mid-1960s. It is the most widely used of the many bankruptcy classifications that exist, and it has stood the test of time. To arrive at his formula, Altman looked at the financials of sixty-six publicly traded manufacturers: Thirty-three had filed for bankruptcy; thirty-three had not. Out of a selection of twenty-two financial ratios, he found five that could be combined to discriminate between the bankrupt and the nonbankrupt companies in his study. Later, Altman created what he calls the four-variable version (see Figure 1). Also widely used, this version is appropriate for both public and private firms, and for both manufacturers and service companies.

To get the Z score, you simply take the figures for the four ratios, which Altman calls X1, X2, etc., from your financial statements. Multiply their values by coefficients Altman has derived, and add up the results. The formula, explained in detail below, looks like this:

$$6.56 (X1) + 3.26 (X2) + 6.72 (X3) + 1.05 (X4) = Z \text{ score}$$

If a company's total score is greater than 2.60, things are looking good. If it is less than 1.10, bankruptcy may well be in sight. Figure 2 shows the financial statements and Z-score calculations for a hypothetical company, the BC Corporation, which, at 5.206, has scored well above the danger point.

The interesting thing about the Z score is that it is a good analytic tool no matter what shape your company is in. Even if your company is very healthy, for example, if your Z score begins to fall sharply, warning bells should ring. Or, if your company is barely surviving, you can use the Z score to help evaluate the projected effects of your turnaround efforts.

To find your company's Z score, first calculate the four ratios.

$$X1 = \frac{\text{Working capital}}{\text{Total assets}}$$

This measure of liquidity compares net liquid assets to total assets. The net liquid assets, or working capital, are defined as current total assets minus current total liabilities. Generally, when a company experiences financial difficulties, working capital will fall more quickly than total assets, causing this ratio to fall.

$$X2 = \frac{\text{Retained earnings}}{\text{Total assets}}$$

This ratio is a measure of the cumulative profitability of your company. To some degree, the ratio also reflects the age of your company, because the younger it is, the less time it has had to build up cumulative profits. This bias in favor of older firms is not surprising, given the high failure rate of young companies.

When a company begins to lose money, of course, the value of total retained earnings begins to fall. For many companies, this value—and the X2 ratio—will become negative.

$$X3 = \frac{\text{EBIT}}{\text{Total assets}}$$

This is a measure of profitability, or return on assets, calculated by dividing your firm's EBIT (earnings before interest and taxes) for one year by its total assets balance at the end of the year.

You can also use it as a measure of how productively you are using borrowed funds. If the ratio exceeds the average interest rate you're paying on loans, you are making more money on your loans than you are paying in interest. In Figure 1, for example, you can see that nonbankrupt firms earned 15.4 percent on their total assets before payment of interest and taxes. Since this performance exceeded the average interest rates at the time, nonbankrupt firms profited, on average, from every borrowed dollar they invested in assets. Failed firms, on the other hand, were losing 31.8 percent on total assets yearly. Even before they paid their interest costs, in other words, the bankrupt companies were losing nearly 32¢ on each dollar they borrowed.

To calculate this ratio in the middle of a fiscal year, use your month-end balance sheet and the EBIT from an income statement showing the most recent twelve months of activity. (It takes extra effort to maintain this moving twelve-month income statement, of course, but you probably will find that the statement provides a view of your business that is valuable in its own right.)

$$X4 = \frac{\text{Net worth}}{\text{Total liabilities}}$$

This ratio is the inverse of the more familiar debt-to-equity ratio. It is found by dividing your firm's net worth (also known as stockholders' equity) by its total liabilities. Notice in Figure 1 that nonbankrupt firms maintained more than twice as much equity as debt—2.684; failed firms managed to accumulate more than twice as much debt as equity—0.494.

FIGURE 1: The Z-Score Bankruptcy Classification Model

Ratio names	Description	Coefficient	Mean ratio values Altman's sample cos.	
			Bankrupt	Nonbankrupt
X1 =	$\frac{\text{Working capital}}{\text{Total assets}}$	6.56	(0.061)	0.414
X2 =	$\frac{\text{Retained earnings}}{\text{Total assets}}$	3.26	(0.626)	0.355
X3 =	$\frac{\text{EBIT}}{\text{Total assets}}$	6.72	(0.318)	0.154
X4 =	$\frac{\text{Net worth}}{\text{Total liabilities}}$	1.05	0.494	2.684

Cutoff values		Mean scores	
Safe if greater than:	2.60	Nonbankrupt	7.70
Bankrupt if less than:	1.10	Bankrupt	(4.06)

Source: *Corporate Financial Distress*, by Edward I. Altman; John Wiley & Sons, 1983.

After you've calculated these four ratios, simply multiply the X1 ratio by its coefficient, shown in Figure 1, the X2 by its coefficient, and so on; add the results; and then compare the total with Altman's cutoff values, also shown in Figure 1.

The BC Corporation in Figure 2, as we've seen, scored 5.206. Since this Z score significantly exceeds the cutoff value of 2.60 shown in Figure 1, the company is safe from bankruptcy, at least for now. Suppose, instead, that its score had been *minus* 2.70. This would say that its financial statements strongly resemble those of companies that have gone bankrupt. If the score had been 1.70, the company would be in a gray area: Companies with higher scores have gone bankrupt, while companies with lower scores have survived.

The purpose of calculating your own Z score is to warn you of financial problems that may need serious attention and to provide a guide for action. If your Z score is lower than you would like, then you should examine your financial statements to determine the reason why.

FIGURE 2

BC Corp. Balance Sheet, December 1986 (All values in $1,000)		BC Corp. Income Statement, 1986 (All values in $1,000)	
Assets		Sales	845
Current Assets		Cost of Goods Sold	
Cash	13	Materials	250
Receivables	109	Direct Labor	245
Inventory	272	Utilities	32
Prepaid Expenses	9	Indirect Labor	28
		Depreciation	31
Total Current Assets	403	Total Cost of Goods Sold	586
Net Fixed Assets	169	Gross Profit	259
Total Assets	572		
		Operating Expense	
Liabilities		Selling Expenses	99
Current Liabilities		General and Administrative	
Accounts Payable	82	Expenses	110
Notes Payable	50	Total Operating Expense	209
Other Current Liabilities	35	Earnings Before Interest and Taxes	50
Total Current Liabilities	167	Interest Expense	14
Long-Term Debt	130	Earnings Before Taxes	36
Total Liabilities	297	Taxes	8
		Net Income	28
Stockholders' Equity			
Common Stock	110	**Stock Data, December 31, 1986**	
Retained Earnings	165	Stock Price (in dollars)	3
Net Worth	275	Shares Outstanding	100
Total Liabilities and Equity	572	Market Value of Equity	300

Z-Score Calculations

Ratio	Description	Formula		Result		Coefficient		Z Score
X1	Working capital / Total Assets	$\dfrac{403-167}{572}$	=	0.413	×	6.560	=	2.707
X2	Retained earnings / Total assets	$\dfrac{165}{572}$	=	0.288	×	3.260	=	0.940
X3	EBIT / Total assets	$\dfrac{50}{572}$	=	0.087	×	6.720	=	0.587
X4	Net worth / Total liabilities	$\dfrac{275}{297}$	=	0.926	×	1.050	=	0.972
Z Score:								**5.206**

Start by calculating the scores from previous periods, comparing them with your current score. (Graph them if possible.) If the trend is down, try to understand what has changed to create ratios that are dragging your scores down. Monitoring the trend in your Z scores can also help you evaluate your turnaround efforts.

Another way to analyze your score is to compare your results with those of other companies. Figure 1 shows the mean (average) ratio values that Altman found for bankrupt firms in his study. Compare these ratios with your own. You could also refer to the Robert Morris Associates (RMA) *Annual Statement Studies*. These studies, to which your banker probably subscribes, provide detailed financial ratios by Standard Industrial Classification code. (Ratio X2 cannot be calculated from RMA data, however, because retained earnings aren't included.) Compare your own calculations with industry ratios, and find the ones that are out of line.

When you make this comparison, however, I've found it's very natural to excuse low ratios by saying, "We're different." Suppose, for example, that your X3 ratio is lower than your industry average. You might say, "We've made a much greater investment in production equipment than our competitors, giving us an advantage." But if this additional investment provides a truly competitive advantage, the other ratios should more than compensate for the low X3 ratio. If not, your competitors may actually have the advantage because they are able to achieve similar profits with a smaller investment in assets and correspondingly smaller debt.

The Z score, you will soon learn, takes a very stern view of your financial statements. To the Z score, profits are good, assets are bad, liabilities are worse, and current liabilities are worst of all. If yours is lower than you would like, you can improve it considerably by selling marginal assets and using the cash to reduce current liabilities. This will improve ratio X1 by both increasing working capital and decreasing assets; it will improve ratios X2 and X3 by reducing assets; and it will improve ratio X4 by reducing liabilities.

In real life, of course, this action can also make perfect sense. Reducing current liabilities often lowers interest costs and reduces the possibility that an unhappy creditor will force you into bankruptcy. Reducing assets can often lower overhead costs and improves your return on the assets invested in your company.

When you use bankruptcy classification models, including the Z score, keep this reservation in mind: They are by no means infallible. The fact is, one doesn't necessarily agree totally with another. The models can provide valuable warnings of trouble and useful guides to ways of avoiding trouble ahead. And they can complement the other reports and analyses that you use within your company. Seldom, however, should you use any of the models as your only means of financial analysis.

—CHARLES W. KYD

PRESELLING THE COMPANY

Amid the celebrity of last year's megabucks mergers, nobody paid much attention when one of the country's best-known microcomputer-software publishers acquired one of the country's most obscure microcomputer-software developers. The snub was understandable, since the payment of 500,000 shares of Ashton-Tate common for all of Forefront Corporation appeared on paper to be the conventional outcome of a typical high-technology venture. But in fiscal fact, the clever folk at Forefront added a Lewis Carroll twist to the annals of start-up financing. And, for their part, the people at Ashton-Tate added a touch of patience to the annals of acquisition—and product development. You have to admire the *Through the Looking-Glass* sequence. First, Forefront's founders sold the company to Ashton-Tate for a nifty profit. Then they started it up.

In mid-1983, when this unusual saga began, Robert Carr and Martin Mazner had recently left positions elsewhere and were designing the elements of a sophisticated software package they called Fred. Carr possessed programming skills and Mazner marketing smarts, but infant Fred demanded pure capital—a minimum of $5 million, they figured—to form a business strong enough to enter the software market. To be sure, they could have tapped a venture pool, since in those days a person needed only a key to a garage to whet investor appetites. But the pair decided that they didn't want to go that route.

One concern was that to part with that kind of money, venture capitalists would seek a huge payback, achievable only through building the proposed company into a massive vertical entity. And anyone who aspired to such fast growth, Carr fretted, would hold that the goal of business was return on investment. "We had the same end in mind," he admits, not entirely berserk, "but we wanted to create a special place for software development along the way, attracting top talent, removing them from money worries, and creating a nest." Of course, that would be a different culture from the one venture capital would spawn. "We can do it better," Carr urged Mazner with enthusiasm, "and let's have *fun* while we do it better."

More to the point, before you design ambitious five-year business plans, they reasoned, you ought to get the product at least partly working. Even then, you're going to have to go out and sell the damn

273

274 / VALUING, BUYING, AND SELLING A BUSINESS

thing, and that means spending venture capital on management and salespeople—excess baggage in the nest they envisioned. Since their program was well enough along to suggest its finished state, Carr and Mazner decided to get Fred a hearing at an extant software publisher whose treasury might accelerate the development process. They had nothing in particular in mind, except that the goal would be toward symbiotic benefit: Like a shark and a pilot fish, if one fared well, the other would, too.

The pair studied the list of corporate associations they felt might appreciate Fred's mutual potential—among them VisiCorp, Digital Research, MicroPro International, Lotus Development, Ashton-Tate, Software Publishing, and Microsoft. Not wanting word to spread, they contacted only two of the companies for starters. By the luck of the draw, one was Ashton-Tate, a quick trip down the coast in Culver City, California. The other was Lotus Development Corporation in Cambridge, Massachusetts, whose head, Mitchell Kapor, was scheduled to be in California the same week. At first Ashton-Tate's then–chief executive officer, David Cole, in the process of bringing his company public, turned them down. Ironically, Lotus almost got a peek at Fred first—with who knows what consequences, since it was but a few months before Lotus's own competing Symphony came out.

But the fates of free enterprise decreed that integrated software should have two prime contenders. Cole consented to a one-hour audience, and the rest is history. Ashton-Tate kept Fred—soon to be called Framework—and its two guardians for forty-seven additional hours. In that interval, a letter of intent was drafted, capitalizing Forefront as a going concern, and a formula was devised to determine the amount of the cash-out three years down the line, in August 1986.

Ashton-Tate had proposed buying everything outright then and there, as any normal company would do when faced with the opportunity to add immediate substance to its product line. "We said no," Carr relates. "Their eyebrows raised, and they looked baffled. We said we want to do something different: start a company around the product, and then have you buy the company in a few years. We believe in Framework so much that we're willing to bet on the come."

In this case, the come was no vague roll of the dice, but a strict formula that at merger time would factor the profitability of the start-up times an earn-out ratio (relating to how well Framework performed within the Ashton-Tate line) times Ashton-Tate's average price/earnings ratio. Pitting it measurably in open contest against Ashton-Tate's stalwart dBaseII and dBase III in the end-user arena would demonstrate Framework's profit potential, Carr calculated. Deferring to the company's P/E ratio would be a shortcut to appraising Forefront: How Wall Street assessed Ashton Tate's market value in relation to its earnings should apply to Forefront as well. And, even more brazenly, Forefront's profitability (essentially, net profit over sales) would give the savvy of the to-be-acquired talent its proper due. Hastening to seal the deal, Ashton-Tate presented Carr and Mazner with $25,000 in earnest money—enough, surely, to phone the luckless Kapor person-to-person and tell him next Sunday's dinner was off.

Ashton-Tate agreed to invest $975,000 toward the completion of Framework by plowing $750,000 into development and buying 15 percent of Forefront for $225,000—sufficient for the tiny company to gear up and plunge ahead. But when Framework was done, Forefront would need a revenue stream. So Ashton-Tate became Framework's publisher, being granted marketing rights in return for which it would pay Forefront royalties. With the tail now wagging a salivating dog, the public company was held to minimum performance standards by which it was obligated to roll out Framework as soon as development was complete, and to spend a stipulated minimum on advertising in the first year. There was also a floor price of acquisition below which the deal would not be consummated, even if Framework fizzled but Ashton-Tate still wanted to own the development company.

For its troubles, Ashton-Tate received an option to buy the remaining 85 percent of the formative company in August 1986. At that, those three years were a concession by Forefront's principals, who hoped for longer exposure before the final price was calculated. "But considering that they wanted to buy us that same day," Carr generously cedes, "we were willing to let the chips fall where they may."

The bones of that setup are not unfamiliar to commerce: A big company buys a small fraction of a small company, accompanied by rights to purchase a larger interest in the future. Ashton-Tate, for one, has since made similar arrangements with private enterprises, but the rights provisions are based on the latters' projected revenues, not on arcane calculations relating profitability to the whims of Wall Street. Even rarer, neither are the target companies apt to consist of a "handful of recruits," as Carr affectionately saw his yet-to-be-gathered cadre, but are solid businesses such as East Hartford's MultiMate International Corporation, which Ashton-Tate recently bought—for straight cash. "[The Forefront formula] remains unique," acknowledges Norman Block, Ashton-Tate executive vice-president for finance and administration. "I know of no other. They didn't even have seed capital. Nonetheless, they had the kernel of an idea and had some development work done already. And they were supremely competent people."

The chips fell a year ahead of schedule, and resoundingly at that. By the turn of 1985, after Framework was finished and had been shipping for only six months, it was clear that the five-function program was a smash hit. Framework was chipping in a healthy 18 percent of Ashton-Tate's annual revenues.

But the resultant royalty income to Forefront muddied the buyout waters in ways the drafting attorneys had not anticipated. Since Forefront's sales consisted of Framework royalties alone, how much should fairly be expensed for more development, favoring the buyer? How much should be brought directly to the bottom line as profit, favoring the seller? "There was a lot of uncertainty around the one-time shot that looked simple but actually left a lot of things unclear," Carr says on reflection. "To be frank, that would be the one thing I'd change if I were doing it again."

Partly in light of such complications and partly to cement ongoing development of additional products, Ashton-Tate offered to throw the formula to the winds and merge early. Why not, replied Forefront, all eighteen of whose employees held uncashed-in equity in the on-paper-rich company. But considering that TATE (as it's publicly listed on NASDAQ) common had fallen to around $10 a share, at what reward? "It was an excellent piece of timing," Carr admits with relish. "Both parties felt the stock was a good buy, but we argued that we can't take the risk on counting on it going up, so we need to get a number of shares that at ten dollars would constitute a fair price. Ashton-Tate said, 'My God, you guys want five hundred thousand shares? If it goes to twenty dollars, that's an incredible amount.'" And so it was: By the end of January, TATE was trading at over 20.

Among the assets Ashton-Tate had received in return for its 1983 commitment to the unorthodox contract were intangible dividends paid back instantly from Forefront's spanking new offices in Sunnyvale, California. "We were more highly motivated because our price had not yet been determined than if we already had the money at a fixed price," Carr recalls. "We wanted to work motivation into the structure, and the logic seems to have been successful. It helped bind us together. We knew we were going to be rewarded in three years."

American dreamy as that sentiment is, in retrospect Forefront stockholders undoubtedly could have gotten more if they had cast their lot with venture capitalists and had built a vertical company. But, Carr believes, the morning-line odds were stacked against them without Ashton-Tate's entry. "There are a number of things that you really can't put a price on: the name, the expertise and experience they have in the microcomputer marketplace, established goodwill, established public reputation, the ability to get people to listen to them. These are things we would have been foolhardy to feel we could build from scratch. It's hard to go out there and say, yes, there are another five hundred start-ups but, listen to me, I'm different. It seemed to us there was less promise for added risk."

Devoted exclusively to software development, the idealistic founders understood that their creation was not an organism that could survive on its own in the open market. Instead, like some creature with an inescapable place in the food chain, Forefront's charter was ultimately to merge. A corporate guardian was needed, since no self-respecting venture capitalist would have funded a start-up if the only payoff was going to be the price of merging the little company into a big one. Now a designated Ashton-Tate "development center," Forefront yet lives on in the Valley, its nest intact. The blending was so seamless that nary an employee, including the founders, has departed. "The only thing that has changed," says Carr, "is that our business cards and paychecks now say 'Ashton-Tate.'"

—ROBERT A. MAMIS

THE LEVERAGED BUYOUT BOOM

I t was too perfect a symbol, too convenient a metaphor to slip into the first paragraph of a story about leveraged buyouts, but there it was, sitting on the top of Leonard Shaykin's desk: a croupier's stick—that long, graceful object with the slightly curved tip that croupiers use to maneuver gambling chips. Lacking a pointer at a speech he had given, Shaykin had improvised with the stick, which he had found in the bottom of a closet. Since then he has kept it in his office.

Now the stick was in his hand, punctuating his remarks about leveraged buyouts, or LBOs. The principal purpose of the capital-raising technique, he was saying, was to maximize the number of chips while significantly reducing the risks.

"In a leveraged buyout," Shaykin explains for perhaps the dozenth time that week, "we take a financial risk, but, hopefully, not a business risk." Shaykin, who had set up Citicorp's leveraged buyout unit before joining with venture capitalist Fred Adler to form Adler & Shaykin (a partnership that is raising $100 million to do LBOs), has been talking about leveraged buyouts a lot recently. The LBO has become a phenomenon, a device whose popularity is attested to by everything short of buttons and bumper stickers.

Every other day, it seems, the *New York Times* or the *Wall Street Journal* reports on another LBO development—the bidding war over Norton Simon Inc., the purchase of the McCulloch Corporation by an investment group headed by McCulloch president Donald V. Marchese, the creation of LBO units by E. F. Hutton Group Inc. and Oppenheimer & Company. *The New York Times* observed, parenthetically, that in an LBO, "a management group puts up a relatively small amount of money and uses the company and its assets as collateral to borrow a relatively large sum to buy the outstanding equity."

"There's still a need to explain what LBOs are," notes Shaykin, "but that's changing quickly."

Specifically, LBOs are transactions in which buyers borrow against a company's assets at extraordinarily high debt-to-equity ratios, sometimes as high as twelve-to-one. LBOs also happen to be one of the hottest items to hit the business and investment communities in nearly a decade. W. T. Grimm & Company, a Chicago-based merger broker that tracks management buyouts (the purchase of a company by members of the management team), many of which are highly leveraged, reports that the number of management deals has more than doubled since 1980, while the size of the average deal has shot from $24 million to more than $33 million during the same period. The Merrill Lynch White Weld Capital Markets Group, which has itself invested around $30 million in LBOs, has tracked a 116 percent increase in LBO activity since 1979, and believes that the volume will be up significantly this year. "As much as twenty percent of all the acquisitions done this year," predicted James J. Burke, Jr., of Merrill Lynch's LBO team in 1983, "will be financed as leveraged buyouts." Shaykin expects that number to eventually approach 50 percent.

Shaykin, thirty-nine, a tall, trim man who refers to himself as "the better-looking half" of Adler & Shaykin, compares the situation to the one that prevailed in venture capital in the early seventies, when that industry was still finding itself. "I remember having a series of discussions back then," he recalls. "We were all relatively young, and we'd been making investments and doing all of the right things, but we weren't making any money—and venture capital began to look fragile. If Federal Express, which had tied up seventy million dollars of the total venture capital pool, had failed, it could have seriously affected the shape and direction of the entire venture capital industry. And the question we were asking was, 'Is this really a business, or are we just a group of smart young men making a mistake?' "

In the case of LBOs, that question has already been answered. "It *is* a business," says Shaykin, who, during his four years at Citicorp, oversaw the investment of $30 million in twelve transactions. During the same period of time, between 1978 and 1982, the LBO market shot to between $4 billion and $5 billion a year, more than twice the size of the venture capital market. And it kept growing. In 1984, some 252 companies were involved in deals valued at $18.8 billion. In 1986, there were 329 transactions totaling $44.9 billion, according to *Mergers & Acquisitions* magazine.

Why LBOs? Why LBOs now? The explanations are as numerous as the deals. They were triggered by inflation, with buyers hoping to pay off the debt in ever-cheaper dollars from sales that were inflating at double-digit rates; they were created by the banking community's desire to lend money at above-prime rates; they were sparked by "deconglomerization," the increased spinoff of divisions by U.S. corporations; they were fueled by changes in Federal Reserve regulations in 1981, which enabled investment banks to arrange financing for the acquisition of stock in public companies. But Shaykin sees something simpler at work. "I don't think it's inflation-driven or economy-driven or interest-rate-driven," he says. "I think it's really driven by the American dream—the desire of management to own a piece of the company they're running, to control their own destinies. . . . It has to do with the entrepreneurial spirit."

Adler, best known for his role in the founding of Data General Corporation and Lexidata Corporation, agrees. "I really don't even like the phrase *leveraged buyout*," he says. "To me, the key phrase is *man-*

agement buyout, because management is what these deals are really all about."

In fact, LBOs are used to achieve a number of ends: to take a public company private, to buy a division shed by a corporation, or to satisfy the needs of a founder who is selling a privately held company and is concerned about liquidity.

In the first case, explains Shaykin, an otherwise solid company may be out of favor in the public market, resulting in low prices and possibly inviting takeovers by "the sharks that swim in the water." Or, the company may feel that it needs to make strategic changes that won't sit well with stockholders. "Does it allow itself to be taken over or to make the wrong decision, or does it say, 'We have to maintain control by going private'?"

An LBO snatched the Signode Corporation from the jaws of financial wheeler-dealer Victor Posner. Another, engineered by Citicorp vice-president David Thomas, resolved a major dilemma for the Devon Group Inc., a Stamford, Connecticut–based company with graphic-arts and wine-distributing interests. "We were traded on the American Stock Exchange and had about one million shares outstanding," says Devon president Marne Obernauer, Jr., "but no more than three hundred thousand to three hundred fifty thousand could have been actively traded." Institutional investors were uninterested, and the research community didn't bother following the stock. As a result, outside shareholders saw few benefits. "We couldn't get up any momentum," Obernauer concedes.

The solution was a $50-million buyout by company management, subordinated debt holders, and Citicorp (which took an equity position) that gave stockholders double the market value—$28 for stock that had been trading at about $14 one month before the deal was announced—and freed Devon from its public responsibilities and concerns.

"[The buyout] took care of a very difficult problem for stockholders," notes Obernauer.

The second scenario, involving the purchase of a corporate division, is by far the most common type of LBO. During the past three years, many of the conglomerates that spent the 1960s and early 1970s acquiring are now divesting in order to make for a more compatible mix of companies, implement new strategies to address changing markets, or to improve their cash flow. In 1982, W. T. Grimm recorded no less than 875 divestitures (37 percent the number of acquisitions), 115 of which resulted in management buyouts.

Beatrice Foods Company and Gould Inc. are among a number of corporations that have recently been busy spinning off. Faced with a sharp decline in profits, Beatrice has put some fifty companies on the auction block; Gould, moving from a diversified manufacturing base to strengthen its electronics group, may divest 75 percent of the company. And, observes Shaykin, "GE is moving away from middle-tech into higher-tech—so you could say that GE itself is up for sale."

Among the recently liberated is Universal Electric Company, of

Owosso, Michigan. Founded in 1942 to manufacture gyro motors for the Norden bomb sight, UE moved into the HVAC (heating/ventilation/air conditioning) market after the war, and was acquired by ESB Inc., of Philadelphia, in 1969. ESB, in turn, was acquired by Inco Ltd., of Toronto, in 1974. A solid, slow-growth company that served as a cash cow for Inco, UE led a rather autonomous existence until 1980. Then the parent, eager to regroup its resources in Canada and to return to what it did best—"pulling things out of the ground"—announced a program of divestiture, beginning with UE.

"I was taken completely unawares," recalls president Bill Lawson, an electrical engineer who had joined UE straight out of college, "and my first thought was, We're going to be sold to somebody else." Later, it occurred to management that it might buy UE itself, but the $11 million to $22 million of up-front cash that would be required for an ordinary purchase was out of reach, and, at the time, Dawson had never heard of an LBO—a situation that an acquisitions expert at the accounting firm of Coopers & Lybrand corrected.

"He mentioned the LBO as a possibility," says Lawson, "and noted that he had a friend who was gaining quite a reputation in this area, that being Leonard Shaykin." Lawson arranged an "audience" with Shaykin, who was still at Citicorp, and came away "utterly amazed."

"I sat down with Leonard," Lawson recalls, "and he asked me a number of questions—about our annual sales, rates of return, the market we were in, the growth aspects of that market, our market share, why we were successful, who our key players were. At the end of a thirty-minute conversation, he astounded me with his concluding comments. He said, 'Lawson, we want to do the deal. We'll make all the arrangements, we'll take care of everything. We'll handle your equity financing, your debt financing. . . . We want to do the deal.'"

Eight members of management applied a total of only $250,000 of their own cash to the $45-million purchase price, but obtained 25 percent of the equity. In order to ease UE's heavy tax burden, Shaykin suggested a reverse merger. "He said, 'I've got a few companies with NOLs [net operating losses] that I'd like you to talk to . . .'" Lawson remembers. One such company was First Wall Street Settlement Corporation, a clearinghouse for brokerage firms. First Wall Street had run up a $50-million NOL. In a reverse merger, 51 percent of UE was acquired by First Wall Street.

The complex transaction, some three months in the making, was closed on June 26, 1981. "It took a lot of time, and put quite a strain on my family life," concedes Lawson, "but it was well worth it. This little company was worth any price I could have paid." UE, which employs some 2,000 people, will do more than $80 million in sales this year, clearing 3 percent to 4 percent in after-tax profits, and has already retired $9 million of its $34-million debt.

"I can't begin to tell you how excited we are," says Lawson. "The company's performance has improved incredibly, because everybody's working so damn hard. . . . And the reason is that they've all got a piece of the action now."

Inco, for its part, was so pleased with the way things went that, following the UE sale in 1981, it quickly did three more divestitures as leveraged buyouts.

The third context in which LBOs may make sense are situations involving liquidity. Generally, the owner of a private company who is growing older decides that he doesn't want to leave his company's destiny to fate, that he wants to sell during his lifetime. "And it often works out best," says Shaykin, "if he sells to his own management, to the people who have been working for him and been loyal to him for all those years."

The company doesn't have to be shopped, won't be absorbed by a competitor—a blow to a founder's ego—and the owner can generally get his price and get it quickly.

Jim N. Brown, president of GP Technologies Inc., in Philadelphia, a manufacturer of typewriter elements and print wheels, notes that founder Calvin Page decided, in 1981, that he wanted to get out of line management; he wanted to devote himself to other interests and, at the same time, effectively convert his ordinary income into capital gains. He also wanted, Brown explains, to protect his company—"a very healthy firm, with good products, good markets, and good distribution" when Brown joined it in April 1982.

The company was presented to several likely purchasers, among them Gillette Company and American Brands Inc., without luck, before Page heard about LBOs. Then, during nine months of "dancing," he shaped a deal with Citicorp and individual investors that gave him most of what he wanted. He has reduced his equity position from 100 percent to 30 percent of the company and is less active in daily operations, although he serves on the board of directors and remains vice-president of GP's research and development. And he knows that his "baby" is in competent hands.

LBOs have been around in one form or another since the early 1970s, but it was only several years ago that the theories, language, and mechanisms came together in a cohesive whole. ("The one thing we're lacking at this point," interjects Shaykin, "is a word to describe people who do LBOs.") Since that time, the technique has swept across the U.S. marketplace and has been utilized to move companies as diverse as Tenneco Chemicals Inc. and Expediter Systems Company. The press has often described it as "the salvation of sunset industries," but that definition is being superceded by the LBO's success; Adler & Shaykin, for instance, plans to add high-technology prospects to its shopping list.

Even now, LBOs seem omnipresent: The list of deals features Congoleum (flooring), Mid-Atlantic Coca-Cola Bottling (soft drinks), H. G. Parks (sausage), Chris-Craft (cruisers and sportsboats), U.S. Repeating Arms (rifles), Hood Sailmakers (sailing equipment), Converse (footwear), Ray-O-Vac (batteries), National Psychiatric (mental hospitals), and A-1 Tool (mold builders).

The insurance companies, banks, and investment firms that pioneered the field—Prudential Insurance Company of America; First

Boston; Oppenheimer & Company; and Kohlberg, Kravis, Roberts & Company—are now part of a greater LBO community that includes Merrill Lynch; Morgan Stanley & Company; Aetna Life & Casualty; Travelers Insurance; Northwestern Mutual Life Insurance; Forstmann Little & Company; Bankers Trust; First National Bank of Chicago; Lehman Bros. Kuhn Loeb; General Electric Credit Corporation; and Oregon Public Employees' Retirement System. "There's an entire infrastructure for doing LBOs now," says Burke of Merrill Lynch, who notes that investors are increasingly inclined to become equity partners.

For lenders, LBOs are attractive for a variety of reasons. Unlike the venture capital–funded company, the typical LBO company is older, established, and has proven products and markets and a seasoned management team, all of which reduce the business risk. Because it generally doesn't have the clout or credit rating of a *Fortune* 500 company, it is willing to pay above-prime rates. And, because management is newly invigorated, the deals make for close and rewarding relationships. "It gets back to those things bankers wish they still had with major corporations," notes Shaykin. If they take an equity position, lenders may serve in an advisory capacity (Adler intends to share a lot of his high-tech expertise with A&S concerns, showing them how they can use technology to improve profit margins); they get a hedge against inflation, and may see the value of their investment soar.

Although the rags-to-riches multiples that feed venture capital dreams are less likely, some LBOs have yielded impressive returns. In January of 1982, an affiliate of Wesray Corporation purchased Gibson Greeting Cards from RCA Corporation for $81 million, all but $1 million of it financed by bank loans and real estate leasebacks; in May 1981 when Gibson went public, the 50 percent interest held by Wesray's two principals (one is former Treasury Secretary William E. Simon) was worth an estimated $140 million.

Sellers like LBOs because they are easier to arrange, generally produce the desired price, and reward the management team. For the buyers, LBOs represent what Shaykin calls a "Horatio Alger mechanism for the middle-aged manager."

"When he's sitting quietly behind his desk, or heading home on the highway at night, [the manager is] thinking, 'Gee whiz, I wish I were running my own company,'" says Shaykin, sketching the vision that drives him. "Do you realize how many people like that there are? They've got all the corporate marbles, but it simply isn't satisfying."

An LBO gives such individuals an opportunity to buy into a company they otherwise couldn't afford, and it gives them the freedom to run it as they think best—"not for all sorts of exogenous reasons like quarter-to-quarter earnings," he says, "or emphasis on earnings instead of cash, or to defend some piece of the business that the president finds 'cute.' . . ." And, Shaykin continues, "what happens in every case is an unleashing of entrepreneurial spirit. . . . A seasoned management team really becomes young again."

He points to cases in which LBO owners have saved a company that might otherwise have faltered. "During the recent recession, Universal Electric suffered a major shortfall in business," Shaykin explains, "but they managed to reduce inventories much faster than the reduction in sales . . . and, throughout the whole sales decline, continued both to make money and to generate cash. . . . I'm not so sure that they would have been so diligent if the business wasn't their own."

And, as the company pays off its debt, management's equity position may become quite valuable.

The pitfalls are those that attend any investment phenomenon: namely, that enthusiasm will take precedence over financial considerations, and bad deals will be struck—a seller will find that he has been underpaid, a company will see that it can't handle the debt load. "There used to be more reservations about huge debt-financed purchases," concedes Shaykin. "There are fewer filters, inhibitions, and restrictions now." A few LBO businesses have failed—Brentano's Inc. and a food distributor funded by General Electric Credit Corporation among them.

For the moment, though, Shaykin is consumed by the golden outlook: "I feel very, very lucky because I've come across something that I absolutely love doing and that lends itself to entrepreneurial formation—to having a fund and doing it in such a way as to control one's own destiny."

Shaykin's vision, that of a frustrated corporate executive sitting in rush-hour traffic considering what might have been, has a personal source. Not long ago he was that executive. Now, for the first time in his life, he is an entrepreneur. He has traded a plush office at Citicorp for a spot at the table and a croupier's stick.

—CRAIG R. WATERS

THE DREAM MAKERS

If you just sort of stumbled into this place—admittedly a little difficult, since it's on the thirtieth floor of a skyscraper near Wall Street, but let's say you did anyway—and you happened to overhear a conversation, you might have a very hard time figuring out whether you were in a "little shop of horrors" rather than a leveraged buyout boutique.

LBO HOTSHOT #1: You look depressed. What's the matter—you break your pick [exhaust every conceivable possibility]?

LBO HOTSHOT #2: Just about. The diversion looked great—I mean it was covered with hair [problems concealing opportunities]. But the new product they were working on just tanked [failed]. They tried all kinds of tweaks and twoks [fine tunings and major adjustments], but they had to put a pin in [terminate] it anyway. It absolutely cratered [messed up royally] their projections.

LBO HOTSHOT #1: Guess we'll have to shoot this puppy in the head [reject the deal].

LBO HOTSHOT #2: It's too bad. I thought it could be a screamer [a great investment].

Good Lord, what manner of men are these? Imagine, little puppies. The fiends.

Fortunately, underneath all this metaphorical mayhem, there lies a far more palatable reality, which, in its own way, is still no less shocking.

The fiends in question are actually six young, rather mild-mannered men, clean-cut and listing toward preppy, representing Weiss, Peck & Greer (WPG), a private merchant banking firm. They are: E. Theodore Stolberg, thirty-seven; Kim G. Davis, thirty-three; Wesley W. Lang, Jr., thirty; Stephen L. DeMenna, thirty-four; Peter B. Pfister, twenty-eight; and intern Bradford Peck, twenty-five. Despite the tough talk, they have no noticeable inclination toward wanton violence. Quite the contrary, it can even be said they are possessed of a rare and distinctly humanitarian sensibility. Superficially at least, they might be mistaken for any other group of LBO hotshots on the prowl in Wall Street, but that would be a regrettable error, since there are a number of important differences.

Rather than focusing on huge deals like a $6.2-billion Beatrice Companies buyout or a $4.25-billion Safeway Stores transaction, WPG concentrates on small to midsize opportunities with purchase prices generally ranging from $10 million to $100 million. And where many buyout specialists never involve themselves beyond the sheer mathematics of the initial financial leverage, and still others rapidly liquidate the underlying assets to pay down debt, this group attempts to build value through ongoing operating improvements in the portfolio companies themselves.

Finally, and perhaps most surprising, they do this by emphasizing what they call "human motivation" much more than numbers. They believe—and their results appear to bear them out—that the buyout must serve a higher calling, which is to nourish the passionate, occasionally miraculous, commitment of employees suddenly become owners. By placing people before figures, they look to create what might be called leveraged buyouts with heart—an offering not often associated with Wall Street.

"It's beautiful to watch," says Stolberg, the group's founder. "There's a vast ocean of frustrated middle managers out there, and we're helping them become entrepreneurs. It may sound arrogant, but I really think we're dream makers."

Dream makers?

Well, maybe so. After all, look at forty-three-year-old Robert J. Morrill, now part owner of Microwave Radio Corporation, in Lowell, Massachusetts, a manufacturer of portable television broadcast equipment. Twenty years ago, after he got out of the Navy, Morrill started up a small roofing business, today recalled fondly as the entrepreneurial bug that bit him. But life, as it will, had different plans, and Morrill spent most of the next two decades working for a huge corporation. Even so, he never gave up on the idea that one day he might still have his own company. In December 1985, he got his chance.

Then a divisional vice-president with M/A-Com Inc., Morrill convinced his employer that it would make sense to let him buy a single product line within that division as part of a companywide restructuring. The line was burdened with various corporate overheads, bruised by an unwieldy and ineffective service department, and excluded from potentially lucrative government business because M/A-Com was too big to qualify for the small-business set-aside program. None of these problems, however, was attributable to any inherent deficiency in an otherwise robust product. So high of heart, Morrill, most often in the company of his collaborator, Edward Dahn, an M/A-Com marketing manager, set out on his quest. For six months he wandered around Boston trying to find financing. He saw twenty different venture capitalists, all but one of whom rejected his petition. For some, his projected growth rate of 15 to 20 percent a year was too slow; for others, his potential market was too small, or his idea fell into an unacceptably murky area somewhere between a bona fide start-up and a de facto refinancing of an existing business.

Ultimately, Morrill found his way to Stolberg and friends and also found the fit he was looking for. "It was a question of chemistry," Morrill says. "I need people around me with a sense of humor, and all those other guys couldn't crack a smile."

On its part, the LBO group was not only sublimely indifferent to the venture capitalists' point of view, but also nearly ecstatic that the deal should come with such interesting "hair." In the end, though, and in keeping with the group's people-centered ideology, it was Morrill's strength of character and commitment that made the difference. Within sixty days, the leveraged buyout was complete. And since then, Morrill and his partners—Dahn and Fredrick Collins, who originated the product line twenty-eight years ago—have been meeting their projections regularly, with new orders now approaching $7 million.

"You know that fairy tale character, the frog prince?" Stolberg asks. "Well, sometimes I think that's the best way of describing what we do: We take frogs, give them a kiss, and watch them turn into handsome princes."

At first such whimsical notions are difficult to reconcile with Stolberg's outward demeanor and appearance, but he is a man of many parts. Although he is fashionably svelte and prone to wearing double-breasted suits of stylish cut, and although his features are sharp and angular, all of which suggest a cool, professional reserve, he is, instead, affable and warmhearted. He is also, according to his own analysis, "twitchy," which in this case translates as enthusiastically high-strung. When he gets excited, which is frequently, he sputters and sparks with colorful turns of phrase and decidedly mixed metaphors. And there are times during particularly anxious moments when all he seems able to do to moderate the considerable energies within him is sit at his desk and flip number 2 yellow pencils into the cork panels of the ceiling above, hoping they'll stick.

When Stolberg came to Weiss, Peck & Greer in 1981 to organize the firm's leveraged buyout capability, he brought impressive, if varied, credentials to the job. He had been a small-college, All-American football player and first in his MBA class at Indiana University. He took a job as a corporate finance specialist with prestigious First Boston Corporation, and as part of his duties became manager of a corporate development project for the National Commercial Bank of Saudi Arabia.

Once freshly installed at WPG, Stolberg spent his first year and a half building up a network of contacts and carefully evaluating the buyout market. Then, backed by an exploratory allotment of $5 million and eager to make a good impression, he was at last ready to engineer his first buyout. It was not an auspicious beginning. "Out of all the companies I've been involved with," he says, "I'm particularly proud that this one's still in business. It's kind of like having survived the Bataan death march."

In this case, Stolberg had spotted a division of a Cities Service subsidiary that seemed an ideal buyout candidate. The division extracted copper and sulfur in Copperhill, Tennessee, but its operations were suffering from neglect and its products limped into markets that received them indifferently. "It was a chance for our Statue of Liberty play," Stolberg says. "You know, give us your tired, your weary, your hungry, and we'll give 'em a new life." But only months after his $50-million buyout elevated the division into a freestanding company called Tennessee Chemical Corporation, the new owner-managers called to report a catastrophic mine cave-in. It had spared human life but forever buried $25 million worth of equipment under a quarter mile of Tennessee dirt. Even though Stolberg and management were eventually able at least to stabilize the company's operations, the incident hardly inspired confidence in his luck, if not judgment. Stolberg is sure he would have been fired except that shortly after the disaster he completed another buyout that turned out to be a genuine screamer. And from there, Stolberg's enterprise grew steadily in funding and staff.

Currently backed by a $50-million fund specifically dedicated to buyouts and able to draw on another $150-million general fund if necessary, the team has completed eight buyouts since 1981 with a total purchase price of $225 million. That amount also includes Weiss, Peck & Greer's original equity participations totaling $15.3 million, an investment that has since appreciated to $105 million. Of this performance, Philip Greer, one of the firm's founders, was moved to remark, "It's simply the best thing we're doing."

Not surprising, they that actually do the work are also very well rewarded. Counting base salary and bonuses and various distributions from the funds, an individual's annual compensation can easily exceed $1 million. But that's not all. They can also invest personally in the transactions, and therein lies the path to truly extraordinary gains. In one case, an investment of $35,000 has since grown to roughly $850,000 in less than four years. Leveraged buyouts with heart, it might be useful here to observe, may be humanitarian, but they can hardly be called charity.

The six "corporate development associates" at Weiss, Peck & Greer are, in effect, a company within a company. Not only do they have their own income statement—largely composed of the 1 percent to 1¼ percent of the purchase price they charge clients as a fee for services and the management fee on the limited-partnership pool—but they also have their own culture, characterized by its vigorously descriptive vocabulary, a demanding commitment to superior performance, and a fraternal camaraderie. Much of their time is spent on the road prospecting for deals. Of the nearly 300 deals the group sees each year, almost 85 percent are rejected in the first twenty minutes, usually because they have been shopped around so widely that a "bakeoff," or competitive bidding war between buyout shops, is almost certain. The remainder are considered at least worth a plane ticket, but of those only a very few become active candidates. "They're up there on the shelf percolating," says Davis, who prior to joining Weiss, Peck & Greer was a vice-president of acquisitions with competitor Dyson-Kissner-Moran Corporation. "Every couple of months we come in and tweak them [get updated]. There're maybe ten or twenty of these things up there percolating, but then one comes down onto the front burner and the fun begins."

While it is common in the corporate finance business to find aggregations of specialists arrayed around one individual whose presence and influence rule the overall effort exclusively, this group seems to have developed a kind of tribal collaboration that is far more democratic. In practice, that collaboration even seems to produce a pulsing syncopation of its own as team members convene informally, then wander off to pursue individual initiatives, then reconvene to compare notes and digest meanings. As a given deal's deadline approaches, the pulse quickens under severe, spastic pressures, and the group's focus intensifies to accommodate marathon, around-the-clock deliberations that sometimes go on for days. During the final moments of their most recent buyout, for example—a fertilizer plant in southeastern Idaho—the group had to resort to techniques more common to a tag team of wrestlers than a band of sophisticated financiers. Assembled in a New York City law firm, the team met continuously over three days, scrutinizing every last word of the buyout's closing documentation. When one member's eyes glazed over, he would call up a fresh replacement and slink off to get some sleep under a conference table.

Over time, the combined experience of the team's individual members has coalesced to produce a rather formidable paradigm known as the "Screen." Wesley Lang, who came to the group after extensive experience in corporate finance with Manufacturers Hanover Trust Company, describes it as a "set of shared beliefs compounded of philosophy, anecdotes, and practical advice," a definition that at least hints at the diversity and reach of the Screen's unwritten precepts. Most often the Screen enters conversation as a device similar to a radar display that is scanning, always scanning, to detect the presence of a potential screamer—like Microwave Radio.

Philip Greer, the founding partner, first heard about the company at a dinner party and later mentioned it to team member Steve De-Menna, who paid Morrill a visit. The results of that initial contact got Morrill and his partner, Edward Dahn, an invitation to the firm's New York office for a more extensive irradiation under the Screen's illuminating glow. Morrill might even have experienced a slight electrical tingling as he approached the conference room where the associates had assembled, in effect already adjusting the sensitive controls of their instrument.

Even at the most elemental level, Morrill's deal met two important criteria. First of all, although M/A-Com's asking price of roughly $3 million placed the proposed buyout a bit under the group's favored range, it nonetheless shared the intent of their overall strategy. Buyouts with purchase prices under $100 million, the team has found, generally attract far less attention than monster undertakings and are, as a result, more realistically priced; they require fewer layers of financing and thus can be completed quickly; and they are small enough that the new management can have a noticeable and immediate impact on operations. "Also," Davis adds, "in huge deals you don't have the time or the setting to really understand in every business unit what the human-motivation factors are. You do the numbers and pray every Sunday that the human stuff is right."

Second, Microwave was the right type of deal—a product line within a division rather than an entire company. As a rule, the team avoids company buyouts in which the original owners cash out and go home because the second-line management's understanding of the business is often underdeveloped. The value of this particular observation was reinforced not long ago when the group acquired, for $20 million, Superior Manufacturing & Instruments Inc., based in Long Island City, New York. Here the original owners had aged to the point where they were more interested in personal liquidity than in running a business. After they cashed out, the new management team decided to expand by developing a line of sophisticated high-voltage power supplies. Unfortunately, after signing several large contracts, management discovered they did not have the operational depth to perform, particularly in engineering. "We disappointed a lot of people," says Stolberg. "I badly underestimated how much the old president knew about the business. I should've involved him more and put him on the board, but I didn't and so we broke our pick." The lesson was more than merely academic. According to Stolberg, the team's initial $2-million equity investment is now worth only half as much, the only loser in the entire portfolio.

But back to Morrill. After the first coarse sweep, the group turned up the dials for a more detailed look at three major areas: management, company operations, and the financial structure of the deal itself. Of the three, the quality of management is by far the most important. "The biggest problem a deal will face," says Stolberg, "is whether the divisional manager can make the transition to becoming president of an independent company and do that under leverage. You know, it's very difficult betting on people. That's the art of this business." It is also its greatest risk. Over the years, the team has put together a Rogues' Gallery of Undesirable Management Types, any one of which will cause the Screen to crackle ominously.

First, there is the general manager in a large corporation who has several business units reporting to him and takes on delusions of grandeur. "This is a little tricky," Stolberg says, "because a guy like that will always say to you, 'I'm responsible for four hundred million in revenues,' or 'I run four businesses.' But after some probing you find out that all he's got is a monitoring role. He's not an operating guy; he's a group 'staffee'"

Next consider the general manager who actually does have operating responsibility—but no guts. "He says everything he thinks you want to hear," says Steve DeMenna, "but pretty soon you'll find out that he doesn't really want to take a risk and invest his money. He really wants a teed-up deal—twenty percent of the company for nothing, a big salary and a bonus, a country club membership, and a car."

From Wes Lang comes a description of yet another classic type—the general manager who thinks he's a chief executive officer but always needs strong direction. "This is the guy who can't make decisions on his own," Lang says. "He needs the consensus of a president and a board of directors. If you do his deal, you'll get a phone call from him every other day saying that he's got a problem at the plant or this machine's not working and what do you think. He doesn't put the bit in his mouth."

And finally, there's the manager whose ethics are a little loose. "This one manager was bidding on his own division," Stolberg recalls, "but at the same time the parent asked him to show it to other bidders. So what did he do? He wore a big red carnation. On the right lapel, it signaled his people that competitors were around and to talk the place down. On the left, it meant his own backers were there and to talk it up. If he'd do that to his own company, you can be sure he'll do it to you. We passed."

The team expects more than mere technical competence from its managers—that is, something more than a thorough understanding of the business and industry, dexterity with basic business skills, and a record of demonstrable effectiveness. Above all, members say, they are looking for "good human beings with the right stuff," a rich discovery unearthed more by intuition and feel than by hard analysis.

They may be hard to find, but at least there are a few clues to look for. Successful candidates invariably display the same characteristics, including an optimistic world view heavily colored with a sense of fair play, initiative coupled with calm persistence, and a willingness to commit "emotional equity" as well as the personal financial investment routinely required of every manager-owner. The one question the team must always answer positively before it will proceed any further is, "Will they make good partners?"

"It's not always easy to tell," says Stolberg. "You've got to cut through the cosmetics, and that can be difficult when everybody's wearing their Sunday best. The key is to ask the open-ended question and just listen. It doesn't matter which question you ask—keep it general, keep zeroing in on the human motivations on why he wants to do the deal, are his motivations right, is his background relevant, and then you get into how bad does he want it."

It was against this backdrop that Morrill began to talk about his successful, eighteen-year management career with M/A-Com, about how the dream that had started with the roofing company suddenly came alive again. But he didn't know anything about venture capital, let alone buyouts, so he checked books out of the local public library. And then, what a letdown when he asked that first bank for help and they gave him a form to fill out as if he were applying for a MasterCard.

Unbelievable. But oh, man, it was nothing compared with the long, frustrating hegira through the offices of the venture capitalists. He used to bring a rented videocassette player and a brief tape about the product to every meeting, but eventually he got so sick of seeing it that he had to leave the room. But no, he never allowed himself to get discouraged, not really. Someone sooner or later would surely recognize the merit of his proposal. It was simply the right thing to do, so right that he was willing to leave behind at M/A-Com nearly $300,000 in accrued bonuses and deferred compensation.

"And that," says Stolberg, "was the sound of the right stuff talking. Plus, that man had the smell of Yankee honesty all over him."

It would be difficult to exaggerate the group's emphasis on management. Indeed, were it not for this emphasis, its entire approach to the LBO marketplace would be a ridiculous contradiction in terms. Since 1981, Stolberg has seen the market explode as the success of early pioneers attracted competition from newly formed LBO shops, whose numbers are now counted in the hundreds. In the process, the scramble for the best turnkey deals—those free of operating or other problems—became so intense that purchase prices, in many cases, passed beyond economic logic.

"There's simply too much money chasing too few deals," says Stolberg, "particularly the bigger deals. I think deals driven purely by the mechanics of finance have about run their course." Rather than follow the pack, the team adjusted its focus to emphasize building value through operating improvements in smaller deals that were a little too hairy to be bid out of sight. And to do that, they needed the best managers they could get—managers like Morrill.

Scanning, always scanning, the Screen now moved on to contemplate the specific operating environment of Morrill's product line. And here, too, the buyout conformed to the team's specifications.

Perhaps it would be too much of an exaggeration to say that it does not really matter to the team what business a division or company is in, but it is nonetheless relatively insignificant. Of far greater importance to those who read the Screen are the requirements that the product line in question have some defensible competitive edge, an appreciable share of the available market, and, of course, significant opportunities for future growth that at the moment of acquisition are not, for one reason or another, being adequately exploited. Viewed from this perspective, the product line that would soon be called Microwave Radio was very well qualified. At the time of the buyout, Microwave offered a complete line of portable microwave equipment primarily used for electronic news and sports gathering. Steve DeMenna and Wes Lang, who did much of the original number crunching, estimated with $4.5 million in revenues, the business unit was either first or second in its $10-million industry, with roughly a 40 percent share and an opportunity to move easily into much larger markets worth some $100 million. M/A-Com, for its own reasons, had decided that the highly specialized nature of the equipment did not fit in with its newly re-modeled business objectives.

For a moment, the team worried that Microwave might not fit in with their interests, either. Maybe the market was too small after all? And how could anyone really fathom the operations of a product line that had not had its own independent profit-and-loss statements during its twenty-five-year history? But right here, at a point where many another firm had done the opposite and walked away from the deal, Stolberg and associates put Morrill before the numbers and thereby put a little heart in the buyout. They were convinced he had the right stuff, and they were not to be disappointed. It soon became clear that Morrill had conceived a plan that would allow the company many years of profitable and rapid growth before the presumed market ceiling became a threat, if ever. All he had to do was remove some of the hair.

Almost every WPG deal features some kind of depilatory ritual in which problems become opportunities, just as frogs become handsome princes. It is the very stuff of dream making. In fact, the team insists that management be able to list four or five specific improvements they can make in the business after the buyout is done, or else they're not interested. "If they can't do it," says Stolberg, "they're probably not good managers anyway." But in this case, Morrill and his partners, living up to the team's expectations, had already spotted the right improvements: Get out from under the burdensome corporate over-head, move into less expensive quarters, develop international sales, apply for government business, streamline marketing by trimming the product line from twenty items to ten, and institute a new customer service program that could reduce repair turnaround time from thirty days to two days. Once some of these adjustments were factored into the first-year *pro forma* projections, like magic, Microwave, which had lost money in the previous two years, turned an operating profit of $600,000. And with that, M/A-Com's asking price of roughly $3 million began to look very attractive indeed.

"In the old days," Stolberg says, "back when doing deals was a slam dunk, I could buy a good company for four times earnings. But now there are a lot of people around who don't mind paying eight times, or ten, or even higher. It's gotten ridiculous." The Microwave deal's multiple of five times EBIT (earnings before interest and taxes) was like buying a gallon of gasoline for 50¢. Moreover, the team's computer model predicted that the company could easily be worth $15 million in only a few years. All that was necessary now was to build the financial bridge to get there.

Most of the calculations that ultimately produce a given deal's financial structure assume a five-year period of operations. The team first projects a profile of what the new company's operating results will look like in the fifth year and then hypothesizes what value is likely to be placed on those results if the company were to use any one of three so-called "paths to liquidity": taking the company public, selling it, or having management buy out WPG's interest. That ending value must give WPG a compound annual rate of return over the five-year period of at least 50 percent, and it must also make the equity position of each of the top managers worth at least $2 million—a wholly pleasant experience for managers known in-house as "the equity pop." From these premises, mathematics alone will reveal the deal's basic debt-to-equity ratio, which then must be tinkered with to make room for future growth, particularly through acquisitions.

The final Microwave structure was a model of economy and efficiency, employing as it did a line of reasoning common to many buyouts. The WPG team put up $150,000 in equity representing a 75 percent ownership, while Morrill, Dahn, and Collins contributed the required cash for a 25 percent stake. The team then added a $1-million revolving loan from a bank and took back a note for $1.35 million fully subordinated to the bank debt. The type of debt used was, in itself, extremely important, because the bank will view the subordinated debt as permanent capital that both decreases the bank's overall risk and encourages it to expand the "revolver" again after the balance has been paid down should an acquisition present itself.

In other ways, too, the final structure served Microwave's best interests. For example, the team's projections indicated that cash flow would cover interest charges by a factor of two and that the company would be able to reduce its total debt to within 50 percent of the capital structure within eighteen months. Moreover, $2.35 million in debt against $200,000 in equity represented leverage of roughly twelve to one. Because the team also agreed to allow M/A-Com future royalties representing 5 percent of sales of the acquired product line in excess of $4.5 million, the value of that concession, in effect, pushed the total purchase price to roughly $3.2 million. But here, too, the terms worked to Microwave's advantage, since the company's products would be sold by M/A-Com's sales force, among others.

After six months of frustration and twenty rejections, but only sixty days after their first meeting with the team, Morrill and Dahn became entrepreneurs. For Morrill, the process of building value had just begun. "I found that the sense of responsibility to the people who work here was nearly overwhelming," he says. "Things are much more real. They're just not numbers on a piece of paper anymore." More than anything else, Morrill discovered that the activities he had once taken for granted in a large company now required an extraordinary amount of personal attention. Today when he loses a piece of business or when a receivable starts to get a bit moldy, he's quick to pick up the phone and talk to the customer personally. "You can't keep yourself aloof from your business," he says. "You take nothing for granted. You take it personally. You're scrapping all the time."

When they work right, the magic of leveraged buyouts with heart can work wonders. They can, as in Robert Morrill's case, breathe new life into a dream twenty years waiting or, as happened one day near Soda Springs, Idaho, restore 400 jobs and repair the tattered prospects of an entire town (see "High Noon in Soda Springs," page 296). No doubt there are still more wonders to perform, but they're getting harder to find. Indeed, in recent years as the scramble for deals intensified all around them, the team's attention has been drawn ever more inward toward their concept of partnership. Even as they cull for new screamers, the team has redoubled its efforts to build value in the companies already owned, using such methods as refinancings, acquisitions, and sale and leasebacks.

And here, too, their results have been impressive. Not long ago, the team engineered an acquisition for TransLogic Corporation, which immediately doubled its size—and the company continued to grow rapidly from there. Late this year, TransLogic is slated to become the first company in the team's portfolio to translate its paper return on investment into hard cash. Stolberg estimates that the company's initial public offering will be valued in excess of $50 million. Of that amount, Weiss, Peck & Greer will realize roughly $25 million on an original equity investment of $1.25 million. At the same time, the manager-owners will themselves become multimillionaires.

But for all the success of a TransLogic, there are many other times when—despite the team's considerable insight and experience—the magic just doesn't seem to be there. Once, for example. Stolberg met several times with the president of a subsidiary of a much larger company who was contemplating a leveraged buyout. The deal looked promising, but for some reason Stolberg just couldn't decide whether this manager had the right stuff, and the group subsequently rejected the deal. But this man went elsewhere, got his buyout done anyway, and went on to manage his way to great success. After a polite pause just long enough to let his accomplishments sink in at WPG, the man, still a friend of Stolberg's, jokingly sent him a memorial plaque on which were two tiny metal balls and the following engraved inscription: "The Badge of Uncourage to E. Theodore 'BB Balls' Stolberg. Let it be known that in the face of great adversity, difficult decisions, and monumental unknowns, 'BB Balls' Stolberg crumbled, thereby allowing opportunity and great personal wealth to escape."

Stolberg is still amused to read it. "Well, give us a break," he says. "I mean, we're still learning."

Manager Without a Company

Charles P. Gallagher is nearly bald, which may explain why he loves fixing companies with "hair," which in turn definitely explains why the Weiss, Peck & Greer buyout team loves Charlie Gallagher.

"When it comes to revitalizing tired assets in a variety of different businesses," says Kim Davis, a leveraged buyout specialist with Weiss, Peck & Greer, "Gallagher's the best CEO I've ever seen."

So good, in fact, that the team backed the forty-nine-year-old management wizard for nearly a year and a half despite the fact that all that time the redoubtable Mr. Gallagher didn't even have a company to manage.

When Davis first met the man, Gallagher was engineering a spectacular turnaround as president and chief executive of publicly held Susquehanna Corporation. Gallagher wanted to sell Davis one of Susquehanna's business units. Davis thought the business was a dog and declined, but he was rather more impressed with Gallagher's overall accomplishments at Susquehanna. In 1980, when Gallagher arrived on the scene, Susquehanna, a manufacturer of various building materials, had been sorely battered by the cyclical nature of the building industry. That year, the company reported an operating loss of $14.2 million on revenues of $110 million, and its book value per share was a negative $2.80. Five years later, though, after Gallagher had cut staff, closed plants, and excised nearly $40 million in unprofitable products, Susquehanna reported a profit of $14 million, and its book value per share had risen to $6.

Shortly afterward, Gallagher resigned, intent on doing for his own account what he had just done for Susquehanna. He set up an office in Denver and set out to buy a company in which his own equity position would profit directly from his turnaround talents. In the process, he interviewed several investment bankers. He chose the buyout team at Weiss, Peck & Greer.

"They were more creative than the others," says Gallagher. "They were aggressive without being reckless, and they brought a lot of diversified experience to the deal. It was definitely a collaborative effort."

Between June 1985 and October 1986, Gallagher and the team looked at more than a hundred companies until they acquired the industrial products division of International Minerals & Chemicals Corporation in a leveraged buyout worth an estimated $100 million. Once again, Gallagher, now CEO and owner of an enterprise renamed Applied Industrial Materials Corporation, performed prodigies of turnaround artistry. He recharged a weary mix of mineral, metal, and carbon products and nearly doubled gross margins to the point at which his new company earned $18 million on some $400 million in sales. What's more, in only eight months, Gallagher paid off the entire $90-million debt load used to finance the buyout in the first place.

The WPG team, however, saw more to Gallagher than numbers. They also saw the mother lode of "emotional equity."

By way of explanation, WPG's Ted Stolberg offers the following tale. In the fall of 1986, Gallagher had planned a trip with the team that would include visits to nearly twenty different plants owned by the division in question. The trip was crucial to Gallagher's understanding of the business. Just before he was about to leave, he developed an excruciating crick in his neck. Not wanting to change his plans, Gallagher consulted a number of medical experts. He brought along various remedies, ranging from portable traction equipment to what one team member remembers as "Spanish radish root pills" of a size that seemed better suited for horses than people.

On the road, Stolberg and Davis watched in awe each day as

Gallagher swallowed the giant tablets. And they were no less fascinated by the large chain Gallagher had taken to wearing around his neck, the better to realign certain bodily magnetisms that might relieve his discomfort. But the most incredible demonstration of Gallagher's commitment to the buyout effort always took place after dinner. Every evening, the group would sit together in Gallagher's hotel room and discuss the day's events. Gallagher, however, observed the proceedings from an unusual vantage point: He sat in a chair in the middle of a doorway with his neck, stretched in self-inflicted traction, attached to a cord attached to a heavy water bottle dangling from the doorjamb above. Only after the plant fly-around was over did Gallagher have the time to get proper treatment for his crushed vertebra.

"I'd like to say it was more complicated," Davis says, "but the simple truth is that we just wanted to put some assets behind this guy. You can see why, can't you?"

High Noon in Soda Springs

Recently, the LBO team from Weiss, Peck & Greer engineered a deal so manifestly benevolent that a troop of Eagle Scouts turned out to honor it. Here's what happened:

In 1984, the C. F. White agricultural fertilizer plant near Soda Springs (population 4,051), in southeastern Idaho, is making money—as it has every year for the five years before that—earning $6 million on sales of $70 million to $75 million. By the spring of 1986, however, when the team from WPG first learns of it, the plant is about to close down.

Beker Industries Corporation, the plant's parent company, files for Chapter 11 reorganization, and the shadow of its collapse falls heavily on the town. Nearly 300 workers are laid off. Stores start closing in Soda Springs, as nearly 800 people move away to find a better life.

From any angle, the predicament presents the team from WPG with a formidable challenge. The market for agricultural fertilizer is in ruins, the victim of another cyclical disaster in supply and pricing; there is a large and contentious group of creditors involved in the bankruptcy, all with their own axes to grind; and the plant is about to miss its mining season, which means that it will have to be mothballed. That, in turn, will greatly increase the difficulty and cost of a future start-up, if ever.

Still, the team has fallen in love with the thirty-eight-year-old general manager, Craig Harlen, who, along with Mack Barber and Cleve McCarty, both former Beker executives, proposes a leveraged buyout. "He was definitely the heartland of America," recalls WPG's Ted Stolberg, "like he just stepped out of a wheat field." If ever a buyout needed a little heart, this one certainly does.

In July, the team makes a bid for the place. The judge supervising the Beker bankruptcy in New York City rejects the offer because the creditors can't reach consensus. The plant is shut down. Almost a year goes by. The team tries unsuccessfully to influence the creditors. Meanwhile, a Chicago-based investment group enters the lists. The team decides to let them play their hand. One day in June 1987, Stolberg reads in the *New York Times* that the Chicago offer has indeed been made, and that competitors have ten days to counter. Stolberg is stunned. He has counted on having thirty days to respond.

As expected, the ten days run out and the team's counteroffer is nowhere near done. On a Friday, WPG's lawyer goes into court and asks for an extension. Sure, says the judge, you've got till Monday. Not to worry, the lawyer says, I'll work around the clock. But that Sunday, the guy calls Stolberg, reports a conflict of interest, and quits. On Monday, Stolberg comes into work with no lawyer, no deal, no nothing, and he has to be in court that afternoon. What to do? They love Craig Harlen, but, hey, let's be realistic.

At the last minute, the team finds another lawyer, a genius at bankruptcy law. He goes into court, says the other lawyer is a jerk who misrepresented his deserving clients, and gets three more days. Pandemonium at Weiss, Peck & Greer—number crunching, phone calls, frantic meetings, Stolberg flipping pencils into the cork ceiling—very crazy. Somehow they put a proposal together. They will offer $48 million in cash, preferred stock, and various kinds of subordinated debt. Bridge financiers will pick up a $15-million chunk of the package until the team has time to involve a senior lender. No problem.

Then the bridge loan falls apart.

Heavy breathing and hard swallowing at Weiss, Peck & Greer—but what the hell, the team decides, we'll find it later. They go into court anyway. The boys from Chicago are very upset. A bidding war breaks out in court. Back and forth, back and forth. WPG comes out the winner. "I've never been on a roller-coaster ride like that in my life," says team member Kim Davis. "I mean, there were many times when we were sure this wasn't going to go through."

On August 10, nearly 500 people come to Soda Springs to celebrate the reopening of the plant—now a freestanding company called Nu-West Industries Inc.—the restoration of nearly 400 jobs, and the rejuvenation of an entire town. Governor Cecil D. Andrus shows up and speechifies for a while. Then he joins Craig Harlen and various visiting dignitaries, including the entire WPG buyout team, to watch the Soda Springs Eagle Scouts raise the American flag.

"It's a new day," says thirty-three-year-old Donald K. Kuhn, a rehired filter operator at the plant. "It's as if the sun has just come up."

"I don't know," says Stolberg, "but I think we done some good."

Financing the LBO

Financial engineering is a lot like building a bridge," says leveraged buyout specialist Ted Stolberg of Weiss, Peck & Greer. "You can build it any way you like as long as it doesn't collapse when heavy trucks run over it, and you can add additional lanes when you want more traffic to go over it. And when it's all done, it should be a thing of beauty, like the Golden Gate."

Sounds simple enough, doesn't it? Not always.

Typical was the architecture of a $27.5-million LBO involving TransLogic Corporation, a Denver manufacturer of conveyer systems. It began with $1.5 million in equity put up by WPG and the managers, to which was added (1) a $10-million revolving loan from a bank, (2) $6.2 million in industrial revenue bond proceeds from a second bank, and (3) an $8-million chunk from a Massachusetts insurance company.

Usually, as a deal gets bigger, so does the financial construction crew—and the help doesn't come cheap. Indeed, the terms behind some of the financing components make loan sharks look like goldfish.

Consider the "mezzanine" financier. This enterprising character, usually an insurance company, takes a subordinated debt position between the senior secured lender and the equity interest (and hence the name mezzanine). Maybe the view isn't quite as good as the senior lender's, but it's not too bad. In exchange for a long-term note, the mezzanine money gets an interest rate of three or four points above the prevailing prime rate, plus an equity kicker that can run as high as 25 percent of the company.

More profitable is the lender who provides the "bridge" financing that holds until a long-term lender is found. While mezzanines normally do not require principal repayment for roughly seven years, the bridge expects to be repaid in less than one year. And just so they won't get bored waiting, bridge financiers are given an interest rate of four to five points above prime and hefty equity kickers generally ranging from 10 percent to as much as 25 percent. In addition, the bridge financier charges sizable up-front fees for the service. Not surprising, over the past three years bridging has turned into a lucrative sideline for several large brokerage firms.

—LUCIAN RHODES

GOING WITH THE FLOW

At fifty-four, Alfred L. McDougal was still having a good time running his $28-million Chicago textbook company, but his co-founder and the other eleven original investors were ready to cash out. To get the funds, they could have sold McDougal, Littell & Company, but that would have left McDougal out in the cold. They could have gone public, but they felt that that would be an expensive hassle and, besides, the risk was high that within a year the company would become a takeover target for one of the mammoth publishers. Again, McDougal might be left out in the cold. They left it up to him to find a solution, and the one he came up with gave him control of the company and gave them their money. He arranged a leveraged buyout calculated not on the company's assets, which were limited, but on its cash flow, which was strong.

While cash flow–based LBOs have been around for several years, their use has mushroomed recently. PruCapital Inc., for example, the Prudential Company of America's corporate capital group, arranged 80 percent of the LBOs in its current portfolio in just the past two years. More than half of these are in the Midwest. The beauty of cash-flow LBOs for such low-asset companies as McDougal's is the amount of money that can be raised. In asset-based LBOs, a lender looks at the book value of a company's assets—inventory, fixed assets, receivables—and lends against them to approximately 80 percent with the loan secured by those assets. Cash-flow lenders base their loans on a projection of revenues and earnings, and can provide as much as three times book value, usually in a combination of debt and equity financing.

Most companies that use this sort of financing are looking to transfer the business from one generation to the next (resolving estate tax problems in the process), or from one founder to another, as in the case of McDougal. Often the financing is set up to provide the new owners not only with the purchase price, but also with additional capital to undertake expansion plans. An example is Consolidated Stores Corporation, a Columbus, Ohio–based "closeout" retail chain. Through a cash-flow LBO, some of the original shareholders sold their holdings in the company to the remaining original shareholders and to some venture capitalists. They used the capital raised beyond the purchase price to enter an aggressive growth phase. Consolidated expanded from 40 stores in the fall of 1984 to 104 by November 1985. With the business well established and sales growing, the company went public, and ranked ninth on *Inc.*'s list of best-performing new issues of 1985. Another major user of cash-flow LBOs are managers who want to buy profitable divisions being cast off by larger companies.

Part of the reason for the flurry of activity these days in cash-flow LBOs is that while financiers will consider almost any type of company that can demonstrate strong cash flow, definite projections, and good management, they do have an ideal profile in mind. And it's one that happens to fit many of the companies founded in the Midwest in the 1950s, whose founders now want out. Star Forms Inc., a company in Moline, Illinois, is typical.

Star Forms was founded by John H. Harris in 1959, first producing general business forms, but since the mid-1970s specializing in continuous-feed forms and paper. With the boom in personal computers, sales, which had been growing steadily, began to soar—shooting up from $20 million in 1979 to $100 million in 1985. Last year, at age seventy, Harris decided to cash out, and his son Hunt, who had been active in the business since 1971, looked for a way to buy out his parents and siblings. Like McDougal, the Harrises decided against either going public or selling Star Forms. They looked into traditional lending sources, but found that the book value wouldn't give them what they knew the company could provide in earnings. Then they turned to PruCapital, and arranged a cash-flow LBO in May 1985 that brought them about three times the book value of Star Forms.

Star Forms was in many ways a perfect candidate for PruCapital. It was a stable company with high revenues and high earnings, yet low fixed assets—exactly what any cash-flow lender would like to see. Even though the founder was leaving, the company's management was solidly in place. And it was the right size. According to Marc J. Walfish, the regional vice-president of PruCapital in Chicago, the firm favors transactions in the middle market, companies with purchase prices from $10 million to $150 million. PruCapital finds smaller deals less appealing because of the expense involved in arranging any LBO, regardless of size. And there aren't that many closely held companies in the region that top $150 million.

To help determine Star Form's value, the first thing PruCapital asked to see was the company's audited financial statement for the past year and a financial history for the previous four years. While that's a common stipulation among cash-flow lenders, formal audits are not necessarily a rigid requirement. Each deal is individually structured, and much depends on how the lender views the company's strengths and weaknesses.

While PruCapital had Star Forms prepare a five-year business plan, "the rest of the due diligence on the industry and markets is done by PruCapital," Walfish explains. "In evaluating them, we look first for good cash flow, and for us that means that it shows the ability to pay off between one-third and one-half the debt portion in a five-year period.

"Second, we look at earnings, because they convert to cash flow. Price is calculated as a percentage of earnings, and averages between four to six times operating earnings before interest and taxes."

Both the Harrises and PruCapital declined to discuss the specifics of their deal, but, according to Walfish, PruCapital's cash-flow LBOs generally take the following form:

- About half of the debt financing is arranged at a fixed rate. The rate is a function of the risk, and currently at PruCapital averages from 3 percent to 4 percent over long-term Treasury securities on a ten- to fifteen-year loan.

  "While the rate is usually a bit higher than the conventional loan rate, you must remember that a company involved in this kind of financing is a highly leveraged, not a conventional, borrower," says David Katz, an associate investment manager in the Chicago office.
- The remainder of the debt financing is arranged on a floating rate.
- A "blind spot" is often applied on the fixed-rate portion of the loan for three to five years. Principal payments are not required during that period, so that the burden of the financing doesn't hit the new owners all at once.
- PruCapital takes equity in the form of nonvoting common stock, and its average debt-to-equity financing is in the neighborhood of ten to one.

PruCapital's share of stock has been as low as 20 percent and as high as 70 percent. "It depends on the transaction and what managers put in," Walfish explains. "Our shares are nonvoting and held for investment purposes, and this is where we make our long-term gains, whereas in the loan portion of the financing, where our return is capped, we earn current yield." Some lenders like PruCapital require equity, but that is not always the case. It all depends on how the deal is put together. McDougal, for instance, got an expanded line of credit from the Harris Trust & Savings Bank, in Chicago, and bought back equity from the other investors. They hold unsecured personal notes to be paid out over six years. And it is common, in cases such as his, to receive part of the financing from the seller.

David Katz points out that PruCapital's financing to a company like Star Forms is basically unsecured since "we don't want to depend on assets to repay the debt. Because we are involved in all levels of the financing, including equity, if times get tough we have an additional incentive to work with management to overcome problems." PruCapital takes no part in the day-to-day operating control of an LBO portfolio company. Though it is not a requirement, PruCapital does prefer that third parties sit on the board as voting equity holders. These may be key managers or outsiders knowledgeable about the particular industry, and the expectation is that because of their own financial commitment, they will do whatever they can to keep a company on track.

Standard covenants in the loan agreement require the company not to pay dividends or pledge assets, and to maintain a minimum amount of working capital and abide by restrictions on future borrowing.

"Through such a structure, we can finance, for every dollar needed for the purchase price, ninety cents in debt, a debt-to-equity ratio of about nine to one," says Walfish. "These financings make it possible for an individual or management team to own a significant portion of the equity in a company by coming up with as little as four to five percent of the purchase price."

Cash-Flow Lenders

Cash flow–based leveraged buyouts are by no means limited to the Midwest. If you want to look into one, your accountant's office is a good place to start. Alfred McDougal, of McDougal, Littell & Company, went to Touche Ross & Company, which prepared his financial statements and projections. In addition, it gave him recommendations and introductions to put together his financial package. Your accountant may also know of specialized cash-flow lending partnerships and venture capital firms that will arrange LBO financing. If you work with venture capitalists, you can often get better rates on the fixed portion of your loan than you can get from institutional lenders. On the other hand, if your time is short and interest in financial details is slight, you may prefer the large, one-stop shops. These include General Electric Credit Corporation and such big insurance company subsidiaries as Equitable's Equitable Capital Management Corporation and Prudential's PruCapital Inc.

—SANDRA CONN

THE PERFECT ACQUISITION

When one business acquires another, the tenets of Western commerce have it that the acquired entity be paid for with cash or stock. Though basically unchanged, the rules are being read more loosely in this era of greenmail and white knights, and some intriguing turns have been taken. It's not unheard of, for example, that a seller may be so delighted to discover that someone is interested in its proffered operation—a failing division of a large corporation, for example—that the seller actually gives the *buyer* some money if only he'll take away the hapless enterprise and run it somewhere else.

So far, though, there's precious little in business texts that describes how a modest private company can purchase a going public concern for nothing down; how that buyer at the same time can convince the seller to guarantee to buy *him* out in a few years for several million dollars; and how the initial acquirer ends up not only awash in cash, but owning more than half the consolidated entity—whose shares by then presumably will be soaring in the public market. The scheme sounds too good to be true, but if and when the founder of New York City's Perfect Courier Inc. emerges unscathed from the convoluted deal he forged last summer with competitor CitiPostal Corporation, he intends to have everyone—buyer, seller, and stockholder—going home rich and happy.

It takes the mind of a lawyer and an accountant to have devised this flawless chain of events. And, according to the pair of certificates framed and hanging in his midtown office, that is exactly what Perfect's Norman Brodsky possesses—plus a swashbuckling sense of business adventure. "I don't do this for money," Brodsky insists, referring mainly to the time he puts in figuring out how to make money. "If I did it for the money, I'd sell my business today and go to Tahiti."

Brodsky entered entrepreneurship in 1979 and now, eight years later, expects to take in close to $30 million. His courier service has been listed on the *Inc.* 500 ranking of private-business growth for the past three years, yet its forty-four-year-old founder works only three weeks a month. "You have to be insane to drive yourself," he preaches to the deaf ears of his brethren.

If all goes well, Brodsky's sanity will win out on or before September 30, 1990, the last date on which CitiPostal can exercise its option to buy out Brodsky's Perfect Courier for $6 million. And CitiPostal's new chairman and president—none other than Brodsky himself—is confident that it will.

The two companies in finance's version of "I'm My Own Grandpa" are among the many wheeled fleets that collect packages in urban areas and ship them by specialty carriers, such as Federal Express and Airborne Express, for next-day delivery. Because they can consolidate the packages and earn discounts from the carriers, they are able to offer individual users customized service at a savings.

Both Perfect and CitiPostal work the streets of mid-Manhattan. But judging by their results, you'd never know that they did the same thing in the same place (although the former does it in eight cities). While Perfect was briskly expanding by means of internally generated funds, CitiPostal lost some $880,000 in the past year alone, and in less than two years had run through the $1.4 million it had raised in a stock placement. Aside from a $2-million tax loss carryforward, there were few assets left. As far as Brodsky could see, the five-year-old company was functioning only by dint of a factor's happily lending against receivables at six points over prime. CitiPostal stock, unable to qualify for listing on a regulated exchange, was stuck in the tundra of the over-the-counter's Pink Sheets, barely trading at 50¢ bid, $1 asked. The company clearly showed little promise.

"They were losing money, but they had a better customer base than I did, and better prices!" Brodsky reflects incredulously. "It shows there can be a business that's a natural profit maker, yet someone can lose money with it." The "someone" in CitiPostal's case was its two free-spending founders, who, overstaffing, overbenefiting, and overpaying, according to Brodsky, "had a lot to learn."

But Brodsky wasn't about to teach them. Instead, he flushed out the corporation's three major investors and reminded them that the company they owned was going down the tubes. "But I am here to tell you that I can bail you out," Brodsky proclaimed at their first meeting last March. "The only thing is, it won't be for charity: The executive officers have to go, and you have to give me half the company. Call it fifty-three percent, and I'll make us all a fortune."

Since those investors already had dropped more than $1.5 million on a similar promise two years back, they were doubtful. "We want to *see* you make a fortune" was the gist of their reply. "Well, for fifty-three percent," Brodsky took up the gauntlet, "I'll guarantee that, in the first fiscal year starting July 1, CitiPostal will do ten million dollars in sales and one million dollars in pretax profit. If it doesn't, I'll give you back part of the stock." That sounds fair enough, the about-to-be-minority stockholders agreed. Brodsky's portion—more than 8 million shares of common—would be placed in escrow pending the end-of-year financials as of June 30, 1987. If his projections failed to materialize on that date, Brodsky would relinquish ownership in proportion to the shortfall of his vision.

Given a customer base expanded by 600 new businesses, each sending 2.5 packages per night and generating $6 million a year, a shortfall would be unlikely, since the profligate CitiPostal operation could be intertwined with lean and mean Perfect's. "They had only one problem," Brodsky concluded—"overhead that would choke a horse." Where one section of Brodsky's service was employing four people, a similar operation at CitiPostal had sixteen people running four specialized departments. "They were sitting around all day doing nothing," Brodsky says. "Their explanation was, 'We're going to grow bigger.'" Not wanting to lose more ground, he took over as president of CitiPostal on May 1, 1986, even before the deal was final, and started to trim the payroll. With Perfect Courier performing (and getting paid for) services for CitiPostal, that very June CitiPostal posted a monthly profit.

But Brodsky had more in mind than simply a miracle turnaround. He wanted to be majority owner of a public company. Being public automatically would place a price on and provide a market for Perfect should Brodsky want to cash out. And it would enable him to reward faithful employees with something more meaningful than a Christmas turkey. "For them to own shares of a private company doesn't mean too much. They could wipe their backsides with the paper if something were to happen to me," says Brodsky, who, nominally through his wife, Elaine, has retained 100 percent of Perfect Courier and Perfect Air Inc., a spin-off he created to help smooth the transition. But he isn't allowed to give employees stock in the publicly held company based on past performance in his private company. Key employees are, however, being granted stock options in CitiPostal.

CitiPostal was already public—albeit barely. To achieve Brodsky's ends, CitiPostal's financials first had to be shaped up to where the company could qualify for a listing on an exchange. "With a public company, you have something that's real, something to look at," Brodsky feels. On NASDAQ, his chosen market, CitiPostal's visibility would enable him to go to the market for financing, which in turn would allow him to make yet further acquisitions.

With both scenes in mind, Brodsky granted CitiPostal an option to buy Perfect Courier for $6 million, exercisable between May 1988 and September 1990. If that happens, the short of it is that Brodsky will have sold his company to a public entity, yet have a majority interest in the combined corporation.

Handily, the company that is to decide whether to buy Perfect Courier for $6 million is controlled by the would-be recipient of the $6 million—seemingly a nifty fail-safe. Unfortunately, the rules of the SEC and the IRS tend to frown on such *faits accomplis* and won't allow Brodsky to buy his own company. So, in 1988, an arm's-length appraiser is to be hired to evaluate the deal and make sure it's good for CitiPostal. "They'd be crazy to turn it down," predicts Brodsky. "They'll get a terrific deal, because now they'll have one whole company with earnings such that Perfect is probably worth more as part of the public company. I won't have to increase my overhead a nit to pick up their business, and I'll end up with a chunk of money for ten years' work."

Brodsky's bravado aside, there's a risk that the bottom will fall out of the local-courier industry, and CitiPostal (presuming it still exists then) may turn down the purchase option. If that's the case, in hindsight Brodsky would have done better taking cash and running to Tahiti. While the option is active, however, Perfect Courier cannot be sold to a third party, no matter how enticing the offer. On the other hand, if Brodsky decides he doesn't want to sell to CitiPostal after all, he could make Perfect's books look so nasty that stockholders would turn it down.

A person has to marvel at how little else is left to chance. And Brodsky does: "The big score for me is not the six million dollars," he says, "it's the stock. That's where the leverage is. The cash gives me enough security so I don't have to worry." CitiPostal has been given the better part of two years to make up its mind, because it will take time to get an evaluation and then arrange to come up with the capital. If it turns out that when CitiPostal pays up, Brodsky's company is actually worth a lot more than the $6 million, then the price of the common stock, reflecting the combined value of a consolidated operation, will rise. With 8,281,344 shares in his portfolio, Brodsky is not apt to suffer from an inadvertent undervaluation of Perfect.

How will a company that has no net worth now be able to come up with $6 million in two years? By borrowing or floating more stock. In order to do that, however, its performance must merit the new financing. First, CitiPostal has to be rescued from the Pink Sheets and become a reporting company on a bona fide stock exchange. Thus, one of the first things Brodsky did, after the deal was sealed and he had installed himself as CitiPostal's president, was to apply for NASDAQ listing, among whose requisites are standards for assets, equity, and shareholders. First-quarter results showed pretax income of $621,910 on sales of $2,429,880. "I don't think I'll have a problem earning the one million dollars," Brodsky concludes.

To accomplish the turnaround, Brodsky paid off the factor and loaned CitiPostal money himself at a lower rate, renegotiated vendor contracts, plugged procedures into his own automated system, and—perhaps most important—severely pared CitiPostal's payroll. Like most courier companies, CitiPostal's pickup fleet was comprised of independent owner/operators. "They started these part-time people at seven dollars for a job description that calls for five dollars an hour," says Brodsky. "That's not so bad. But soon they went to nine dollars. Still not that bad. But instead of the five hours of actual work, they clocked them in when they came in and out when they left. So they were working forty hours a week. Still not bad. But after thirty-five hours, they paid them overtime. *Still* not bad. But they gave them vacation, sick days, and other benefits that a part-time job didn't call for. Add it all up, and they were paying tantamount to twenty dollars an hour. That's bad!"

Perfect Courier undoubtedly is salable today for a substantial sum. But simply disposing of a business for the sake of putting a few million dollars in the bank is not Brodsky's style. "Most people don't take calculated risks, but I'm a gambler at heart," he admits. "I guess that's what an entrepreneur does."

PERFECT'S PRIMER
How to Not Sell Your Company for Fun and Profit

1. Start with your own growing private company.
2. Find a struggling public competitor.
3. Tell its major stockholders you can save their investment.
4. Demand control. Take over as operating officer.
5. Grant them an option to buy your company in the future.
6. Clean up the public company, preferably by melding its operations into your own. Make your company more profitable by charging the other company for services.
7. Use the improved financials of the public company to go to the market for more money to buy your company out.
8. End up owning the consolidated entity.
9. So why not do it all over again?

—ROBERT A. MAMIS

HE TOOK THE MERGER ROUTE

One sunny California morning in January 1978, Jerry Casilli, thirty-nine, president of fast-growing Millennium Systems Inc., received a startling telephone call. It was from David Kratter, a director of Millennium and president of Western Venture Resources Inc., which represented 38 percent ownership of Millennium, then a $5-million-a-year electronic instrument maker. Would Casilli consider taking Millennium public, Kratter asked, to increase capital and gain investor liquidity?

"He told me that a New York investment banker was ready to get on a plane and fly out here," Casilli recalls. "Three days later the banker was here. I hadn't even thought about going public. I didn't know what a public offering entailed. I didn't know everything that investment bankers actually did."

Five months later—on the verge of going public—Casilli changed direction and sold Millennium to American Microsystems Inc., of Santa Clara, California, for $9.4 million in AMI stock.

How Millennium Got to the
Merge/Go Public Decision Point

The seeds of Jerry Casilli's dilemma—whether to go public or sell out—were planted at the founding of Millennium Systems Inc. in 1973.

Casilli and William Kirn, electrical engineers at General Telephone & Electronics Corporation's Sylvania subsidiary, launched Millennium with $50,000. "Our goal," Casilli said, "was to be part of the microprocessor revolution."

Headquartered in 1,000 square feet of garage-like space, Millennium secured a $150,000 credit line from Crocker National Bank of San Francisco. But its major source of capital was its customers' advance payments.

The company's first big break came in 1974, when Millennium signed a $750,000 contract to make video display systems for shopping centers. Most important, Millennium was given the chance to apply microprocessor technology.

Pioneering Intel Corporation had introduced the microprocessor in 1971. Subsequently, Intel developed a device that simulated a microprocessor for use in designing microprocessor-based products. But Intel's product could only be used to simulate its own microprocessor.

Millennium decided to develop a system that could simulate *any* company's microprocessor—a market no other company had attempted. The strategy paid off when Signetics, a subsidiary of U.S. Phillips Corporation, ordered 200 of Millennium's systems for $1.4 million.

Signetics' contract increased the company's revenues and enhanced its credibility. But management remained thin, and the marketing, sales, and distribution staffs were virtually nonexistent. Millennium desperately needed new capital to build the company and sell its product.

Then, in October 1976, Millennium and Tektronix Inc. signed a contract making Tektronix the exclusive worldwide seller and distributor of Millennium's universal development system. As a result, revenues shot from $1.7 million on a break-even year in 1976 to $5.1 million on net income of $582,000 in 1977.

Still, 95 percent of Millennium revenues derived from selling one product to one company. To reduce reliance on Tektronix for the company's stability, Casilli wanted to provide a full line of test instruments and services that would allow electronics manufacturers to design, test, and maintain microprocessor-based equipment. So Millennium developed its portable testing device—called the MicroSystem Analyzer—for tracking down faulty electronic components. Like its universal development system, the tester was an industry first.

The transition to selling a number of products and services to many customers was a critical turning point in Millennium's history. It also marked Casilli's renewed search for capital.

He recognized the need to plan in advance for capital requirements—but the company's two-year projections didn't show capital needs exceeding Millennium's borrowing power, which Crocker Bank had extended to a $1-million credit line. Still, Casilli wanted to "reduce the business risk we saw over the twelve to eighteen months to follow." One investment banker estimated that Millennium would need between $3 million and $5 million in permanent working capital, to finance inventory and receivables, by 1982.

As Casilli saw it, the major problem was that the company's markets were beginning to expand perhaps more rapidly than Millennium could service them. He estimated that the market for test aids, of which the MicroSystem Analyzer was a part, would grow from about $64 million in 1978 to as much as $370 million in 1982. And the market for field service was projected to increase from only $18 million in 1978 to $250 million in 1982.

The necessity to market and sell its new MicroSystem Analyzer, however, had exposed the same weakness in Millennium that had forced Casilli to sell Tektronix the rights to market its universal development system. "The marketing channels in our company still simply didn't exist," Casilli explains.

Casilli knew, too, that unless Millennium aggressively expanded its market share, the giants of the microprocessor industry, such as Intel, might eventually choose to compete and leave Millennium in the dust. At that time, he was beginning to notice competition from smaller companies. "A high-technology, rapid-growth business offers the chance of the big win," Casilli says, "but also the possibility of the big loss. I saw that a small firm could easily be left behind."

Thus the stage was set for the sale of Millennium to American Microsystems.

Why would Casilli sell so promising a company as Millennium? It seems inconsistent with the hardy resolve of the classic entrepreneur who fiercely guards the independence of his company. Yet the recent wave of small-company acquisitions and mergers indicates that staying independent is becoming more the exception than the rule.

As every successful entrepreneur must, Casilli recognized a basic truth: To maintain growth, a firm requires constant capital infusion. Bank loans are the prime source at the outset, but they are principally for the short term. Later on—particularly for firms growing faster than their return on equity—greater cash flow is needed and other sources are sought.

Companies on a high growth curve, such as Millennium, often turn to venture capital financing. But that alternative has a major pitfall. Pressure from the venture capitalists for a return on their otherwise illiquid investment soon builds. Inevitably, such growing companies have only two choices: to go public or sell out. That was Jerry Casilli's predicament.

David Kratter's call set off one of the most hectic and critical periods in Casilli's entrepreneurial life. He learned how difficult and costly it could be to get capital and to stay independent. He recognized how financially tempting were the merger offers of larger firms willing to pay many times a company's book value and make the founders millionaires. And he concluded that the disadvantages of going public outweighed the advantages.

At the time of Kratter's call suggesting that Millennium go public, Casilli had already recognized a need for more capital. That need had been growing since Millennium was launched in 1973. "The retained earnings and borrowing power were there," he says, "but marginally."

That made Millennium vulnerable. So did the fact that 95 percent of Millennium's revenues were derived from selling one product to one customer, Tektronix Inc. "We were lopsided," Casilli says.

Millennium's product was a special one, however. It was an instrument that simulated a microprocessor—the computer on a chip—in an electronic product under design. It allowed an electronics designer to develop software and hardware for microprocessor-based products such as video games and computerized copiers. Since it could replace any company's microprocessor, this "universal" development system was unique in its industry.

But in early 1978, Millennium was set to expand ambitiously into

new products and new markets. Specifically, it was launching a portable testing device that could track down faulty electronic parts of
microprocessor-based products. Substantial additional capital would
be needed, especially to set up critical marketing operations.

Also lurking in the back of Casilli's mind was the possibility of an
economic downturn. That would bring increased difficulty in expanding the firm's borrowing power and a higher cost of borrowing. And any
downturn in the business fortunes of Tektronix, which had the exclusive rights to sell and distribute the Millennium development system, would cause Millennium's earnings to plunge.

Casilli was optimistic that Millennium could grow. But how to
raise additional capital? One possibility was new investors—if he could
find them. But that solution would dilute the holdings of existing
investors.

Casilli also considered a long-term bank loan, but he didn't want
to finance the company's growth with debt. So when Western Venture,
the Seattle-based venture capital arm of National City Lines Inc.,
began pushing for liquidity from its majority stock ownership position,
Casilli had to consider going public.

He began by investigating the public offering process. The investment community was a breed unknown to him. "I read books. I talked
to investment bankers until I was blue in the face. I talked to company
presidents," he says. One president he talked to was Glenn Penisten,
head of American Microsystems, located near Millennium's Cupertino,
California, base.

At the beginning, Casilli was optimistic about the prospects of a
public offering. The investment community seemed finally to understand the company's development system and its potential. Millennium
was coming off a healthy earnings year, with 1977 net income of
$582,000. And an earlier $500,000 investment by Time Inc. for 8
percent of the company had enhanced its credibility with the investment community and added to Millennium's still meager book value.

Indeed, Casilli saw going public as insurance against any financial
instability that might jeopardize the company's survival. He realized
that with increased equity the company would be able to borrow more
money if it needed to—and at less risk. "I knew that you could overin-
sure yourself, but you also have to be sure you have enough insurance,"
he says.

But the public marketplace, which had been so receptive to emerging high-technology companies in the late 1960s, was sluggish in early
1978. Only fifty-eight companies went public for the first time in 1977.
And the battered Dow Jones industrial average was still in a fifteen-
month slide, with small companies especially hard hit. "Such a volatile
market was a dangerous place for a company making its first public
offering," Casilli says.

Nevertheless, Laidlaw, Adams & Peck, the New York investment
banking firm that had solicited Kratter, encouraged Casilli to take his
firm public, They contended that a window could be found in the

market, particularly for a glamorous technology company like Millennium. Pointing to the successful public offering of Tandem Computer, Laidlaw proposed that Millennium be valued at $10 million and seek $3 million in the market for 23 percent of the company's stock.

Casilli became convinced that Laidlaw, which was concentrating on emerging companies, was capable of handling the offering. But he had one reservation. The underwriting team at Laidlaw, although comprising experienced investment bankers, had only recently been formed. Casilli felt that the experience of an investment banking firm was critical for a small company like his. So he decided to meet with other firms before making a decision.

On February 2, he flew to New York to meet with James Furneaux, senior vice-president of L. F. Rothschild, Unterberg, Towbin, another underwriter specializing in small companies. Furneaux advised Casilli that a public offering was premature. By waiting a year, Furneaux believed, Millennium could do a $5-million offering with no more shareholder dilution than would be realized with an immediate $3-million offering. Furneaux suggested a private placement with his firm first.

Casilli came away from the meeting more skeptical than before. "They [Rothschild, Unterberg, Towbin] had just come off a very difficult offering," Casilli wrote in a memo to his board. "They had the client convinced they could take the offering out for higher than they were then able to, because of market conditions." Casilli concluded that the climate wasn't all that great for "a risky deal such as Millennium."

Casilli was also concerned that the investment banker might not be able to successfully complete an offering. And he knew that underwriters won't guarantee a successful offering. "I realized that we could get to the altar, but we might not consummate the marriage," he said. "How well would the stock be traded afterward? Six months later would it be trading at two dollars instead of ten dollars?"

Casilli also totaled up the costs entailed in a public offering. He estimated that filing fees for registering with the Securities and Exchange Commission, legal and accounting fees, printing costs, and other expenditures would come to $200,000. And the investment banking firm would take an additional 8 percent to 10 percent of the offering as a commission. In addition, there were the ongoing expenses of going public—complying with SEC regulations, preparing reports, and doing other regulatory paperwork. Casilli estimated these expenses to be $50,000 a year.

He also wasn't overjoyed at the prospect of the increased responsibilities he would face as president of a public company. "I was ready to go public," he said, "but I wasn't looking forward to entering that fishbowl. Your salary has to be made public." And he wasn't looking forward to continuous dealings with the Wall Street financial community or with the increased number of shareholders.

Casilli was publicly quoted as predicting Millennium sales of $20 million by the end of 1979. Now he sees $13 million to $14 million as more likely. "You can see what would happen if a disgruntled share-holder walked in and demanded to know why I was so wrong," Casilli says. "That's the fishbowl."

Still, the liquidity that could be achieved through a public offering was very tempting to him and his investors. As part of a secondary offering, Western Venture would be able to sell about one-third of its $1.8-million investment. Within a year, through SEC-regulated sale of stock, Western Venture would be able to extricate its entire initial investment and still own a hefty chunk of Millennium.

Casilli had other reasons for seeking liquidity. He had a $250,000 personal debt resulting from his buying 8 percent of cofounder William Kirn's former 51 percent holding. A secondary offering would allow Casilli to sell enough of his 23 percent ownership to settle the debt.

Yet even a public offering wouldn't give him instant liquidity. Under SEC Rule 144, an investor was restricted to selling 1 percent of his stock every six months (since changed to 1 percent every three months). "Suppose I wanted to sell. Suppose I needed to sell. I felt I might be trapped by the restrictions," he says.

Meanwhile, Glenn Penisten of American Microsystems had approached Casilli with a merger proposal. The idea of selling to Penisten's company was now becoming more attractive to Casilli. But he asked himself if he really wanted to give up his independence. "My goal was to start a company, build a company, and make a contribution to industry," Casilli says. "Another objective was to reach a certain level of financial security and make sure I didn't lose it. Whenever you start a company and see where it is today, you have a personal attachment to it. It's part of you. Was I emotionally ready to give it up?"

He also asked himself what he would be giving up if he placed Millennium under the umbrella of a larger company. "The glory? The power? I didn't feel I was giving up that much because those qualities have never appealed to me. But I didn't want to give up our posture of growth. I did feel selling would give Millennium a secure base to build on. Should I falter, I could draw on the larger company to help me out of the bind."

Western Venture was still pushing for a public offering, but when Casilli proposed the sale to American Microsystems, Western Venture gave its support.

The $9.4-million sale price meant Western Venture's investment had tripled in only one year. As Casilli logically notes, "Why should they risk staying around to get a possible six-times gain on their investment when they had a sure and immediate three-times gain?"

In the end, Casilli sold Millennium for some of the same reasons he had earlier sold rights to the company's development system to Tektronix—to obtain more working capital and to get access to more extensive marketing operations.

The deal was attractive to American Microsystems, too. Its customer base was similar to Millennium's, and its 1977 sales were $71 million. The acquisition of Millennium promised an impact on its bottom line.

Today, Millennium is a wholly owned subsidiary of American Microsystems, with 1978 sales of $9.3 million, and on its way, Casilli projects, to $40 million by 1983. The only real change since the merger, says Casilli, is that he now reports to a different board of directors.

—BILL HENDRICKSON

ANATOMY OF A MERGER

When he is there, which is most of the time, Bard Heavens answers the telephone himself at the still-tiny company he and his wife, Shirley, started less than a year ago. "Good morning, Shim-It Corporation," he says enthusiastically. The call might be someone with an order.

He wakes up optimistic every morning, probably too optimistic, in Shirley's view. If her husband's earlier hopefulness had been well founded, today she would be spending more time with her two teenage daughters. And Bard would be honcho-ing the international expansion of a multimillion-dollar manufacturing business while anticipating an active, early retirement in just a couple of years. They still don't know what went wrong. Whatever it was, it began three years ago when they decided to sell American Shim & Die Inc. (AS&D), the company they started in 1975.

Bard had spent fifteen years with a company called U.S. Gasket & Shim Corporation (USG&S), in Cuyahoga Falls, Ohio. By 1974, when he was forty-one, he had been president of USG&S for three years, during which time the company's sales had grown from $2 million to nearly $4 million. He foresaw continued growth for the company, but he also foresaw problems. He wanted new managers in a reorganized management structure. He wanted a computer. The chairman, the majority stockholder, disagreed. Bard went to the bank, arranged a $400,000 loan, and offered to buy the company for $1 million with the balance to be paid over ten years. His offer was turned down, and in January 1975 he resigned.

"The only alternative," says Bard, "was to start a company of my own. So I did, and I knew it would be up and running in a year. I was Mister Shim. If God couldn't do it, I could." He and Shirley had been married two years, both for the second time; they threw themselves into the new business.

A shim, usually made of stamped metal, can be as thin as 0.0005 inch, less than the thickness of aluminum foil. Bard calls it "an engineer's eraser." Shims are used in the construction of machinery to fill a space between adjacent parts that, by accident or by design, is slightly larger than need be. Shims make things fit together, everything from toasters to rocket engines. U. S. manufacturers buy about $50 million worth of these custom stampings every year from scores of suppliers, mostly small machine shops, although three companies probably account for nearly one-third of the industry's sales.

The growth of the shim industry is tied to the needs of its traditional consumers. Shim makers can't create new markets as, for example, computer makers did by moving their machines into the home. So any new shim maker grows only at the expense of its competitors. And, since a shim is a shim, the only way to take business away from the competition is to offer lower cost, higher quality, better service, a bigger smile, or some combination thereof.

The new company, AS&D, grew, albeit at a slower pace than Bard had optimistically projected. By 1979 the company had twenty-two employees producing and selling $750,000 worth of shims from the Kent, Ohio, plant. Pretax profits reached $100,000, according to the Heavenses, even after they pulled out $40,000 in combined salaries for themselves. The only serious glitch was an angina attack Bard suffered in 1977. With him in the hospital, Shirley had to quote prices to buyers and watch over the shop. Had it been Shirley in the hospital, Bard would have had equal difficulty stepping into office details. They resolved thenceforth to be better understudies for each other.

Despite the company's respectable growth rate, Bard was impatient. He had started American Shim only because he couldn't be the manager he wanted to be while at USG&S. He wanted American Shim to grow. Since shim suppliers must be reasonably close to their customers to provide quick delivery and frequent plant visits, growth meant opening new plants in other geographical locations. "We figured the Ohio plant could do about $1.5 million. If we could get a California plant doing about $1 million, then we could look into another market, maybe Texas."

Bard looked, unsuccessfully, for someone who could manage a new West Coast plant. In an industry as small as shim stamping, experienced plant managers are few in number and almost certainly already working for the competition. The man Bard decided he wanted had just switched jobs and wasn't ready to switch again soon. The Heavenses put their expansion plans on hold until, Bard says, "I heard that C.E.M. West was in trouble and maybe for sale."

C.E.M. Company, based in Danielson, Connecticut, had entered the shim business in 1977 by acquiring USG&S, Bard's old employer. The acquisition included USG&S's Westminster, California, and Ohio plants. Both Bard and Shirley were familiar with the California plant, now called C.E.M. West Inc., Bard from inspection trips made while he was president of USG&S and Shirley because she had worked in the plant's office. In fact, they had met for the first time there in 1969.

Bard put out feelers and in early 1980 got a telephone call from Hans Koehl, chairman of Spirol International Corporation, C.E.M.'s parent company. No, Koehl said, C.E.M. West wasn't for sale, but he would like to meet Bard and talk about the shim business some day. He would call, he said, the next time he was coming to Ohio to look in on C.E.M.'s plant there. Events, however, eventually took an unexpected turn. About eight months after that first telephone conversation, Koehl bought American Shim & Die from the Heavenses, and Bard and Shirley became employees once again. It looked to them, at the time, like a very sweet deal.

When Bard and Koehl met for the first time in March over dinner at the Silver Lake Country Club near the Heavenses' Stow, Ohio, home, Bard says Koehl spoke openly about the problems C.E.M. was having in the shim business. C.E.M.'s West Coast plant was much talked about in the industry. The rapid turnover of chief executive officers there had prompted one jokester to suggest that they form a President-of-the-Month Club.

"Koehl," Bard says, "talked about personnel problems, about misquoted jobs, about a lot of things I wouldn't want a competitor to know." When he got home, Shirley says, Bard was puzzled. "He couldn't figure out why that man was telling him all those things."

Koehl had, as Bard recalls the meeting, indicated indirectly that he could use someone like Bard to tackle the problems besetting C.E.M. West, adding that, of course, there would have to be some sort of merger or acquisition if Bard ever became interested in taking on a challenge like that. "He didn't make a proposal," Bard says, "he just slipped the suggestion in, almost as an aside." However casually Koehl might have meant it, his suggestion planted an idea in Bard's mind that took root and was nourished in subsequent conversations and negotiations.

After their first meeting, Bard and Koehl talked by telephone a couple of times, and, as Bard recalls, while no proposals were exchanged, each conversation fanned the flame of his interest in pursuing a deal. In mid-April, as part of another business trip, he visited C.E.M.'s Connecticut facility. "We didn't negotiate that afternoon," Bard says. "There was some talk with C.E.M. president Terry Tobias about whether I might be interested in running their West Coast plant and if so did I think I could straighten it out. I think that what Koehl really wanted to do was to impress me with his operation in Connecticut. Koehl was flying back to Ohio in a Piper Aztec and offered me a ride. I took it." Soon after, Bard had his accountant work up an estimate of AS&D's market value—$878,050—and he mailed this workup and a cover letter to Koehl. The cover letter suggested a price tag closer to $750,000.

For nearly a month little of substance passed between Bard and Koehl, and even at dinner on May 15 at the Silver Lake Country Club they ate without discussing hard numbers.

But the following week, on May 21, Koehl wrote to Bard. "Again," the letter opened, "I enjoyed talking 'shims' with you last Thursday. It gave me some further basis for consideration." Koehl then suggested three alternative ways of computing a value for Bard's company, based, the letter said, on the average price of companies sold during 1979: (a) sales divided by 1.8; (b) 1.6 times net worth; (c) 10.9 times after-tax earnings.

Applying these formulas to the financial figures Bard had given him, Koehl derived three different values, in this order: (a) $424,000; (b) $481,700; (c) $490,500.

"After deliberating on this subject off and on for the last four days," he wrote, "taking into consideration more thoughts, guidelines, and factors than I could reasonably set forth here, I have come to the conclusion that based on what I know and what I assume, a fair value would be $450,000." His "thoughts" were, he wrote, to offer 40 percent down, followed by six annual payments of $45,000 in principal, plus interest at 10 percent. "Part of the sale, as we discussed," Koehl said in his letter, "would be an employment contract for five years together with covenants not to compete for the term of the contract and for a reasonable period thereafter. . . . I am considering you a valuable addition to our Group and I am *not* considering the employment contract part of the purchasing cost."

Since what Bard really expected to get was about $500,000, he says, Koehl's tentative offer looked good.

They worked out details of salary and position, and in a letter written June 20, Koehl formalized the offer he had suggested a month earlier. Bard, according to Koehl's letter, would be paid $45,000 annually as president of C.E.M. West, plus $15,000 annually as a vice-president of C.E.M. Company. Wearing his vice-president's hat, he would act as a consultant to the corporation's other shim-making facilities.

The letter contained some contingencies. Koehl still had not seen AS&D's plant, its customer lists, or a full set of financial statements, and no offer would be firm, the letter indicated, until these had been inspected by Koehl and other C.E.M. executives.

Bard was excited. "There was nothing negative about the deal at all. My accountant and my lawyer both said it was really super."

But more to the point, Koehl's offer promised to catapult Bard several years ahead of where he might take himself as owner-CEO of single-plant AS&D. "Bard really wanted to manage a staff. Part of him," says Shirley, "is entrepreneur, but part of him is trained manager."

"I had never thought I'd be running my own business," Bard says. "Being an entrepreneur was not my ambition."

Between his first meeting with Koehl in March and the day he and Shirley signed over their company to C.E.M. in September, Bard convinced himself that he was making not only the right financial move, but the right career decision as well.

"We had," he says, "just gone through the building of American Shim and Die, and it was working well. But what if something went wrong? Here was [Koehl] telling me all his problems, and I'm thinking, 'Hey, I could walk in there and be a hero!' I knew that in five years I could solve the problems at C.E.M. West and still have a nice piece of change for myself. The California house would be paid for, and, with some wise investments, we could do anything we wanted. So we were selling the company a bit earlier than we thought we would. . . . It was a good time to sell. We were at our business peak—and we had someone who wanted to buy. In many respects I thought selling out and going to work for C.E.M. would give me more freedom, because I wouldn't be operating so close to the financial edge. Besides, I thought I would be a director of American Shim and Die, able to keep an eye on the operation. We wouldn't really be leaving it, we would just be picking up more responsibilities. I thought I was also going to be vice-president of shim operations at [C.E.M.], in charge of adding shim-making to the plants in England, Canada, and Mexico. In many respects, working at C.E.M. was going to give me what I had wanted at American Shim and Die: the opportunity to manage a multiplant operation. I was diminishing my risk with a guaranteed payout and a five-year employment contract. I was having my cake and eating it. This was it. We had it made."

At C.E.M., Bard could see himself as a real manager—traveling, setting up overseas operations, juggling competing claims for company resources, taking on new markets. The prospect, he says, was attractive.

On July 22, Koehl and a contingent of C.E.M. vice-presidents flew to Ohio to inspect the Heavenses' plant, their books, and their customer list. A week later, on July 30, Koehl, C.E.M. president Terry Tobias, and Koehl's wife again flew to Ohio to make the terms of the deal final. Bard picked them up at the Kent State University Airport, waited while they checked into their hotel, the Brown Derby Inn in nearby Boston Heights, then drove them home for drinks. Shirley met Koehl for the first time. They chatted, and all five went to dinner at the Silver Lake Country Club where, after they had eaten, Koehl told them that a closer look at the company had convinced him that $450,000 was too high a price. He said, Shirley recalls, that he would be paying for "blue sky." Instead, Koehl offered the Heavenses $350,000 for their company. He felt that even that was high, but it was part of the price he was willing to pay to move an able president into the trouble-plagued California plant. While he reduced the offer on the plant, he sweetened his salary offer to Bard and suggested that employment was available for Shirley, too.

"We were upset," says Bard.

The talk that evening ended abruptly and Bard and Shirley dropped the other three at the Brown Derby. Shirley wondered what the tax consequences of Koehl's amended offer might be. In effect, the new offer shifted $100,000 from capital gain to ordinary income.

"I was also worried about what if something happens to Bard," says Shirley, since death or disablement nullified his employment contract.

The next day Bard went to the plant, and Koehl negotiated specific dollar amounts in the proposal with the Heavenses' accountant. The accountant, Bard says, advised them that the tax consequences were not significant, "so I decided to go ahead. I thought it was risky, but you don't go into that type of situation thinking that the other guy. . . ."

"Congratulations!" began Koehl's letter of August 1 to the Heavenses. It outlined the terms of the agreement, and on September 17, at their attorney's office in Cleveland, the Heavenses sold all of their stock in American Shim & Die to C.E.M. for $100,000 in cash and a promissory note (see box). Bard agreed to accept a salary totaling $305,255 and consulting fees totaling $75,000 over the next five years. Shirley's two-year employment contract specified an annual salary of $27,500. The entire package came to $832,000—$435,000 in salary and fees and about $397,000 in principal and interest payments. Taken as a lump sum over five years, Bard points out, the salaries and payments of principal and interest in the final contract came very close to matching the price Koehl had first discussed with the Heavenses back in May.

"I saw Bard having such plans," Shirley says, "and such dreams. Finally there was a company behind him with enough resources, so that, for him, the sky was the limit."

FINDING A WAY TO MAKE A SHIM DEAL FIT TOGETHER

Before inspecting the American Shim & Die Inc. plant or its books, C.E.M. chairman Hans Koehl tentatively proposed to buy the company for $450,000 and to give Bard Heavens a five-year employment contract at an annual salary of $45,000, plus an annual consulting fee of $15,000. The offer wouldn't be firm, he stressed, until he had verified the data Bard had supplied. The terms of the proposed deal, spread over six years:

	Principal	Interest	Salary + fees
At closing	$180,000	—	—
Year 1	45,000	27,000	60,000
Year 2	45,000	22,500	60,000
Year 3	45,000	18,000	60,000
Year 4	45,000	13,500	60,000
Year 5	45,000	9,000	60,000
Year 6	45,000	4,500	60,000
	450,000	94,500	360,000

TOTAL: $904,500 over six years

After inspecting the books and plant, Koehl revised his offer. He said he would pay only $350,000 for American Shim & Die but that he would pay Bard Heavens a higher salary and offer Shirley Heavens a two-year employment contract. The deal Koehl and the Heavenses agreed to:

	Principal	Interest	Salary + fees	Salary
At closing (9/17/80)	$100,000	—	—	—
1/2/81	70,000	7,291	65,000	27,500
1/2/82	60,000	18,000	70,000	27,500
1/2/83	50,000	12,000	75,500	—
1/2/84	40,000	7,000	81,550	—
1/2/85	30,000	3,000	88,205	—
	350,000	47,291	380,255	55,000

TOTAL: $832,546 over 4.5 years

Barely twelve months later, Bard and Shirley each applied to the State of California for unemployment benefits of $130 per week. C.E.M. protested their application, and Koehl flew from Connecticut to Los Angeles to testify personally against them at the hearing. They had been fired—whether properly or not the courts have yet to decide. Each side accuses the other of failing to meet the letter and the spirit of their contract. Bard and Shirley feel abused. So, too, does Koehl.

Bard's employment contract did not specify his duties and responsibilities at C.E.M. West, saying only that they "shall generally be those of President of the company," and that they could be increased, decreased, or changed at the board's discretion. He could be dismissed, according to his contract, if he knowingly and willfully violated any instruction or policy of the board, or if the board judged him to be "culpably negligent or inefficient." Shirley's two-year contract, defining her duties as "those of general office manager," had the same two provisions for dismissal, provisions that they see now gave them little protection. "I guess we didn't pay enough attention to the what-ifs," Bard says.

It never occurred to Bard that the management style he had developed over fifteen years at USG&S, the same management style he had used to build AS&D from zero to a $750,000 business in four years, wouldn't work at C.E.M. The Heavenses' style is paternalistic but not authoritarian. Tom Corathers, now twenty-six, first went to work for the Heavenses in Ohio back in 1977, when they were just getting AS&D off the ground. "It was an easy place to work," he says. "No whips were cracked, and everyone policed themselves well. We took a lot of pride in what we did. Bard helped along with everybody else. He wasn't an outsider in the shop, he was more of a friend.

"Bard and Shirley could have fired people, but they gave them a chance; they were willing to let people learn. The real losers would quit on their own. Nobody ever said, 'This isn't my job.' Wherever you were needed, you went. Nobody had to ask. Eventually we lost our shop foreman, so we ran things by committee. Five or six of us would meet every week. No one person knew enough by himself to take over. If we decided we needed a rule—maybe people were starting to come in late—we'd talk about it and make it a rule. We may not have owned it, but it seemed like *our* company.

"When C.E.M. took over, most things changed. They appointed a foreman, they dissolved the committee, they stopped giving incentive raises. Before, you could grow with the company. But after C.E.M. bought it, people didn't feel like that anymore. Bob Kuhar [AS&D's new president] was a C.E.M. man. If something was against C.E.M. policy, even though we had been doing it for years, we'd change." Corathers followed the Heavenses to C.E.M. West. He is now one of Shim-It Corporation's two shop employees.

Turning C.E.M. West around, Bard thought, would be easy. "It was just a matter of realigning it the way it was when it was [U.S. Gasket's] shims division. Hell, they were losing money. They couldn't keep a president. If anything needed changing, that plant needed changing."

The plant was profitable when C.E.M. acquired it in 1977, but in the fiscal year ended September 29, 1980, C.E.M. West lost $166,000. The Heavenses arrived on October 9 to take charge. They found most of C.E.M. West's problems not on the shop floor, but in the bookkeeping, sales, and administrative systems. There were, Shirley says, too many office people, and most of them were untrained, unsupervised, and sullen. But changing people or policies proved difficult. Often, they contend, they were told whom to fire and whom not to fire. A young woman, who did telephone sales work, frequently came to work in dirty blue jeans and with a bare midriff. The Heavenses found her work unprofessional, but, they say, they were told to keep her on. She was, Shirley says, one of the employees that visiting C.E.M. executives would ask out for a drink when they were at the California plant. Shirley found the plant bookkeeper, an older woman, adequate and, unlike some other employees, willing to learn and to accept suggestions. Corporate headquarters pressured Bard to fire her. He did.

Some employees apparently enjoyed a direct line to corporate headquarters in Connecticut, and the Heavenses were criticized and, they feel, second-guessed by Tobias and corporate vice-presidents on the strength of complaints lodged by their own subordinates. During a dispute over office procedures, C.E.M. West's outside salesperson told Shirley she would "tell Terry Tobias on you." The same individual, Bard says, frequently challenged his authority to make decisions and to set policy and spoke disrespectfully of him to the junior office staff. But the Heavenses had been warned against taking any action against the woman. "Tobias told me," Bard says, "that she could do the company a lot of damage if she went over to the competition. 'She thinks you're trying to fire her,' he told me. 'Take it easy.'"

In January, Bard says, C.E.M. executives began suggesting that Bard and Shirley were overpaid.

By February, Bard's self-confidence had frayed. "Mister Shim," the man who was going to be a "hero," began himself to doubt that he knew what he was doing. When a Connecticut executive insisted that a particular production job should take only a fraction of the time Bard estimated, he had to go to the shop and do the job himself to confirm what he thought he already knew. "We found ourselves playing a game," Shirley says, "that we didn't know the rules for."

"I'd been in this business," Bard says. "I'd run this plant before, but these guys kept giving me orders. At one point I told [headquarters executive] Mike Martin that I could just stop thinking and take orders from him. 'Oh, no,' he said, 'This is your show.' I kept trying to get some kind of handle on how these people were thinking," Bard says. "I couldn't believe this was happening."

"Monday mornings," says Shirley, "were always a new beginning. We both believed it would turn around, so we boosted each other. Neither of us could believe that Hans Koehl really knew what was going on. It all appeared so obvious to us, so we were sure that when he found out he would straighten things out in a hurry."

The Heavenses began seeing an industrial psychologist. They needed help, they say, in handling the stress of the situation. "The psychologist's basic message," Shirley says, "was to trust our own instincts, to believe in what we knew."

Finally, in June, Bard says, "I asserted myself. I'd finally had it with all this crap." In a ten-page memo to Koehl, Bard addressed point by point the criticisms that he thought had been unfairly leveled at him and Shirley. He recounted the progress he thought had been made toward profitability. He said that, unless otherwise ordered, he would proceed along his own course. And he asked Koehl for an expression of support.

"He never answered that memo," Bard says.

In August, the C.E.M. board approved a resolution giving Tobias authority to suspend the Heavenses at his discretion, and a week later he exercised his discretion.

"At four forty-five," Bard recalls, "he came in, plunked himself down in my office, and said, 'It isn't going to work.'

"'What isn't going to work?'

"'You as president,' he told me.

"'When is it going to be? End of the week?'

"'No,' he said, 'Now.'

"'And what about Shirley? Does she stay, or do you want her out, too?'

"'She can go, too,' he said.

"I called Shirley over the intercom. 'Okay, Shirl,' I said, 'This is it; we're all gone.'"

"When I came in I smiled," says Shirley, "and said, 'Am I really free? You're not kidding? I can go?'" The emotion she felt the strongest, she says, was relief.

While Tobias watched, they packed personal effects into cardboard boxes and carried them out to the car.

"In the car," says Shirley, "the first thing Bard said was, 'Well, I guess we're back in our own shim business.' I made him promise that wasn't true."

On October 1, just one week shy of a year after his arrival at C.E.M. West, Bard was officially notified that his contract for employment with C.E.M. had been terminated. A telegram on October 15 delivered the same message to Shirley.

Eleven months later, in September 1982, the Heavenses opened Shim-It Corporation in a small suburban Los Angeles machine shop. Along with the equipment, they had bought the shop's existing accounts, which amounted to less than $6,000 monthly. But the time between the telegram and the opening was more painful, Bard says, than he sometimes thought he could bear.

"I was still hopeful," he says, "for a reconciliation. Letting us go solved none of C.E.M.'s problems. Besides, I had a house in Ohio that still wasn't sold, a house here, two kids in private school, [daughter] Diane's ballet lessons, legal fees. The stock market was down. Our oil and gas partnerships weren't paying out. Shirley told me I had to face up to reality."

He looked for a job through executive search firms and by responding to ads in the *Los Angeles Times*. "Even when there was some interest, as soon as people got my résumé," Bard says, "that was it. Every company I'd ever worked for was now owned by C.E.M."

In February they went back to Ohio for a visit. Bard's best friend there, whose own business had failed, had taken to spending his days in front of the television wrapped in a blanket.

"After the trip," Bard says, "we thought about going back to Ohio to live, but we'd seen the empty shopping centers, my friend. There was nothing for us there. What the hell was I going to do? For the first time in my life, none of my usual escapes was applicable. Having a drink, going to a movie didn't help. I actually thought of getting the hell out, of just getting in the car and disappearing . . . maybe to Colorado, or to Texas. But then I'd think, What'll I do when I get there? I couldn't get a job. Mister Success couldn't get a job. What do I say to Shirley in the morning? What did I have to say the night before? The highlight of my week was 'Hill Street Blues.' When Shirley is down, she's down. What do you say to a person who has no more strength than to pull a blanket over her on the floor? She had had her own plans. Two years at C.E.M., and then she was going to go to school, open a dress shop. She had already worked herself stiff at American Shim and Die. She would say then, 'When does *my* life begin?' I had guilt trips about what I had done to Shirley. We had days of total silence. There was a lot of isolation. Who can you talk to at a time like that?"

Bard was a pilot, so he looked into aircraft sales. There was nothing there or in boat or car sales. He and Shirley investigated fast-food franchises, salad-bar restaurants; they even made a beginning on a janitorial service with a couple of small accounts, but that didn't work out either.

"We walked," Shirley says, "and Bard would spend hours puttering in the yard. Some days I would pray fifty times. We wasted days, weeks. We'd sit here and go over it and over it. . . . What had happened? What if. . . ? If only we had. . . . Why did we ever do this? But in the end, it brought us closer."

In March the Heavenses found a small, well-equipped machine shop in Hawaiian Gardens, a suburb whose name is its loveliest feature. Bard and the retiring owner took four months to agree on terms. Financing, however, was a problem. The Heavenses could not obtain a loan.

"Bard went to every bank around with his proposal," Shirley says. "They all said no. Finally he found one that seemed interested. We went back together. I could see when we walked in that the man was going to turn us down. It was terrible to watch Bard just short of begging. That hurt me more than anything. Eventually we had to get my father to cosign. It was very painful for me, at the age of thirty-eight, to have to go to my dad for help."

Besides the Heavenses, Shim-It now has two employees who can easily handle the workload in the shop. Bard and Shirley share the sales job.

Things are slow in the aerospace industry now, but Bard says that slow time is the best time to solicit these companies. They have time to listen to you, to inspect your plant, and put you on their approved list so that you are there when business picks up again. He is already worrying about how he will finance his receivables if too much business starts coming through the door too soon.

"C.E.M. was the first time I'd ever had to look at failure," says Shirley. "It shook my foundations—temporarily, but not anymore. I know we can do it again. It may take selling the house and everything else. But we've decided this is our best chance to climb above it again."

The Heavenses have sued C.E.M., alleging that they were dismissed without cause and that C.E.M. deliberately harrassed them and interfered with their attempts to solve problems that existed at C.E.M. West before the Heavenses took control. C.E.M. will try to show that Bard was ineffective and had to be removed to save the company's West Coast plant. Both expect the case to remain in the courts for years.

"When this thing is all put to bed," Bard says, "I'm sure that I will come out the better person."

"Not I," says Shirley.

"I can't forget how it felt back then," Bard says. "We'd signed the papers. This was it. We had it made . . . and here we are today, starting all over again."

—TOM RICHMAN

BREAKING AWAY

Last year my wife, Sandee, and I parted company with one of our children. Letting her go was a difficult decision for us, maybe the toughest we've ever made. But the kid was twenty-six years old and maturing fast. You know how these things go. She had wants and needs her parents weren't sure they could meet anymore. After some tense moments, and a whole lot of soul-searching, we swallowed hard and said good-bye. It seemed like the best thing for her—and us.

Our "child" was "Bugs" Burger Bug Killers Inc., the nation's largest independently owned extermination company. It reflected everything Sandee and I believed in, and the company's success revolved totally around the notion of guaranteed customer satisfaction. Clients hired us to eliminate their pest problems not because we cost less or worked faster, but because we guaranteed results. Unconditionally. It was really pretty simple. When you bought a "Bugs" Burger service contract, you bought our personal commitment to a job done right. If our people failed in any way, you got a refund on every nickel spent with us during the previous year—plus a year's free service from one of my competitors.

When it came to selling our company, however, there were no such guarantees. Our biggest fear had always been that new ownership would mean a relaxation of the standards it had taken us a quarter-century to perfect. For a long time, in fact, Sandee and I had resisted the notion of selling at all. Two of our children were actively involved in the business. We had more than 500 other dedicated employees who shared in the company's profits—and in its commitment to excellence.

And we had fought so many wars. In 1960, I made a speech to members of the Florida Pest Control Association about standards of excellence and service that I felt had to be set. They all said, "Come off it, Al, that's not the way things work," and laughed me out of the room. I left in tears that day, vowing to prove them wrong. And I did. Later, when "Bugs" was expanding to the other southern states and into the Southwest, I took a lot of abuse for being Jewish. One restaurant owner in Fort Worth kept telling me I'd never make it there, that I should go back to Miami with the rest of the Jews. We'd call her up every time we signed another Texas client on, just to let her know we weren't going away. By 1986, "Bugs" was doing $1 million worth of business in her backyard.

In the long run, the stress of managing the company took its toll on both Sandee and me. Still, it was nothing compared with the stress of contemplating selling our business—our baby—and seeing it change value systems under someone else's control.

Despite these concerns, we had begun to bump up against some fairly formidable ceilings. "Bugs" was a growing company with not much in the way of rapid upward mobility for many of our district and regional managers. We didn't want to lose these people, either to other job offers or to the opportunity to start their own businesses; yet there was little room for them to grow with us. Expansion into overseas markets would help, but that in turn raised problems of dealing with foreign languages, different cultural values, and the overriding issue of quality control. Also, the better we performed, the more large companies set their sights on our market. And we faced such minor crises as our liability-insurance premium going up $750,000 in a single year.

So, starting about two years ago, Sandee and I began listening to the would-be suitors more intently. We had a few nonnegotiable criteria for any potential buyer. One, it would have to be a family-oriented company that cared about its employees the same way we did. Two, it would have to guarantee its work unconditionally. Three, it would have to keep our people on and provide them liberal opportunities for advancement. And four, it would have to be willing to pay a premium price for what we considered to be the finest company in the pest-control industry.

Money wasn't everything, of course. But it mattered. If I were to retire from "Bugs," I never wanted to have to work again. In fact, I wanted enough money from the sale so that if I dropped a hundred-dollar bill on the floor and had a backache, I wouldn't think twice about having to bend over to pick it up.

Several prospects came calling me as soon as they heard we might sell. One offered a very generous financial package—more than we actually ended up settling for—but the vibes weren't right. I remember the president of this company telling me, "You've got a great company, Al, but we feel we can triple your profits." When I asked him how he'd do that, he said, "By cutting out all the waste." "Right," I said, "and I know just what kind of 'waste' you'll cut. You'll start with the fringe benefits and the size of the workforce. Then you'll slash the pay scale, which is thirty percent higher than yours, followed by the performance bonuses and the profit-sharing. You might even water down the chemicals we use. In the end, my company will deteriorate to the level that yours is at." He started screaming at me—in my accountant's office. Five more minutes of that and I'd have showed him what pest control was truly all about.

All in all, I probably met with, checked out, or otherwise dealt with seven different would-be buyers. Even though I had relinquished most of my day-to-day operational responsibilities with "Bugs," the effort was taxing. Taxing in terms of time and money, yes, but also emotionally. I'd talk to these people, and inevitably something would pop up that would make me feel as uneasy as a parent seeing his kid join up with a cult of lunatics.

Dealing with Johnson Wax was a completely different experience. Here was a company I'd always admired, one that seemed to approach business with the same "family" orientation and sense of ethics we had. Its mergers-and-acquisitions representative first phoned me in May 1985. I was sitting on my sun deck in Miami, dreaming of what I wanted to do with my company. I tossed him a fantasy figure that was at least 50 percent above the industry value and said, "We're not for sale anyway. Call me in a year." He promised he would.

Over the next twelve months, while we were checking Johnson Wax out, it was doing the same with us. It was a good fit. Johnson Wax has product distribution in forty-five countries and a large chemical division that produces, among other things, pesticides. We had absolutely the best reputation in our industry. I felt confident that if chief executive officer Sam Johnson wanted a foothold in our field, he would only want the best company our industry had to offer. Nothing I've seen since persuades me differently.

Serious negotiations finally began in May 1986. Almost all of these took place at our Florida home, overlooking the swimming pool and flower gardens. That was a psychological boon. I'm not a very formal person—visitors don't wear neckties on my patio—and this wasn't easy on me emotionally, even under the best of circumstances. Being in my own home, my own element, helped enormously.

When we announced the sale to our division vice-presidents and regional sales managers, in fact, it was over brunch by the pool. I told them we'd signed a letter of intent to sell, and that I had individual employment contracts for each of them. If they didn't sign, the deal was off. That was really the moment of truth. Johnson Wax didn't want the company if there was going to be a mass exodus of the top people. Nor can you sell a company like ours, in which your employees—their feelings, their ambitions, their financial comfort, all the things that make up who they are—mean everything to you, if money is the only object. I knew I couldn't. I had to know they felt as good about the deal as I did.

So what was their reaction? Shock. And disbelief. But we also told them about Johnson Wax and the kind of company we knew it to be. I said that, though I was still a relatively young man, I'd have to live to age 123 to accomplish the goals that they would achieve under Johnson Wax in the next five years. And that I looked forward to seeing many of them traveling the world, directing large new divisions of "Bugs" Burger.

In five minutes, every one of those contracts was signed.

Until then, only a small handful of corporate people had been in on the discussions. Secrecy was necessary because at several junctures the whole deal could have been aborted. We closed on October 31, 1986. During the course of that one day, I went from my lowest low to my highest high.

I'm an optimist, you see, and Sandee is a pessimist—or, for the sake of argument, a realist. At the last minute, Johnson Wax's lawyers stuck in some stipulations that made her a little paranoid. She balked at going to the closing. If she didn't go, I didn't go, and there was no deal. Considering that it was Halloween, you could call this my waking nightmare. Rarely have I felt lower. It got a little hairy there, but finally she agreed to go.

The highest high? That's easy: when the cash was transferred to our personal bank account. I may not leave hundred-dollar bills lying on my bathroom floor. But if I chose to, I'll tell you one thing: I'd have a hell of a time finding the sink.

This was not the end of tough times, though. Two weeks after the pool meeting and four days after the closing, we threw a big cocktail party for our eighty-five home-office employees at a local restaurant. I broke the news of the sale to them then. It was horrible—funereal, even. Everyone was sobbing, including me. Some wanted to return their bonuses and have me buy back the company. That wasn't about to happen, of course, but I was extremely touched. Since I'm still on the board now and have a three-year consulting contract with the company, I drop by the office from time to time. Some of the women come up to me saying, "You're not my boss anymore, so I guess I can kiss you." And they do. That's a pretty good feeling.

It's been six months now since the sale went through, and everything I'd hoped for has come to pass. Johnson has made good on everything it promised. Many of our people have been invited up to Racine, Wisconsin, for tours of corporate headquarters. The attitude at "Bugs" is extremely positive, and profits are good.

I have my own new ventures to look forward to. One of them is a group I've founded called the Society of Ethical Entrepreneurs (SEE). In order to join this group, an entrepreneur must subscribe to two basic tenets: "I and my company have an ongoing obligation to be fair, scrupulously honest, and ethical with my customers, suppliers, employees, and creditors." And, "I and my company have the obligation to give the highest-possible quality goods or services to the customer and to *unconditionally guarantee the foregoing*." Members must also list written policies and contracts that pertain to the quality of service, supply all relevant data on bankruptcies, and so on, and provide affidavits of support from a cross-section of the population they do business with.

Through membership fees we hope to provide scholarships, loans, and grants that will further SEE's goals. But getting into the group is not supposed to be easy. That's why I'm especially pleased that my charter partner in SEE is none other than Sam Johnson, the CEO who bought my company. Getting Sam on board is the closest thing I can think of to an unconditional guarantee that parting with "Bugs" Burger is an act I'll never regret.

—ALVIN L. BURGER

INDEX